# NORTHROP
# FRYE

# NORTHROP FRYE

## A Biography

## JOHN AYRE

VINTAGE BOOKS · A DIVISION OF RANDOM HOUSE · TORONTO

First Vintage Books Edition, October 1990

Originally published in Canada in 1989 by Random House of Canada Limited, Toronto.

**Canadian Cataloguing in Publication Data**
Ayre, John
  Northrop Frye: a biography

Vintage ed.
ISBN 0-394-22178-8

1. Frye, Northrop, 1912-    . 2. Critics—Canada—
Biography.  I. Title.
PN75.F7A96 1990        801′.95′092        C90-094330-0

COVER DESIGN: David Wyman
COVER PHOTOGRAPH: Nigel Dickson

For copyrighted material, the author wishes to thank the following publishers:

Lines from "Edmund Blunden on his Sixty-Fifth Birthday" from *A Woman Unashamed and Other Poems* by Paul Engle, copyright © 1962, 1963, 1964, 1965 by Paul Engle, reprinted by permission of Random House, Inc.

Lines from "The Truant" by E.J. Pratt from *E.J. Pratt: Complete Poems Part 2*, 1989, reprinted by permission of University of Toronto Press.

Lines from "The Anagogic Man" from *Poems Twice Told* by Jay Macpherson, copyright © Oxford University Press Canada 1981.

Drawing by David Levine. Reprinted with permission from *The New York Review of Books*. Copyright © 1982 Nyrev, Inc.

Printed in Canada

To my parents,
Joan and Alan

# CONTENTS

## PREFACE

The idea for this book really goes back to the fall of 1969 when I was editor of the literary magazine at Victoria College. As an anthropology student, I was deeply interested in the way religion organizes and impels human culture. It seemed obvious that I should interview such leading campus lights at Toronto as Marshall McLuhan, Gregory Baum and Northrop Frye, all of whom had serious connections with religion. McLuhan, however, had reached the upper realms of media celebrity and wasn't available to undergraduates. Theologian Baum was in Rome on Vatican business. That left Northrop Frye who, unbeknown to me, was just starting a difficult project on the symbolism of the Bible which would lead to *The Great Code* over thirteen years later. Frye was willing to be interviewed and—with courage born of ignorance—I blundered into probably the fullest and most spontaneous interviews I've had in some twenty years as a writer.

In dealing with him then it was painfully obvious that Frye deserved much more attention than he was receiving. Astonishingly, there was almost no biographical material available on him. What I'd heard of his history, however, seemed not only fascinating, but certainly very much at odds with his image as an excruciatingly shy scholar whose clever but dry mind supposedly spun archetypes like the wheels on a one-armed bandit.

1

Through the early seventies I kept wondering what kind of a man would write such important but unquestionably eccentric works as *Fearful Symmetry* and *Anatomy of Criticism*. Why in the late twentieth century was this scholar struggling to resurrect the arcane science of biblical typology, a vestige of the Middle Ages and the Renaissance? I did a long magazine profile of him in 1973 to answer some of these questions and then, after an interview for a cancelled article in 1976, thought the next logical step would be a biography.

When I approached him about a book in the fall of 1978, he demurred. He was uncertain about his suitability for a full-length book. He'd already warned off biographers by claiming that he had led an uneventful life. Moreover, I had hit him with a request for interviews when he was still struggling with his now unruly and long-overdue project on the Bible, *The Great Code*, which he feared he might never finish. By coincidence, I bumped into him outside the west door of the Old Vic building of Victoria College and talked to him about his concerns. I was unnerved by the effects of his struggle: his ashen face and the steel-wool swatch of long grey-brown hair which incongruously reminded me of a nineteenth-century American frontier lawyer. It was obvious that any biography at that time, certainly involving interviews about his often tragic family background, would constitute another burden he didn't need.

I convinced him that, unlike the Victorian or Edwardian periods, this was not an age of confessional diaries and massive family correspondence, and that important material about the background and influences of any major figure had to be collected through interviews. This certainly turned out to be true in the first third of the manuscript which is substantially based on the memories of Frye himself, his first cousins, his school and college classmates, and Saskatchewan parishioners. Because Northrop Frye is a person who has always valued his privacy, this process at first involved a fair bit of turmoil. Although he confessed to another journalist that the process was sometimes "nightmarish" for him, he submitted to one-and-a-half-hour interviews which over eight years totalled over forty hours. Despite his initial turmoil, I came to believe that

Frye almost always told the truth about himself. He was not like a psychological onion, hiding his "true" self below ever deeper layers. While this will disappoint Freudians, I never felt I was dealing with anyone but an unusually honest man.

The importance of personal interviews also proved to be crucial in ferreting out Frye's intellectual influences such as Colin Still, Gilbert Murray, Francis Cornford, Emile Mâle, Wilson Knight, and C.S. Lewis, none of whom, unlike Spengler or Frazer, receive much attention in Frye's own writings. I consider these influences important in the creation of a genuine context for his way of thinking. By ignoring this background himself, Frye has to some degree been his own worst enemy, isolating himself in an academic environment which is often ignorant of the territory he has been working. As a result, Frye's writing has been seen to be more eccentric than it really is.

From the start, however, I've been acutely aware of entering dangerous ground. As a journalist, I knew that scholars would resent amateur poaching. But I also felt that my strength lay precisely in my weakness. Most academics trained in English often seem squeamish about basic journalistic techniques, preferring to deal with documentation which is already published or comfortably tucked away in an archival file. If it were left to a scholar, a biography of Frye would probably have taken another twenty or thirty years when most everyone connected with Frye was dead. Whatever documents remained would not provide a rounded picture.

There has been, moreover, a tendency on the part of Frye's academic contemporaries to take ideological positions for or against him which inevitably color any view of his career. I can hardly claim to be dispassionate but it is inevitable that my interests are different from a scholar. I like to think that any insights I have managed to produce are the consequence of my own non-specialized approach. As a result, I hope that what I have to say about Frye's work will represent an entry point for many people who are curious about Frye but are not conversant with the eternally raging Battle of the Critical Schools.

Basically, I have followed a thoroughly ordinary biographical premise that a writer and his work are intimately linked. Although Frye's opposition to the biographical method is well-known, I have taken my cue from Frye himself who has confessed that everything he has learned he has derived from either Blake or his evangelical Methodist background. Frye has even connected the two by admitting that it was Blake who made sense of evangelism for him, thereby heading off the kind of sour and futile rebellion which blighted the life of a friend. It's obvious in the first chapters that I have tried to outline the dimensions of Frye's own religious background, both ancestral and familial, to show how his personal adaption to militant Protestantism moulded his thinking and values. His writing, in turn, inevitably projects many of the same positive, often romantic, qualities. In writing the book, I also came to realize that the crucial element of Frye's literary theories, dialectic re-creation or "the eternal newness of the same," is his own personal accommodation to both religion and middle-class life. In an odd way, the work of one of the most impersonal critics of this century has in fact been intensely personal. Although I thought it ridiculous at first, I now agree with Frye's own contention that his work *is* his autobiography.

Like nearly all biographies, this is not a fully balanced work. There are the inevitable gaps occasioned either by a basic lack of material or by my personal decision to limit research time which might have added further weeks or months to an already overdue, and decidedly underfunded, project. Although I had access to the absolutely crucial letters he sent his wife, Helen, in the thirties, I have not seen everything. While his personal friends have been overwhelmingly generous with letters from Frye, I have not by any means seen all the letters he may have written over the years. One friend at least has withheld correspondence about a crucial period.

There are other gaps and deficiencies. Because Frye has written so much, I have had to be highly selective in the essays I have noted and commented on. My focus has been inevitably idiosyncratic. While I hope I have been faithful to Frye's intent, my comments on his work are shaped by the needs of the biographical narrative. It will be obvious, for example, that I am more interested in the way Frye developed major themes from a very early stage, projecting them *towards* major works. This has been quite deliberate, and academic readers who wish more critical detail on the major works like *Anatomy of Criticism* should consult Robert Denham's *Northrop Frye and Critical Method*. Denham's *Northrop Frye: An Annotated Bibliography of Primary and Secondary Sources*, published in 1988, lists hundreds of critical articles and reviews on Frye's work including much material on the recent *The Great Code*.

This book took me eight years to complete and has inevitably instigated cabin fever and oxygen starvation. For her patience, I would like to thank my wife Mary Ann Evans. I would also like to thank my writer friends who know that in an age of instant production, a biography is not.

# PART ONE

## NEW JERUSALEM

Northrop Frye once described his own critical tendencies as Odyssean—comedic and romantic—rather than that of the darker Iliad type of tragedy and irony. Because of Frye's early and pervasive interest in satire, this is not entirely true but its near accuracy does put Frye comfortably in the realm of radical Protestantism which has always been interested, even obsessed, with the glittering comedic finale of the Bible, the New Jerusalem of Revelation 21. Eagerness to effect this vision historically of course has often instigated a whole range of non-conformist sins, from Cromwellian tyranny to the pie-in-the-sky escapism of storefront fundamentalists.

But despite its sometimes ugly associates, the search for a New Jerusalem has remained a central Protestant quest which Bunyan definitively encoded as a harrowing, Evangelist-inspired journey by Christian from the City of Destruction to the glories of the Celestial City. Not coincidentally, this quest features the destruction of Giant Despair himself, and the Doubting Castle, which enslaves energy and vision. The fundamental quest, with all its mythic informing qualities, manages to reach through the centuries, linking the early left-wing Puritans, the evangelistic Methodists, Blake, and eventually Northrop Frye himself who has applied the same apocalyptic vision to the total range of western literature.

9

Not surprisingly, Frye realized early in his career that the evangelistic Blake would always be first in his regard and the Puritan Milton always second. Despite this, he never has given much attention to one obvious factor behind his interest, his own connection on both sides of his family with persecuted seventeenth-century Protestant dissenters who quite consciously left the Old World to undertake the basic Puritan goal of "regeneration and sanctification" in a New England. The first great Puritan leader, John Winthrop, quite explicitly envisioned the Revelations dream of a "city upon a hill" which would be viewed by the whole world as a project of God's grace. Though this dream became the root of early New England, and possibly of America itself, contemporary English Puritans like John Owen, Joseph Mede and Hansard Knollys likewise saw Zion appearing in Britain. Although Milton became disillusioned with the zanier forms of millenarianism of this period, one scholar argues that the vision of a Kingdom of Christ also provided him "with a definite point of reference in the future and a focus for his idealism." Jerusalem, of course, refused to appear from either the clouds or Massachusetts soil, but over a century and half later, Blake, who significantly claimed to take Milton into his foot, was again audaciously ready, sword in hand, to build "Jerusalem/In England's green and pleasant Land." Spiritual son of Blake and Milton, twentieth-century Frye would take in this essential vision and, like Blake, call for a "mental fight" which would build Jerusalem in a real time and place.

There are reasons for Frye's tepid interest in his ancestry. Frye knew that, while his ancestors on both sides of the family were Puritans or Huguenots, it was preposterous in the depths of his own family's poverty to congratulate himself—as other pretentious cousins did—on something so distant and elusive. And Frye was always more impressed by the imaginative rather than factual basis of such past associations. His own ancestry was merely a given with which he could not quarrel. What was important was how to fit himself imaginatively into a tradition which is predicated on spurning corruption and building anew. For Frye this has meant a uniquely Protestant form of British tradition, "the tendency to anchor apocalyptic vision in a direct individual experience, as the product, not of sacramental discipline, but of imaginative experiment." Although culturally based, this practical apocalyptic sense had its greatest merit when internalized and reborn by anyone who cares to understand it: "Scholars will assert that the famous 'Jerusalem' hymn is crypto-Anglo-Israelitism or what not; but when it was sung in front of the Transport House at the Labour victory of 1945 the singers showed that they understood it far better than such scholars did." This in itself points to a central aspect of radical protestantism which Frye has adapted for his own literary theories, the idea of possession, which represents the same internalization and reenactment of mythology which motivated the early Puritans.

The various colorations of fact about ancestry both by Frye and other family members for convenience and ideology were often, in fact, as important in his development as any presumption of an ancestral voice. Frye has always preferred to believe, for example, that his original New World ancestor, John ffrie, was a preacher from Andover, Hampshire, when in fact he was a wheelwright. ffrie did have one son who was a prominent church figure in New England but it was another son, Frye's own ancestor, Samuel Frie, whose descent included army men, Indian fighters and even a prominent politician. All of these ancestors were numbingly antithetical to Frye's own image. It is interesting, though, that in warping facts, Frye adjusted his ancestry to its own original vision.

Frye is not alone in his vague comprehension of family history. Nearly all the Canadian Fryes were sufficiently ignorant about their own background to turn key information around. When Frye's grandfather, Samuel, a third-generation Canadian, retired from farming in Quebec to his son Austin's place near Lowell, Massachussetts, he would sit with another old in-law, Charlie Noyes, and refight the Bunker Hill battle. With passion born of ignorance, Samuel volubly took the British side, apparently unaware that his own great-grandfather, Timothy Frye, was an authentic Lexington Minuteman who later fought as militia lieutenant at Bunker's Hill in the regiment of his cousin Col. James Frye. When this connection was recently rediscovered, Frye's distant cousin Roland Mushat Frye, himself a scholar of Milton, Shakespeare and the Bible, sent Frye a lead figurine of a Minuteman as a joke. Upon receipt, Frye faithfully kept the figurine on his desk, but when the muzzle of the gun was knocked upwards in an accident at a 90-degree angle to the stock, Frye left it that way for months, unconsciously making a Loyalist protest.

His first known ancestor was John ffrie, a Puritan dissenter who left southern Britain at the tail end of the Great Migration of the 1630s. He left on the *Bevis* in May 1639 from Southampton with a small group of artisans. The voyage took much of the summer, but like other shiploads of Puritans in the well-organized and -financed Great Migration, they were welcomed by an already established community of coreligionists who were convinced that they were building not only a New England but a New Jerusalem. John ffrie and his family moved up the coast and then inland to Andover along the banks of the Merrimack River where he was listed as eighth on a list of settlers.

Burning religious mission may have spurred the initial drive to emigrate thousands of miles from Britain, but ffrie settled down to a perfectly routine life as wheelwright and farmer and lived to be 91. Besides his land and property, his estate included the works of the liberal Puritan theologian Dr. John Preston. His childless son, John Frie, became a Congregational minister and a powerful magistrate. Pressured by John himself, his wife became briefly victimized in the Andover witch trials which were nearly as ferocious and socially traumatic as the more celebrated trials in Salem. Northrop Frye's direct ancestor, Samuel Frie, was a third son who produced a line of militia colonels, mandarins, and pragmatists that included one of Washington's militia generals, Joseph Frye, and the jingoist, William Pierce Frye, interim Vice-President of the United States in the McKinley-Roosevelt administrations. Colonel Joseph Frye who served briefly as Brigadier in Washington's Continental Army, inadvertently stumbled into New England legend. His harried escape from the Indian-seiged Fort William Henry, later outlined in Hoyt's *History of the Indian Wars,* is a probable source for James Fenimore Cooper's *The Last of the Mohicans.*

Although the clan was overwhelmingly revolutionary, Col. Samuel's most prominent son, Peter Frye, was a resolute Tory who left the United States for England as a Loyalist. His nephew and namesake likewise had a powerful urge to leave the American experiment behind. Family myth, heavily embroidered by the fierce Loyalist prejudices of Frye's own mother, had it that he had to abandon his properties in Massachusetts because of a direct threat by revolutionaries. Since he was all of five years old when the Revolution started and since his own father was the Minuteman, Timothy, this story is hardly credible. Like many young American farmers, Peter probably emigrated to pick up cheap land in Canada.

Shortly after the turn of the century, Peter Frye was listed as one of the first settlers who occupied the heights overlooking the St. Francis River north of Sherbrooke, Lower Canada. In essence he relived the whole immigrant experience against the raw wilderness. His son Hermon and grandsons Abbott and Samuel held and farmed the land which now comprises the central and northern section of the town of Windsor (formerly Windsor Mills), despoiled today by a huge paper mill. In the 1850s, though, it was conventionally idyllic. Abbott had a beautiful brook running through his pastures and built a red brick home. He farmed, ran a butcher shop and became mayor between 1876 and 1880. By family tradition Abbott taught in the winter in a boys' school in Vermont and at some point met an American girl, Abby Northrop, the daughter of a farmer from Danville, Vermont. Like the Fryes, the Northrops descended from a Puritan. Joseph Northrup emigrated from England in 1637 in the same wave of religious dissenters.

Although Abbott and Abby Frye were both rather flamboyant people, their younger siblings, Samuel Fletcher Frye and Sarah Ann Northrop were quiet and reserved. They married each other in 1861 and first had three daughters, Etta, Carie and Ella and then three boys, Herman, Alfred and Austin. Sarah Ann had worked in Lowell, Massachussetts at the J.C. Ayer patent medicine plant and, like a whole generation of factory girls from farms, lived in boarding houses on the Corporation when Lowell was a major textile centre. By the 1850s Lowell was already losing its importance but Sarah Ann brought her children up to believe that Lowell was the golden city to head for in life. Although this was colored by her American upbringing, English and French Quebeckers traditionally looked "across the line," the virtually open border, for opportunities.

Sarah Ann's directive was so compelling that when she died in Windsor Mills at 61 in 1895, two of her daughters and her three sons were living in the Lowell area, within miles of the home of the original ancestor, John ffrie. None of the boys was interested in farming and ultimately, when their father retired, his land passed out of the family to the chagrin of at least one niece, Lillian, who remembered the beauty and value of the property from childhood visits. The Frye boys were eager to rise out of their farming past but all three were curiously unsuccessful in life. After graduating from the Belleville Business College in 1891, Northrop Frye's father, Herman, started as a clerk for hardware stores in Lowell but faced a blighted business future. Austin was a pharmacist in Lowell but became ensnared in legal problems when a partner was caught dealing in illegal drugs. Alfred was a Congregationalist minister in marginal parishes and was noted in the family for his tedious sermons. At one time in the thirties, he was even unemployed.

**THE HOWARDS**

As bastions of the Methodist church in Windsor Mills, the Fryes were of course inextricably bound up with the ministers who arrived and departed in the usual three-year cycle. In the late 1880s, Rev. Eratus Seth Howard was posted to Windsor Mills and by immutable social chemistry, one of the Frye sons, Herman, and Rev. Howard's second daughter, Catharine, married a decade later and had a family of three children; their youngest was Northrop Frye.

Rev. Howard came from an intensely Loyalist background, and instilled his family with unshakeable and often numbing convictions of Tory and Methodist rectitude and superiority. At least two of his daughters, Dolly and Hatty, took up the refrain and continually congratulated themselves—without a shred of evidence—on their alleged connections with various Howard aristocrats in Britain. An item planted by Dolly in a local paper in Wellington, Ont., claimed: "Coincident with the visit to America of the Dowager Duchess of Norfolk, widow of one of the wealthiest English Peers, come some interesting reminiscences ... concerning the Canadian branch of this old and distinguished British family. Mrs. Dolly Garratt, now living in Wellington, Ont. is a daughter of Rev. Eratus Seth Howard, born in 1833, whose paternal ancestors were directly connected with the Duke of Norfolk."

Actually the origins of the Howard family are unknown. Frye himself has said that the Howards were descendants of Catholic Howards who came over with Lord Baltimore to settle Maryland, but there is no more proof of this than the conjecture of his Aunt Dolly. It's interesting nonetheless that Frye would relish the notion that *all* his ancestors were America-bound seventeenth-century religious dissenters. His first known Howard ancestor was in fact his great-grandfather, Eratus Howard, who died by falling through ice before his last child, Rev. Eratus Howard, was even born in 1833. If there was any documentation of his background—English, Canadian, or American—it was lost in a house fire when Rev. Howard was a small boy. Despite his obscurity, Eratus senior did marry Catharine Demorest whose father was Gilliam Demorest (dem-or-ray), who controlled the then flourishing mill town of Demorestville in Prince Edward County, Upper Canada.

In 1865 Eratus married Harriet Hersey of Kingston. Variously stern and indulgent, the two parents raised a brood of eight children, all of whom were quite different from each other in personality. Despite this, there were obvious family traits, most notably high intelligence and the odd outburst of murderous impatience and humorlessness which became known even in the family as "the Howard grouch." Although Eratus doted on his eldest daughter Elthea ("Dolly"), she was sufficiently eccentric and domineering to be thoroughly disliked by her siblings. She married a well-liked but meek Quaker called Rufus Garratt who she promptly railroaded into the Methodist Church as preacher. She became associated with a radical wing of the Methodists, the Holiness

Movement. By contrast, the eldest son, Daniel Hersey ("D.H."), was a quiet, likeable printer in Montreal. Although just barely successful in business himself, he had two brilliant sons, a PhD geologist, Waldie, and a millionaire Westmount lawyer and financier, Wilbert, whose princely mansion overlooked lower Montreal and the vast sweep of the St. Lawrence River beyond. The sibling leader who inspired and prodded all the children was the third child, Eratus ("Rate"), who first taught grade school, then earned a gold medal in math and physics at McGill University, and then went on to win another gold in law. He set up a law firm and became a judge briefly in the early thirties before he died in his mid-sixties in 1934. His own daughter, Alma, created a modest sensation in Montreal papers in 1938 by earning a PhD in biochemistry on scholarship. In the late forties in the Hammersmith Hospital in London, Alma managed to discover a crucial link in genetic research, "the timing of DNA synthesis in the cell cycle of ordinary tissue cells," which became important in cancer research.

The next child was Northrop Frye's mother, Catharine ("Cassie") Mary Maud. Cassie was recognized by most in the family as the perhaps most intelligent and certainly most formidable in both bearing and personality. Her photos as a young woman show her beautiful but stolid, suggesting an inner-directed resilience that would be depressingly appropriate to her tragic married life. She lived the sheltered life of a pastor's daughter, teaching grade school for a year in Wellington, Ont., then as matron in the mid-1890s at the Methodist Stanstead College before marriage. She considered those years to be the happiest in her life. Cassie possessed an attractive contralto voice and if the opportunity for training had ever existed in the primitive cultural conditions of rural Canada, she might have developed into a serious singer. As a woman of her generation, though, she could not expect either training or education and would, outside of raising her family, lead a wasted life, plagued by ill health and anxiety over her husband's chronic business failure.

Cassie herself was close to her second youngest sister, Mary, who was mannish and well-read. Mary left the family for a church school mission in a new Ukrainian community near Edmonton called Sniatyn where she worked until cancer hit her in 1932. Between Cassie and Mary was Theresa ("Tessie") who was the most reserved and in a family of unrepentant eccentrics, the most ordinary. She married a lumber merchant in Granby, Quebec, and like Eratus, died relatively young. Harriet ("Hatty"), the next daughter, sometimes resembled Dolly in her pretensions but was well liked. She became a bookkeeper in Lowell, Massachusetts, and married her boss, quickly had a family and returned to Canada with her children. She separated from her husband and ran a small farm called "Two Oaks" and then a boarding house in Montreal near McGill University. Finally, there was John. Gifted with lavender-colored eyes which drove his adoring sisters crazy with jealousy, he was the best looking. He had a happy-go-lucky personality that was entirely out of sorts with the proprieties of his home. He feuded with his father, and eventually moved to Lowell where he managed his own parcel delivery service. His own son, Donald, became a minister in New England and upstate New York.

In the numbing tradition of the rural pastor's family, the Howards moved every three years to a new location. The list of towns reads like a railway schedule—Kingston, Brockville, Wolfe Island (where Cassie was born), Aultsville, Sydenham, Elgin, Nepean, Inkerman, Iroquois, Inverness, Windsor Mills, Farnham, Phillipsburg, Lawrenceville, West Brome, Minton, Marbelton, Odelltown and Lawrenceville again for five more years past retirement. Even with all his own failures in life, Herman Frye considered his father-in-law a genuine Lord-inspired innocent who failed to jockey for the big, well-paid city congregations. Certainly, there was an obsessed nature to Rev. Howard. In the 1950s old-timers in West Brome, where Howard's great-granddaughter Wilma vacationed, still remembered that he was so dedicated that when snow storms made horse travel impossible, he insisted, like John Wesley himself, on trying to complete the circuit on foot. Nor did he ever retire. A month before his death in Oct. 1923, *The Detroit Free Press* ran his picture with Harriet, both in severe Victorian black, on the top front page with headline "HAS PREACHED GOSPEL FOR SIXTY-THREE YEARS."

Yet he was hardly the innocent of Herm Frye's characterization.

Cassie alluded to a bitter disappointment in his early career when he lost an attractive parish in the Ottawa area. When he subsequently moved to nearby Nepean, Cassie felt that a certain sourness crept into the family that permanently affected everyone. He even suffered religious doubts. When he was dying, he surprised his daughter Mary with the wrenching confession, "I don't understand God."

Congruent with his dedication to poorly paid rural parishes, Rev. Howard was nevertheless conventionally pietistic. At the dinner table at home, he insisted on Bible readings around the table that included even the very youngest of grandchildren. If the youngest faltered, an older sibling took over. He also required family prayers after breakfast and dinner. The family knelt down away from the table, facing their pulled-out chairs. Because Rev. Howard had an eye for his own comfort, he liked to have a pillow handy to protect his knees. If there was none, a fleeting look of disappointment passed across his face and he would spread a handkerchief on the floor instead. The family would be happy that, with that inadequate barrier on the floor, the prayers would be abbreviated. In church, he showed a similar propensity for drawing out his rhetoric without regard to the increasing boredom of his congregation. Not surprisingly, no living grandchild can ever remember his actually laughing. According to family lore, the closest he came to humor in his services was the result of a great yapping of dogs outside the church during a very rare moment of silence. He lifted his head erect creating a minor tizzy in the congregation which realized that history was being made: the Rev. E.S. Howard was going to crack a joke. With a straight face, he proclaimed the line from Revelation 22, "Without are dogs!"

He was also obdurately vain. When he began losing his hair on top, he started wearing a large skull cap which he kept on at all hours wherever he went. He even refused to take it off for photos. He stood up beside his oldest son Hersey and asked people, "Who is the youngest?" He was apparently not joking, and failed to understand the devastating effect on his son. To one grandchild he represented the ominous image of the Old Testament Jehovah. By the time he was elderly, however, the hard edges of his eccentricities were more endearing than frightening. The parsonage at Lawrenceville was for some reason infested with flies and Eratus surrounded himself with fly paper only to get murderously stuck in it. Visiting Two Oaks, he used to try to count the freight trains going by, and then got riled with himself if he lost count.

His wife Harriet fit into the Methodist mould, explaining sinners in grinding simplicity: "That's how they git when they dance." Yet while she complied with the Methodist Blue Sunday, there was a degree of protest. A short stout woman who would lend her features to some of her grandchildren in their own old age including Frye, she would wind up the piano stool as far as possible and sit down. She would then place a large Bible on the closed piano lid and read passages with such a whimpering voice that it indicated to at least one grandson that it was duress not piety which made her read.

It was perhaps significant that only the values and not the rituals survived into the next generation. Generally there was a slow disintegration of the whole rural Methodist ethos in the family. In her involvement with the Holiness Movement the eldest, Dolly, was obviously retrenching. Cassie and Mary remained convinced Methodists, though like everyone, saw no need for compulsory Bible readings or agonizing family prayer sessions. The more sophisticated, like Eratus, or socially aspiring, like Hatty, converted to Anglicanism. Yet despite the weakening of content, the form, particularly of the evangelical impulse, survived intact through Cassie to her son Northrop. Although he would bitterly reject the fundamentalism, even in rebellion he would carry on its central aspects of left-wing Protestantism.

## A NINETEENTH-CENTURY HOME

In a family round robin letter published in 1913, Cassie remembered her marriage in Oct. 1897 with an almost sentimental fondness which belied the difficult times she had already faced. She

was married to Herm Frye at Philipsburg, Quebec, in the old
Methodist Church where her father was just finishing a three-year
posting. Travelling by train up to Stanbridge, the family dined in
the "old parsonage of many happy memories." The family escorted
the newlyweds down again to the station and pelted them with so
much rice they escaped up onto a flatcar protecting themselves
with an umbrella. Born on the same day, Aug. 30, 1870, they were,
at 27, late for marriage. Alluding to the Victorian paternal hold in
the Howard family, Cassie noted that she was the first of the girls
to leave her parents' home on her own.

Setting up a home in North Chelmsford near Lowell, the couple
had every reason to slip easily into the American Dream as had
tens of thousands of Canadian immigrants before. Cassie, however,
was quickly disgruntled with the United States. Perhaps it was the
suddenness of independence from her family circle or the insoluble
accretions of Loyalist sentiment. Whatever the case, Cassie developed an almost pathological hatred of America. She later confessed
quite seriously that she had been so depressed and chronically ill
with flu she feared that she might die. She told Herm's niece
Lillian Noyes that the Stars and Stripes was a repugnant sight
to her. Her younger sister Hatty, who soon joined the general
Howard-Frye migration to Lowell, had a better sense of humor.
To the disbelieving outrage of her neighbours, she truculently
raised the Union Jack outside her home on Queen Victoria Day.

Cassie's anglophile sourness certainly troubled the beginnings
of an otherwise conventional family life solidly centred on family
and church. The Fryes quickly realized the rice symbol of their
wedding day by having two children, a boy on March 29, 1899,
and a girl on Christmas Day, 1900. They called the boy Eratus
Howard after his grandfather and the girl Vera Victoria. Since
Queen Victoria died soon after Vera's birth, Victoria seemed appro-
priately British and Loyal, unlike the first choice of Sarah which
was too redolent of the shanty Irish in Lowell. Vera never appreci-
ated the gesture and always tended to lean to her American birth
and eventually her Frye ancestry for her identity.

By the time that Vera was born, the family had moved in from the
outlying town of North Chelmsford to 19 Varney St. in downtown

Lowell and Herm could now get to work without commuting. Lowell was experiencing a second boom and Herm found little trouble in establishing himself economically. He held jobs with two hardware firms, first with Adams on Middlesex when he was boarding with his sister Ella and then for a larger firm, Thompson, where he was a senior clerk. At some point, he also travelled as a salesman for Moses ("Hugh") La Hue, an American of Jersey Island ancestry, who manufactured mechanical loom attachments and married Cassie's sister Hatty. Although Herm rarely talked about his experiences as a commercial traveller, he once erupted into a negro dice chant in a family card game he'd learned on a trip into the deep south. On other occasions, he displayed a substantial knowledge of southern geography which startled the family for the suggestion of an exoticism they never associated with him. Otherwise Herm's life seemed totally directed to a settled middle-class American life. The extended Frye family, in fact—Herm, Austin, Alfred, Ella and Etta—were now all so thoroughly settled in the Lowell area, that their father came down from Quebec to retire with Austin on a small farm outside the city in the early 1900s.

Nevertheless, Cassie's venomous anti-Americanism did not abate and in 1904, with her children approaching school age, Cassie insisted on a return to Canada. It was not just that the States had proved so disagreeable for her. There was also the lingering trauma of a boy born two years before who was either stillborn or died soon after birth. Herm and Cassie had planned to call him Northrop after Herm's mother's family. Like most stillborns, he was not totally forgotten and lived on in Cassie's dreams. The family settled in Sherbrooke where Herm first rented a flat on Wolfe St. from a widow. They then moved into their own home at 30 London St. in 1905. It was on the outskirts of the city then and looked down into the deep St. Francis River valley with a view to the high eastern bank beyond. Now she was delivered back to Canada again, Cassie's emotions settled down. She was once more close to her parents in Lawrenceville who frequently visited. Cassie also quickly became absorbed into a solidly anglophile Methodist congregation headed by a wealthy lumber merchant, B.C. Howard, whose huge park-surrounded estate, Howardene, was just a few blocks away. The Methodist community was extremely close and supportive of its congregation members. The Howards, who were not related to Cassie's family, allowed the Fryes to graze their cow, which Howard and Vera tended when they were older, on the fields of their estate.

As in Lowell, Herm found work as a hardware clerk in the large firm of J.S. Mitchell, another of Sherbrooke's benevolent merchant princes. After the disruptions of Lowell, the family again seemed to be settling into a prosperous lower middle-class life. The Fryes could even afford a French-Canadian servant and their duplex house on London St. provided the cushion of extra rental income from the other half of the house. There seemed to be few immediate worries. When enrolled in school, Howard and Vera, already coached by Cassie, did extremely well. The family was prosperous enough to look after the orphaned children of Herm's sister Ella who had died in childbirth and whose husband subsequently died in a tragic accident. The Fryes took in the two youngest children, Dorothy, and for a while, her brother, Austin, without a thought.

For Dorothy, who had so recently suffered the trauma of losing both her parents, the chance of quickly entering a settled family existence again was a great relief. Although both Herm and Cassie were affectionate, she observed Cassie as the stricter family head who insisted on unwavering obedience to routine, regular piano practice, homework and particularly to the rituals of the Methodist Blue Sunday which Dorothy found particularly onerous and boring.

The Sabbath began on Saturday evening when Herm portioned out little white candies into dishes for each of the children to literally sweeten the way through the long quiet hours after church on Sunday. In the morning the family went together to the Methodist Church down the hill off Montreal St. After the service there was little to do except read, go for a walk, play tiddly-winks or Methodist surrogate card games like Old Maid. Although there was no dogmatic insistence on the Bible, it was an omnipresent tome which could be consumed in the King James and Revised Standard editions or in a children's condensation, *Hurlbut's Story of the Bible*. The advance of the Bible, of course, was not that it was approved but that in the context of evangelical Christianity, it was *interesting* narratively and symbolically. To Dorothy, who was extroverted, her adoptive family was quiet and almost reclusive, oriented to books and the piano. Howard had a particularly deep interest in the piano and developed into an accomplished classical player. Athletically competent, Howard also skied and mountain climbed in the ancient volcanic mountains of the Sherbrooke area. Vera was more home-centred and to earn pocket money, made marmalade and peanut butter for family friends. Despite this domestic industry, she rebelled against the ordinary household discipline of Cassie with whom she quietly feuded for most of her life. She indulged in subterfuge: conveniently disappearing upstairs to the bathroom when it came time to do the dishes, often leaving such chores to Dorothy.

Just as her children were entering adolescence, Cassie found herself pregnant again at 41. It was not a pleasant prospect. The birth of Vera had been difficult and there was, of course, the tragedy of the third child, Northrop. As Cassie entered the final stages of pregnancy, she tried to minimize domestic complications by sending Dorothy and Vera down to a maiden cousin of the Northrop family who lived in Danville, Vermont. While Dorothy luxuriated in the new environment, Vera became homesick and, echoing Cassie's earlier reaction to Lowell, soon headed back.

## NORTHROP

On July 14, 1912, after a difficult labor which nearly killed her, Cassie gave birth to a son. Herm and Cassie called their baby Herman Northrop after his father and the earlier dead brother. It was ironic that from the start they called their baby by the formal, and very American, name of Northrop rather than the familiar Herm. Their new son, however, was an attractive reflection of the Howard-Demorest side of the family with light blue eyes and eventually a healthy mop of blond hair which was so light that he was often assumed to be of German extraction. On Oct. 17, Cassie's father came to Sherbrooke to baptize him, outlining the implacable symbol of the cross on his forehead in the Methodist Church. In a certain sense, he was claimed by that baptism and never escaped its association.

As a baby, Northrop suffered crying fits and rather serious teething problems that disrupted the family. Dorothy and Vera, who were nannies to Northrop, regularly had to leave their dinner when they heard him howl and go upstairs. Rocking his cradle they sang anything they knew, including hymns, in an effort to quiet him. Barely would they get downstairs before he'd let out another howl and they would have to go upstairs again. Unfortunately his problem endured and the following summer the family cancelled a plan to go to summer camp because of his teething. Dorothy, however, remembered her cousin as an otherwise adorable and good-natured child on whom she and Vera loved to dote. That impression is certainly confirmed by photos of his early years which show a boy alert and emotionally open within the circle of his family.

Despite his own generally reserved nature, Herm was prone to fits of optimism about his own ability to make money with grand schemes. Fortunately he never acted on these fantasies. After nearly ten years as a senior clerk in the Mitchell firm, however, he took an uncharacteristic step at independence by setting up his own business. On May 15, 1915, he signed papers to establish the Frye and Cross shop at 187 Wellington St., not far from his formidable former employer, J.S. Mitchell. Despite his partnership with lumber merchant Arthur Cross, it appeared that Herm really ran the business. At $960 a year, his rent was very steep but the shop was in a central location. What Herm didn't count on was that the wartime economy would not allow another hardware store to compete with the established Mitchell firm. While none of this was immediately obvious, Herm's bold decision was a catastrophic mistake which would completely undermine the happiness and well-being of his family for the next quarter century.

Despite its central importance to the well-being of the family, Cassie did not encourage her children to work or even spend time down at the store. Her own attentions were centred solely on her family and on church activities. Howard and Vera were now doing extremely well in high school. As she had done with them, she began tutoring Northrop, now three, in both piano and reading. For reading she used a text *I Want to Read* which emphasized word identification. In casual kitchen sessions, Cassie would ask her son to go into the dining room, study the book and come back and point to all the *thes, thems,* and so on. For the piano, she would ask him to point out and play particular notes.

When he was four, Northrop began piano lessons with B.C. Howard's adopted daughter Gladys. At his première performance he played a piece called "The Acorn" and created a modest sensation when he bowed in the wrong direction when announcing the composition. Later in life, he considered Cassie's attentions partly the result of a conspiracy by Vera who wanted to have him occupied and out of the way when she was entertaining friends from school. Although Cassie was more ambivalent towards Northrop than her adored first children, she was actually just following the established pattern of intensive early education. Northrop's reading precocity allowed him to start on the family's Altemus editions of children's classics. His absorption in books was immediate and so pervasive that in the normal troubled sleep stage of four-year-olds, he awoke one night with a searing image from an illustration in the Altemus edition of *Pilgrim's Progress* of Faithful being burned at the stake.

Northrop was also being groomed to the gentility basic to the English upper middle class of the city. This meant tea and crumpets and the hushed good manners of gentlemen and ladies. While Methodism elsewhere maintained a proud rough-hewn image, the church in Sherbrooke flirted with Anglican pretension. A Christmas party for some 275 children of the congregation in 1917 involved "a sacred cantata" followed by "a substantial and varied 'high tea' [which] was served in the tea room ... " Against this cloistered effeminate existence, there was, of course, the foil of the outside world. Because Northrop never fit into the standard boy pattern of fishing and hiking expeditions, this conception of outside freedom inevitably had an urban, though no less compelling, cast. Northrop was very early interested in the names and patterns of the streets in his neighbourhood and the small downtown. Reflecting the omnipresent religion of his home life, he indulged in a bit of imaginative heresy, speculating that the place of heaven was close by, on the other side of the St. Francis River. From his own look-outs on the streets around his house, he could see the hills of the opposite bank. Up in the sky, he imagined Jehovah on a throne in the image of Rev. Eratus. This geography became so much a part of his fiber, he would always consider himself a Quebecker.

A year and half after opening, Herm's business ran into so many financial problems that he had to sell both sides of the family duplex to raise capital. His tenant, J.F. McKenna, bought it in Sept. 1916 and in what must have amounted to a bruising reversal, the Fryes became tenants in their own house. The following July, Herm's business deteriorated even further and his partnership with Arthur Cross broke up. Herm renamed the store H.E. Frye, advertising his specialties in the *Sherbrooke City Directory:* "builders' hardware, cutlery, tools, sporting goods, mantels, tilings, gratings, paint and oils."

An odd descant to Herm's declining fortunes was the war fever which had spread throughout the jingoistic and obdurately anglophile population of the Eastern Townships. The Sherbrooke Exhibition Ground across the river from the Fryes was, in fact, a staging ground for troops going overseas. On June 4, 1915, "10,000 people from all parts of the Eastern Townships assembled in Sherbrooke to bid God Speed to the gallant lads from the townships, the first distinctive Eastern Townships unit to go overseas." The following spring another unit encamped on Exhibition Grounds and headed off for Saint John after an obligatory and rousing march through the city. The ghoulish appetite for young men for the front continued unabated. In January 1917, Lt. Gen. Sir Sam Hughes pleaded for more men at a "patriotic rally."

In April, a Lt. LaBreque placed a brash ad in the *Record:* "30 YOUNG MEN WANTED FOR MOTOR CYCLE SECTION ... Special authority granted for organization of Motor Cycle section to be composed of Eastern Townships' young men of good character and intelligence ... No infantry drill ... Join at once." The *Record* followed LaBreque's enlistment drive with coverage appropriate to a high-pressure charity drive, counting down the number of men still needed to bring the unit up to strength. Just two weeks past his eighteenth birthday, Howard Frye answered the siren call.

Although he was bright and athletic, Howard was an unlikely warrior. His one letter home, published in the *Record* as part of a series of soldier letters, showed a kindly middle-class boy concerned like a good Methodist with group morale. He explained how the massive troop congestion in Halifax was backing up troop trains as far back as Truro. Except for bread and butter, there was no food for soldiers. The ministers in Truro appealed from the pulpits and the troops, mostly boys, were fed cake and doughnuts by the local ladies. Everything in his letter offered reassurance to Herm and Cassie: while he had left home, he carried his home life and values with him. "I am beginning to feel as though I ought to be petted by the home folks. Nearly every soldier who has left a fine home and position feels the same ... So far I have not been homesick. One poor fellow cried most of the first day in the train."

When he was overseas, his family followed his progress through correspondence and every so often reported his activities in the City News column of the *Record*. He finally arrived overseas in mid-May and, probably because of his youth, trained for an entire year at Aldershot in the Boy's Battalion. He visited his cousin Wilbert Howard at Shorncliffe who was convalescing from trench fever suffered at the Somme. Wilbert's own negative experiences on the front did nothing to dampen Howard's desire to go to war. He even turned down an offer from his superiors to remain in England as a motorcycle training sergeant. In early August 1918, the Fryes reported in the *Record* that he had been transferred, still a private, to the 14th Battalion in France.

The year that Howard was overseas was an especially trying one for Herm's business. Among the local merchants Herm presented every appearance of ordinary success. He donated a silver cup for the local junior baseball league championship. He regularly advertised in the *Record*. Unlike the cool, correct ads of the established J.S. Mitchell Co., however, Herm tried various degrees of promise and sensationalism. He offered substantial discounts to raise sales volume, chopping a dollar off the price of $6 lawn mowers. In one ad, he even sensationalized a manufacturer's warranty: "RATS! RATS! ONE THOUSAND DOLLAR REWARD." The ad claimed that if a particular rat poison did not kill rats without odor, the manufacturer would pay out a $1000 reward. Although he made a determined advertising campaign in the summer of 1917, the business continued to flounder.

There was a cruel edge to his failure. Despite his own bitter struggle to keep the business going, the established businessmen of the city, the Howards, the McKechnies, the LeBarons and the Mitchells seemed to have it absurdly easy. The City News was full of chit-chat about their jaunts, unruffled by recession or war, to winter havens like Coronado Beach in California and West Palm Beach and St. Augustine in Florida.

By fall 1917, Herm was so broke, he could no longer afford the rent of his former house and had to move the family to a small fourteen-acre farm, Two Oaks, in Lennoxville run by Cassie's sister Hatty. It was a beautiful property just four miles south of Sherbrooke on the edge of Bishop's College overlooking the Massawippi River. Moses LaHue had bought it with the intention of settling permanently in Canada but after his family moved he decided not to join them.

In the meantime, Howard's battalion was brought up to the front near Amiens and immediately took part in the savage August 8, 1918, offensive. They were so successful that in one day, they hauled away 10 field guns, 46 machine guns and 8 mortars from the increasingly demoralized Germans. The next two days they enjoyed a couple of days of good weather, quiet and no casualties. August 18th would have been the same except for some early morning artillery fire. In the regimental diary, the adjutant noted drily, "Situation was quiet during the day, with the exception of a few shells which landed in our area very early in the morning, one of which killed two and wounded eight other ranks." One of the two dead "ranks" was Howard Frye, dead at nineteen. To the adjutant, he was just another nameless boy blasted to scraps by a random shell.

When Herm and Cassie received the news by telegram from Ottawa on Aug. 28, they were brutally crushed. Howard was their

adored son, destined for a brilliant future. Coming on top of Herm's
bleak business prospects, both Herm and Cassie fell into a deep
depression from which they never recovered. The day the news
came, Herm sat in the summer kitchen of the Layhew farmhouse,
staring blankly into space for hours. Thereafter, the sight of military
uniforms made him agitated, even furious. Years later when Hatty
showed off her twins Hugh and Lew in the military-style band
uniforms of Stanstead College, she made the mistake of asking him
what he thought of them. With an icy stare, Herm contemptuously
snapped, "I hate that uniform." When Northrop himself participated in compulsory cadet training early in high school, there was
a distinct unease about another son in uniform.

Characteristically Cassie kept emotional control of herself and
cried discreetly and quietly throughout the day. But the loss of
Howard cut so deep that to the end of her life, she often wrote
letters to relatives close to Howard's birthdate, March 29. A year
before her own death in 1940, she wrote her nephew Donald
Howard, making a rare confession: "I began writing to you because
of Howard's and your birthdays coming so close together and I
could not get over the terrible loneliness of losing Howard." Vera
too, who had been a childhood companion of Howard, was stunned
and traumatized by his death.

After the war, the city fathers put up a huge war monument on
the steeply banked avenue of King St. A sculpted swirl of bare-
breasted Winged Victories arch towards the river below, a curious
monument for teenagers who were slaughtered before most of
them knew women. On the back, facing his own home, Howard's
name—spelled wrong—is on a plaque. By then, the Fryes had
departed from Sherbrooke, never to return to the valley which
Peter Frye had settled 120 years before. For Northrop who'd
just turned six, the death of his brother presented a complex of
confusions he was too young to comprehend. He had only a dim
recollection of his brother as an amiable good-looking soldier in
uniform who headed off to war when Northrop was still only four.
But in the long term, Howard's death had major repercussions for
him because he became Howard's replacement without the luxury
of being allowed Howard's conventional boyish interests.

At first, this protectiveness created no major problems. In Lennoxville, Northrop continued to amaze his cousins Lew and Hugh with his precocity in reading. Northrop carried around the copy of *Pilgrim's Progress* like a teddy bear and would read from it with little prompting to his twin cousins who were three years older than he. They were so proud of him that they invited him to their grade two class to perform by reading from their reader or from anything that the teacher cared to produce for him.

Finally in mid-1919, Herm could no longer carry on his business and, after four expensive years of failure, he closed shop. Since his creditors did not force him to file bankruptcy, he must have settled or evaded his debts. Nearly 50 and without money to show for three decades of work, Herm now had to start a career once more as a commercial traveller. There was little option. He couldn't be a hardware clerk again in Sherbrooke. Returning to Lowell where his brothers and sisters lived was impossible because of Cassie's obvious distaste for America. To hunt up business, he disappeared for days during which there was often little food in the house. Vera also was in a difficult position when she graduated from high school and seemed to have no prospects for the future until she landed a job as a clerk in the new Sherbrooke Pure Milk Company which was owned and managed by the ubiquitous B.C. Howard.

Although the Fryes managed to move into a large rented home called the Reid house on the other side of the river, monetary pressures made them move again into a cheaper house on the main road. Northrop had passed it many times, loathing its ugliness. He now recognized the significance of having to move into it. Through the moves, Cassie kept the family's basic cultural infrastructure intact. The Weber piano went along everywhere, as did the books and a 1912 American encyclopedia, but there was an undeniable vulnerability to their poverty. In their third move, to the ugly house in Lennoxville, a sour group of movers deliberately cracked a pane of glass in a cabinet because they thought the household wasn't properly packed up when they arrived and resented working longer hours than they expected. Although he would face many more moves in childhood, Northrop never got used to the domestic disruptions and always carried an anxiety with him about the permanence of home.

All of this, of course, was extremely hard on Cassie. Not so long ago she'd been a leading member of the strong and prosperous Methodist circle in Sherbrooke, a friend of the wealthy Howards who dominated the city. She had a husband with a steady position, two very bright older children with strong prospects, her own duplex home with extra income from tenants, even a maid. Now everything had disintegrated: husband unemployed and penniless, son dead, daughter unhappy and restless, no financial security and no real home.

## MONCTON EXILE

Slowly Herm began to build up a business representing "Upper Canadian" (Ontario) manufacturers in the Atlantic provinces. He belonged to a small army of nearly two hundred agents in the east who served contractors, hardware stores and wholesalers, each of them representing three or four Canadian, British or American companies. With their catalogues and sample cases, they travelled mostly by rail, seeing customers at their offices or hotel rooms to draw up specifications. It was difficult and uncertain work. As a defeated man who was temperamentally unsuited to life on the road, Herm was hardly a star salesman.

Eventually, however, he felt that he had established enough business to relocate his family in the Maritimes rail centre, Moncton, and boarded them in the house of a bad-tempered old woman whom Northrop loathed. Once again, Herm could not meet basic expenses and Cassie and Northrop had to return to Quebec, this time to stay with another of Cassie's sisters, Tessie, who was married to a genial well-to-do lumber merchant, Albert Solomon, in Granby near Montreal.

The Solomons had one son, Willie, who was a little older than

Northrop. Because Willie was allowed a good deal of freedom, he was baffled by the housebound cousin who was so very different from Howard who Willie had adored. Howard had visited a few years before, and after Sunday service took Willie and some friends on a fishing expedition up the Yamaska River near Granby, eating their catch by a fire. To Willie, who was still quite young, this all-male expedition, led by his glamorous older cousin, was exotic and thrilling and he naturally expected Northrop to share the same interests. But Northrop did not fit the mould. In Victorian boy's style, Cassie kept his curly blond hair long and insisted on formal deportment. When Willie and two close friends, both sweaty and filthy from fishing, returned to the house once, they met a prim, clean Northrop. Seven-year-old Northrop responded to the round of introductions with "I am pleased to make your acquaintance." Instead of more conventional outdoor activities, Northrop rooted through the Solomon's encyclopedia to add new names to a list of different types and species of trees, a list which eventually ran to over 600 names. He also kept a stamp collection, and more exotically, a collection of chocolate bar wrappers which managed to combine indulgence with a sense of order. Willie was under specific orders to collect wrappers from his own friends to add to Northrop's special scrap book, which eventually ran to about 100 wrappers.

Like most people who did not know Cassie intimately, Willie saw his Aunt Cassie as a stiff, formidable woman. Yet ironically the most serious run-in he had with her happened when he had the temerity to tell Northrop that there was no Santa Claus. For Cassie, obviously, there was a generous area of fantasy which she considered inviolable, despite its obvious ideological inconvenience to Christian orthodoxy. In contrast to Cassie, Herm was a genial, quiet man who could get right down on the floor and play with children in their own element. Except in the one obvious area of making money, it always seemed that Cassie was in control. Despite her domination, there was much to weaken her resolve. As well as her continued grief over Howard, she had troubling health problems. The latter included a massive subcutaneous tumor which covered the back of her shoulders. The Solomons were so concerned about it, they paid for an operation in Montreal to have it removed. While the operation was not complicated, the tumor may have indicated a propensity for cancer.

Cassie's teaching of her son nevertheless continued as before with more emphasis on literature, history, rudimentary arithmetic and Bible knowledge. Despite her own deep religious interests which inevitably led her to concentrate on the Bible and writers like Josephus, she had a genuine interest in Thackeray, George Eliot and Dickens. Fully utilizing her contralto voice, she loved to read out loud novels of Scott and Dickens to Northrop. She even tried some Milton but when it made no impression, she quickly abandoned it. She in fact confessed many years later that she was not much interested in poetry. "It seems that straight simple prose says it better—yet how much poetry there is in reading the Bible!"

For history she used Dickens's querulous but dramatic *A Child's History of England*. Dickens's invective aroused at least one flare-up. Cassie would have nothing to do with his poisonous view of Henry the Eighth on the grounds that Henry had brought Protestantism to England. This obviously had infinitely more weight than the scandal of Henry's political and marital machinations. The obvious twisting of facts to suit ideology impressed Northrop even then.

Another book which left a strong impression on him was the common storybook of ancient myth, Charles Kingley's *The Heroes: or Greek Fairy Tales for My Children*. It's interesting to see how Kingsley divided the three basic "stories," of Perseus, the Argonauts and Theseus into distinct narrative phases, indicating the rise-and-fall shape of tragedy. In his introduction, he even suggested that "fairy tales" called *mythoi* by the Greeks were told by all nations "when they are young," thus implying the primitive focus of imaginative language.

Fortunately not everything was so assiduously bookish. Probably through the generosity of relatives, Cassie and Northrop were able to rent a cottage in the resort village of Ayers Cliff on Lake Massiwippi south of Sherbrooke where for the first and really last time, Northrop was initiated into the art of being a boy. In a free and unstructured setting which he would always consider idyllic, he discovered the wonders of clam shells, digging in the blue clay, rowing a boat and fishing for perch.

Finally Herm re-established himself solidly enough again to move the family back east to Moncton. For Northrop, the day-long trip from Granby through Quebec and the northern wilds of Maine was vivid and exciting. But for Cassie, it was a final move into exile. She would now live permanently hundreds of miles from her family and because of the high rail fares, would find it impossible to return to Quebec or Ontario where her parents finally settled on retirement. In fact, the only trip she would ever take again was to visit Vera after she later settled in Chicago.

When they settled into a house on North Street, Cassie decided to put Northrop in school, which in Moncton was a grimy building dating back to 1890 called Victoria School. Although the school inspector approved him for grade three, his reading ability proved to be so advanced in class, he was quickly skipped to grade four. At eight, he was one to three years younger than the rest of the class and this unfavorable age discrepancy would stay with him right through university. Because of Cassie's tutoring and his own intelligence, he floundered in miseries of boredom. Through the years his view of his early education which he viewed "as a form of penal servitude" was consistently savage though not entirely humorless: "I saw children lined up and marched into a grimy brick building at nine in the morning, while a truant officer prowled the streets outside. The boys and girls were sent through sexually separate entrances: it was regarded as a matter of the highest importance that a boy should not go through a door marked 'girls' even if no act of excretion was involved. They then filed into their classrooms, found their desks and sat down with their hands folded in front of them in what was referred to as 'sitting position.' At that point a rabble of screaming and strapping spinsters was turned loose on them, and the educational process began . The deterrent to idleness in this set up was being kept in, or having one's sentence lengthened."

Much of this, written for a public speech, was of course exaggerated. Frye later acknowledged there was actually so little interest in the floating population of itinerants like his own family, that he could have stayed out of school indefinitely. Once placed there, however, he impressed his teachers with his easy command of historical facts. His grade four teacher, Miss Stannard, reminded him in his early teens of his propensity even then of devouring history and his confident prediction that he would someday write a history book.

In the summer, the family moved once more south to Sussex and in the fall, Northrop started grade five in a school where his teacher in fact was a screaming, strapping spinster who couldn't seem to get through the day without beating one or other of the boys. Northrop escaped the strap but his taste for school was hardly enhanced by this reign of terror.

Once again Herm's business took him back to Moncton and for the third time, the family moved into the city. Their move into an upper duplex at 24 Pine St. was this time permanent. The flat, which had an entrance on the southeast corner, was cramped and Northrop had only a poorly heated alcove. Bitterly cold in the winter, it had been built onto the house and was just large enough for a bed. The rest of the house was plainly furnished but Cassie still had managed to salvage the piano, the encyclopedia, Howard's music, an extensive library of classics and children's books including Howard's *Chums* annuals. The books were neatly lined up in two bookcases, one in the front parlor and the other in the dining room. While recognizing its impossibility, Northrop harboured a secret ambition to have his own study.

Vera never liked Moncton and actively avoided it by studying and residing at Mt. Allison University in nearby Sackville and summering with her Aunt Tessie in Granby. Compared with Sherbrooke and Lennoxville, Moncton must have been a serious disappointment for Cassie. It developed quite suddenly as the main regional centre of the Transatlantic Railways which was absorbed into the much grander Canadian National Railways in 1925. It is physically distinguished by a tidal bore which daily reverses the Petitcodiac River, then drains out, leaving a monstrous deep trough of glistening mud which looks like an intestine split open. Frye once confessed that it had given him the visual sense of Leviathan.

The ambience of the northwest sector where the Fryes lived

was one of prosperous working class, the fathers often mechanics, machinists, test engineers or blacksmiths who worked on the loco-motives and cars in the huge shops nearby. At five in the afternoon, a flood of men came down through the streets from the shops. Because the population was predominantly Maritimer, people were sensitive to the arrival of "upper Canadians" like the Fryes who usually worked for the railway, Eaton's or other national companies. There was no hostility towards them, just an observa-tion of differences.

As she had always done, Cassie depended on the church to fill her time. Wesley Memorial Church was just two blocks away on Cameron and St. George and because the congregation was basi-cally working and lower middle class, it tended to be more evangel-ical than the fancier Central Methodist a half-mile downtown. For someone of her background, the evangelical element was hardly troublesome, but there was a residual snobbery in Cassie. The original wood structure of Wesley Memorial, soon to be razed for a bland brick structure, had a towering, blue-painted dome which Cassie considered the design of an extreme Pentecostal sect.

Although the ladies of the church in her circle kept up certain rituals like afternoon tea, it was Cassie who distanced herself by serving a distinctly foreign condiment: crumpets. She retreated behind ritual, and constant chatter in the church's sewing circle about her own illustrious Howard and Demorest forebears. Clearly she was creating a barrier to shield her shyness and loneliness in a foreign city. When Frye later read *Adam Bede,* he saw much of his mother in the figure of Hetty Sorrell. Yet in style she was severe with plain dresses and short straight hair. When she walked north to the corner of Pine and John for groceries, she looked straight ahead, never greeting anyone whom she didn't know from church. Her isolation was aggravated further by her growing deafness which not only cut off social ties but diminished her one strong area of personal achievement, her singing.

For the rest of grade five, Northrop returned to Victoria School which was just across the Cameron St. park from his new home. His progress was disastrous. He exhibited such an unco-operative attitude to learning arithmetic that his teacher gave dire warning that he might fail. Cassie angrily reminded him that Howard and Vera had made effortless progress in school. While he did make the year, he never lost his sensitivity to the hazards of enforced curriculum.

Although he liked Moncton immeasurably better than his sister did, Moncton was sports-obsessed. It was hardly the best place for a boy suffering from poor eyesight, balance and coordination. Unlike his brother, he was defeated by the simplest sporting skills, including skating which was central to all recreation in the long New Brunswick winters. His mother and father never seemed to encourage him in the usual boyish tinkering. As a result the crystal set craze passed him by and gave him the lifelong conviction that he was incompetent in all mechanical tasks.

There was a murderous ambivalence to this, particularly since his own idea of heroism was strongly associated at first with physicalities. He greatly admired athletic prowess and strength. The apparently effortless sports triumphs of his classmate and neighbour on Cameron St., Jim Davison, seemed the epitome of golden-limbed youth. Davison's sister, Dorothy, remembers Northrop making a few exuberant attempts at kicking a football around the Cameron St. park with the ineffectual clumsiness of a girl.

Even in his reading of *Hurlbut's Story of the Bible*, Frye's fantasies easily connected with Samson-like heroics. Later in life, he scribbled an autobiographical fragment admitting to suffering from a Napoleonic complex that put him in the role of "a future military commander simultaneously with knowing that I was the least military of males, and would always be." By college years he was sufficiently distanced from his adolescent fantasies to joke that he once soaked himself like a Spartan in a cold tub when he was twelve "to acquire the cool nerves and steady resolution characteristic of Sir Walter Scott's heroes." He did this for half an hour "keeping warm by a glow of self-righteousness."

There was however a more crucial intellectual aspect of Scott's oeuvre which went beyond a purely physical dimension. The fact that Scott had written an interconnected *library* of books was for Northrop an exciting notion and gave birth to a fantasy that he would write a similar cycle of novels. This, of course, represented a more plausible fantasy. His heroic notions shifted from the model of the fictional good guy whom he could never imitate to the figure of the writer. Although he first thought of it as early as nine, it wasn't until "the owlish solemnity of fourteen" that he gave individual names to the historical sequence of novels. "The first was to be called Liberal: it was to be satire, a witty comedy of manners. The second I called Tragicomedy, and thought of it as a panoramic novel: I had always been fascinated by complicated plots with great numbers of characters. The third, Anticlimax, I thought of as austere and forbidding; the fourth, Rencontre (I liked the nasalized French form) was to be a war novel. The fifth, Mirage, had no particular characteristics; the sixth, Paradox, was to be the most dizzily complicated of them all; the seventh, Ignoramus, the profoundest (because I was an agnostic by then and had started to read Hardy), and Twilight, subtitled Valedictory, was to be my Tempest, the work of my old age." His own deep interest in music also gave rise to "a fixation of wanting to be a great musical composer—I call it a fixation because I did no work at it. I remember my Opus 2 was to be a series of eight concerti—a sequence of eight masterpieces in the same genre ..."

Despite all this precocity and pretension, Frye wasn't at all isolated from the ordinary cultural influences that most Canadian boys faced. He consumed a steady diet of church-promulgated fiction such as the novels of Horatio Alger and the internationally celebrated Canadian, Ralph Connor. While he refused to repudiate this kind of fictional diet for children, he confessed that there was a hazard connected with his own photographic memory. The words of Alger's insufferable little boys came up at him like computerized junk for decades, usually early in the morning. He realized quite soon that in Alger, he was really reading the same story again and again. He also was a regular habitué of the movie houses whenever he could raise money from his parents. He took in the cheap westerns and slapstick comedies of Chaplin and Keaton, impressed by the ever repeating plot gimmicks.

For someone so intensely shy, Northrop was oddly ambitious to promulgate his own idealistic notions, and boldly formed a boy's club called the Royal Club as a haven for boys who were not interested in sports. The club of about 10 or 12 boys used to meet in a member's house once a week to give and hear talks on subjects usually cribbed from encyclopedias. Ostensibly to learn parliamentary procedure, they debated political issues, but in venerable Maritimes tradition, the club split into warring Liberal and Conservative factions. The rivalry was sufficiently intense at one point that the club's typewritten, carbon-copy newspaper was published in two editions. Northrop took an anxious view of membership and tried to beef it up with a few stars like Jack Grainger, the son of an executive of Eaton's department store. When the club appeared to be heading awry under the wrong leadership, Northrop and his best friend, John Branscombe, devised a scheme of marking ballots during a club election to figure out who was supporting whom. To Branscombe, Frye relished the role of backroom manipulator who would avoid face to face confrontations but liked to get his way. If anything the club's problems seemed to have the exact opposite effect on Frye because he subsquently avoided practical political involvements. When one of the members, a crippled boy called Andrew Mackinnon, died, Frye and Branscombe were among the pallbearers in their capacity as club leaders and the club was mentioned in the local paper. Mackinnon's funeral was coincidentally the first time Northrop heard any extended piece of serious music: the High Requiem Mass.

By grade eight, his school performance had greatly improved but the contempt for the "penal servitude" remained. In his class picture taken with everyone at their desk, Northrop appeared with his head cocked back in weariness. His blond hair, shorn in the early school years, was long again and he wore an uncharacteristic, bulky turtle neck and round horn rim glasses. By the blackboard in the back, across the faces of the other students was his teacher and principal, Arthur Robinson, who was the first teacher to actively encourage Northrop in outside interests. Robinson talked him into subscribing to the *National Geographic* to feed his fascination with foreign places.

Because of obvious repercussions with classmates, Frye assiduously avoided the role of teacher's pet. Robinson nevertheless assigned him the role of monitor with the task of listening to the after-hour lesson recitations of poorer students. Branscombe, who was often in the latter category, invariably tried to get his name assigned to Frye so they could conspire to fudge Branscombe's knowledge and so get out of school as fast as possible. After school they would often pore over the reference books at the Frye's, plotting fantasy itineraries to places all over the world. Reality, of course, was much less grandiose. On the weekends, they sometimes took the train ten minutes out to Steeves Mountain and hiked three miles to the farm of Branscombe's uncle, Albert Brown. Brown used to tease Frye about his eating habits. Frye would cut up his food and eat each particular item entirely before trying something else.

Frye also developed a conventional middle-class boy's interest in Scouts in grade eight and continued with it in high school until the troop at Wesley Memorial disbanded. He pestered Branscombe for manuals on achieving badges. Although he suffered one requisite, mosquito-filled night camping in wilderness to earn his overnight badge, he set his own typically urban style to his badge acquisition. Accompanied by Jim Davison, he went over to his teacher Robinson's house, to be tested for the Entertainment badge and performed "a variety program of piano, readings, jokes, recitations, presented easily and with finesse."

Frye also put pressure on Herm for a bicycle, then largely a middle-class luxury. Because of a poorly diagnosed back ailment which left him laid up for weeks, Herm's business had once more stagnated and the request was an unusually difficult one for him but he eventually managed to put together the then enormous sum of thirty-five dollars. Leaving early in the morning, Frye travelled out on the dirt roads of Albert and Westmoreland counties, along "curious lonely roads," to ghost towns and farms abandoned because of the poor thin soil. The landscape was not so much real as an abstraction of hills rolling away in ranks of omnipresent pine and spruce. He was usually gone all day, and lunched in the towns he passed. He pressured Branscombe to buy a bike as well, but Branscombe's family could not afford it. Branscombe was satisfied to listen to the formidable range of his friend's explorations.

Oddly these trips did not seem to meet much opposition from

the usually protective Cassie who controlled so many other aspects of his life. Although she never told her son, Howard had uncannily possessed an identical wanderlust in adolescence and had disappeared on day-long bike trips away from Sherbrooke. Faced with the penury, reclusiveness and now old age of his parents, Northrop enjoyed the freedom and openness that the bike provided.

One inevitable area of conflict, however, was religion. Cassie was deeply involved in church activities. As well as attending the usual Sunday morning service, she was president of the Women's Bible Class which met on Sunday afternoon, and a member of the sewing circle which met on Tuesday afternoon. Invariably she also attended a weekly "Prayer and Praise Service" on Thursday evenings. If Branscombe were over at the house, she encouraged them both to come with her. Although both were to become ordained ministers, prayer meetings were hardly to anyone's adolescent taste. Cassie had her revenge when she came home. She sat down at the piano and played hymns with sufficient force and volume that Branscombe got the message and was soon heading out the door.

But even surprising to Branscombe, who was Baptist, were Northrop's very liberal notions about religion. He had already showed contempt for itinerate Methodist preachers who visited Wesley Memorial, preferring more liberal preachers from Toronto who occasionally turned up at the more sophisticated Central Methodist downtown. His precocious liberalism even erupted once over the piano. When Branscombe wearied of Frye's serious classical playing, he tried to turn Frye towards gospel or popular music. He particularly liked the famous missionary hymn "Greenland's Icy Mountains" by Reginald Heber and Lowell Mason. While the tune was catchy, some of the lyrics were archly Calvinistic and racist:

What though the spicey breezes/Blow soft o'er Ceylon's isle,
Though every prospect pleases/And only man is vile
In vain with lavish kindness /The gifts of God are strown
The heathen in his blindness/Bows down to wood and stone.

As a good Methodist, Northrop objected strenuously to the
Calvinist notion that man was vile and the two friends argued
heatedly over the comparative depravity of man.

In the meantime, Vera had graduated from Mount Allison College in 1924 and once more found herself in an enforced hiatus,
not knowing how or where to get a job. She was adamant about
not staying in Moncton, While she had done well in her first
three years at college, her last year was plagued with bad health,
apparently aggravated by emotional problems that were unclear to
her brother. She was lucky however when a classmate managed to
tip her off about a position as registrar and librarian of an osteopathic college near the University of Chicago in the States. Frye
was very attached to Vera and was unhappy to see her go, but her
comparative prosperity there soon had important repercussions.

## ABERDEEN HIGH

In his high school entrance exams, Frye stood fifth in all of Moncton
and while this was a distinct improvement over his earlier record,
Aberdeen High down on St. George St. opened few glowing doors
of knowledge. He found the shallowness of the curriculum, particularly in English, appalling. Over fifty years later, Frye could sputter
at the mention of such fare as *Uncle Tom's Cabin*, *Lorna Doone*,
*Lady of the Lake* and a volume of execrable neo-romantic Canadian
poetry. Latin offered the first book of Virgil's *Aeneid* but the process
involved so much construing as to dampen interest. French class
taught the rudiments of grammar but left the spoken language a
permanent and baffling mystery. Geometry was an accretion of
memorized solutions which had to be regurgitated for the class on
the blackboard. Frye's chief eccentricity here apparently was that
his pianist fingers were so long he could dispense with the blackboard pointer. Even then by grade ten, his marks were seriously
divided between literary and mathematical subjects. While he was
receiving 98 in history, 95 in composition, 92 in English literature,

90 in grammar, there was the sorry spectacle of 51 in bookkeeping, 47 in arithmetic and 33 in geometry.

Socially Frye succeeded at a difficult balancing act, coexisting between teacher favourite and erstwhile rebel. There was, however, an undeniably disdainful, even prissy side to Frye. He was proud of his name Northrop because it sounded beyond the ordinary, the name of an intellectual. His friends referred to him as "the Professor" for sounding off on arcane and esoteric topics which none of them could ever follow. He teased classmate and neighbour, Dorothy Davison, who'd just plucked her eyebrows for the first time, "When you grow those eyebrows out again, you'll look much less like an Egyptian sorceress." Nor in class would he be drawn into any of the usual adolescent teacher harassment games like pitching pennies from the back, or stamping into class with the rest of the boys with open, buckle-chattering galoshes.

On the other hand, he also had to handle his own formidable boredom and sense of disaffection. When the mood struck, he was known to grab the curls of the girl in front and dunk the ends unappetizingly into his inkwell. During quizzes, he would gingerly subvert the system by whispering answers to anyone within earshot who was having trouble. Likewise, he was an uncommonly soft touch for anyone who genuinely wanted help with assignments. For a debate in his church's boys' club, he quietly slipped an outline to one of the members, Earl Steeves, who was in a fix. This was a central character trait quite directly connected with his Methodist backgound: if someone deserving asked for help, he gave it. It was both a strength and a bedevilment all through his later life.

Not surprisingly his approach to school was accomplished with a furious concentration. The sooner he got there, the sooner he could get out. Usually alone, he charged down Pine St. to St. George St. A Catholic boy his age, Ned Belliveau, who Frye did not know, later became a journalist and described his memories of Frye's passing by: ". . . his wildly blowing reddish hair today would go unnoticed, but in the late 1920s it seemed the essence of artistic eccentricity. He never seemed to move at anything but a half-running pace. His books stacked under an arm, obviously concentrating, he seemed to look neither to right nor left; just straight ahead and determined."

It was during one of those furious walks to school that he had a decisive religious experience that was a parody of the Methodist conversion experience his Howard and Demorest predecessors so earnestly demanded of themselves. Although it had the vibrancy and finality of a genuine epiphany, it wasn't particularly touched off by any immediate thought or incident. He "remembered walking along St. George St. to high school and just suddenly that whole shitty and smelly garment (of fundamentalist teaching I had all my life) just dropped off into the sewers and stayed there. It was like the Bunyan feeling, about the burden of sin falling off his back only with me it was a burden of anxiety. Anything might have touched it off, but I don't know what specifically did, or if anything did. I just remember that suddenly that that was no longer a part of me and would never be again."

Frye was not completely free, however, and the anxieties, now more personal than theological, would continue, strongly repressed for years. Cassie of course never wavered in her attempt to inject every able-bodied male relative into the ministry. Her belief overwhelmed common sense. She'd earlier hoped that her younger brother John would become a minister even though his personality militated against it. Her hopes for Howard were most probably in the line of the ministry. As she became older she was more and more anxious to draw Northrop himself into her own structure of faith. Once more, Frye achieved a balancing act in which he would participate but only on his own terms. He bitterly hated the current minister of Wesley Memorial as a pettifogging boor who was trying to ruin the congregation, yet raved about his replacement, Harold Tomkinson, who was liberal for his time in guiding open discussion groups for younger members of the congregation. It was Tomkinson's positive image that abated Frye's anxieties about signing up later as a church student headed for the ministry. Frye also had a strong admiration for an elder of the congregation, Paul Kingston, who discussed the Bible with rare intelligence and sensitivity.

Very early he had set a pattern which would show up consistently throughout all his involvements in life: do not be an anarchist; accept the social and cultural institutions for their strengths, revealed by thought and imagination, and fight their weaknesses with precisely those strengths. In terms of religion he made this clear later in life to a friend, Roy Daniells, who was battling the dragons of his own fundamentalist upbringing in the Plymouth Brethren: "In early adolescence I suddenly realized, with an utter and complete conviction of which I have never lost one iota since, that the whole apparatus of afterlife in heaven and hell, unpardonable sins, and the like was a lot of junk. There remained, of course, the influence of my mother, and the fact that I had already agreed to go on to college as a church student. My mental processes were pretty confused, but restructuring them by hindsight I think they were something like this: if I go though the whole business of revolting against this, I shall be making a long and pointless detour back to where I shall probably come out anyway, and will probably have acquired a neurosis besides. I think I decided very early, without realizing it at the time, that I was going to accept out of religion only what made sense to me as a human being. I was not going to worship a god whose actions, judged by human standards, were contemptible. That was where Blake helped me so much: he taught me that the lugubrious old stinker in the sky that I had heard so much about existed all right, but that his name was Satan, that his function was to promote tyranny in society and repression in the mind. This meant that the Methodist church down at the corner was consecrated mainly to devil-worship, but, because it did not know that, it would tolerate something better without knowing what that was either."

Although Cassie was most often a barrier to Frye's growing desire for religious freedom, she was also, curiously enough, an ally who transmitted some of her own unconscious doubts about the old-time religion. While she saw nothing wrong with her son's signing the standard temperance pledges "by the gross," she did resist an attempt of a meddling church member to pressure Frye into open activism. In retrospect, Frye felt that this really extended to all her beliefs. "I realize now that my mother did not actually

believe what she was teaching me, but she thought she ought to
believe it, because she got it from her father, and so something
else got through as well as that fundamentalist teaching."

The crucial element of his life at this time was music. As early as
1924, Frye started subscribing to *Etude* magazine, a sophisticated
American publication which promoted 19th century Romantic
music and reproduced piano and organ music. Frye pressured his
father for lessons with George Ross who was organist for St. John
United Church downtown. A former student of Sir Hubert Parry
who wrote the music for the hymn "Jerusalem," Ross was probably
the best music teacher in the Maritimes. Herm rarely pronounced
about what his son should be doing with his life but he did feel
that musical ambitions were not proper for a man. He could be
quite generous, but this time he refused to help. Vera, who was
now in Chicago, had no deep interest in music herself but her
memory of Howard's fondness and competence at the piano made
her eager to send money home so that Frye could take weekly
lessons at Ross's studio on Archibald St.

A reserved Scot, Ross had a somewhat enigmatic personality,
but because of his deep knowledge and interest in music, he had
an inspired quality, the only teacher of any kind in Moncton who
Frye knew was not a dilettante or a fool. A graduate of the Royal
College of Organists, he also worked on a doctorate in musicology
for the University of Toronto. But he was consummately bourgeois,
his world delineated by his organist job, his teaching and family.
In the summers, he simply parked himself at the nearby beach at
Point-du-Chêne.

Instead of working his students up into frenzies for ego-inflating
recitals, he encouraged a quieter absorption and love of music.
Frye later claimed that it was Ross who gave him the idea that a
teacher should be ideally transparent so that the art itself could
shine unobstructed by the shadows of ego. Despite Frye's own
overbearing enthusiasm and ambition, Ross never pushed him
towards a musical career. In later years Frye realized that since
he started too late, he could never have made a serious career
anyway but in the short run, through his teens and his twenties,
the piano was a great release. It provided a crucial focus of emotion

and even a slightly priggish mandarin identity which insulated him from an environment which could never accept him on his own terms.

Although he never much liked it, Frye practised so hard that it became a cause of annoyance among his friends. One of them, Fred Kirby, with whom Frye sometimes cycled over to Point du Chene, would come around the house and ask Frye to knock off his work and go bowling or cycling or picking up girls at a band concert. But Frye was usually adamant that there was no point in going out, either because he had piano practice or, as he got older, an accumulation of school work which he increasingly saw as his ticket out of the Maritimes.

Kirby, who was very much attuned to the fads of the twenties— bowler hats and ukulele and saxophone bands—also tried to draw Frye into one or other of the pick-up basement bands in which he was involved. Frye came to a few early sessions but like most classically-trained musicians, he proved inept at the kind of syncopation that the Tin Pan Alley idiom required. While he was the only player who could easily play from a score, he always insisted on a note-perfect rendition which is always fatal to any real jam session.

In the summers when the windows were open, the sounds of Frye's practising drifted out to the neighbourhood. At the Davison's across the street, Mrs. Davison, herself a pianist and organist, complained to her family that his playing was mechanical. "But oh," she added, "the accuracy of it!" Her daughter, Dorothy, with whom Frye played duets, found this frustrating. "Once, when Northrop and I were playing a duet, I stumbled over notes or phrases. It maddened me and I gave the keyboard a good, banging slap. Northrop gave me a scalding look, fixed his eyes on a small bust of Beethoven sitting on the piano and delivered the punch, 'That fellow would never have advanced to immortality if he'd had *your* puerile attitude to things'."

In the summer of 1927 following grade ten, Vera sent her brother a ticket to come to Chicago to practise his piano full-time for a couple of months. Because she had no piano herself, she boarded him with the family of an osteopathic doctor called Wallstrom she knew at the college. Once he got there, he headed for a music store in the Loop and bought the sheet music for all the Beethoven sonatas. So exhilarated was he with his purchase, he walked the entire way back clutching them and taking in the pulse of the huge exciting Sandburgian metropolis. He had to walk through a black section which in the twenties posed no great hazard. Mrs. Wallstrom nevertheless severely scolded him when he got home.

In his final year, his musical obsession abated somewhat and became balanced by a newer and ultimately more important interest in literature. This was partly the result of two coincidences, the opening of the new library in early 1927 and the apparent temerity of New Brunswick school officials in putting a first-rate poetry reader on the senior curriculum.

The library, set up in the old Archibald mansion at the end of Archibald St., was a wooden gingerbread palace that was an obvious firetrap. Frye naturally gravitated there and became very friendly with the sister of a classmate, librarian Marjorie McCleeve, who encouraged him to keep up with book reviews of the latest works of such contemporary figures as Galsworthy.

He became a volunteer at the front desk checking books in and out. The job gave him an opportunity to preview the new books which included a complete set of Shaw's plays and prefaces. He had already had a little exposure to Shaw through *Plays: Pleasant and Unpleasant* which his Aunt Mary had given the family but it was the collected works, particularly the prefaces, which touched off a crucial intellectual reaction. Since there was virtually no live theatre in Moncton, Frye in fact had little idea about real drama. The closest he came to it was an all-girl mufti production of *As You Like It* for which he was prop assistant. Frye was immediately fascinated by the odd combination in Shaw of the arch-Methodist, preachy teetotaler, with the socialist curmudgeon-eccentric. More than a Napoleon or Beethoven, this was a role model which was relevant to his own concerns and character. Shaw's work, in fact, became a theatre of his own irreconcilable tensions and, coincidentally, a model for his own early prose style. What fascinated Frye was Shaw's very direct, hard-hitting approach which was close to spoken language. He also tasted two poets who were absolutely crucial to his later career, Wallace Stevens and William Blake, but neither made a great impression on him at that time. Ironically, he found Blake impenetrable and had no idea that he would one day replace Shaw as a guide through the dark wood of Frye's own evangelical protestantism.

His literary interests received a decisive boost in his grade eleven senior year when the school authorities put *Palgrave's Golden Treasury of Song and Lyrics: Book Two* on the curriculum. Frye would always bitterly contend that the supervisors had so shocked themselves by doing something fundamentally right, that they retreated in blind panic and promptly removed it the following year. By the contemporary standards of Canadian high schools, it was an exceptionally good text which concentrated on the sixteenth- and seventeenth-century English poets with a breezy disregard for the capabilities of the poor student. Without prompting, Frye read the entire book and in the index, placed asterisks beside the names of Dryden, Herrick, Jonson, Marvell and Milton. Milton's own representation included Nativity Ode, Lycidas, On His Blindness, L'Allegro and Il Penseroso. Frye was so enthralled by Milton, in fact, he beleaguered friends like Dorothy Davison with his ability to recite his poetry from memory. Frye later claimed that the book was a key element in his eventually becoming an English teacher. Its removal the following year engendered a permanent feeling that the high school apparatus was inherently anti-intellectual.

It was the purest irony that the only girl in Moncton with whom Frye ever developed a serious romantic tie, Evelyn Rogers, hadn't the slightest interest in serious music, deep thought, reading or academic achievement. They met in youth activities at the church and their attraction became immediately personal and romantic. Evelyn, in fact, was an indifferent student, interested in the usual teenage pastimes of skating and dancing. Frye sometimes arrogantly dismissed her notions as stupid but she had power over him. She possessed a full and boisterous personality with an uproarious laugh which seemed to soften Frye's sometimes grating pretensions. She was the only person his age to draw him out of his shyness into a wider circle of social life he had so far missed outside of the church. She even tried to get him to skate and he willingly went out one day with her only to collapse on his ankles. He gave up quickly and Evelyn recognized the hopelessness of the situation. Inwardly she blamed Cassie's over-protectiveness.

Frye had little money to take Evelyn to the movies and often just came over to her house on Friday night. He was quite easily accepted into the Rogers family. He often played checkers with Mr. Rogers and queried him about left-wing thinking which, through Shaw, he found increasingly interesting. A machinist in the nearby railway shops, Rogers was an intensely committed unionist leader who followed socialist thinking. In a sense, he was an exemplar of the old working-class aristocracy who had a solid job, social ranking and his own home on Cameron St. just north of the Fryes. Despite his union activities, he was conservative enough to sit on the board of Wesley Memorial Church during the change from the old wooden Methodist church to the new brick United Church.

When Frye would talk with Evelyn later on, he revealed a more personal side which virtually no one saw. Reflecting the pressures at home, he seemed hostile about the idea of his becoming a minister. He seemed to doubt even orthodox views about the divinity of Christ. This was probably symptomatic of the murderous personal and social juggling act Frye had to perpetuate with religion. Far from becoming a convinced agnostic, he was, in fact, just on the point of signing up as church student for the ministry. He even assumed the role as "Devotional President" of the church's Young People's Society for 1929. Of course, the latter gave Cassie a sense of rightful progress and she noted his giving a talk one night on a church calendar she sent to Donald Howard, the son of her brother John who recently had taken a pulpit in New England.

**CHAMPION TYPIST**

When Frye graduated from Aberdeen, he jumped to fourth place overall, one position higher than when he entered. At fifteen he now had a meagre seven and a half years of formal schooling behind him, none of it as good as what he himself or his mother had provided. For standing first in English, he was offered a scholarship in stenographic training at the Success Business College in the Knights of Pythias building downtown. For someone as young as he was, the three months of useful training would represent only a small inconvenience. If all else failed, including the ministry, he could provide for himself and his parents with a well-paid job. Male secretaries were still the most highly valued executive assistants.

In the fall, Frye started his course in shorthand and typing. Presumably because of his facility with the piano, Frye picked up typing with astonishing ease and quickly worked up to 70 words a minute. With such a prodigy on their hands, the manager and owner decided to get some promotional value out of Frye by offering him a free trip to Toronto to compete in the National Typing contest run by the Underwood Company in April 1929. This was the heyday of the typing contests which, like all Jazz Age extravaganzas, were conducted with high publicity and consummate bad taste. Contestants enjoyed the full glare of publicity, including newspaper interviews redolent of the sports page. Professionals who could type up to 140 words a minute on manual typewriters made comfortable incomes from contests and demonstrations.

After Frye's graduation from Success, the college owner provided him with freelance secretarial jobs in Moncton. Frye wrote a prospectus for the inventor of a patent medicine, who was stunned that Frye knew how spell "belladonna." He prepared a report for a General Motors official assessing the local market for the new Marquet auto. He took dictation at an executive meeting of the Brotherhood of Locomotive Engineers and so capably trimmed down an executive's wordy speech that he was complimented at getting all his golden words down exactly. Of course, he was hardly fulfilling any kind of destiny with this kind of work but he rather enjoyed it. He also managed to keep up his piano and at the urging of George Ross played four works, including pieces from Schubert sonatas, on the CNRA. It was a good deal. His professional earnings were a then hefty $5.00 and there was no embarrassing archival recording to immortalize his efforts.

The typing contest was to be held April eighth. A few days beforehand, Frye left Moncton on the 2:30 train with a borrowed Underwood in a wooden case. It was the first of many wearying and expensive trips to and from Toronto. Travelling second class, he stayed up the entire day and a half journey. In Toronto, he registered at the Ford Hotel and was a bit taken aback when the clerk insisted on prepayment. On the evening of the eighth, Frye sat on the crowded stage in Massey Hall with a New Brunswick pennant and typed his way to a second place finish in the novice class with an average of 63 corrected words per minute, barely ahead of a girl who had 62. It was not a vintage year: the winner herself only attained 69 words a minute. After heading off to Chicago again to see Vera for a couple of weeks, he returned non-stop to Moncton across half a continent. At home the owner of the college planted a photo of Frye in the Monday edition of the Saint John, N.B. paper with a long news caption of his second place finish before a crowd of 4,000 against a field of more than 60 rivals. As far as the free press would allow, the message was clear that he was a product of the superb training of Success. The photo shows a serious young man of 16 in suit, shirt and tie standing erect with his left arm resting on the carriage of the black typewriter. The round lenses of his Harold Lloyd-type glasses emphasize a rather quizzical gaze which suggests neither enjoyment nor discomfort. Significantly, his usually unruly hair is plastered down in a tight, almost coiffed mound. The college also rushed out a pink-colored promotion blotter with his cherubic face. When he married, "the pink blotter" became a joking ikon of his lost youth.

Despite the interlude, both Cassie and Frye were determined that he get out of the Maritimes for a proper university education. There was the opportunity for him to go, like Vera, to the local Methodist college, Mt. Allison, but Victoria College in Toronto was infinitely more attractive. Still, Cassie was torn by ambivalence. Nearly 60, she was very worried about her own future. When an attractive job opened in Moncton as private secretary to an executive of Eaton's, both Cassie and Herm strongly urged Northrop to take it. It was in fact more the rule than exception that boys took time out between high school and college to work but Frye was adamant this time about furthering his education. He was sure he could scrounge together enough money from secretarial work to go to Victoria College in the fall. He was helped by a lucky coincidence: the international typing contest that year was again going to be in Toronto and the genial owner of Success was once more willing to put up the stiff $50 return ticket. Frye's status as church student also meant reductions in store prices in Toronto and an automatic scholarship which defrayed his residence expenses.

After a month of working in offices, Frye returned to the business college to work up his typing speed. He found that he had gained over his earlier average and was peaking at 85 words per minute. On Wednesday afternoon, September 18, 1929, he headed off for Toronto with a suitcase and a very reassuring invitation to a freshman breakfast on Friday, the morning after he would arrive.

## VICTORIA COLLEGE

Coming to Toronto from the parochial Maritimes, Frye feared the high academic standard which he felt awaited him. To enter the elite stream honors courses, Frye needed two more years than Moncton Grammar offered. As a result, he could only enter the Pass Course, a devalued dead-end stream. Even then, the administration stamped his lecture card with a brutal "ON PROBATION" as if to remind him daily of his shaky credentials.

Frye was shucked off into a mouldering firetrap called Charles House. The college had just built a line of stone-faced Oxonian residences down the eastern edge of the college campus, but generally only students with good marks or family connections got in. Despite its lowly standing, Charles House had a tremendous *esprit de corps* which helped incorporate Frye into college life. A

freshman, Bill Conklin, from a wealthy lumber family, shocked
Frye by thrusting a visiting card into his hand. Frye, who'd only
read about them in Victorian literature, momentarily panicked. He
quickly recovered by fishing in his pocket for a complimentary
ticket to the typing contest which Conklin graciously accepted.

With his scrawny frame, pale complexion, thick horn-rim glasses
and wild blond hair, Frye was an anomaly among freshmen who
were often large, well-built farm boys from southern Ontario who
were already sizing up the game field for soccer and football. His
hair was so long and wild that one visitor, spotting his mop of sun-
colored steel-wool, wondered if there wasn't a shortage of bobby
pins on campus. Unlike the smooth-rolling cowboy style favoured
by men then, his gait seemed pigeon-toed (actually toe-out), and
angular. There was a bit of the Alice in Wonderland rabbit in him.
In his later career, in fact, he several times referred to "the panic
of time" as if this were a common anxiety.

Because of his resemblance to a verbose and silly figure in a
current college movie, Frye won the nickname Buttercup, which
was a term of mild opprobrium but which became more affectionate
as people got to know him. Though the nickname stuck for years
without embarrassment, it continued to baffle him because he
thought he rather looked more like a dandelion or bird of paradise.
He had changed his mind about the attractiveness of "Northrop"
and encouraged people to call him "Norrie," a name which stayed
with him for life.

Either by design or good luck, the seventeen-year-old Frye, one
of the youngest freshmen, was roomed with the oldest, Del Martin,
who was 23. Martin had taught grade school for a few years but
decided on the ministry which now required a BA. Frye was
perceived as a boy, scrawny, emotionally explosive, naive about
sex jokes and—except for sparse blond whiskers—smooth cheeked,
but Martin was the house's big brother, diplomatic and gifted with
a solid physique which had seen him through years of hard work
at the family farm near Honeywood to which he took Frye on
Christmas holidays. He was a grown man among teenagers, and
played a decisive role in calming down his skittish roommate,
protecting him from the excesses of house rakes who wanted to

drag Frye into panty-raids and other expeditions. Martin never had the temerity to ask Frye, but quickly discerned that he was very nearly penniless. Their room was in the third-floor attic and their fire escape was a curious rope ladder they were supposed to throw out the window.

With a modicum of tolerance, Frye endured some innocuous initiation rites which included cold showers and wearing yellow ties (one of the college colors) which sophomores sadistically cut off with scissors. Typically, Frye stayed clear of all this and quickly established a reputation for playing classical music on the piano in the Charles House common room. For some of his new friends, whose idea of serious music was Gilbert and Sullivan, his knowledge of music was a revelation. Here was Bach and Mozart on a piano which usually responded to the honky-tonk jazz of another freshman, Pete Cosgrove. His facility with big words and ideas, which were new to them, virtually elevated Frye into intellectual house mascot. He agreeably took up a bet, which he won, to write out 2,000 words without repeating himself.

Nevertheless, there was an attempt, even by Frye's most loyal friends, to draw him into mainstream activities, which in the fall included early-morning intramural soccer. Like a befuddled child, Frye had to be instructed step by step: to first get some durable shoes, then present himself on the field. The intramural league was for average ability but Frye was lost even there. Friends feared for him, yet felt immensely proud if he appeared as it was clearly a concession to their own interests.

Frye took his classes in the nearby college building, now called Old Vic. Symbolic of the quixotic taste of Victorian-era Toronto, it combined Victorian lumpiness with embellishments from just about every period of Western architecture: squat, pink-marble columns with Corinthian capitals, a large Romanesque arch over the south main entranceway with the biblical motto "The truth shall make you free," and some anaemic-looking gargoyle reliefs set high on the eastern wall. The fortress walls were made of pollution-stained red stone from the Caledon Hills. Upstairs, almost like the soul of the place, there was a dingy chapel with a row of incongruously aesthetic stained glass windows at the front representing four Protestant saints. Wesley, Milton, Newton and a very sour Martin Luther, with requisite five o'clock shadow, faced towards the plain oak benches and organ pipes at the back. By contrast the lecture rooms were airy with high ceilings and huge ten-foot windows which opened in the autumn and spring to the fresh air and the sounds of the robins which inhabited the surrounding yard. Students were enthralled with the place.

Victoria College, which is always called "Vic" on campus, was an autonomous college of the University of Toronto. The university taught the physical and social sciences and the professions, but left the humanities to the separate colleges which generally had church ties. Because of this college system, which was unusual in North America, Frye had entered a self-contained college with its own identity, history and range of activities which had nothing to do with the university at large. This had some very positive ramifications for him.

Because Vic had always been the premier Methodist college in Canada, it benefited considerably from a circle of Methodist multi-millionaires in Toronto who included many of the scions of the Massey and Eaton families and the controversial "Holy Joe" Flavelle, a magnate of pork processing whose mansion was barely fifty yards from the college on Queen's Park Cresent. The student union, Wymilwood, the former mansion of E.R. Wood, was one door north from the Flavelles. Despite this, the students for the most part tended to be the least affluent students at the university, though rarely, like Frye, poor. Students were often parochial but with an unquenchable and easily satirized energy. Right up to the sixties, Vic students were abused in other colleges as Protestant bumpkins. Yet through the decades, the college earned a formidable reputation for producing a range of student activities which included drama, operetta, debates and a celebrated undergraduate literary magazine *Acta Victoriana* which is the oldest continuously-published magazine in Canada and which provided the first space for many of the major writers, poets and journalists who developed in the country.

After his initial discomfort, Frye entered a euphoric phase as he sensed that he had shucked off all the pressures and woes and parochialism of his Moncton years. He felt that he had finally found a community which represented his own interests, that was willing to accept him for what he was. Instead of dilettantes he faced interesting minds. Even his attitude to religion became more accommodating. Most of his new friends in Charles House were students for the ministry. All of them including Kingsley ("King") Joblin, George Birtch, Don Amos and Martin would become United Church ministers who would represent a circle of life-long cronies with whom Frye could relax as he could with few others. He wrote home about his new friends, calling them "theologs," the common and sometimes negative term for arts students heading for the ministry. Following the exhortations of Dr. Cochrane of the Home Missions Board, he even seriously considered, like Martin, doing summer work as a student missionary. Confronted by this unexpected excitement, Cassie was surprisingly neutral.

Religion was not only hard to escape in Vic, it was not, in comparison with the raw intellectual climate of Wesley Memorial, an altogether unpleasant involvement. On Saturday nights, the students in Charles House decided by consensus which of the main downtown churches they would hit the following morning. In these expeditions, Frye became acquainted with a sophisticated style of preacher which had nearly missed him in Moncton. The important ministers such as Richard Roberts of Sherbourne and Robert Slater of St. Andrew's were men of letters who wrote about literature in their spare time. To Frye this signified that one could be a minister without also being a pietistic evangelical fool who resented the probing intelligence.

With so many new involvements at college, the typing contest lost its burnish. Out of obligation, Frye occasionally slipped down to the Underwood office downtown to practise. The contest took place on Saturday night, Sept. 28 and was an extravaganza covered by newspapers all over North America. A reported 3,000 spectators crammed Massey Hall. Behind the curtain, five professionals sat at desks on a top tier at the back with silver laurel wreaths suspended above their heads. The amateurs sat across the front of the stage and the novices, including Frye, filled the anonymous middle ground. Frye had a big blue placard on a stand beside his desk announcing that he was the champion of New Brunswick, an invented title. The 75 typists started working their machines and when the curtain went up, there was a veritable "Niagara of continuous sound."

The contestants copied an original story, "Cactus Country," by the 76-year-old master of ceremonies, J.N. (Pop) Kimball. The novices typed for fifteen minutes, the amateurs for a half hour and the professionals for a whole hour. The scene was organized pandemonium, with contestants ripping out each page, flinging it away anywhere and trying to stuff in a new page in only a second. The audience burst into applause when contestants started a new page. At the fifteen minute whistle, Frye stopped and exchanged his pages with the girl from Missouri for marking. Within the international context, his results were poor and he finished towards the bottom of the group. Despite this, the rumor persisted for decades around Vic that Frye's achievement had been Herculean: he had been a world champion.

At Victoria, he soon discovered that his initial anxiety about high standards didn't materialize. Dismayed by his own Pass Course, he sank back into a phlegmatic routine which amazed his roommate Martin who was struggling just to keep up after seven years outside school. While Martin worked both late at night and before breakfast, Frye was consistently first to bed and last to rise. He was genuinely baffled by Martin's difficulties because they seemed too elementary for him to understand. Often he escaped to the room directly downstairs to talk with Don Amos and King Joblin, or the common room to play the piano. He also took to taking long hikes through the city streets and once ended up at the corner of Sherbourne and Queen, which, an alarmed friend later noted, just happened to be the heart of the red light district.

Still, with his probationary status, Frye could hardly be frivolous about his own work. Once more, he faced the drudgery of subjects which had no appeal for him. His French slumped to a borderline B and he had to rely purely on rote memory to achieve a B in a compulsory course in mathematics. But in Latin and Religious Knowledge he did well and his highest marks were in English, which unfortunately offered little new material.

One of his English instructors was a future colleague, Kathleen

Coburn, temporarily back from Oxford where she was writing a BLitt thesis on Coleridge. Her work turned into lifelong labor. His other professor of English was John Robins who was the first of three important English professors at Vic who made an enormous impact on Frye's later career. Robins, who was part black, worked his way out of a poor family in Kingsville, Ont., as a railroad porter and laborer, eventually earning a PhD from the University of Chicago in German Philology. While he taught the college's difficult courses in old English, Robins had a fascination for folk literature which was then considered academically eccentric in North America. He did not publish many scholarly papers and was looked down upon by other professors at other colleges. But despite fits of deep gloom he was probably the most popular teacher at Vic. He had a welcome tendency to wander off topic in his undergrad courses by reciting folk literature including Paul Bunyan and Uncle Remus tales which he told with appropriate black dialect inflections. Though Frye's own later interests in literature were academically orthodox, it was Robins who presented to him the scrappy sub-culture of ballads and folk tales which was not blessed by academe but yet needed a place.

Robins was also greatly attuned to the cultural trends in Toronto and pointed his students, most of them ominously ignorant about art, to the Toronto Art Gallery's small but growing collection of Group of Seven paintings. In his college office, he had his own J.E.H. Macdonald painting, *Montreal River*. While Frye had already built up a formidable knowledge of music and to a lesser degree literature, art itself meant little more than the salon paintings of his Aunt Hatty or Cassie. In Moncton there was no art gallery. Color art books were almost unknown. At the art gallery in Toronto, one of the two best in Canada, Frye found the Group of Seven paintings so vibrant against the rest of the collection, mostly third-rate Italian Baroque, that he developed an enthusiasm and loyalty to Canadian art that was never matched by a commitment to Canadian literature. His taste was significantly enriched by one of the Group of Seven, Arthur Lismer, who was a genial English-born enthusiast in charge of education at the gallery and regularly guided his own tours.

In the last days of November with the newspapers full of stories of investors jumping out of windows, the Great Crash had rather a "muffled thud" at Victoria College. Frye's math instructor informed the students that the crash was merely an adjustment of an over-heated stock market. For months, Frye barely pondered the impact of the market collapse. Back home, however, construction began to dry up and the business for independent hardware salesmen evaporated. In another rail center near Moncton, Amherst, where most of the hardware travellers lived, there was catastrophic unemployment. Herm managed to stay nominally in business, but was eventually forced to sell calendars to old customers and friends. This strategy hardly proved adequate and he fell badly behind on grocery bills and rent. His inability to pay his milk bill occasioned a sputter of disgust from Cassie who felt it reflected as much on Herm as the economic situation. To Frye's later exasperation, both Herm and Cassie felt that the Depression was the will of God and that blaming the capitalist system or the honor of Messrs. Hoover or Bennett was inadmissible.

The obvious fall-back position for the family was Vera but she too was struck by uncommonly bad luck. She had left the osteopathic college and had started teaching elementary grade school in the Evergreen Park district of Chicago. The chairman of the board of education, however, had lost millions in the stock crash and the board failed to meet its payroll first for months, then years. Although the whole affair became a national scandal, Vera faced weeks of no money.

Frye deliberately insulated himself from the difficulties of his parents because he was afraid that worries would inevitably conspire to destroy the college life which was becoming so important to him. In college, he could escape direct anxiety. Most of his friends, in fact, who came from Ontario farms, were comparatively sheltered from the Depression. In Ontario, there was no drought and a reliable market remained for produce. Students, who'd usually suffered bleakly puritan existences in high school, enjoyed the social rounds which included the famous Victoria Promenade and—more illicitly—the Silver Slipper dance club.

Frye's one major extracurricular activity was dramatics but his interest seemed at first curiously unliterary. He approached John

Bates about a part in a play he was producing, *The House with the Twisty Windows,* a one-act play by Mary Pakington ominously set in a cellar in Petrograd during the "red terror." Frye's motive for joining the cast, he said, was to attain poise in front of audiences. Bates cast Frye in the role of Moore who is described as "a man of forty ... so remote from the powerful vision of his thoughts that Roper [another character] can only stare dumbfounded." Moore is thrown into an incarcerated group of westerners in danger of their lives and launches into a four-page speech presumably to calm them down. When Bates rehearsed Frye it was only a matter of Frye's quickly looking over the speech and he had it memorized but he recited his lines so fast, they were impossible to follow. Although Bates calmed him down in rehearsal, Frye leaned back on a table behind him during the performance and upset a water-filled soup bowl which spilled onto the stage. Panicking, he again recited his lines so fast, the speech was lost. Frye continued to involve himself in bit parts in other plays including an A.A. Milne drama. A friend remembers his acting as wooden but his enthusiasm for dramatic production genuine.

## SCHERZANDO

Through his acquaintance with the college librarian, Dr. Frank Barber, Frye was able to get a summer job pasting labels into new books at the Central Reference Library. The job was menial but meant that he could finance the next year as well as buy himself a new suit. When the residences emptied out, he felt a certain loneliness and frustration but inured himself to it. He ate on the chop-suey circuit, carefully watching every dime. Decades later, he would remember that breakfast was 15 cents, lunch a dime and a four-course dinner was 35 cents, if he chose the lowest item on the menu.

The library job was consummately tedious and, despite its utter simplicity, he never developed any skill at it. Still he managed to

squirrel away new books that interested him, the most important
of which was Denis Saurat's 1924 book *Blake and Modern Thought*.
Frye later repudiated it but it awoke his interest in Blake. Fascinated by the reverberations of the book, Frye came in a half-hour
early every morning to read it. Although absorbed to an excessive
degree with Blake's occult and mystical background, Saurat
planted a golden seed in Frye's mind that, once these sources were
understood, "Blake's ideas ... considered as a whole, are perfectly
coherent and reasonable."

Frye also fell to the dubious charm of the tales of Richard
Garnett, collected in *The Twilight of the Gods*. Although Garnett
had family ties with the Bloomsbury group, his fiction re-created
an ancient Magian atmosphere of trickster gods, priests and popes
and devils, magicians and aged philosophers. Although the contrived thee-and-ere style was no better than a self-conscious smirk
in the Jazz Age, the stories entranced Frye so much that when he
later tried fiction, he used them as a model. This indicated how
pervasive and unshakable was the romantic cosmology which
defined Frye's imagination.

Because he stood fourth among all the students in the Pass
Course at Vic, he could now transfer easily into the much-vaunted
honors stream, which, until its crude dismantling in 1970, made
Toronto probably the best undergraduate university in North
America. Instead of honors English, Frye wanted to take the philosophy (English or History) course which the philosopher George
Brett had set up at Toronto to copy Oxford's Great Moderns. It
was intended as a difficult course for elite students but, because
of a technicality, rarely entered at Vic except by students heading
for the ministry. For Frye it was an intellectual windfall—the
course his "theolog" friends had entered. But while it managed to
balance his anarchistic intellectual interests, the course created
problems in the long run by providing thin preparation in English.

There was a temporary setback when Frye discovered that the
philosophy department hadn't yet approved his application. He
became very depressed about this, but it was only a bureaucratic
delay, and he soon enlisted in the course. Essentially, he jumped
two academic years into a bracing world of high university stan-

dards. Commensurate with his rise in the college, he received a private room in Gate House, one of the men's new residences.

In his second-year Shakespeare course, Frye encountered another of his great Victoria College mentors, Pelham Edgar. At the still-strongly-Methodist college, Edgar was an anomaly. He was an Anglican who looked like a British major with moustache and correct air. His father, Sir James Edgar, had been Speaker of the House of Commons in Ottawa. Edgar was not wealthy but inherited the family mansion. There was an illusive rakishness about him and one inaccurate legend had him taking a corner so fast in his car that he pitched a visiting duchess out of her seat and over a hedge. His close friend was E.J. Pratt whom Edgar rescued out of a minor instructor's job in psychology on the premise that Pratt seemed to know something about literature, though his PhD, improbably, was on speculative theology. Together, Pratt and Edgar played golf and drank liquor with a clear conscience that was positively idiosyncratic at the Methodist Vic.

The professors at University College who ran the English department considered Edgar a dilettante. He hadn't, in fact, published much except for a pioneering study of Henry James, and his area of interest, the Romantics, was unpopular in academe. Another of his problems was his first wife who made him miserable and insomniac with her severe attacks of depression. But Edgar had two unusual qualities. His knowledge of literature was vast, and included the contemporary work of D.H. Lawrence and Eliot, which was spurned as degenerate at other colleges. He also had a weird ability to push people in exactly appropriate directions. He served as guardian angel over his friend, Douglas Bush, who wanted to transfer from classics to English. Very early, he sensed something Coleridgean about Kay Coburn, and sent her on her way to preeminence as editor of Coleridge's notebooks. When he saw Frye, he thought Blake.

In class, he had a diffuse air about him and often wandered off into areas—particularly in contemporary literature—that had nothing to do with the lecture. This approach attracted some University College students who used to drift over to Vic to hear lectures by Edgar or Pratt. In one lecture, Edgar began a discussion about Blake which was exciting enough to involve Frye a little further in Blake's work. Above all, Frye admired the depth of Edgar's knowledge. Edgar once electrified him when he impatiently told a student talking about an obscure poet to sit down. He then launched into an amazingly detailed analysis, starting with "The facts about Crabbe are these."

Despite an indifferent childhood reading of Lamb's *Tales of Shakespeare* and dissatisfying high school study of *As You Like It,* Frye sent up a barrage of questions and comments in Edgar's Shakespeare class which impressed his classmates and the lecturer, who quickly discerned a protégé. In fact Edgar seemed unable to start his classes without scanning the class to confirm whether Frye or his other favourite, Munro Beattie, were there. Edgar loved the romantic qualities of Shakespeare and, wrapping his legs around the chair legs, used to read lyrical passages from *Antony and Cleopatra.* But both Frye and two friends, George Birtch and Art Cragg, sensed a hollowness in Edgar's approach to Shakespeare and early in the term, marched over to Pratt's office for a three-hour gabfest to receive a more positive view of the poet.

A contributing factor to Frye's own early curiosity about both Shakespeare and mythology was his discovery that year in the Central Library of Colin Still's book *Shakespeare's Mystery Play.* Still dropped the reasonable suggestion that the play might have been based on a 1609 Spanish novelette *Noches de Invierno* about a magician king who flees with his only daughter Seraphina to a submarine palace until the wicked deposing emperor dies. Still however discounted the possibility, applying the thesis that the sixth book of *The Aeneid* was an account of the Eleusinian mysteries, making *The Tempest* a 17th century variant.

As an undergraduate, however, Frye was most interested simply in the possibility that there *could be* a timeless theme. Still posited the suggestion that this might be so because Shakespeare was a receptor for a free-floating dramatic-religious form which periodically adhered to new writers. Frye would always stay clear of eccentric psychological explanations but never failed to be impressed by structurally sound evidence which linked improbably distant works. That same year he was coincidentally fascinated with the bald statement in his *Hamlet* text that Hamlet was really the successor to a line of similar figures from Norse mythology. Despite Still's crankiness, there were theories he held which were close to myth critics of his own period and which would reflect deeply in Frye's own thinking: "[*The Tempest*] is a synthesis of the main features of all mythology and ritual whether Christian or non-Christian. It tells the story of man's upward struggle partly in Biblical terms and partly in terms of pagan myth and ritual. It not only presupposes but actually demonstrates that there is one universal tradition underlying all religious and semi-religious concepts. In short, having regard to the manner in which its theme is handled, *The Tempest* is an almost perfect essay in what we should call today Comparative Religion."

While Frye was tepidly interested in a history course on the Tudors taught in orthodox linear fashion by Donald Creighton, he discovered in the small Hart House library a work of historiographic expressionism that was to have a monumental impact on his thinking. It was the recently published translation of *The Decline of the West* by Oswald Spengler. At four different times in his later career, Frye tried to come to terms with this youthful exuberance over Spengler, admitting he couldn't put the work to rest. In a 1955 radio talk, Frye called *The Decline of the West* "a vision rather than a theory or a philosophy, and a vision of haunting imaginative power. Its truth is the truth of poetry or prophecy, not of science ... If it were nothing else *The Decline of the West* would still be one of the world's great romantic poems."

In a 1974 essay "Spengler Revisited" he had to admit: " ... it is still true that very few books, in my experience, have anything like Spengler's power to expand and exhilarate the mind. The boldness of his leaping imagination, the kaleidescopic patterns that facts make when he throws them together, the sense of the whole of human thought and culture spread out in front of one, the feeling that the blinkers of time and space have been removed from one's inward eyes when Greek sculptors are treated as the 'contemporaries' of Western composers, all make up an experience not easily duplicated ... Some of his comparative passages, such as his juxtaposing of colors in Western paintings with tonal effects in Western music, read almost like free association. Any number of critics could call these comparisons absurd or mystical balderdash. But Spengler has the power to challenge the reader's imagination, as critics of that type usually have not, and he will probably survive them all even if all of them are right."

What is interesting here is that it didn't appear to matter to Frye how turgid or difficult the text could be (of Spengler or any of his later heroes like Blake or Yeats) so long as it yielded a pattern which extended to infinity and absorbed all of man's creations. Spengler in fact was an arch-idealist who insisted that through "countless shapes that emerge and vanish, pile up and melt again, a thousand-hued tumult ... the keener glance can detect those pure forms which underlie all human becoming ..." Besides its obviously thrilling personal effect on Frye there was a crucial cultural concept of organic growth and decay, the simple cycle of the seasons. Spengler applied these to the phases of history. Frye later applied them to literature: comedy, romance, satire, irony and tragedy. There were other major legacies too: Spengler's distaste for progressive Darwinian history, his insistence on history as philosophy, his use of "polar" dichotomies, his Blake-like differentiation of "clever systems" against a philosophy which finds the "soul" and form of the time, his proto-structuralist ideas of civilizations' developing nearly identical features in isolation of each other. Like Blake who saw "the same characters repeated again and again," Spengler claimed that the expression-forms of world history are limited in number, and that eras, epochs, situations, persons are ever repeating themselves true to type.

In this second year Frye busily exerted himself with the proliferation of college activities. The drama group, Vic Dramatics, fell apart organizationally and Frye helped to pick up the pieces and organize the year. He involved himself in the debates club and became a sub-editor in charge of alumni notices for the college literary magazine, *Acta Victoriana*. A much more important personal involvement came out of his tendency to loiter around Music Club productions in which his friends like Del Martin were involved. The club yearly cranked out a bright, well-produced Gilbert and Sullivan opus which later drove Frye into frenzies of opprobrium. But one of the rehearsal pianists of the Music Club was Helen Kemp, a Pass Course student in fine art. Helen was a Torontonian who lived in the Broadview area on the east side of the Don River. Her father was Stanley Kemp, a commercial artist who had written an MA thesis in 1908 on the Palladian architectural style and personally knew the Group of Seven artists, including Arthur Lismer, who had worked at an engraving firm, Grip Ltd. A commonly published photo of artist Tom Thomson at Grip, in fact, is not Thomson at all but Stanley Kemp.

At Music Club rehearsals, Frye took note of Helen, who he considered the kind of girl he would like to know. Their relationship was upgraded when Frye took the job of arc light operator in the wings during the Hart House production of *The Gondoliers,* with Helen holding the prompt book in the other wing. In a magazine profile, Frye quipped, "It wasn't love at first sight, but it was a very effortless operation." It took about another year before they were commonly identified as "steady." Helen didn't have the same literary and philosophical interests as Frye and although he later urged her to read his patron saints Spengler and Blake, it was Helen who was most often successful in transmitting her own enthusiasms, particularly art, to Frye. Like Evelyn Rogers before, Helen was a much more extroverted person who didn't take Frye too seriously. She quickly saw the person beneath the then formidable crust of pretension and impatience.

As summer approached, many of Frye's friends planned to go out west on summer mission and once again Frye applied for work in Manitoba and this time was accepted. Because his Aunt Mary, seriously ill, had left Alberta precipitously the previous autumn to live with Herm and Cassie in Moncton, most of her possessions still lay in storage either in her rural village of Sniatyn or at a friend's in Edmonton. When she died, she wanted these disposed of. Frye agreed to do this but since it would interfere with the first few weeks of his mission, he cancelled it. Cassie assured herself that the following year "he would be more anxious to go."

In late May, he left Union Station in Toronto with George Birtch and Del Martin, sitting up in the coach section and eating food they'd stored in the train kitchen. They travelled non-stop to Moose

Jaw where they shared a room in the YMCA and Martin headed south to his field in Crestwynd. Frye and Birtch travelled on until they split up, Birtch heading for the fabled cattle country of the Cypress Hills and Frye up to Andrew, Alberta, near Sniatyn. When he arrived, he realized he'd made a mistake. A Ukrainian family, the Palamarchucks, had stored Mary's largest possessions such as her washing machine and trunks in a decrepit shed used for chicken feed. The door had been left open and everything was dusty and weather-beaten. A missing record player had found its way to better use in the community. None of his aunt's larger possessions could be sold or transported East. There was better luck in Edmonton where Mary had stored her books with a friend who helped Frye pack them up and ship them off along with the trunks of the more portable possessions from Sniatyn. To fill time in the hotel in Edmonton, he borrowed Spengler's *Decline of the West* from the library. His reacquaintance with it set off the first of several epiphanic experiences which turned vague personal ambitions into one great vision. There was little specific about his experience and it had no real connection with any particular passage or state of mind. Rather it was a boundless sense that Frye suddenly felt about what he could accomplish with all his resources and knowledge.

Back at home in Moncton for the first time in two years, he practised on the piano and waited for news about scholarships which would alleviate the financial burden of the next academic year. He had stood first among the twelve in his course, but he needed the supplementary income which he would have earned from the summer mission. Spending much of his day at the library, he researched an essay called "Eccentricity" to compete for the Lincoln Hutton essay prize worth $100. In a sense he had become a professional student who had to appraise every award and prize essay for its relative financial strength.

Frye's subsequent attitude to "Eccentricity" was complicated, so much so that he refused publication the following year in *Acta* even when the college chancellor himself, E.W. Wallace, appealed to him. In choosing a compulsory pseudonym for himself, he decided on Scherzando to indicate to the judge, Pelham Edgar, that it was not to be taken too seriously. Eventually regarding it as juvenilia, he threw it out. But in the summer of 1931, it was an important exercise which indicated Frye's intense proclivity towards typological thinking.

When he explained it to Cassie, she was fascinated enough to sketch out the schema for her own interest and then sent a copy to her nephew Donald.

clown    connoisseur    crank
buffoon    jester    satirist        fanatic    hermit    freak
medicine [man]    prophet    genius

The polarized schema, based on his own categories, was as wide and complex as the margins of possibility. It was populated not by the symbolic equivalents which would fascinate him later but by actual figures from history, music and literature. It was his first all-encompassing pattern and it possessed a complete lack of regard for the limits of historical period or art or religion. The concept of "individual phases of human existence with encyclopedic ranges of association around them" was still very much fresh in his mind when he wrote *Fearful Symmetry*.

Soon after Frye came home, the trunks from Alberta also arrived and filled up the five-room flat, making it difficult to move around. When she opened them to air and shake out the contents, Cassie started coughing and wheezing and had to go to bed one Sunday with a bad cold. She estimated 400 books in the lot. Not long after, Frye received a round robin letter from Del Martin reporting from his mission in the Palliser Triangle in southern Saskatchewan where the drought was unrelenting. It gave Frye an eery sense of what he had missed himself.

Riding his circuit on a black charger called Nigger, Martin wandered a surrealistic landscape visiting homes and schools. He was lonely and disturbed but tough. "The country south of Moose Jaw is hilly and looks like the Sahara at present. Along the track we saw men lying with their knapsacks under their heads. There was not a green blade of grass to be seen. All was dry and dusty. Farther south the soil has drifted until the fences are completely buried ... There has been no crop for almost four years. This year is the worst yet. Only one rain has come and the winds are terrible. The wind has blown this last day and a half. The house is full of dust. There is dust everywhere even in my toothbrush ..." Cassie was so impressed with the letter, she copied it out for her Bible class.

By the end of the summer Frye had accumulated a patchwork quilt of scholarships which would carry him through the next year without anxiety. As first in his class, he won a token $50 but his standing meant other prizes including half of the War Memorial Scholarship worth $100 and a John Trick scholarship of $250 would cover most of his residence fees.

## OWL AND BIRD OF PARADISE

Frye started off his third year at a blistering pace. He became president of the debating club with the tragic diplomat-to-be and scholar of Japanese history, Herb Norman, as treasurer. He rejoined the Vic drama club and the *Acta* staff as associate editor and leading contributor. The strain of the heavy school and extracurricular activity had an alarming effect. Cassie noted "some sort of breakdown" or at least slump which resulted in Frye's resigning from many of his extracurricular activities. His mother was clearly worried. Before Frye went on Christmas holiday, once more to the Martins' farm, he ominously reported to Cassie that "if the professors wanted to pluck him they could easily."

His academic load was nearly all philosophy and included Ethics, Philosophy Texts, History of Philosophy and Aesthetics. Because the curriculum was set rigidly by the staff, there was no escape from this preponderance of philosophy. It did manage, however, to provide Frye with a fundamental knowledge of the major thinkers like Plato and Aristotle who permeate his later work. His one English course in the Romantics with Pelham Edgar proved to be utterly crucial. Among the assigned subjects for seminar papers was "The Mysticism of William Blake." Although he'd spent the summer leafing through Blake's prophecies, Frye was still baffled by the poet. Edgar, however, encouraged him to take the topic on. Frye knew the Saurat book, but found this a confusing quest. Some of the inevitable dyspepsia is clear in an essay he wrote in 1962 about his collision with an obtuse passage from *Jerusalem*: "What is Above is Within ... The Circumference is Within, Without is formed the Selfish Center,/And the Circumference still expands going forward to Eternity ..." The bemused Frye noted, "Something moves, anyhow." Frye produced a mammoth seminar paper which took two or three sessions to read. When his fellow students were beleaguered by the torrent of ideas, Frye later considered this more the result of his own confusions than any deficiencies in his classmates. Edgar nevertheless found the essay so impressive, he sent it over to G.S. Brett, the editor of *The University of Toronto Quarterly* as a serious submission. Brett was interested but rejected it as too immature.

Although Frye kept up all his old theolog connections, he fell in with a new friend, Norman Knight, who introduced him to the far-left radicalism which was spreading among students on campus as the Depression deepened. Knight, who was a year behind Frye, had a circle of friends, centred on brother and sister Kenneth and Sylvia Johnstone, in his working-class town of Weston, just outside Toronto. One of the chief attractions of this group was Sylvia who had a *femme fatale* aura, attractive yet extravagantly distant and who managed quite unintentionally to create enormous romantic tangles within the circle.

As part of a discussion group which formed at the Johnstone household, Frye gave a talk on literature which started with Greek tragedy. Not long after, Ken Johnstone heard of a Marxist called Maurice Spector who'd been a founder of the Canadian Communist Party. Spector, who lived in a boarding house of a fellow worker of Johnstone, had walked out of a Stalinist party meeting in 1928 after expressing enthusiasm for the heretical views of Trotsky. He subsequently tried to establish a Trotskyist cell in Toronto.

Spector came to one of the Johnstones' meetings and totally charmed the group. The one exception was Frye who was visibly annoyed, and amazed that Knight and the Johnstones could be so easily taken in by Spector's line. As a result of Spector's persuasion, the Johnstone group quite quickly became the nucleus for the Trotskyists in Toronto and, under the impetus of Knight, eventually infiltrated and took over the campus chapter of the leftist but non-communist League for Social Reconstruction. Frye was deeply dismayed by Knight's involvement and hoped that since "humor and virility are not allies of communism," Knight would be saved either by his sense of humor or by a love affair.

All of this put Frye in a curiously radical centrist position. His biting sarcasm for conservative politics was well-known but now he found himself easily irritated by the far left. His friendship with Knight nevertheless thrived. Knight was the type Frye always liked: emotionally effusive, intellectually quick and generous. They frequently knocked off the day by going over to Murray's Restaurant on Bloor in the evenings to argue politics over coffee. Knight called Frye an idealist and abused Frye's adored Spengler as a "decadent bourgeois ideological apologist." Frye returned the favor by attacking Knight's simplistic notions of dialectical materialism which he thought were irrational and nonsensical. Like a wild card in the pack, a history major called Ernie Gould impartially heckled them both.

Sensing that Frye was a prize catch, Knight and the Johnstones persisted in their conversion attempts. Sylvia who was soon the leader of the youth wing of the Trotskyists, the Young Spartacists, hung around the campus even when she was still in high school. Like Knight, she attended Victoria College debates as a spectator in which Frye was the dominating figure. In the process of converting a graduate student, Earle Birney, she took him to see a debate. Birney was so impressed with the rhetorical command of Frye that he wrote on a slip of paper to Sylvia, "Who is this?" Johnstone replied, "Norrie Frye." Birney queried again, "What is he?" Sylvia, who remembered Frye's talking about a Spengler disciple, Egon Friedell, who wrote a two-volume survey of western civilization, answered, "A Friedellian." It was an exotic even funny tag but in its odd, meaningless way it demarcated his own distance from prevailing Marxist enthusiasms.

As a member of the *Acta* staff, Knight also covered the same debates and, a year later, provided a fascinating portrait of Frye in a debate which weighed the motion that a distinctively Canadian culture can be developed: "The government found itself defeated for the first time this year and Canada found herself denied the power to develop a distinctive culture.

"The chief credit for defeating the motion and thus raising the Opposition to the dizzy heights of power must go to the latter's leading speaker, the redoubtable Norrie Frye. The equally redoubtable Cragg (Arthur, or Large) had opened the attack for the government. He had built up an imposing thesis to the effect that Canadian energy plus British traditions plus American influences plus the pioneer spirit plus the French-Canadian contribution would equal a distinctively Canadian culture. He concluded effectively with an attempt to confound his great antagonist by quoting his [Frye's] remarks from a previous issue of this august journal with reference to a 'distinctly Canadian civilization.' But Mr. Frye was undismayed. He calmly arose, propped himself against the back of his chair, and proceeded to demolish his opponent's case. He pointed out that his writings on the subject had said nothing about the country's power to develop a distinctive culture. His words had been the expression of a hope that such an achievement was possible; but a dispassionate analysis of the problem had driven him to the conclusion that it was not to be. Thereupon Mr. Frye, calling upon his patron saint, Oswald Spengler, proceeded, with his well-known machine-gun delivery, to survey the whole field of Western culture, and to show how the future could produce nothing that had not gone before. By the time he reached the post-Scriabin era in music the House was groggy, and when he sat down he left an uneasiness in the Cabinet and an awed silence in the government back-benches that boded ill for the fate of the motion."

Because they lived in the same residence, Knight also managed to see an almost volcanic physical energy inside Frye which may have reflected his own tearing and pulling ambitions. One Saturday night in the spring Frye and Knight set out to walk the length of Toronto's main east-west axis, Bloor St. They reached the western limit of the city at Jane and turned around and walked back to the

eastern, returning to the college by dawn. It was a trek of about
sixteen miles and what stunned Knight, a middle distance runner,
was the speed and endurance throughout of his ostensibly scrawny
companion. When they returned to residence, Knight remembers
curling up in a heap in a shower stall and putting his feet under
a stream of hot water, but Frye seemed unaffected.

A more immediate hazard, of course, was the annual orgy of
exam studies which so thoroughly depressed and enervated Frye
that in his capacity as the next year's *Acta* editor, he wrote an
editorial for the April issue bitterly condemning the whole system.
Irrespective of its merit in exhibiting his own distaste for an insidious system, which he excelled at, it revealed how innate and deep-
seated were his concerns about education. There is a clear notion,
which Frye never abandoned, that university is a precious time of
remaking individuals, separating them from mob mentality and
providing for them "a poise and culture resulting from moving in
an intellectually stimulating society."

Frye was consistently scathing: "The periodic warping and twisting of life brought about by May examinations has long been
accepted [but] ... the sheer magnitude of the injustice involved in
asking the hopes of our civilization to stake their most valuable
years on the fortunes of a few hours at the end of each is sufficiently
appalling in itself to dismay the stoutest, and when this is backed
up by a mob psychology of a small college centred in residences,
in which the leaders are always on the side of panic, the result is
a distorted and almost inhuman existence."

Final exams in fact sabotaged real education for both ordinary
and serious students. The former "find examinations an insuperable
barrier in the way of getting an education ..." As for protean scholars, whose work "is necessarily careful, labored and systematic ...
a random and time-limited quizzing is an impertinence." Using
the Spenglerian image of the seasons, Frye saw the blight: " ... the
possessor of a really fine mind who goes to college to have it
orientated is at a hopeless disadvantage. If he gets a flash of genius
towards the end of April, he might just as well have an attack of
measles for all the good it does him. It is probably for this reason

that the fine arts, which require real talent, genuine love for the work, careful and properly balanced and regularized study, and to which examinations are consequently fatal, have been so rigidly ruled out of the 'arts' courses. Literature still remains, however, mainly for the benefit of women. As a result Canadian literature is decadent and commonplace, for the literature of a young country needs to be young too, and what is done in Canada, though it may partake of the stifling heat of summer, the cheap gaudiness of autumn, and the sterility of winter, can never reflect the awakening enthusiasm of spring which those educated here have always missed—for the average man brought up on May examinations knows as little about spring as he does about a sunrise."

When the summer came, Frye was so penniless that he had to borrow money from the bursar, W.J. Little, to go home. As usual, he stoically faced the one-and-a-half-day train journey and then at home fell into torpor and slept off the accumulated exhaustion of the academic year. The job prospects in Moncton were miserable. Herm himself was idled by a complete stoppage of construction work and he was trying to land an agency in Montreal to get the family out of the Depression-wracked Maritimes. Frye saw his chances at a library job blocked by a board member with "five enormous and unmarried daughters." As for a stenographic position, the one or two openings were for permanent work. He suspected that part-time work would be impossible without a tie with the business college. The only prospect was the utterly unattractive possibility of genteel begging, selling ties at offices, as Cragg had already done from door to door.

Instead, he hid for the summer. He worked at the piano, discovering his brother's copy of Czerny's opus 740. He even made a determined effort to write poetry and wrote to Helen: "I have already sprained a couple of convolutions trying to produce a poem and the damned Muse is still too stuck-up to come. I keep kidding myself that I have too strong a sense of humor to write poetry." Two weeks later, the effort completely collapsed. He realized his lack of technique and tendency to work himself into sentimentality in order to compose would only guarantee doggerel. He ripped his lines up, and took solace at the library with a book of modern American poetry which reassured him that "there are bigger fools in the world."

By mid-June, the mail brought early rumors that he'd led his class again but failed his academically inconsequential Religious Knowledge course in New Testament because he had missed the term test at Christmas. Hearing that the hard-working Art Cragg had failed to beat him, he lashed out again against the "undignified" exam system. To Helen he complained, "I know that from experience that laziness is a very slight hindrance on exams and that hysteria, general physical debility, eyestrain, nervousness, constipation, panic and lassitude ... are determining factors."

As a refrain to his gloom, the rain outside was persistent and unending. His nerves suffered the abuses of Cassie's loud radio playing and the wailing of a newborn in the downstairs flat. He stayed inside and became morbid, thinking "very clogged thoughts about uninspiring subjects." Helen worried about his growing moodiness but when she suggested that he get out walking more, he reacted with a plea that it was still raining and his brain was water-soaked. He added, " ... The natives stare at me, wherever I go, as though I really were the combination of owl and bird-of-paradise that I resemble."

Everything that summer seemed unfocussed and inconclusive. Even his reading was undirected and non-academic. He did not mention Blake once in his letters. He read J.M. Barrie and the recent novels, *Babbit* and *Arrowsmith*, of Sinclair Lewis whose "execrable" style seemed to clank "along like a surveyor's chain." This led to a diatribe against Lewis's *Elmer Gantry*, which he considered a failure both as satire and polemic. Frye was confused about Helen's association of satire "with dusty pedantry" and considered that satire about the church "must bite, not bark." Lewis, therefore, failed to write a great novel: "Think of what he overlooked—Protestant individualism clashing with Protestant bigotry, Catholic anti-intellectualism cloaked by Catholic urbanity, mysticism in its last ditch, the clergy slowly retreating from their hell-fire vindictiveness to a vague and emasculated ethical sentiment, the slight but apparent rise of superstition and occultism." This kicked off a discussion of a "Representative" denomination in Canada which Frye volubly identified as the United Church which capably combined a concatenation of thoroughly Canadian virtues: "in its good nature, in its tolerance, in its conscientiousness, in its vague and sentimental combination of Socialism, Imperialism and Nationalism all at once—a very appealing mixture, unpalatable though each individual constituent may be—above all in its determination to apply the old traditions to new surroundings which makes Canada sturdier than England and more coherent than the United States."

Finally at the end of July, he received his official results and found that the advance rumors of his technical failure proved correct. He feared that with both his failure and his harsh editorial on exams, he might lose the crucial Trick scholarship which paid for his residence fees at college. Because he refused to go into personal debt, he was uncertain about whether he could return to Vic at all. It was the perfect realization of his criticisms of the exam system. The slaughter of many of his classmates moreover drove him into a fit of self-lacerating guilt: "Well, I can't keep pouring out undiluted genius much longer, when I am living the life of a misanthropic clam." There was a curious conclusion: "I wish I wasn't so DAMNED lazy."

He was also driven into a curious self-defensiveness by Helen's accusations of his being paternalistic in giving her advice. He launched into a classical apology of his own values and hopes which were still surprisingly anti-academic. In a fit of despondency he admitted, "I guess I am going to be a professor after all. Which is a horrible thought. I seem to be anchored to my chair by my guts." His loyalty was not to the universities and schools themselves but to the arts, which were neglected: "Our fine arts training in Canada is so childish, and the general background of culture provided by our schooling so negligible, that it is rare to find a professional in one of them of broad outlook and culture. And when I see the beautiful and good things of life entrusted to a crowd of chattering jackals I see red. I don't care whether they have good hearts or not—a great artist is necessarily *sans peur* and *sans reproche*. As a custodian of beauty he has a great tradition to sustain—if he ignores that tradition he is a nuisance."

His posturing often seemed like whistling in the dark of Moncton but it's obvious that he continued to look for a Nietzschean purification of sham in both society and himself. He'd already established that he had "a definite message to give," but worried about his own cowardice and propensity for discouragement. "I would make a very graceful shadow boxer, but little more ... what I want is a thick skin."

As term approached and he had assurances of academic support, his mood shifted to one of anticipation. He began to plot out areas of concentration in the courses he would take. He planned Romanticism as a topic for his philosophy thesis and, for Pelham Edgar, an essay on Browning who he called his favourite poet, adding that his "very definite heroisms" in literature were Donne, Milton, Bunyan, Swift, Blake, Dickens, Browning and Shaw. As a function of his Blake interest he even started to study astrology, but lapsed into writing a short farce about a backward walking Cancer crab who runs into a Capricorn goat with sufficient force that the Astrologer permitted all Cancers to walk forward "providing they wear their *collars* backside to show their descent ... And that is the origin of the ministerial dog collar."

## GOLD MEDALIST

When he arrived back in Toronto, Chancellor Wallace pulled Frye and Cragg into his office together to try to fathom their surprising incompetence in New Testament Greek. Frye, who had never liked Wallace, shrugged the whole matter off, thinking it was his own fault, no matter how harmful it was to his future. For Cragg, however, it was an indelible mark on his record which Rhodes Scholar interviewers found suspicious. Frye quickly tried to repair some of the damage for Cragg by writing a rare piece of panegyric for *Acta*, praising Cragg as the model for both college and church. Extravagant to the point of nonsense, it nevertheless revealed Frye's impervious notion that culture's "cradle" was religion: "In [Cragg] we can see reflected, like the surrounding country upon a quiet deep lake, those qualities which have made Victoria the cradle of the United Church, the Church which inevitably will be the cradle of all future Canadian philosophy and culture." A necessary corollary was that "the old Methodist tradition of the bespectacled theological student of immense energy and occasional stodginess is giving way to a new conception of the United Church scholar, of keen, penetrating intellect, wide outlook, and occasional mistiness of thinking." It's clear that Frye was really looking into his own mirror.

Shortly after the run-in with Wallace, Frye got a taste of revenge when he received a rush request to write the script for the annual college review, the "Bob," which impartially satirized Vic's leading figures, including Wallace. A classmate, Blair Laing, was in charge of the script that year but when he was unable to come up with material, he asked Frye. Frye stunned Laing by turning out a script in a few days. With apologies to Samuel Butler, Frye called it "The Way of All 'Fresh' " and improbably set the first act, The Pound of "Fresh," in the "College Bar Room" where the characters of Chancellor Wallace, Prof. Auger and Mr. Little, all abstemious in real life, examined the learning of a group of new freshmen. In Act II, They Shall Not Pass, set in "Examination Hell," the professors were so disgusted with the freshmen's ignorance that they decided to write the papers themselves, thereby displaying their own ignorance.

The script was so full of *double entendre* that the Bob committee prudently submitted a bowdlerized script for administration approval, keeping the off-color material intact for the performance. Two of the professors, for example, were called Headgear and Halfcocked. Even then, much of the material was lost to the audience. One remembered gag involved the college's fetishistic collection of Queen Victoria memorabilia which included the Queen's baby mug. Frye had the figure of the college librarian, Dr. Barber, come on stage carrying a chamber pot supposedly used by the

Queen. Someone asks him, "Is that some mouldy Etruscan urn?" Dr. Barber replies, "Oh no, it's quite empty." Urn, of course, was pronounced as dangerously close to urine as courage would allow.

As editor of *Acta*, Frye occupied a precisely similar role of Shavian curmudgeon and wrote some of the most acerbic editorials which have appeared in the magazine. In the first issue, which had been seriously delayed by lack of ads because of the Depression, he stated flatly (and accurately) that "the typical Victorian's interest in literary matters is about equal to a coal pony's interest in chorus girls. For that reason we depart from the usual editorial *cliché*. We do not welcome 'criticism.' "

He followed this up with a longer editorial in the next issue called "The Question of Maturity," prompted by a remark of a professor that students were no longer as mature as they had been. Given Frye's obsessive self-ruminations in the summer, he should have agreed. To test the proposition, he hauled out an 1899 *Acta* and noted that while students of that period were eager to acquire beard and moustache and an "adult's solid respectability which lends such force to dogmatism," they were clueless about the age they lived in, "a period of sophisticated and artificial disillusionment, of effeminate posings and universal hopeless doubt." Similarly a review of Tennyson's poetry demonstrated a Sunday School sentimentalism: "One's final impression of the whole magazine is that it is an extended sermon." Frye then revealed ideas which would prove remarkably durable in his thinking: "Two separate periods cannot be comparatively evaluated in themselves. The 'old fogy' and 'mid-Victorian prude' attitude must be dismissed without serious consideration, and so must the opposing pretence that the youth of today has had its morale uprooted by the war (the present author was two years old when it broke out) and that Tennyson is at any rate 'healthier' and more 'wholesome' than Aldous Huxley ... The best of our [Acta's] contributors ... strive at impartiality of survey rather than judgement in terms of preconceived attitude." Already Frye was writing the introduction to his *Anatomy of Criticism*.

In the following issue, Frye not only discussed the historical tension of poetry forms, he initiated his long-enduring habit of telling poets how to work: "If anyone is really interested in the writing of poetry, it behooves him, not so much to be 'up to date' as to express himself, as he lives in a certain definite age, he must necessarily express that age through himself. To this extent he must make an exhaustive survey of the kind of work done by his most distinguished contemporaries, and trace out the precedents and traditions they follow." Contemporary poetry, in other words, was not a facile newness but a re-creation.

Frye managed to accomplish one task set the previous summer, the long essay on Romanticism for G.S. Brett in philosophy. Although Brett had no business indulging precocious undergraduates, he was sufficiently good-humored about Frye's mammoth 100-page essay that he gave him a high mark. Written in one sustained blast, the essay was faithful to Frye's epiphanic experience in Edmonton and drew on his knowledge of music, literature and philosophy to produce an overview of Romanticism which was heavily influenced by Spengler's opus and Neitzsche's *Birth of Tragedy*, which coincidentally insisted on the power of myth in history: " ... without myth every culture loses the healthy natural power of its creativity: only a horizon defined by myths completes and unifies a whole cultural movement."

Despite the precocity of his ideas, Frye couldn't seem to express himself except in an untamed sprawl. Certainly when he produced another grand opus on Browning for Edgar, Edgar was concerned enough to sit down with Frye for an hour and a half to sort out his labyrinthine sentences. Although Frye was enthusiastic about Browning's work, it left a minuscule impact on his later work, except to suggest a key idea which Frye kept trying to develop in later years, the musicality of poetry which would reverse the usual clichés about sing-song rhythm.

When Frye graduated in May, 1933, he captured two gold medals in English and philosophy. While he stood first-first again, his average was a stunning 83, five percentage points higher than his previous best. His highest marks were in philosophy and ethics in which he received 89. In the thirties, however, there was no automatic advancement into graduate school. Even the "gold" medals, received months later, were silver-plated and worthless.

Theology school, the usual poor man's route to cheap post-graduate studies, was also blocked because of funding. His graduation, moreover, came at the worst possible financial time for his parents. Cassie tended to conceal the extent of their hardship but just before Frye's graduation, she quietly alluded to their destitution: "A High School and the Post Office promised for some years were scheduled to have been built this spring and summer, but for some financial reason postponed again. Makes a big gap of a prospective living Herm expected." Ironically for someone who was anti-Catholic, the most active business came from spending on new Catholic construction.

Planning at first to hitch-hike home, Frye decided to head for the engagingly "adolescent" Chicago to see Vera and the World's Fair. His plans were vague but he thought he might stay for six weeks and enjoy a leisurely trip home with Vera in a new car if she managed to secure her massively accumulated back salary from the board of education. While still teaching, Vera had had to depend on dressmaking and assisting University of Chicago students with theses to earn a living.

Frye surrendered himself to the Fair with a boyish sense of fun which was shared by most of its other eight million visitors looking for an antidote to Depression gloom. Like most such extravaganzas, it mixed progressivist ideology with an eclectic fantasyland of buildings and exhibits—the Hall of Science, the replica of the Golden Pavilion of Jehol from China and the palace of Uxmal, the walls of the electrical group, "one depicting the light and the other the conquest of time and space." Frye stood for what seemed like hours in front of a golden chalice in the Irish exhibit, surrendering to its aesthetic magnetism. Although normally uninterested in plants, he was excited by the horticultural exhibit with its "twenty-odd varieties of gardens—rose gardens, rock gardens, formal gardens, Italian renaissance gardens, Versailles gardens."

Yet inevitably there were the people to offset the pleasure of his visits, the hot, tired and stupid crowds, the "young women tastelessly over-painted." Like a Puritan in a bazaar, he spurned the "stinking food stands, with their noisy brass-throated women and steamy unsavoury-looking kitchens." And overall, there was that nemesis for a "heliophobic blond," the merciless heat. The 21-storey Havoline Oil thermometer looked down on him, registering the ninety-to-a-hundred degree heat which hung day and night over the metropolis. That combined with Vera's roommate's loud radio drained him of energy.

To flee the commotion, he managed to rent a room across the street with a piano in the hallway to practise on. But the evening he moved in, a "brick-red insect" climbed over his pillow. He later awoke to find 18 bedbug bites. After a battle with insects and an apologetic but intransigent landlady, he moved back to Vera's in the midst of redecoration and constant visits of the mother and sister of Vera's roommate. Beleaguered, he finally found a bugless rooming house near the university with piano and quiet lady guests. Borrowing music from the library, he worked on early Italian music, Bach Chorales, Scriabin, the Keltic Sonata by McDowell.

By early July, he joked he was "homesick enough to compose a set of variations on Rule Britannia." He was in fact enjoying such a diffuse sense of priorities, he seemed almost careless about his future. He reported that he had a couple of good but unspecified ideas for writing, later mentioning a Platonic dialogue on the nature of music. Mostly, however, he continued visiting the Fair and the Art Institute for its Italian renaissance art, particularly the work of Tintoretto, Titian, da Vinci. He saw the first full exhibit of Picasso and was fascinated by the metamorphic evolution of phases.

For his birthday on July 14, Vera took him and two of her friends to a restaurant, A Little Bit of Sweden, and as it always seemed to do on his birthday, it rained so heavily, the storm sank boats on the lake. Yet with a weird purple sunset hanging over the city afterwards, he pronounced himself happy. The droll mood was oddly reinforced the following day when the fascist strongman, Italo Balbo, flew into Chicago with his trans-Atlantic fleet of 24 planes. Frye, who'd already become sensitive to fascist buffoonery in the plane-shaped Italian pavilion, saw propaganda easily feeding on the naive minds of the Americans.

Vera's extravagance in taking him out to an expensive restaurant was a brave gesture. By the end of the month, Frye reported to Helen that his sister was down to "two bucks" excepting the money for his train trip home. His stay now depended on the possibility of a bank loan. If it didn't come soon, "Norrie ambles off home by himself, feeling foolishly but quite naturally, like a sponger and parasite." To tide himself over, he helped Vera by typing "a very long and very dull" MA thesis by one of her friends. Raging at the poor quality of thinking and writing, Frye nevertheless surrendered himself to a regime of typing all through the day and indulgently reading detective fiction at night.

On his way home, he stopped off at the Kemps' cottage and enjoyed a reunion with Helen for much of August. He accompanied her back to the city but soon left for Moncton on a filthy, crushingly uncomfortable train. He found his parents in near destitution. Herm could not pay the rent or the milk delivery. He sometimes had to disappear to avoid special constables assigned to harass debtors. The constant economic worry aggravated Cassie's deteriorating health. For an undiagosed ailment, she fed herself cod liver oil, spurning the pleas of Herm to see a doctor. Despite his complete inexperience, Frye seriously considered writing for the magazines. His one concrete idea was to do an article for the weekly *Saturday Night* on the CCF movement in the Maritimes.

Despite the devastation of the Depression, he hadn't moved any further left. Puckishly but quite accurately he placed himself "on the fence between the Liberal and C.C.F. battalions, exactly where a follower of Spengler ... ought to be." He outlined his ambivalence about socialism: "I think, with the C.C.F., that capitalism is crashing round our heads and that any attempt to build it up again will bring it down with a bigger crash. I think with the Liberals that Socialism, as it is bound to develop ... is not a remedy ... In short, any 'way out' must of necessity be miraculous." A personally satisfying antidote lay with the church: "We can save ourselves only through an established co-operative church, and if the church ever wakes up to the fact, that will constitute enough of an miracle to get us the rest of the way."

His direct political enthusiasms, in fact, were never very deep. When the father of his old girl friend, Evelyn, took him to a local CCF meeting, the stirrings of the political fanaticism he saw intimidated him enough to quip: "... why in hell should I get

entangled with daughters of paid agents of Moscow and conse-
quent emissaries of the devil?" Despite his joking, it was the
unsavoriness of blind ideological commitment which made him
leery. It was also the death of his journalism career. He made no
further attempt to write his article.

Instead, he started practising his shorthand again with an obvious view to landing a secretarial job. He wrote and typed a letter
for Herm as he hoped that obtaining a paid agency with a central
Canadian manufacturer would shake Herm's own inertia. He was
becoming inured to the notion of not returning to Victoria. Unlike
the morbid enervation of the previous summer, his letters revealed
placidity. Besides his separation from Helen, his great regret was
simply that there was no copy of Spengler "east of the Don Valley."
To cheer up Helen, he wrote a story called the "Parable of the
Brown Agate" with a full cast of boasting jewels, precious and
semi-precious—diamond, ruby, sapphire, emerald, opal—which
ultimately cede to the bumptious self-assurance of the agate:
"There is sanity and intelligence in brown, a sympathy and understanding in it, at least, which cannot be found in the brilliance of
your glittering variety. Above all, there is self-reliance in it. I
belong to myself, not to the whim of the sun."

# PART TWO

## EMMANUEL COLLEGE

Although Frye tried to assure Helen that he had explored several possibilities of returning to Victoria, it is not likely that he did. When his friends heard he was not returning to college, they were stunned. They thrashed around the idea of putting together a fund for him and lobbied sympathetic professors. Wilmot Lane, who had taught Frye Ethics and was the 1933 class' Honorary President, arranged a reader's job for him to mark freshman essays, the equivalent today of a teaching assistant. The job paid only $250 but this would cover his basic fees. The registrar at Emmanuel, Dr. Langford, told him not to worry about money in the future. Somehow it would be found. His friends sent him $50 to travel in the luxury of a berth, but in his seat-of-iron tradition, he took coach class to save the money.

For the next three years of Emmanuel College, the theology college of the United Church on the western side of Vic, Frye held a curiously indentured position. While he tended to do what the Victoria administrators suggested, he was obstinately independent in his own ideas of what he should be learning.

He moved into Fifth House, now Bowles House, on the south wing of Burwash Hall which was allocated to theology students. As in Gate House, he had his own room, on the second floor. While most students tended to have a personal rug or photos to personalize the plain, poorly furnished rooms, Frye lived in monastic austerity. The don who lived across the hallway, Jim Lawson, was an art collector who managed with negligible salary to put together one of the earliest private collections of the Group of Seven paintings. Lawson encouraged artistic interests in the Emmanuel students whom he saw as cultural illiterates. He loaned Frye a German expressionist painting for his wall and Frye quietly defended and explained it to the curious.

Academically at Emmanuel, Frye felt like he was back at high school. To test student knowledge about the Bible for his course in the Old Testament, the Emmanuel principal, Richard Davidson, held a test for overconfident students, many of whom were flabbergasted by failure. With his absolute retention from childhood of the Bible, Frye breezed through and with Davidson's blessings, abandoned the course.

It was not so easy with the homiletics (preaching) instructor, Alfred Johnston. Frye and Johnston quickly developed a distaste for each other that was chemical. Frye had complete contempt for Johnston's intellectual powers and balked at the fundamental need for a course in preaching. The first time Frye gave a trial sermon in class, Johnston volubly congratulated Frye for both spirit and content. But the second time, Frye committed the error of looking longingly out the window, inwardly savoring the New Testament promise of a better land. He abandoned the course as he eventually did them all. While Davidson and the college's professor of religious history, Kenneth Cousland, didn't care in the least, others had to query the value of their lecturing when Frye did better than the regular students. Of course, there was no big secret in Frye's success. The professors usually dictated their lectures at writing speed so that at exam time, Frye simply read the often identical notes of his friends, quickly memorized them and regurgitated them for an easy A while friends, dismayed by Frye's memory, received Bs. Through the three years of Emmanuel, however, Johnston was unforgiving. In staff meetings he obstinately criticized Frye and came close to depriving him of full academic status by insisting class attendance was crucial for passing. To fill a required obligation to take on a "field" Frye did take charge of a group of Sunday school boys at St. Andrew's where, on the pattern of Harold Tomkinson at Wesley Memorial, they worked out religious principles in relation to contemporary living.

Frye's primary academic interests were increasingly focussed on English literature. Like Art Cragg, he hoped to write an MA thesis along with his Emmanuel studies. This ultimately meant avoiding the rigor of the elite Bachelor of Divinity stream with its compulsory Hebrew and Greek. While this had little significance at the time, it had repercussions decades later. His priority in English was a graduate seminar in Blake held in the University College quadrangle by the Oxford-trained Herbert Davis, who was a scholar of Swift and a polite but cautious champion of Frye at Toronto. The seminar was held in the late afternoon and at the first session, another student, Margaret Roseborough, came in to see Frye sitting by the window. The low sun caught the mane of hair which glowed around his head so that Roseborough became the first person to apply the word halo to Frye's hair with all its boyish angelic connotations.

Although the pressures of work forced Frye out of nearly all extra-curricular activities, he did review Pelham Edgar's long delayed book on the novel, *The Art of the Novel*, for the Christmas 1933 issue of *Acta*. The two-and-a-half page review was disconcerting for its slapdash style and meaning. Like nearly all of Frye's reviews before or since, it rarely bothered to take notice of the book. It nevertheless indicated how advanced and pervasive his theoretical thinking was already.

Edgar's book was really the lame product of a man who had run out of energy. Despite its theoretical weakness, Frye leaped with approval on Edgar's statement that his aim was "to present a systematic study of the structural evolution of the English novel." Frye ignored Edgar's failings by continuing to talk about an ideal book. Fundamentally, such a book should be objective: " ... everything which has any communicative value in criticism is objective; because it must appeal to aesthetic principles which transcend a purely individual collection of likes and dislikes. The more subjective the criticism, the nearer it tends to aesthetic anarchy."

Before finishing he suggested an essential idea that both aesthetic and theoretical authority lay precisely *inside* the work of the major writer. Already Frye was positing the notion that the source of theoretical notions about literature was literature itself. Its form informed. It offered its own "keys to the gates" which opened out the wider imaginative realm. A single line of Shakespeare could be more crucial in critical theory than a whole book by an irrelevant Freudian critic.

For the Christmas holidays, he again went up to the Martins' farm in Honeywood, taking a two-and-a-half-hour sleigh ride uphill from the station at Creemore through bitter cold. As before, he made himself vicariously sociable by playing through *Piano Pieces to be Popular* on the family piano. Bach and Haydn, he thought, were "too elusive." For three days solid after Christmas Day, he worked so ferociously on an anthology of Blake borrowed from Helen he claimed it looked like a blizzard hit it. For the first time, Frye tried to create an all-inclusive schema of symbolism which reflected an almost cabalistic intensity. "My head is spinning trying to figure out a phonetic alphabet for the symbolic figures I'm pretty sure exists."

He finished the Minor Prophecies and got through half the Four Zoas with an increasing feeling of panic. His work was immediately intended for a paper on *Milton*, the most difficult of Blake's prophecies, which he had to give for the Davis seminar in February, but few of the problems resolved themselves. Despite the pressures of the paper, Frye didn't attempt a written version until the night before the seminar. As he confessed years later to Pelham Edgar, "At about two in the morning some very curious things began happening in my mind. I began to see glimpses of something bigger and more exciting than I had ever before realized existed in the world of the mind, and when I went out for breakfast at five-thirty on a bitterly cold morning, I was committed to a book on Blake." This startling Pisgah-vision took place in one of his haunts, an all-night cafeteria on Bloor St. called Bowles Lunch which sold cheap doughnuts and coffee to the rubbies and insomniac students who wandered in to warm up along a shabby row of classroom-like tables.

Later that day, Frye gave his paper to the seminar and was

relieved that Edgar turned up uninvited to hear it. Frye sensed that neither Edgar nor Davis followed his argument, but Edgar, as always, seemed proud. Frye was already so deep into theoretical thinking which could at once be pedantic, confusing and exhilarating, that there was nothing overtly distinctive about this particular paper. Surviving members of the group do not in fact remember it. Clearly this victory was personal.

The original essay has since vanished in a complicated series of metamorphoses which ended in one of the most interesting sections of *Fearful Symmetry*. In retrospect, however, Frye remembered his basic insight to be that Blake's specific work, *Milton*, was fed by Milton's work and both in themselves fed off a central source, the Bible. Frye later claimed that Blake's borrowing from the Bible was about 90%. Their work was new, even revolutionary, and yet relied on an old source which itself might reflect a wider western mythological and symbolic base. It was a tunnel-of-mirrors image which reflected images from a deep mythological source. This, however was a process of sometimes dazzling recreation through time. Nearly forty years later in *The Critical Path*, Frye would call *Finnegans Wake* "that tremendous hymn to the eternal newness of the same." This revolutionary conservatism of Blake and Milton and Joyce was also precisely the image of Frye's own personal adjustment to the world. It would remain a basic element in both his thinking and identity and would endure even the anti-western hysteria of the late sixties.

Frye tried out another paper on the Davis seminar at the end of the term on Blake and Romantic philosophy. Writing it overnight in one sustained blast, he gutted ideas from his "Romanticism epic" from the previous year and worked in new ideas on Blake. He described the class as simply "overwhelmed." Once more he had to confess that monomania was creeping over him, and recognized that his planned full-length work, which he now called "the Blake thesis," was definitely going to be a book for publication. He fantasized about it. He'd publish his ideas with photos of some Blake paintings copied by Helen's photographer brother, Roy. As a result of the book, the university would give him a job and with a job, he'd marry Helen. The idea made him so happy that in the same breath, he considered the incongruous short-term prospect of renting a small apartment in the autumn and bringing Cassie to live in Toronto. Clearly Frye was now thinking more positively in terms of an academic career. His value was recognized by the English department which doubled his salary to $500 to mark papers and lecture one hour a week the following year. This seemed to make theology irrelevant and certainly neither of his mentors, Davis or Edgar, looked favorably on his continued association with the church. Davis told him that it might be embarrassing in the academic world.

Unfortunately it wasn't so simple. Walter Brown the principal wanted him to keep on with theology. The rationale was that he wanted "a man in each department who was something of a philosopher; who can give the theoretical and speculative background of each subject taught in the college, and he thinks theology is a good approach to it." Unfortunately Brown reinforced his idea with the faint promise that if Frye would comply, there was a chance of a position in a couple of years.

Frye had no innate hostility to theological studies in themselves. He could simply continue to ignore the bad professors, bad thinking and use theology for his own interests. Comparative theology and Bible studies all belonged to the same mythological universe as the literature of Blake. He was also doing extremely well, capturing four firsts, two seconds and only one third in his year. His don, Jim Lawson, told him that there would be no competition against him for the enticing Travelling Scholarship which took its recipients either to the University of Edinburgh or Cambridge.

Lawson did his own Bachelor of Divinity thesis on the relation of Christian art to dogma and Frye saw the chance of doing a parallel one on music. The excitement of the idea even offset his earlier notion of a thesis relating the ideas of Spengler and St. Augustine. "But there are two things which are absolutely unique about the Christian religion and which guarantee its truth — one is music, the other a philosophy of history, and, though I'll do them both eventually, I don't care which I start on. They're intimately connected ..." His initial interest centered on four "doctors of the church," two who were musicians, St. Ambrose and St. Gregory, and two philosophers of history, St. Augustine and St. Jerome. The project was a quest to resolve Frye's "old problem ... why Bach is greater than Chopin, Frank than Tschaikowsky."

## STONE PILE, GARDEN HEAD

What this exhilarating swirl of ideas failed to conceal was that on May 1, 1934, Frye would be on a night train for Winnipeg and the "dried out" area of southwest Saskatchewan, nearly two thousand miles from Toronto. For five months he would be student minister for the isolated congregation of Stone, Stone Pile and Carnagh. Cassie couldn't avoid noting that if Carnagh were changed to Cairn, the names would be consistent. This was the price of his theology. The United Church, then assiduously low-brow, was not interested in theses on the ancient doctors of the church. It did not see itself in the business of subsidizing scholars, mission doctors or even theologians. In going west, however, Frye was undeniably solving the problem of how to feed himself for the next five months.

Confessing to be "scared stiff" in a letter to Cassie, he spent the last days in Toronto assiduously living a life close to his civilized ideal. In rapid succession he attended music performances at Eaton's Auditorium, Massey Hall and Hart House. A performance of Bach's Mass in B Minor at Massey Hall instigated another all-night talk with Art Cragg. Free of essays and exams, Frye also dreamed of the exciting intellectual future he and Helen would share together.

Helen, in fact, had enjoyed a glorious year. In the fall, Arthur Lismer, who ran the Education Department at the Art Gallery of Toronto, had hired her with National Gallery money to help lecture to visiting groups and arrange loans of gallery material. On March 2, she delivered a lecture on Holbein in the gallery's evening lecture series which was then a standard feature in the cultural life of Toronto intelligentsia. Her above-average audience of 181 must have reinforced the gallery's confidence in her and soon after, she was up at the National Gallery in Ottawa training with Kathleen Fenwick where she pondered graduate work in Britain with a Carnegie Scholarship.

Still pondering the idea of a BD thesis on music, Frye saw a logical intertwining of their interests. He was delighted that Helen, an art critic, had musical knowledge. This, he noted, was "absolutely indispensible to a critic of the fine arts who wants balance and completeness." He extravagantly praised her awakening critical qualities which really projected his own self-image: "You've got genius in you, critical rather than creative. You can't paint like Matisse ... but you can write better than Ruskin or Pater, and with sounder ideas, when you are mature. You aren't affected, hysterical, sloppy or sentimental, not a cheap pot-boiling charlatan ... you are getting your roots deep into the rich soil of art tradition. A woman who can tell Dürer from Cranach, to say nothing of a woman who has heard of both, can write about Canadian art and wither all the mountebanks and self-advertisers in the country, setting in their place enthusiastic students."

As a last gesture to his own cultural identity Frye went out to a concert of the Hart House Quartet concert at the house of wealthy artist Bertram Brooker. While the concert was "gorgeous," the bright effect of listening to the music and chatting with the Brookers was soon dimmed by thoughts of his mission field. His morbid sense of anticipation contradicted the standard church mythology of the student minister outlined in the boy's novel *Sky Pilot* which he had read himself as a child. In *Sky Pilot*, a scrawny but eager student minister from the east turns up in Alberta, wows the local teenagers with baseball skills and soon gets the whole community back on track in piety and clean living. The church elders still held a misty-headed and durable belief that doing the Lord's work cloaked the young recruit with *élan vital* which conquered all hardship. Charles Trick Currelly wrote in his autobiography, which Frye later edited, that in rash evangelical fervor he'd been dumped in Manitoba's desolate Gilbert Plains and nearly froze to death. By his own resourcefulness, he quickly learned to survive, but the experience left Currelly a bitter picture of the doddering romanticism of the Methodist bureaucracy which refused to properly train, equip or supervise minister trainees.

By luck, Frye's initial contact in the field was a reflection of the civility of Toronto. His supervisor met him at the train and took him home to meet his quiet Scottish wife and brood of children. Frye happily discovered their piano and played for the first time, he said, in fourteen weeks, a period lost to exams and essays. But this was a cruelly misleading introduction. Most everything from here on in would be a miserable confirmation of his worst fears. His mission would be a grinding test for all his values and ambitions.

Even to a westerner, this can be a curious and frightening land. The parish consists entirely of a dry uplands plateau called The Bench which seems forced right up against the sky. This is an illusion created by the long rolling hills which close off any distant horizon, creating disorientation, even claustrophobia. Frye early felt a baffled terror in the "fitful tossing country" with farms so large that "you look over the horizon and all you can see is your own farm." Neither the shallow bush-choked ravines, called coulees, or the dry patches of cottonwood shrub relieved its essential brown, sun-baked banality. The labyrinthine roads and trails were all unpaved. Besides two uncertain streams chillingly called Skull and Bone Creeks, the Bench also featured Anxiety Butte on the south and the hamlets of Stone and Stone Pile, which some wit renamed Garden Head. Only on the northeast and on the east overlooking the town of Shaunavon does the plateau fall away to distant plains which are illusory, golden and inviting. Ironically this bleak upland is the north-south divide for the waters of the Gulf of Mexico and Hudson Bay.

Most of Frye's parishioners were American or British immigrants who had few resources other than the ability to work hard. Their lives were as culturally plain as the land, relieved only by dances and folk music concerts. In the winter, the area was closed off for months by snow so that the small regional towns were distant prospects. They helped each other cooperatively, even setting up a primitive phone service at Stone in the winter with fence-post wires. Beyond a Sunday school organized by a couple

from New York, the Bonfoys, the people had to wait for the United
Church student minister for regular services in the summer.
Despite their generosity with each other, they could be cruel to
outsiders and had hounded Frye's predecessor. Western prejudices were a major problem; even eastern farm boys found them
formidable. One farmer admitted that the closer a student was to
a cowboy, the better he got on. Frye's friend, George Birtch, had
in fact been given a mustang on one of his summer missions and
told to break it for his own use. The eager expectancy was that
he would fail but when he did break the horse, his stock rose
dramatically.

Frye's own first experiences were so unpromising that he broke
out in "protest hives," which turned out to be bedbug bites. He
discovered that he would be boarded around at different homes
each week so that the parish could claim Frye's board money.
What this meant was a constant break in routine, trying to study
Blake in loud open kitchens with blaring radios and unfamiliar
people. While Frye's base of operations was the hamlet of Stone,
he had to make regular visits by horse to the outlying settlements
of Stone Pile, eight miles to the east and Carnagh an equivalent
distance to the west, to preach at the schoolhouses and visit parishioners. Frye's innate shyness, total ignorance of farming and inability to make small talk made encounters difficult and futile. His own
dislike for physical labor meant that he shied away from helping
farmers out.

Although he quickly developed a deep "coffee" tan, his image
was more Don Quixote than cowboy. He kept his hair sufficiently
long that the leading lady of the congregation, Mrs. Bonfoy, mut-
tered to Mrs. Meyers that it had to go. On horseback, he wore
regular trousers, ignoring the usual apparel of jeans or chaps. His
experiences with the horses themselves were symptomatic of his
general unease. His first horse, Katie, was a nag as old as Frye
himself. She was as uncooperative as a donkey. Her physique was
like that of an Alpine mountain range. She was so slow and old,
forward progress seemed negligible. Her up and down disjointedness threw Frye's inner organs into disarray. There was the suggestion that Frye could be quickly upgraded to a better horse but he

begged off. Two months later, he did graduate to Bessie, a younger mare who didn't have to be chased around the barnyard like Katie for saddling. Frye early marvelled at the uncomplicated speed with which she crossed distances, but feared her naughtiness in trying to buck him off.

In his saddlebag he carried a Keynes Blake edition, some yellowing stationery and a toothbrush. He followed the trails along the coulees and cursed the patches of cottonwood which were a comic parody of lush eastern deciduous forests. Since it rained only a couple of times in the summer, Frye thought fondly of his bicycle at home in Moncton which could have negotiated the hard pathways more efficiently. A later student used a motorcycle. Hardly a bright-eyed Wesleyan circuit rider, Frye felt foolish and self-conscious. In later years, he joked that across the flat areas of the parish, he felt he couldn't even relieve himself because he was convinced that the ladies of the parish—one especially—continually kept the preacher boy under view with binoculars.

His own gnawing demoralization was a poor foundation from which to cheer up people who were worrying about a new grasshopper plague which badly damaged crops the previous year in Saskatchewan. There were grim stories of sickly green eggs produced by chickens near Regina which could only feed on grasshoppers, and reports of whole South Dakota farms eaten bare in minutes. But the worst danger that summer turned out to be the merciless sun which baked the ground in 102 degree heat. The sky was sterile, producing only rainless thunder and the rare hailstorm, or a savage windstorm which prevented Frye from travelling. Farm wives had to contend with a light coat of dust every day on their furniture. Despite this, the natural subsoil irrigation seemed to prevent the serious dust bowl conditions which plagued other areas of the Palliser Triangle. One resident remembered only crop failure in 1937.

In frequent letters to Helen, Frye detailed every social and physical agony he encountered. He knew that he would commit suicide "without the slightest hesitation" if he had to stay on the prairies all his life. He tried to put Toronto out of his mind because it unbalanced him to think of the disparity of life styles: "God

Himself seems to fade away on these grim prairies: not that He is far away—I never feel that; but He seems curiously impersonal. That, of course, is largely because I left Blake at Stone, the nearest piano a mile away and you in Ottawa." Two months later, he morbidly predicted that perhaps "by 1940 some student will come out and collect my remains." He managed to cheer himself up one evening by reading Shakespeare's twenty-ninth sonnet in a girl's poetry anthology which conveyed everything about his present state. Besides Blake, he immersed himself in the only universally available literature: "I am getting a sound and accurate knowledge of the Bible; the Bible is magnificent, but in spite of what everyone says, it is a book for admiration rather than intimacy, like the natural world."

If Frye was emotionally and physically discomfited, he was at first benignly insensitive to his parishioners. Although he faced a congregation which was usually poorly educated, culturally isolated and beleaguered by drought and plague, he preached to them like Emmanuel College graduates. Without any sense of speaking the unusual, he outlined his first sermon at Stone to Helen on the first commandment against idolatry: "I said that the worship of idols was a worship of spirits, some good, some evil; that it took more effort and energy to try to get the latter on the side of worshippers: that interesting an evil spirit could only be done by making evil actions: hence idolatry ended up in the worst things one could imagine, e.g., Moloch and child sacrifice. That with the collapse of superstition there returned a new kind of idolatry, the worship of men instead of God. The present trend to dictatorships is therefore idolatry, and there is nothing to save us from the same progression toward the evil, which is why Hitler and Co. appeal to the worst and cruelest instincts of mankind."

While he quickly discerned a need "to work from the inside, in their own language and sets of ideas," he couldn't bear the corollary, reinforcing his parishioners' moral superstitions which passed for religion. "For instance, if old Mrs. McCrae knew that a young lady of whom I was most inordinately proud and fully intended to marry danced, smoked, swore and had no moral objections to playing cards she would be scandalized, and in being her minister

I sometimes cannot help feeling that I am tacitly assenting, through lack of courage, to a monstrous and absurd scale of values."

He was less personal when he wrote to his cousin, Donald Howard: "The Methodist prejudices I encounter ... I regard as the most superstitious of fetishes, and merely a way of avoiding the *real* problems of religion. That is the most obvious of rural deficiencies—making piety consist of taboos ... but I think the religious problem is bound up with the cultural deadness. What these poor people use for literature, art and music is to me the source of the whole evil that makes them regard religion as a social convention rather than an experience. I admire and respect the people in themselves ... But they work too hard, and get too little out of their work."

Part of the problem was that Frye was unwilling to backtrack on his gentlemanly cultural refinement to meet the people halfway. Despite his interest in the folk tradition which John Robins presented, Frye seemed utterly uninterested in any local manifestations of tales or popular music. If he had been interested, he really didn't have to go far. One of the chief parishioners, Walter Hickman, with whom he often boarded, was mandolin player for a religious music ensemble in Stone. Yet Frye was hardly predisposed to suggesting a session of folksy spirituals. About the closest Frye got to popular culture, in fact, was a Free Methodist hymnal which he found "all naive, and often vulgar and silly, but the tunes are so light and lilting that they disarm criticism."

Rather than accommodate, he just saw, suffered and reported the worst, the blaring radios, the mice-chewed organ, the bedbugs, the weary banalities of a physically exhausted people. He built up a defence around the piano by playing classical music on the Hickman's piano, playing either what he had memorized or could scrounge out of Mrs. Hickman's *Etude* magazine. Rather than help out on the farm, he payed the Hickmans back by coaching their daughter Carol in piano playing. When he noticed her stuck at a certain level, he outlined a basic theory of notation under the Equal Temperament system in the end papers of her text. For Frye, it was obvious that such an outline of notation could extend to literary symbolism.

Despite the refuge at the Hickmans, he early predicted: "I shall not come out a second summer; if I can show this year that I can get through something I am totally unfitted to do, that should satisfy Drs. Brown and Lane." The decision which came so easily, however, gave him no comfort. In virtually every letter to Helen, he painfully counted off the remaining time first in months, then Sundays, even in the quarters of the moon. He seditiously planned to cut short his stay by filching the Sunday collections as an advance against his last cheque from the church. He tried to allay Helen's own concerns about him with confessions that he was doing better but every so often he would break a line of thought with a furious condemnation of the 100+ degree heat or troublesome bugs: " ... there's a swarm of all kinds of insects flying all around the light, over this letter, and over me, and they're nearly driving me nuts."

It was precisely when his letters to her were becoming less frenetic that his college friend John Bates sought him out and found him still wild with unhappiness. Bates had learned of his problems in a round robin letter and, feeling depressed himself, he set out in a Model T from his own mission area in Robsart about fifty miles away. To Bates it seemed as if Frye had disappeared into a surrealist wasteland. When Bates asked parishioners where he was, they pointed vaguely down the road and said he should look for a grey, sway-backed mare. Finally, Bates came across a farm where the farmer, Walter Hickman, was putting a horse into the barn. Bates pulled up and when he walked to the side door of the house, he saw Frye through the torn screening furiously swatting at flies in the kitchen. When he saw Bates, Frye's face lit up in a way that Bates had never seen before or since. Frye freely confessed that he'd almost believed that "Victoria College and all that that means to me had become a dream."

After dinner, Bates and Frye played some Music Club Gilbert and Sullivan on the old piano to entertain the family and to cheer themselves up. But the exhausted Hickmans registered only polite interest. Bates stayed overnight and when they settled down in the guest bed, Frye told Bates, "I sleep in eleven beds in this parish and this is one of three in which I know there are no bedbugs." He confessed he was troubled that he couldn't seem to get through to people with his sermons. Bates drove Frye down to East End where they looked up a widely-travelled Welsh minister called Evans. Frye was ecstatic to find a gentleman of "broad culture and rich experience" instead of "the species of porpoise that infest most of the parsonages around here." Another unexpected treasure was a restaurant that served delicious food. "It seems an eternity since I've propped my elbows on a restaurant table, wrapped my hands around a coffee cup and talked to somebody like John Bates or Mr. Evans."

His eagerness to get back was aggravated by Helen's increasingly concrete plan to go to Britain to study for an MA thesis before he got back. As Helen's plans became more definite, they began to alarm him. Frye desperately tried to arrange a reunion of at least a day before another agonizing separation. All through the personal confusions there was the dream of how he and Helen could manage to marry. Early on he was eager to affirm the simple ideal that "marriage with the right woman, living together till we are dead—how utterly right and sane that idea is!" But this was a period when women were expected to choose between the role of subservient wife or spinsterish career lady. With a distinct edge of panic, he tried to warn her off the blue stocking fallacy of putting all energy, including sexual, into work. He'd already suggested that one way of unifying themselves personally and academically would be for Helen to take the Davis course in Blake and explore "the art side."

Although Frye wasn't able to achieve the presence of mind to work on his "only devouring enthusiasm," Blake, until late July, he was still confident that a book would buy an engagement ring. Just three weeks later, he had to admit that the impulse had fizzled: "My work is completely demoralized and disorganized. My visiting is far behind; my reports aren't started; my correspondence is tied up; the thesis is in abeyance, and I don't give a damn ..." In his letter to his cousin Donald, however, he revealed the strength of his Blakean enthusiasms: "No great poet, with the very doubtful exception of Shakespeare, has, since the rise of Christianity, been able to write without the inspiration of the Christian religion behind him, and consequently he is forced to give expression to the deepest religious impulses of his age. Hence in every period there is one supreme poet who expresses the very essence of that period's attitude to Christianity. In English literature such were Chaucer, Spenser, Milton, Dryden and Blake to their various times. But Blake is peculiarly interesting because he lived in the time when the French and the Industrial Revolution with all that they signified, were shattering the unity of Christian civilization, and he, and Goethe, are the two great artist intellects who represent the final and culminating effort of Western culture to express that unity ..."

## BLAKE, BLAKE, BLAKE

After the brutalizing summer, the ministry was no longer even an abstract possibility. Frye's considerations were now overwhelmingly academic. Because Davis agreed to continue his Blake seminar, Frye once more had an easy social context to reinforce his interests. With an obsessive disregard for the limits of his time and energy, Frye also took on Davis's course in English satire and yet another on romantic poetry taught by J.R. MacGillivray. In late October, he planned a paper on Blake to present to the Graduate English Club and was already sensitive to his reputation as a monomaniac. His friend Mary Winspear quipped, "If your name is on the notice, what's the use of announcing the subject?" With Nietzschean bluster which masked his own anxiety, he proclaimed to Helen, "So I have got to smash them and establish myself."

While he was sufficiently important now to sit for lunch at High Table in Burwash Hall, he still had the anxieties of an underling. With Charles Auger mortally ill and Pelham Edgar due to retire in two years, Frye at least thought his chances brightening. But there was a cautionary note from Lane who called him into his office to give him a veiled warning that while Vic recognized his scholarly capabilities, the college put heavy emphasis on "getting good instruction across to the undergraduates." Frye related this to Brown's "superstition that mediocrities make the best teachers because they are slow." Frye was being dangerously cocky about this and even his mentor, E.J. Pratt, confessed the same doubts to Margaret Roseborough.

There were two other serious worries overshadowing his hopes. Herm was two years behind in his rent and his landlord told him to pay an immediate $100 or get out, leaving the furniture as compensation. Since Vera was still not receiving her salary, she couldn't help. Frye rushed all he had, $50, to prevent the threatened eviction. The cash temporarily held off the landlord but their unhappiness continued to be a corrosive worry and a threat to Frye's own marriage plans.

On top of it, his own health was deteriorating. To Helen, he threw down his symptoms like a battered pack of cards: "I am now in for a session of headaches, burning eyelids, tired and heavy so that I practically never wake up at any decent time in the mornings, rasped nerves, bad dreams and general debility." There was little hypochondria in this. His friends in the Davis seminar that year confirmed his fragile, wraith-like bearing. With a thin winter coat and no hat, he seemed to shiver his way across campus in a gloomy cloud of stoicism. The "Blake girls," Margaret Roseborough and Mary Winspear who set up a flat on the western edge of the campus dubbed The Bucket of Blood in parody of an English pub, kept him socially active by inviting him over for dinners. But he remained self-absorbed in his personal and family problems: "At present I am excessively morbid, given a great deal to self-loathing almost, certainly self-contempt, engaged in being utterly sick and weary of my apparently inexhaustible capacity to waste time, rush wildly down blind alleys, overexert myself, do all sorts of fool things." Oddly he saw "a fearful lassitude in me, inherited from both parents ... which has been increasing every year of my college life, and is I hope gradually working out. Working out by the simple process of becoming horribly bored by everything except what I ought to be doing."

Even intellectual excitement engendered its own morbid quality. For his Old Testament course, he stumbled upon James Frazer's *The Golden Bough*. The immediate effect of absorbing

Frazer's catalogue of dying god symbolism was exhilaration and panic: "It's a whole new world opening out, particularly as that sort of thing is the very life-blood of art, and the historical basis of art. My ideas are expanding and taking shape so quickly that they frighten me; I get seized with terror sometimes that somebody else will think them out before I do, or that I shan't live long enough to complete anything."

Frye's reaction to Frazer had none of the adolescent swoon of his contact with Spengler. In fact, he was later quite condescending about Frazer's progressive ape-to-Cambridge perspective, as well as Frazer's industrious but fatiguing exposition of a single obsessive idea. It was rather the material of Frazer which suggested the cyclic organization of seasons with its death and rebirth symbolism which immediately excited him. This, of course, tied in with Spengler but it provided new insights all the way from Blake to his own viewing of Walt Disney's *Snow White*.

Ultimately, however, Frye's developing thought was closer to those scholars influenced by Frazer's material, particularly Gilbert Murray and Francis Cornford. Like all myth critics, Murray and Cornford were much more impressed by similarities of myths, stories and character types than by distinct qualities. Murray was famous for his 1914 paper showing the eerie mirror image of Orestes and Hamlet. Murray suggested "a great unconscious solidarity and continuity, lasting from age to age, among all the children of the poets ... significant details are repeated quite unconsciously by generation after generation of poets." Not surprisingly, Murray considered it "the very feeblest of critical errors to suppose that there is a thing called 'originality,' which consists in having no models."

But while Murray was still on the side of elegance and subtlety in his critical writing, Cornford was unapologetic in his categories, lists and plot synopses, neatly packaged with the arcane terminology of classical scholarship. He even numbered basic thematic paragraph sections. Cornford first set out the structure of Aristophanic comedy, summarizing "standard theories of the origin of comedy" and leading to a "Classification of Types." Readers familiar with Frye's later work will recognize such arcane Greek terminology as *agon, eiron* and *alazon*. *Agon* was defined by Cornford as a "fierce 'contest' between the representatives of two parties or principles, which are in effect the hero and villain." This is followed by a *komos*, a festal occasion or "marriage." Following basic Frazerian emphases, Cornford very quickly pointed out the centrality of the natural cycle, the death of winter and the "release and *renouveau* in spring."

With certainly more personal indulgence than *The Golden Bough*, Frye launched into Robert Burton's fat, curious 1621 work *The Anatomy of Melancholy* as part of his satire course. He agreeably acceded to Samuel Johnson's claim, quoted in the introduction of the 1932 Everyman edition, that it took him "out of bed two hours sooner than he wanted to rise." The editor, Holbrook Jackson, quite explicitly points to the anatomy as belonging to a separate class of literary works which were "almost as common then as anthologies are now."

Frye's major enthusiasms, however, lay in modern literature which absorbed the past, particularly the work of Eliot, Wyndham Lewis and James Joyce. Eliot's poetry was so central to his conception of modern poetry that it seemed to adhere pleasurably to his mind. Frye also sought out Eliot's growing body of criticism. And it's obvious that the Eliot of *The Sacred Wood* was a major influence. In "Tradition and the Individual Talent," in particular, Eliot lay down an idea which would transfix Frye for the rest of his career, that "the whole of the literature of Europe from Homer ... has a simultaneous existence and composes a simultaneous order."

Like others of his age group who idolized Eliot's poetry, Frye was stunned and sickened by Eliot's infamous blood-and-soil dogma in his 1934 Page-Barbour lectures, *After Strange Gods*, which insisted on racial homogeneity guaranteed by a "unity of religious background," which would "combine to make any large number of free-thinking Jews undesirable." It seemed to Frye that Eliot was joining the intellectual stampede towards fascism and he was never able to forgive or forget Eliot's *faux pas*. Four decades later, he would say in an interview, "I remember that Karl Barth said that anybody who wasn't completely devoted to the defeat of Hitler didn't know any theology. I would say that anyone who

wasn't completely anti-fascist and anti-Nazi didn't know literature." It was this flirtation of major writers in the thirties with
fascism that showed how a writer could become alienated from the
truth of his own work. "They didn't know what they were producing, what they themselves meant. That's one reason why there has
to be critics, those who know what they are talking about, to engage
literature in a dialogue with society."

Towards the end of the term, Frye could report that, academically at least, things were going well. His Graduate English Club
paper on Blake came and went without comment. Despite earlier
fears, he sensed that the group had been "tremendously impressed." Before Christmas he was confident about working his Blake
ideas into a PhD thesis which he hoped he could finish before going
abroad. He quickly finished another paper on Shelley's idealism for
his Romantic poetry course which MacGillivray volubly praised,
unaware that Frye had spent little time on it. He also positively
assessed his first real lecturing which involved a potpourri of
literature, *Tess of the D'Urbervilles*, *Lycidas*, *Pilgrim's Progress*
and *Erewhon*.

Now that he was teaching he bitterly resented "pandering to
Brown's pro-divinity prejudices," with a full load of theology
courses. Confident that he would replace Auger, he confessed: "I
am getting impatient to get my teeth into the work, collect more
degrees (this last more as a symbol of progress than as anything
intrinsically valuable) and get some real experience as a teacher.
And I don't want to hang on with a mixture of luck, gall, overwork,
patronage, and the grace of God..." Nevertheless, theology
remained and just before Christmas, he attacked it with fury: "I
arose in my wrath the last week ... and smote theology hip and
thigh—I had five essays and three term exams to get done in a
week. So I wrote two Church History essays Monday, two New
Testament essays Tuesday, exams in Systematic Theology and
Church History Wednesday, exam in New Testament and essay in
Religious Pedagogy Thursday. Then I slept and slept."

While it was true that he wanted to direct his energies towards
teaching and writing, his theology studies were deeply integrated
with his Blake interests. He knew, of course, how deeply influenced

Blake was by the form of the Bible. As an extension of this, he was drawn towards the arcane and virtually extinct tradition of typology which connected the Old and New Testaments in a symbolic skein of types and antitypes. The prevailing trend in Bible studies, "higher criticism," was antithetical to this tradition. With formidable skill, scholars for a half-century had tried to thrash every fact to death in the Bible in the rationalist hope that excruciatingly rigorous linguistic and historical analysis would convert the curious stories of the Bible into facts which were more plausible to a sophisticated society. Frye eventually defined "higher criticism" as "straw-thrashing" lower criticism, a necessary preliminary step to establish a text for real scholars who would then enter into symbolic analysis and re-creation. This was precisely analogous to his wariness of historical and bibliographic literary criticism.

Frye's interests inevitably took him towards St. Augustine's typological treatise *City of God*. He had early been interested in a competition essay topic on the work in his undergraduate years but considered himself too immature to attempt it then. St. Augustine again became important for Frye as a purveyor of a particular history of philosophy which could be compared with Spengler. He now had a go at the opus for a theology paper for Kenneth Cousland. He tried unsuccessfully to construe the typological Latin writings of Hugh of St. Victor, which were not well-known then, at Knox College library.

He had more luck with the typological treatise on the iconography of French cathedrals, Emile Mâle's, *The Gothic Image: Religious Art in France of the Thirteenth Century*. Following Hugo's suggestion of the cathedral as a book, Mâle made clear that Gothic was a symbolic art following basic rules which had to be understood systematically. Typological notions showed up repeatedly in motifs which equated Old and New Testament figures. Christ, for example, figured so often as a second Adam that the theologians almost got carried away with it. Not only that, the pattern of symbolism projected a full range of "historical, allegorical, tropological and anagogical interpretations" from both the Old and New Testaments. This for Frye was an initiation into the fundamental, but largely forgotten, medieval structure of four levels of meaning which would eventually permeate Frye's critical writings for decades.

When the Christmas holidays came, he thought he would sleep the term off instead of going up to the Martins. Instead he used the time to work on Blake and apply his new insights from *The Golden Bough* to the Old Testament which he hoped would dazzle Davidson. The determined effort made him feel better than he'd been all year. He even predicted that "I shall work quietly and sanely for the rest of the year." He was confident that a draft introduction for his thesis indicated a final shape.

There was still the hope that Edgar might be able to gouge money out of the Massey clan to finance research at the British Museum. Frye's ostensible reason was to see Blake's original engravings, particularly of *The Four Zoas*, to eradicate the impressions of "the villainous reproductions" available to him in Toronto. The only pictorial resource he had was a collection of Blake postcards from Helen's friend Norah McCullough. A major reason, of course, was the desire to rejoin Helen in London particularly since she was considering another year at the Courtauld Institute. It was not a completely dishonest conspiracy. Always eager to bind Helen to his own interests, he suggested that she seriously consider Blake "generally the greatest Englishman this side of Shakespeare," particularly since no general, comprehensive work had been done on his art. He brazenly reminded her of his help: " ... you happen to have a husband who knows as much about him as any man living."

His desire to see her again was as pragmatic as emotional. He considered that her physical presence had a settling effect on him which he missed all the year she'd been away. Without her, he was prey to "a series of frenetic spasms of activity coupled with inertia and a lethargy so terrible I wonder if I'm losing my mind." Helen simply provided the unity of vitality and hope that Frye saw in the text of Blake. He even combined them by planting her photo in a difficult section of *The Four Zoas,* confessing: " ... somehow I feel as though I couldn't work on such an absolutely sane, gloriously vital human being as Blake at all unless in some mysterious superchemical way you belonged."

For February and March 1935, he closeted himself with "Blake,

Blake, Blake" to wrestle this most difficult of poets to the ground: "I've spun the man around like a teetotum. I've torn him into tiny shreds and teased and anatomized him with pincers.... But what I have done is a masterpiece; finely written, well handled, and the best, clearest and most accurate exposition of Blake's thought yet written. If it's no good, I am no good. There isn't a sentence, and there won't be a sentence in the whole work that hasn't gone through purgatory. Christ! why was I born with brains? And in the middle of it all there are my infernal lectures and my (no adequate adjective) theology."

Nevertheless despite the hellish loneliness and instability of ideas he said "circle and cluster and hag-ride me until they're sloughed off in some sort of formal connection," he was exhilarated that he had "finally bitten the kernel out of Blake."

As always, his crucial contact was Edgar. While Edgar was interested in the draft, he could offer only a vague hint that Massey, just back from Bermuda, might raise some money for Frye. He warned Frye not to count on it. Herbert Davis called the fragment "extraordinarily good" and thought it could set a new standard for MA theses. Curiously Frye was amazed that Davis didn't suspect his wider ambition to publish the manuscript and launch his career. Still certain that his ideas were so obvious that someone might outflank him, Frye was nervously impatient. He understood that, in the short term, he'd have to serve his ideas up for MA and doctoral theses. The problem here was that Frye was short on champions at Toronto. Since Vic professors had very little influence with the graduate school, there was only Davis to guide his thesis. Frye was effectively stranded when Davis left for Cornell in 1938.

Frye was not naive or uncaring about his isolation. He confessed to Helen that the only person who had "the remotest idea of what I'm talking about," besides his new junior colleague, Roy Daniells, was Wilson Knight who taught through the thirties at Trinity College and was himself a study in isolation. Knight wrote with the imagination of a poet and appeared indifferent to small-minded scholarly issues. He didn't add footnotes or indexes to his work, a practice of high eccentricity, then and now, which Frye often copied later.

Knight had published his revolutionary book of essays, *The*

*Wheel of Fire*, just before coming to Canada in 1931. Although the book, with preface by T.S. Eliot, established his reputation in English criticism, he was inspired like a latter-day Puritan to leave the old world behind and teach in Toronto. In his autobiographical confession *Atlantic Crossing*, he saw himself leaving "sodden, secluded Gloucestershire" to "a new life" and "a new age." Knight's fundamentally Biblical vision also suggested the visionary breadth of Frye's own thinking at the time: "The Flood in Genesis suggests chaos threatening to drag back man to the primeval slime. But in the rainbow airy waters mate with sun-fire to create a circular harmony of blending colours ethereally musical, catholic and cathartic. We must integrate ourselves into this pattern so that all intermeshes like machinery, dances, or persons in a play." Not surprisingly, Knight constantly noted parallels of literary and religious symbolism.

Knight's personal naivety, unquenchable enthusiasm and visionary writing were regarded with suspicion, even ridicule, by the University College coterie of A.S.P. Woodhouse, who set a standard of infrequent, soddenly-written works of intellectual history. Frye's friend, Mary Winspear, described Knight as "a weird bird to fly into all that Babbitry." Although he promoted serious Shakespearean drama at the university theatre, Hart House, there was also an exhibitionist side to Knight which didn't help his image. He toyed with plans for acting *Timon of Athens* in the nude. Playing the beaten messenger in *Antony and Cleopatra* in a 1937 production, he rolled around on stage in revealing purple tights in a frenzy of masochistic yelps.

Despite his extravagance on stage, Knight was personally very reserved and undemonstrative. He welcomed Frye over to his St. George St. apartment as a junior colleague who was fascinated in symbolism. He served him hot chocolate and composed his books in the air, and, like Frye, was incapable of small talk. Knight showed a monomania for Shakespeare, which Frye admired, and Frye for Blake, which Knight admired. Even Knight's gossip was Shakespearean. He told Frye of tracking down Colin Still, author of *Shakespeare's Mystery Play*, in London and finding him a reclusive author who simply decided to follow up an idea about initiation rites in *The Tempest* which no one had explored before. Frye was so impressed by Knight's absorption in Shakespeare's work, he once claimed (incorrectly) that Knight was ignorant of such scholarly niceties as the difference between folio and quarto texts. In fact, Frye was most impressed that the only important professional tool which Knight possessed was a single-volume Globe edition which Frye described as covered "with a mass of pencilled annotations." When Frye tried out some primitive ideas he had on Shakespearean comedy, Knight's reaction was simply to urge him to get cracking and write his own book.

Perhaps reflecting their mutually impersonal attitudes, Frye never made the kind of fuss about his relationship to Knight that he did for Edgar, Pratt and Robins. Four decades later, Frye did acknowledge that " ... Knight's books had much the effect on me that Chapman's Homer had on Keats, and the method indicated, of concentrating on the author's text but re-creating it by studying the structure of imagery and metaphor, seemed to me then, and seems to me still, the sort of thing that criticism is centrally about." Yet it was unquestionably Knight's intellectual courage which encouraged an embattled Frye.

In April Frye faced "the annual exam swindle" of theology courses. The futility of theology was accentuated by his reappointment as reader in English with a $500 salary. Although he captured seven firsts and a church history scholarship (also a poisonous third from his nemesis, Alfred Johnston), Frye still refused to let the bad taste of compulsory theology infect his sense of religion. Without hesitation, he countered Helen's flirtation with communism by defending religion: "I propose spending the rest of my life, apart from living with you, on various problems connected with religion and art. Now religion and art are the two most important phenomena in the world; or rather the most important phenomenon, for they are basically the same thing. They constitute, in fact, the only reality of existence. So I must turn a deaf ear to the arguments of your friend about Communism ... Obviously the world is entering a prodigious change, but the new morality will have to be something better than a rehash of the vague deistic and utilitarian sentimentalism of the capitalistic systems the Communists are most concerned to attack. There will have to be something better, for me, than the Communistic exploiting of emotion by intellect. Atheism is an impossible religious position for me, just as materialism is an impossible philosophical position, and I am unable to solve the problems of religion and art by ignoring the first and distorting the second. Read Blake or go to hell: that's my message to the modern world."

Because he failed to obtain money to go to Britain, he settled into a quiet and almost appealing summer. When Roy Daniells departed for Britain, Frye lived rent-free in his room for the summer. "I read heavily and widely, like a schoolgirl at puberty. I rehashed every problem of the universe eight or ten times, and meanwhile dragged my gaunt and celibate body around to engaging in a positive minimum of activity."

In one exceptional letter to Helen it was obvious that after a year of torment he had achieved distance from himself and could analyze all the warring contradictions in his personality and work: "I know perfectly well that essentially I'm still a great yowling infant ... but I'm growing up, don't you think I'm not. I've got tremendous ideas, but they're like the myths in primitive religions, huge but monstrous, not consolidated, disciplined or defined. Only the Blake—I know Blake as no man has ever known him—of that I'm quite sure. But I lack so woefully in the way of subtlety. I haven't got a subtle mind—only a pounding, driving bourgeois intellect. I don't insinuate myself between two factors of a distinction—I push them aside: if I meet a recalcitrant fact, I knock it down; which doesn't get rid of it, but puts it in a different position. Consequently I'm damnably lonesome, intellectually. I resent criticism, because I don't know, in most cases, what the hell I mean myself, so how should anyone else pretend to do so? ... But the real trouble is that all this work is basically critical, and purely critical work doesn't satisfy me. Because if I am to rest content with criticism I have to pay attention to all these stupid distinctions made by facts: my criticisms are not, properly speaking, criticisms at all, but synthetic recreations. Professor Davis was kind enough, or ignorant enough, to remark that what he had seen of my theoretical re-construction of Blake was a damned sight more interesting than the original, as far as the prophecies are concerned at all events. I can draw blueprints for the loveliest castles in the air, miracles of blending size and grace; this is a work of art, creative in essence. It's silly to object that these castles wouldn't stand up if they were built. Who said anything about their standing up? This is one side of me—the synthetic intellectual. I'm a critical capitalist. The English conquered India, the largest richest, most complicated empire in the world, with a handful of soldiers. I can sail into Blake or Shakespeare or St. Augustine or the Christian religion or aesthetics with two facts and a thesis, and I can conquer it. I may be baffled and obstructed: I may get stuck in a Black Hole, as I have been more or less for a year now; but I emerge with my territory painted all one colour, anyhow. But if you paint everything one colour you over-simplify. And so I have to reckon with another side to me, the creative artist side: at least I call it that because it sounds so swell—it really doesn't get beyond the criticism of criticism. And this side says: You're not working with realities, but with phenomena: go write a novel. A few years ago the challenge was even more uncompromisingly direct: go preach the gospel. And it goes on and says that all this student life is frightfully artificial and deracinated, mechanical rather than organic: all professoring ends in pedantry, in social parasitism. If you'd gone into music, says the conscience, or the fiend, whichever it is, you'd be caught up in the rhythm of a genuine art: if you must work with debased coinage, words being simply tones encrusted with various kinds of patina, work with them properly ... And thus I stand more or less paralyzed, wanting badly to commit myself to something, communism, Catholicism, pedantry in any line, and realizing that I can't; that the only thing I can commit myself to is my religion and my wife, one being in the clouds and the other in Europe. So I rush around squealing, like a pig in a fire, or sit around with large ideas and not doing anything about them, like a eunuch with an erection."

This confession managed to anticipate nearly every major hostile criticism that would ever be directed against himself or his work in the future. It is extraordinary that he would prejudge himself in such harsh terms. But the self-criticism acted as a foil to the development of his career and writing. He would eventually even out some contradictions by jettisoning, for example, the notion that his kind of criticism was a debased form of creativity. He would also see the university itself as a realm of vibrant reality rather than a bone yard for eunuchs and parasites. But he maintained a trace of his old romantic notions too: criticism *could* be sterile; universities *could* be parasitic. These haunting doubts merely impelled a greater intellectual honesty, a loyalty to a pure vision of the imagination and its application to life.

Even then, concerns about application revolved around Frye. He indicated to Helen, for example, that his idea of "religion" was irrevocably tied up with "the positive constructive life." He abusively attacked the clichéd association of "religious" with "mystical experiences which are usually pseudo-mystical or quasi-mystical at the most, resulting in little more than a more effeminate kind of sentimental wallowing ..." His view was archly Protestant. He sanctified positive toil: "Life is activity and experience; constructive activity and intelligent experience is without exception religious ... Once you start thinking about religion as a specialized activity, or as a retreat from ordinary living, you immediately think of it as mysterious, ghostly, esoteric ... when most people say they have given themselves up to Christ what they have really given themselves up to is a rabble of confused and chaotic feelings, mostly memories of adolescence, and the best word for the state they get into is maudlin ... as soon as you start to worry about your soul, you're getting away from religion, and as soon as you get to work, you're being religious."

All summer, Frye struggled with many of the implications of his self-analysis. He confessed to Helen that he was not only consuming Rabelais, he was "giving birth to a novel," about which he provided no details. He mentioned another outline for a novel which he felt he was not mature enough to do. It was about a couple deeply in love and while respectful of each other, one is religious, the other communist. Although they try not to force their ideas on their child, the child must necessarily grow up in a warped atmosphere. Despite the apparent inspiration of Rabelais, Frye seemed unaware that his novel was really focussed on ideas rather than interesting narrative.

He kept a firmer eye on his academic priorities. He planned to study Anglo-Saxon and work hard at setting up his teaching for the fall. While the former plan fell through, the latter left him with an unhappy realization of his own "profound ignorance of English literature and total ignorance of any other literature." Yet he cheerfully predicted that the MA thesis would be finished by the end of July, ready for autumn submission. For the first time, too, he worked as an academic editor, writing annotations, preparing indices and copying poems for the first edition of a new poetry text *Representative Poetry* edited by Norman Endicott and scrutinized by a University of Toronto committee including Davis.

It was anonymous and largely thankless work but it garnered him $20 a week and a valuable scholarly credit for his CV. He did well enough on the Blake section; he eventually handled most of the poets between Donne and Blake. There were less attractive duties. MacGillivray dumped about fifteen pounds of summer school exams to be graded in his room and he was immediately driven into despair by the staggering weight of student ignorance. He was now sufficiently visible as an academic, however, that he received his first job offer as instructor at Wesley College at the University of Manitoba where E.K. Brown had just departed. Although he dismissed the job, he showed a surprising antipathy to his own Vic mentors by confessing that he'd rather work with the younger, dynamic Brown than "this Edgar-Brown-Robins combination."

The summer became increasingly muddled with job complications and worry over Helen's return to Canada. Although Frye was prepared for another year's separation, Helen's stay depended on her success in the notoriously stiff Courtauld comprehensive exams. As if to underline his longing for her, he took a hapless vacation up to the Kemp cottage with Helen's brother Roy. As he headed off, he discovered he had no money, only to find Roy in the same position. Through a cold rainy week which aggravated a "geyser" cold, they lived off a box of oatmeal, "some coffee that would have disinfected a pest-house" and eggs and milk from a neighbour. His longing for Helen was murderously accentuated by the sight of her little red swim suit hanging in a corner. His mood worsened in September. He admitted an attack of pessimism and grumbled about his lack of work on Blake. When Helen suggested that she might spend another year overseas, Frye overran his earlier accommodation with angry imprecations.

## LAST YEAR

Finally, Helen did return from Britain, putting an end to a separation of over a year and a half. Although marriage was a chronic consideration, there was no money to allow it. As a result, Helen lived at her parents' home while Frye continued a disagreeable bachelor's life in residence. Helen quickly settled into her old job at the Art Gallery of Toronto where she and Norah McCullough assisted artist Arthur Lismer in the gallery's manifold educational activities. Helen was specifically in charge of arranging tours and lectures for groups from the university and elsewhere and helping to coordinate an evening lecture series of visiting art scholars which was then one of the highlights of the Toronto intelligentsia. She ran a Thursday Morning Members' Study Group and in 1937 initiated a radio lecture series on the local CBC station, CRCT. Although it was not a senior position, it required a great deal of work which often, because of the evening lectures, was an all-day job. Frye inevitably spent a fair bit of time down at the gallery seeing Helen, visiting the small library which had some of the best art books available in Canada and attending evening lectures. Years later, while leaving the gallery, he decided suddenly that a good title for his Blake opus would be *Fearful Symmetry.*

For the most part, Frye was scrambling himself just to keep ahead of his own students. One of his students, Jerome Buckley, remembers his crossing the short distance from Emmanuel College, where Roy Daniells had his office, to his class in Victoria in a threadbare academic gown. Although he would lecture without notes, it was often with a wariness that would always be a characteristic of his impromptu student lecturing. Already in his first full year of teaching, Frye was distinguished by his use of the blackboard. In his exposition of Milton's cosmology in a course on Milton and 17th century poetry, he used big circles to illustrate the layout of the spheres of the heavens in *Paradise Lost.*

There was, however, the difficult question of how Frye would fit into conventional English teaching. Besides his predominantly philosophical background and eccentric interests, Frye was nowhere near even a homegrown MA, then the absolute minimum requirement. Herbert Davis strongly urged Frye to take "the Schools" at Oxford which, after two or three years, would earn him a nicely minted BA (Oxon.) which would superannuate without further work into an MA. Pelham Edgar who controlled the fellowships in English of the Royal Society finally managed to arrange $1,500 for Frye. Although this would provide for Oxford tuition, Frye's fellowship was explicitly funded for research into the "Development of symbolism in the prophetic books of William Blake."

What this meant ironically was that for a year, Frye would enjoy a fallow period from both his graduate studies and his Blake book which he shelved. In fact, he managed to busy himself with every other aspect of his life. While his teaching was central to everything he did, he managed to find time to write criticism for *Acta* and for the first time the journal of Canadian left-wing opinion, *The Canadian Forum* with which Herbert Davis was connected.

When he burst into print again, it was in the odd stance of a live arts critic who covered opera, ballet and music. This was not so much a personal choice as that of the *Acta* editor, James Taylor, who gave the assignments to the compliant Frye. His first effort, "Current Opera: a Housecleaning," a supposed review of *Madame Butterfly*, showed Frye as an arrogant Spenglerian waving the whole art of opera away. Opera, Frye claimed, had a poisonous association "with high society, and its support by wealthy women pretending to culture has also helped to make it entertainment closer in spirit to the circus than to creative art." The great strength of the form, which reached a peak with Mozart, was its comic capacity. The arch-villain who destroyed the form was Wagner, who with Nietzsche stood "as the joint godfather of Naziism." Thanks to Wagner, opera was in "a state of decadence from which it can never be rescued."

Ballet got off easier. In reviewing a performance of the Ballet Russe, he considered ballet innovative and energetic and was clearly excited that it could play to "an intellectual and sophisticated audience which can respond to symbolism and convention, but becomes impatient of explanation." Frye was already giving vent to his now established feeling that art lay well outside the territory of pat allegory or moralizing. In fact, the one dyspeptic moment in the performance for Frye was an allegorical (Temptation, Passion, Fate and Frivolity) treatment of Tschaikowsky's Fifth Symphony. Frye saw this as misuse of allegory. Music, after all, was music "not a warbling of ethics."

Apparently because of the connection of Davis with the *Forum*, Frye was asked to review the Jooss European Ballet three months later. Frye here was trying to negate the romantic image of the lonely genius artist by claiming that "art flourishes when the artist is regarded, not as a long-haired shaman, but as a skilled labourer ... when it can depend on a set of symbols or conventions the public recognizes and is ready to accept ... when it appeals to a large and vulgar audience as well as to a discriminating coterie ... [and] when it can be pressed into the service of religion, for a religion provides both the large audience and the required body of understood conventions and symbols." As a result ballet which is the product of "workmen in music, drama and choreography" inherently outdistanced the work of "a charlatan chewing his nails in a garret."

Frye was overwhelmed by the Jooss performance. He claimed his "critical faculties were to some extent paralyzed by its novelty, and partly because he believed it to possess an unparalleled historical importance for our own time ... one sees growing up under one's own nose a new art-form showing every sign of becoming as expressive for the twentieth century as Elizabethan drama or Mozartian opera ..." Despite this voluble pronouncement, this was the last writing Frye ever did on dance.

After a consideration of Wyndham Lewis's anti-Spenglerian attitudes in the June issue, Frye returned in the August *Forum* with
a consideration of the music of Delius, which again gave him a
forum to attack the romantic genius cult. Like a pathologist, Frye
picked apart three "easily recognized aspects" of Romanticism
which he disapproved, the "arrogant will-to-power doctrine of
Nietzsche caricatured in Fascism today ... Whitman's ecstatic
absorption in nature ... and the langour and sensuousness of the
Swinburnian school of English poetry ..." In an early example of
how he would later work, Frye slotted three works of Delius, *Mass
of Life*, *Sea Drift* and *Songs of Sunset* into each of the categories.
As in his dance pieces, he was impatient for new forms to rise out
of the dregs of a dead Romanticism.

Frye, of course, really knew nothing about dance and was certainly no expert on either opera or contemporary music. The
reviews showed how much Frye would have to develop to purge
hoary collectivist notions and such red-herrings as the health of
individual arts. The reviews did manage, however, to show notions
that would always stay with him. He would continue to exhibit
great antipathy to simplistic allegory in any of the arts. He also
continued to believe in the inherent strength of popularly understood convention and symbolism perpetrated by artisans who knew
what they were doing. It was craftsmanship's aura of impersonality,
not the cult of the genius, which interested him.

For the first time too, Frye exercised his creative urges as a
fiction writer and made an appearance in the Spring 1936 *Acta*
with "The Ghost," a comic parody of a ghost tale. The unnamed
ghost is simply a failed Banquo, who returns from death to haunt
his "enemy" who unfortunately is not terribly frightened. In fact
the enemy says he's rather weary of the show. Firmly placing all
ghosts in a junk bag of occultism, he promptly falls asleep. The
demoralized spook disintegrates and tries again with his old girl
friend but even she's indifferent. She can't, after all, embrace him
so she wonders why she should bother with him anymore. He then
tries the priest who conjured him back to life because the priest
discerned the ghost "simply refused to enter a world where ... loves
and hates would not matter." Even the priest is uncharitable and

offers him only a future of scaring children, beating up mediums and spooking primitive tribes. The ghost himself is so now frightened, he asks like a child for a glass of water and the story suddenly ends. Ostensibly Frye was merely toying with a convention, but his interest in identity between life and death later extended generically to all *bardo* narratives including the Japanese theatre form, Noh.

Frye's practical interests extended even to the *Canadian Poetry Magazine* which began publishing in January under the editorship of E.J. Pratt. To help Pratt out, Frye made a daily trip over to the nearby postal station at Charles and Yonge Sts. to clear out the magazine's Box 491 and then weed out submissions. When articles in the national media about the magazine precipitated a flood of submissions, this almost turned into a pack-horse job. In the short run, it had little personal importance except to provide him with one experience which taught him the dangers of personal response in evaluating art. In a poem about flowers there was the phrase "golden rain" which "made me feel as though my viscera were floating in space." After searching his memory, Frye recalled that in setting off fireworks when he was ten, he experienced "as intense an aesthetic experience as I had ever had, and one of these fireworks bore the title of 'golden rain.' "

As the term came to an end, there was still the problem of Frye's ordination. After Saskatchewan and his now unquestionable academic direction, it was obvious that Frye was never going to be a minister. There was a perfectly valid question as to why the church should bother to ordain theology graduates who weren't going to take a parish. While Frye was ambivalent, his academic mentors were largely negative about it. Yet there was still pressure from Cassie to fulfill the family imperative. He also felt a personal sense of obligation because he had consistently accepted funds intended only for ministers in training. He had lengthy discussions with a prominent older student, Harold Vaughan, who agreed that the United Church, like the Catholic, should accept and ordain a variety of men, including teachers.

Frye would have easily backed down if there was serious opposition to his being ordained but the liberal faction inside the church prevailed. Two days before his actual ordination at a church conference in Toronto in June 1936, the conference president, W.L.L. Lawrence, called ten of the ordinands together to confess their religious motives for a *Toronto Star* reporter. As if talking to skittish adolescents, Lawrence advised them not to be nervous. For the most part he seemed to elicit what he wanted, revivalist confessions of conversion experiences. Repudiating an agnostic boyhood, Frye's friend John Bates confessed, "The irresistible character of Jesus drew me into theology—and Him I must serve all my life." The last subject, Frye, stated bluntly, "I have no mystic experience to relate. I have no thrilling emotions, and I cannot name the date of my conversion." Sensing a mistake, the reporter quickly dismissed Frye by reporting, "He will go to Oxford for two years to further his academic studies."

When it was published the next day, the article created great jubilation among Frye's leftist friends who'd been so hostile to his joining the ministry. Yet in the context of Frye's own struggles with Blake, his remarks were false. In fact, his work with Blake was a real mission, a parody of a holy quest with a full complement of conversion experience, thrilling emotions and read-Blake-or-go-to-hell evangelical commitment. His comments represented the first overt indication that Frye was willing to offer a bland persona to conceal powerful feelings.

For July, Frye worked up at the Kemp cottage on his Blake manuscript. Although Helen disliked Muskoka, he found it a congenial place to work, blessed by quiet and the opportunity of walks up a nearby hill which they called "the mountain." The Kemps had hammocks out in front facing the bay and while reading Swedenborg's *True Christian Religion* during this period, it occurred to him that Blake had derived the names of *Tiriel* from the book.

He eventually had to head home in August and had the usual grim trip. This time, he just managed to grab the last seat in the coach to Montreal. The traveller ahead kept the window open to the blowing cinders which instigated a two-day sneezing fit. At home, he found Cassie physically and mentally aged. Her mind now dwelt on pleasant memories of her early family life before she was married. Everything else had become hazier. Frye wrote to

Helen that "I'm not quite real to her now, except as an after-image of Howard." She was, in fact, consistently calling him Howard.

But she liked to talk and Frye enjoyed listening to her accounts of dreams which were "extraordinarily vivid ones, full of Biblical symbolism and startlingly like Pilgrim's Progress." Frye thought she fancied herself as a kind of Armageddon, a passive receptor of what she thought were external supernatural forces rather than creations of her own psyche. She even related a poltergeist experience she experienced years before in which she was struck down twice by an invisible force in the kitchen. A disturbing reminder of the deep cutting personal tragedies which had marked her life was a dream of seeing her two dead sons together.

Like his explanation of the bleak lives of his Saskatchewan parishioners, he saw his mother's problems as chiefly cultural. "I do wish Mother would let me talk to her as I would like to, but the barrier of her complete self-absorption is always there, besides an unalterable difference of our way of looking at things. Mother, like most of her family, needed a training in some difficult technique like one of the fine arts—all that genuine inspiration and terrific emotional power frittering away in backwoods Methodism is a waste of genius." Yet Cassie did read the essays Frye brought home. Although she confessed she would have trouble relating the ideas to someone else, she claimed to have understood and enjoyed them. In a move which chilled Frye but displayed clear admiration for him, she covered a group photo of her brothers and sisters with Frye's Emmanuel graduation photo.

As for work, Frye was able to summarize a couple of brand new volumes of *The Golden Bough*, which the public library still had hidden behind the counter. One result was the recognition that *The Winter's Tale* had a close affinity with fertility festivals. But besides Cassie's loquacity there were personal worries which seemed to conspire against his working. Helen seemed beset by her family which was under a great deal of financial stress. He was dismayed that as soon as he himself left Toronto, the pressures on Helen had started. He felt impotent that there was nothing he could now do to help her for a whole year. He bridled at the idea that she might lose her independence by moving back home permanently which would be inextricably followed, he thought, by her abandoning the idea of coming to Europe to pass her examinations. He felt anguish when Helen sent him a maple leaf which had turned color. With sadness he guessed, "The mountain must be lonely now."

## MERTON COLLEGE

On the eve of going away, Frye was gloomy. His money had dwindled alarmingly away during the summer and the separation from Helen was an emotional strain. He tried to buoy himself by reminding Helen that after he finished Oxford, they could finally do what they wanted. After agonizing about cost, Helen and Frye decided to meet in Montreal before he left on the small Cunard liner, *Alaunia*, on Sept. 4. For Frye it was the "supreme gift" which helped alleviate the obvious pain of departing.

His trip overseas was distinguished by its boredom. Although he had bouts of constipation and headaches, his stomach, buttressed with fruit salts, held through three days of stormy weather. He was amused by his eccentric shipmates. There was a former architect who planned to settle in Norfolk and "run an electric cable under the soil to warm it up, raise red, white and blue asters before anyone else, and clean up money at the coronation." There was also the missionary "from the headwaters of the Congo" who Frye thought stupid and prudish. She disliked Albert Schweitzer for making "such a point of his having 'sacrificed' a great musical and academic career for Africa."

The Channel was placid but Frye was too exhausted from poor sleep to see Le Havre. A little later he saw the cliffs of Dover. Finally as the little liner moved up the Thames estuary, a brilliant red sunset covered the western sky, dyeing the Thames below. It was an exhilarating experience which gave Frye a fleeting sense like many English Canadians of his generation that somehow he was coming home. Yet he reported a sense of strangeness too:

"...everything I could see of England from the boat looked eerie, subtle and mysterious, like something on another planet. The confused mass of subdued colours all running into one another, the hazy misty air, the arrangements of clumps of trees, hedged farms, and sand, all make it look convincing and still vaguely unreal."

After settling the next morning into the bed and board on Guildford St. where Helen had stayed in her Courtauld year, Frye cautiously explored the city on foot, feeling his way around St. Pancras Station, then heading in the afternoon to Trafalgar Square. Fascinated by the familiar names like Piccadilly Circus, Covent Garden and Charing Cross which indelibly adhered to his memory, he developed a habit of trekking around, feeling as though "I belonged to London." But there were hazards. He caught a bad cold and agonized over "the cat houses of parliament" outside his window. The boarding house, moreover, was full of coal gas fumes and "quite uninhabitable." For the first time his Spenglerian perspective was not intellectual but deeply personal. After a gloomy political conversation with another Canadian student, he felt revulsion for "the extraordinary grey horror of this dying world ..."

Oddly, Frye made little effort to explore the obvious Blakean resources of the city. He didn't visit addresses relevant to Blake. He failed to examine the Blake prints at the British Museum to offset his earlier annoyance at the "villainous" prints in Toronto. This was astonishing because it was still possible for serious students to walk into the museum, sign a simple form and personally handle the collection, some of it stored in ordinary file boxes. His interest in ballet did impel him to look up C.V. (Veronica) Wedgwood, who knew a friend of Helen's, partly to track down the Ballet Jooss and also to inquire about a 1931 ballet based on Blake's *Job*. Wedgwood who was then writing her history of the Thirty Years' War, had Frye to tea, gave him a few names but he failed to look anyone up. The ballet *Job* was essentially irrelevant to his Blake work but with libretto by Geoffrey Keynes, music by Vaughan Williams and choreography by Ninette de Valois, it was a key work of British cultural nationalism which could have given

Frye a taste of real energy to balance the grim student life which awaited him in Oxford.

Before going to Oxford, Frye took an excursion to Cheltenham in the Cotswolds to see Wilson Knight's brother, Jackson, who was a classics professor at Exeter College. The train trip was like "being dragged through one Constable painting after another." Although Jackson Knight was more gregarious than his brother, he had the same intensity of spirit. His own deep interest in symbolism was just being realized in his new book on the labyrinth in religion and art, *Cumaean Gates: A Reference of the Sixth Aeneid to the Initiation Pattern*. Like most myth critics, Knight was an essentially reductive thinker who could breezily announce that "the two most important classes of myth [were] the ocean type, in which the dead are supposed to cross the ocean, and the cave type, in which they are supposed to enter a cave, on the way to their rest." Frye sat for hours enthralled by Knight's conversation and presenting his own ideas. He noted that he had picked up the idea in a recent book, *The Labyrinth*, that some traditional swastika patterns were associated with the Knossus labyrinth but received little response from Knight. He drank so much cider, he said, he ended up pissing pure apple juice. The encounter made him realize once more that "the Knights are the only people I have met who really speak my language..."

Knight made one mistake, however, in inviting a pro-fascist poet to meet Frye. The poet took Frye and Knight to hear Beethoven's Ninth on his radio, expressing an admiration for Beethoven in Nietzschean strongman terms. "Along with this," Frye reported to Helen, "goes a native mysticism like Lawrence—if you get around to reading Lawrence's *Plumed Serpent*, you will see how closely exaggerated respect for nature and her works is bound up with Fascism ..." He admitted the poet was clever, "only he represents everything in this world I detest and fear ... when civilization approaches a precipice, there is always a group seized with an instant desire for suicide. That's what the Fascists represent and what he represents." This confrontation was a prelude of many such encounters in Britain which dismayed and ultimately drove

Frye into depression. When he returned to London, he was buoyed by the news that another Canadian student he'd met had just taken part in a massive demonstration of leftists which prevented a fascist parade through one of the Jewish areas.

Finally at the start of the second week of October, Frye went up to Oxford and settled into an excellent room in the oldest part of Merton, Mob Quad. It was, in fact, a suite the size of the Senior Common Room at Victoria, furnished with "a chesterfield, two armchairs, seven wooden chairs, a bookcase, two desks" and had "two large windows with window seats." It was in the arch near the famous Merton chapel and was later turned into a room commemorating a former graduate, Max Beerbohm. His first reports home must have been quite reassuring to the ever-anglophile Cassie, who approved the church-like round of lunches and teas into which Frye appeared to be settling. She even detailed the minimum crockery each "man" had to have in his room.

Frye soon met his "scout" who wondered whether Frye would ever get used to the newly installed electric heater instead of the fire he had previously tended. Embarrassed by this taste of the British class system, Frye tried to put his mind to rest. Because he was an ordained minister, who received letters from his mother addressed Rev. H.N. Frye, B.A., B.D., he seems to have escaped the traditional hazing of making newcomers drink highly spiked sherry until they threw up. His status, however, backfired later in the term when an ordained Anglican minister who was at Merton simply to receive an Oxford BA, tracked him down, assuming that they could "talk over the heads of the unregenerate." Frye, of course, bristled at this but had to admit a failing: "It's curious that a snobbery which I take for granted when it's intellectual or artistic I resent when it's moral."

Hating his undergraduate status and his isolation, he reported his first week to Helen in the gloomiest terms: "Sunday in Oxford. I am completely surrounded by a shell. I have no curiosity: don't want to see anybody, or go for a walk: just want to sit in my room, devour books nervously and feverishly ... there is no Oxford—not for me at least—except the university, and the feeling of moving like a separate disembodied spirit among lights and crowds, which makes me love a city so, will have to remain in abeyance." Like most overseas students, he found the much younger British undergrads immature and slowly made friends among other foreign students like Rodney Baine from Mississippi and Mike Joseph from New Zealand.

On top of personal misery, there was the shock that the much vaunted English School at Merton itself was going to be inadequate. His tutor, Edmund Blunden, a minor poet and author of a celebrated prose work about the First World War, *Overtones of War*, seemed to have few intellectual resources to handle a murderously impatient young scholar who already appeared to know more about literature than himself. Worse still, like many middle-class Britons, Blunden had a frank enthusiasm for Hitler's accomplishments. This was hardly reassuring to a left-wing student who had already collided with a fascist poet in his first weeks overseas.

Many students, who were at Merton simply to soak up atmosphere, seemed happily oblivious to the failings of the shy, pleasant Blunden. He perceived that most North American students enjoyed the initiation into British life and thought nothing of cancelling a tutorial for a quiet conversation in a local pub or a lesson in the fundamentals of cricket. Blunden was so genuinely well-liked that he inspired a cycle of adulatory poems by one of his American students, Paul Engle, who was at Merton just before Frye. In one, Engle describes how as an "uneasy Iowan" he climbed the stone stairway, "the purgatorial mount" to Blunden's room for his first tutorial:

> Eyes met me, burning through the morning mist,
> Shy creature, burrowing the autumn gloom,
> Who seemed to haunt, rather than hold, that room:
> Warm hand that clenched into a wiry fist
>
> Short, slight, he seemed assaulted by a chair,
> But as he waited, such a radiance beamed
> From his intensity of face, it seemed
> An animated star were rising there.

"Written your essay? Good. Then we won't read it.
Late yesterday I saw you playing cricket.
Now let's suppose these volumes are a wicket.
Just watch. Here's some advice. I'm sure you'll need it."

Frye's first two tutorials were a perverse parody of this. Frye reported that his paper on the early poetry of Chaucer, on which he had worked feverishly for three days, was only tepidly received: "Blunden said very flattering things about it, but he obviously isn't very fresh on Chaucer. That's the weakness of the tutorial system, I think: the tutor has to pretend to know everything when he doesn't, like a public school teacher. Not that Blunden bothers to pretend much. I think he likes me, and spoke of taking me out to see Blenheim palace." Obviously the two were on a collision course.

Still expecting Oxford magic, Frye worked hard on his next essay on 8,000 lines of Chaucer's *Troilus and Cressida*. Once more, however, Blunden met his earnest professionalism with a personable but empty response. It was obvious that for Frye panic was setting in: "I think that Blunden approves all right but his main interest is in things like natural imagery of the 19th c. type. I can't write about that intelligently, as I don't think in those terms, and neither did Chaucer. So what Blunden says is that the paper is a very fine piece of work, that Chaucer was quite a poet, that that picture on the wall he bought for ten pounds at an auction, and the catalogue described it as School of Poussin and dated it around 1710: would I give him an opinion on the date? Also, the next time I pass St. Aldate's Church, would I take a look at the font cover there, which has been varnished out of existence, and which looks medieval, but is, he thinks, sixteenth century Flemish work done in a medieval tradition, and let him know what I think about it? So I get up and stare solemnly at his bloody pictures, and then announce that my opinion on the date of a bastard Poussin is not worth a damn, and my qualifications for pronouncing on Flemish font covers are exactly nil. Well, no, I let him down easier than that, so that he thinks I know far more about it than I actually do— you know my methods, Watson. I can see where I shall have to marry you and make you live with me at Oxford next year in sheer self-defence."

By the end of the term, Frye felt so cheated, he was in a murderous mood: "I have decided not to write a paper for Blunden tonight. I'm going to go in and twist his neck with my bare hands. I've scared the shit out of him, in the Burwash phrase, and I'm just beginning to realize it, and to comprehend why he gives me that dying-duck reproachful stare everytime I finish reading a paper to him. He returned the Blake with the remark that it was pretty stiff going for him, as he wasn't much accustomed to thinking in philosophical terms."

Certainly Frye's own classmates soon discovered that they could learn as much from him as any of their teachers. Frye's best friend at Oxford, Mike Joseph, reported: "He was already knowledgeable about Blake and Spenser, and was throwing out critical concepts like the 'anatomy', which he developed later. Or he would, for example, in talking about *Romeo and Juliet* say: 'It's built (making a shape with his hands) like an arch—Escalus is the cornerstone'— and this would be a whole new way of looking at the play."

Another major disappointment was the uniformly dismal standard of lecturing. After hearing lectures by Blunden and Abercrombie, he complained of "an endless niggling over minutiae." A major exception was C.S. Lewis whose lectures were uncommonly popular throughout the Oxford colleges. Frye read Lewis's just published book, *The Allegory of Love: A Study in the Medieval Tradition*, in which Lewis used bad poems as effectively as masterpieces, and audited his lectures in the first term.

Essentially Lewis was a cosmologist who was interested in using broad cultural evidence—literary, philosophical and scientific—to outline the dimensions and shape of the human universe, which insinuated into and sometimes structured literature itself. Lewis was interested in questions like what is the world which writers of a particular period see again and again in the same way? Where are heaven and the gods, hell and the devil? Are they inside us or beyond in some distant zone? What are angels and spirits and types of human heroes and scoundrels who constantly appear in narrative? How does literature reflect and give meaning to the wider apparatus of culture and religion? In dealing with medieval literature he called this established pattern the Model. In the published version of the lectures Frye heard, *The Discarded Image*, he went on to make a crucial point that it is poets and artists and not philosophers who are innately and enthusiastically interested in the imaginative possibilities of such patterns. As Lewis himself anticipated, this cosmological approach is inherently foreign to evaluative criticism because it is based on objective sifting and grouping of basic elements. Although this was only a suggestion, Lewis was nevertheless insistent that scholarship should always direct the scholar inwards towards the symbolic core of literature and not repel him to the periphery with excessively picky historicism. Lewis was never close to his own students at Magdalen, let alone auditors from other colleges, and so it's not surprising that Frye never had anything to do with Lewis. Had Frye somehow been redirected to Lewis for tutoring, however, the immensity of his unhappiness at Oxford would obviously have been alleviated.

Frye also took a course at Balliol in Anglo-Saxon with J.N. Bryson along with Rodney Baine, and a Texan, Alba Warren. Bryson took his North American students capably through the rigors of old English, thereby filling a serious void in Frye's academic background. At first Frye cursed this compulsory absorption in early literature but, as he became absorbed and fascinated with it, he found it was replacing his predominant interest in Romantic and modern literature.

In the short term, however, he was sunk in the kind of desperate misery he felt in Saskatchewan, isolated from Helen and friends in an inhospitable environment. In a Beckett-like statement of impotence, he reported to Helen: "Here I am sitting with a whisker half an inch long waiting for my scout to take away the water I washed my face in out of my wash-basin and give me a chance to shave. There's no place I can put that water except into my pisspot, and *that's* full of piss." He claimed to be winning a struggle with flu but the bitter cold of his rooms was so bad his shaving mirror fogged up. Because his windows faced only east and west, the sun, trapped for the winter in the south, never entered directly. He defined the English gloom of November "a fitting symbol of the dark underworld to which your absence has consigned me." He claimed to sit indoors like "a convict, and look like one." Everything was "dismally cold, wet, clammy, muggy, damp and moist, like a morgue." The "bogs," the bleak unheated toilets some 200 yards from his room, were so unappealing that he became constipated.

He was worried too about the failure of the Royal Society to send along money installments. The lack of money left him in a state of powerlessness and rage when Baine and Warren headed off on vacation for sunny Italy, cursing Frye for not coming. The only entertainment he could manage was playing the piano and hiking out to Cunmor with a Canadian book designer in Oxford, Elizabeth Frazer, with whom he developed a lonely hearts relationship centred on discussions of art and the damnation of poverty.

Nothing annoyed him immediately more, however, than Helen's apparent failure to send along promised copies of the *New Yorker*. In furious block lettering he admonished her: "WHEN THE HELL ARE YOU GOING TO COME THROUGH WITH SOME NEW YORKERS?" Given Frye's seemingly bottomless taste for esoteric works, this voracious desire for copies of America's quintessential upper-middle-class weekly with its cartoons and satire by Thurber and White appeared mysterious. But within the context of his misery at Oxford, it represented a life-line to an urbane North American perspective which Frye desperately needed.

As the term came to an end, Frye was in a better emotional state. He got to know the Canadian community around Oxford and was surprised to find that there was in fact a Canadian identity so that social encounters with compatriots were effortless. He was elected to the twenty-member intellectual circle called the Bodley Club which heard and discussed members' papers. Compared with the Sir Richard Steele Society which was an ill-disguised drinking club, the Bodley was relatively high-tone, but hardly a haven for teetotallers. The day after his first meeting, Frye went out with his new friend, Mike Joseph, and "drank most of the beer in Oxford." With a new cheque soon after from the Royal Society for £50, Frye's spirits revived further and he promptly celebrated by taking Frazer out to dinner and bought himself some sheet music.

For Christmas, he headed down to London and stayed in the

home of friends of Norah McCullough, Stephen and Edith Burnett, in Bayswater. Because Frye was broke so often, he tended to freeload off the Burnetts, repaying them by house-sitting when they were away. For the long six-week holiday he worked on a weighty assignment of 1,600 lines of *Beowulf* for an examination which Bryson had casually assigned, then cancelled when Frye got back to Oxford. Frye cursed murderously over this imposition but in time came to be very fond of the poem. For pleasure, he toured the museums and travelled down to Hampton Court where he was enthralled for over an hour by the "*glorious* Mantegna." He also took in Eliot's *Murder in the Cathedral* with Frazer and by mistake was placed in the front row of the dress circle where they were "practically breathing down the actors' necks." For Helen, he quickly noted the loveliest of poetry in the chorus.

## BIONDINO INGLESE

In early 1937, Frye and Blunden settled into much the same routine as before. Frye bullied Blunden with his knowledge and Blunden tried to take it graciously. Frye suffered for his grandstanding. He worked so hard on an essay on sixteenth-century poet Fulke Greville his eyes gave out for a week. Even then, a week's solid work was not enough: " ... like Blake, his religious, philosophical and political views are all in one piece, and it would take at least a month's solid work to read all of him and tie him all up in a neat little sack."

Soon after, Frye read his "anatomy essay" to Blunden. Since his undergraduate work on Blake's *Isle and the Moon* and his interest later in Burton's *The Anatomy of Melancholy*, Frye had been playing with the concept of anatomy. Blunden's reaction was unapologetically commercial and he claimed that Frye "had two hundred very saleable pages there." Frye himself suddenly came alive again with schemes for publishing. He saw a possible volume in the essays he was writing for Blunden. He also bought a ream of typing paper "to get a lot of Blake done," earnestly hoping to complete his "general book" before the end of the year. He expected to write the book itself, or at least a detailed outline of it in Italy, and then type up three copies and send one to Geoffrey Keynes, another to Edgar and the last to a publisher. If he managed to scare up money from Victoria College, he would stay in Britain and write footnotes at the British Museum. He played with his original idea of Helen's coming over and writing her exams again while he worked in the Museum. They could travel through "either South-West England or Ireland or Southern France or West Germany." All these fond hopes, however, were interlaced with more pressing anxieties over money and the interminable cold of Oxford, the filthy washrooms, the woefully inadequate electric "fire," the sunless days. Although Frye had won his battle with flu in the autumn, it was now getting the upper hand.

Many of those discomforts were thoroughly resolved in a matter of days, when he and Mike Joseph headed off for Italy. To counter the image of cultivated vagabonding Frye was adamant that this trip was not indulgence and that armed with his Blake manuscript, he would faithfully labor "every evening when he arrived in Rome." From London, Frye and Joseph travelled to Pisa through Genoa without stopping except for hotel layovers. They stopped in Pisa just long enough to view the Cimabue mosaic, the Gozzolis and the tower and raced onto Siena where Frye occupied a room in a former palace with "five enormous pillars with Ionic capitals in a semicircle." Entranced by Frye's blond hair, the hotel maid slipped into his room in the evening. He reported to Helen that she started pulling his hair, "got her kiss and departed gurgling. Everybody wants to pull my hair in Italy. In the train to Genoa I caught the words 'biondino inglese' and a woman's remark 'com'-una signorina.' " They moved on to Orvieto for an afternoon and then Rome.

The presumed rationale for this dash through Tuscany was that Joseph, at the urging of his Catholic family, was eager to reach Rome for the Pope's Easter blessing. By the time they had settled in a cheap hotel, however, the Pensione Flavia on the Veneziale, Joseph's Catholic enthusiasms had faded utterly and when Easter

came, Frye tried to rouse him out of bed to get over the Tiber to
the Vatican where the Pope would rise in St. Peter's imperially on
an automated throne. Although the group did head off for the
Vatican, Frye felt a bout of *turista* coming on and instead of taking
in the Pope, the group was quickly enlisted to track down a
washroom.

What they couldn't avoid, however, was the tail end of a rally
for some quarter-of-a-million fascists. Mussolini had just returned
from Libya where he'd pranced like a buffoon in a new imperial
uniform in front of a cavalcade of white horses, proclaiming himself
the "Protector of Islam, liberator of centuries of Muslim slaves."
Frye arrived too late to see the ceremony but the fascist presence
in banners, black uniforms and fatuous Mussolini aphorisms everywhere set an appropriate tone to his art tours in Rome which gave
substance to Blake's prophetic distaste for the brutalizing art of
imperialism.

After the exhilarating taste of Tuscany, Frye was thoroughly
dismayed. "History of Roman art: bastard Etruscan, bastard Greek,
stolen Greek, bastard Oriental, bastard North Italian, bastard copies of bastard Greek, bastard Dutch, and various kinds of eclectic
bastardy." In viewing the "junk piles" — the Thermae, the Vatican,
the Laterine, — he caught a glimmer of the development of Greek
sculpture but most everything disappointed. Even what was good
was diminished by irritants. The Vatican obsessively plastered fig
leaves on nude sculpture. An Italian mania for "restoring" friezes
had even spread to the supposedly inviolable Sistine Chapel. There
was opportunity, however, of seeing a more enticing contemporary
side of Rome—in its opera and ballet—but on the pretext of
disliking Verdi, Frye passed up the chance to see a production of
*Rigoletto*. Although he was still suffering a degree of intolerance
(Beethoven good, Verdi bad), there were undeniable considerations of money and his still insistent desire to keep working on
Blake.

With a mutual sense of relief, the group of four, Frye, Joseph,
Bell and Palmer moved on to their real objective, Florence, stop-
ping off in "glorious" Assisi where they spent a whole day in San
Francesco: "...those Giottos, that Cimabue and what was left of

Cavallini kept us working hard for six hours." They continued on to the "bloody burg" Perugia and to Arezzo for a quick two-hour visit. Finally in Florence they found the town so overcrowded they had to sleep two nights in the corner of a huge lounge room of the Pensione Rigatti on the Arno River before they were able to land a room.

In the Uffizi, Frye was so entranced by the three Madonnas of Cimabue, Giotto and Lorenzo Monaco, that he spent much of the morning there, proclaiming, " ...I shall return with a profound conviction that Cimabue was the very greatest painter who ever lived, on the strength of two paintings." Bell and the others made only slightly better progress: "We got only to the first six rooms, but we saw most of the pictures in them with care, standing before the great ones, the Cimabue and Giotto *Madonna*, the Simone Martini *Annunciation* and the Botticellis for over half an hour each." The whole group acted collectively as critics to "observe many fine points that a single spectator would overlook." Frye himself was particularly valuable with his encyclopedic knowledge of Biblical imagery. Frye was not, however, infallible and Palmer remembers Joseph quietly mediating arguments of interpretation between Bell and Frye.

After a week of their ten-day stay, they still hadn't exhausted the possibilities of the city. Of the group, Bell was most consistently manic, rising at six to write letters home then hitting the galleries, at best downing a litre of milk in a latteria for lunch and then heading back to the art. Frye, "stuffed and drunk, mentally" by the sensory overkill, regularly allowed himself a leisurely lunch of pasta and fruit and, although he never developed a taste for it, the occasional wine like Orvieto or the red champagne, Lambrusco. After several weeks of Italian painting, he suffered a modest rebellion when he saw some Masaccio: "I went to see the Masaccios in that hideous church across the river, and they knocked me as cold sober as a quart of black coffee. I've never seen anything make such a terrific physical impact on me in the way of a picture—I think it was because Catholic painting, with all its serenity and its conception of beauty as loveliness ... was beginning to bore me a little, and I think I detected the individual in revolt in Masaccio—

I may have been wrong. Anyway, the third time I went back to the
Uffizi I went to the Flemish room first—previously the Flemish
pictures looked so ugly and twisted after the Italians. As soon as
they began to soak in I got a bit restless—the next time I go forth
in search of paint it will be to the Low Countries."

A comic relief to all this intensity was the decadent art of the
Pitti where they giggled over the sado-masochistic rendition of the
martyrdom of Ste. Agathe whose large and decidedly unsaintly
breasts were being tormented with pincers. There was a convenient male equivalent, nearly as distasteful, which showed a cupid
reaching determined little hands up to the testicles of a Hercules
figure. This appeared coincidentally with an elevated sensitivity to
the bawdiness in some of the art Frye was seeing. When they took
a side trip down to the mountain fortress of San Gimignano in the
south, Frye was vastly intrigued with the hell scenes of Taddeo
di Bartolo, showing "a Freudian riot" of fiendish lechery and
defecation, which was sufficently sensational to make Frye vow to
return. In Ravenna, Frye particularly noted the famous Byzantine
mosaics. But again they collided with vulgar decadence in Tiepolo's
baroque riot of cupids and naked, full-breasted angels in San Vitale.
Frye quipped to Bell that when he got to heaven, "his first request
of St. Peter will be to let him rape a baroque angel." The line stuck
in Bell's memory and he borrowed it for a character from the Deep
South in his novel *The Half Gods*.

Their continued thoroughness, however, sent them on an expedition five miles under "a blistering sun" from Ravenna down to
Porto Fuori on the coast to see the chapel with frescos from the
Giotto period, the Basilica of St. Apollinare in Classe. The group
was eager, however, to catch a train to Padua, and already late,
they had to take the five uphill miles back at a dog trot. Although
Frye and Joseph wiped sweat and volubly cursed, Bell became
exhilarated because the hot dusty scenery reminded him of his
own Delta home in Mississippi. They arrived just in time for the
train but when they travelled on to Padua, Bell threw the wrong
bag out for Frye and Frye's luggage with his only copy of the Blake
"thesis" travelled on to Venice. The next day, he recovered it and

reported that Padua was the hometown of St. Anthony, "the saint who finds lost things."

After a day and a half of seeing Giotto and Mantegna, they moved on to Venice, which distressed Frye nearly as much as Rome. Frye cursed the dishonesty of the tourist-jaded Venetians and the art which traditionally followed the beleaguering commercialism of the city: "The only time somebody like Tintoretto or Veronese gets really emotional is when he can depict gods dropping gold and jewels and crowns on a broad-bottomed blonde sow with a smirk representing Venice ... I can see now that Venice has no money she does nothing but grab it, because when she had money she had nothing else." He reread *Merchant of Venice* "on the spot," previously failing to realize "how much money was in that play." Virtually every evening, however, they went out for gondola rides and even intrepidly went swimming on the Lido a couple of times. Frye also caught up with home in Venice with some letters from Helen who was eager to come overseas to join him. This, of course, just drew troubling attention to Frye's penury and his complete impotence until he heard from Brown about financing his second year. Although he stayed in Italy for five weeks on just £20 including railway fare, he was close to being broke.

From Venice, they moved on to Verona and Mantua where the food was "ambrosial." Unfortunately bitter cold descended on the swamp-surrounded city and Frye caught the worst sore throat he'd had since getting his tonsils out. As before, he was faced with the bruising irony that after a trip partly intended to clear up the poor health which had plagued him in Oxford, he was heading back feeling worse. After a brief stay in a German-crowded Milan, the group boarded a sparkling-clean Dutch carriage and went through the mountains by night to Basel and on through Alsace-Lorraine and Brussels where Frye was delighted with the news that in recent elections the Belgians had badly drubbed the pro-fascist Rexist party.

After the trip to Italy, Frye was broke, enervated and terribly unhappy. His immediate impulse was to cable Helen with a desperate plea: MUST COME HOME CAN YOU LEND ME SOME MONEY. When he calmed down a little, he analyzed his situation. He anticipated another £30 from the Royal Society but this would leave him only £10 after debts. Agonizing over the costliness of living in Britain, he anxiously awaited a letter from Brown. But when Brown finally wrote, he seemed to prevaricate, alluding to the financial needs of other students. Brown promised $600 but didn't make it clear if this was an immediate grant which would help Frye through the summer. Because of the slow overseas mail, Frye realized it would take another three weeks to clarify the point and by then, he would be even deeper in debt. Blunden had little encouraging news about Oxford subsidies. If Frye did well on his exams, he might pick up £20 but this was hardly the windfall he needed.

Frye played with the idea of making a living writing in London but quickly let it drop. He still hoped that somehow he could prod Edgar into action on his behalf. He sent him the essays he had written for Blunden. He also sent off the recently rewritten first chapter of his Blake book. Possibly worried that Edgar's silence was censorious rather than negligent, he now approached his mentor, he reported to Helen, with what he considered self-abasing rhetoric. He even promised to dedicate the book to him when it was published. Still his letters seemed to disappear into the Atlantic and he never received a reply. The truth is much less spectacular. Frye did in fact write a concise note to Edgar explaining he was now sending off "the first chapter of the Blake, expanded into six because of the number of footnotes." But there was no self-abasement and his only apology was for the delay in sending it along. He gave a distinct impression that with Blunden's support of it, and his own confidence, it would be published. It's not clear what Frye expected of Edgar, yet he clearly did expect some magical solution.

Faced with the total muddle of options, Frye plunged into his work on Blake. He informed Helen that the first two chapters, which represented half of the total, were approaching final draft. Blunden was now more accommodating about it and suggested that Faber and Faber might be interested and he would try to provide an introduction. Again, he tried to raise his morale by dreaming about the book's success which would salve his growing resentment and isolation: " ... the book, if it comes out, will be a damned important one, and when Victoria College sees H.N. Frye splashed over the Times Literary Supplement they may be less worried about my correspondence." As in 1935, the effort became a quest for personal salvation. "The Blake is the only thing I can do now to recoup myself. I am sure it will be published, and that it will attract a lot of attention." He would, moreover, be unworthy of Helen until it was done.

But there was too much strain and worry. He complained of bad eyes since coming back from Italy and confessed that he was very tired and "heartily sick of Oxford." He acidly reported Blunden's enthusiasm for Nazi Germany after a trip in May and he mentioned an unfortunate dinner with the wistful Merton warden who seemed alarmed that the college was going intellectual on him. Because of his exhaustion, he simply wanted to borrow a hundred dollars from Helen and come home instead of soldiering on or joining Helen for a tour of Germany. " ... I don't know when my vitality has been lower—and I don't think I'd last the second year if I spent the summer freezing my feet in the B.M., or, for that matter, in Germany." It was becoming clear, too, that the hope of landing another teaching position at Victoria was no more speculative than the evaporating assurances of financial help from Edgar, the IODE, or Victoria College. In any case, struggling on at Oxford would be academically meaningless because he wasn't "getting enough out of Oxford to make sacrifices worthwhile to finish my course here."

While all this was going on, Frye's American friends were indulging in venerable Oxford rituals. On the day Frye was writing Edgar, Bell and friends punted up the flower-banked Cherwell in two boats and had a picnic tea after a swim. The following day, they rounded up Frye to drive in Lou Palmer's mother's old Chevy to Fairford to see the famous St. Mary's Church with some of the rare stained glass which had survived Puritan iconoclasts. For Frye, it was a revelation. He had read Emile Mâle's book on the iconography of the Gothic cathedral but was uncertain how it actually worked. The church took several hours to see and while

the typology was not nearly as elaborate or as obvious as that of
French cathedrals that Mâle studied, Frye was fascinated with
how the Biblical outline could be set into architectural design.

Most of the vivid imagination of the glassmakers went into the
Last Judgment scene with its purple, brown and red devils raging
below an imperial four-ringed mandala of angels and saints revolv-
ing around Christ whose body was nearly completely haloed. The
huge window was in the western nave end with complementary
window of the crucifixion in the chancel. The Fairford Last Judgment was similar to many such scenes in medieval art, which Blake
himself painted as late as 1808 and worked into his writings with
obsessive attention. A glowing Christ with His ranks of angels,
apostles and martyrs dominated the light-filled top half, with black-
ened devils and naked damned souls wrestling and cannibalizing
each other in the bottom right nearer and nearer a marine-monster
Devil. At the bottom left, the saved souls, the elect, passed from
death and damnation upwards on a gold stairway away from Archangel Michael who divided the underworld of the dead. It was in
fact an inclusive medieval visualization of the apocalypse and
would lend some not-altogether-coincidental features to Frye's
own "circle of stories" in the *Anatomy of Criticism*. For Frye
tragedy, satire and irony lay at the bottom among the damned.
While the bleakest expressions hung below, the force of the quest,
suggesting the sweeping power of Christ's "harrowing of hell," led
up into the brighter areas of comedy and romance.


**TORONTO ILLUSION**

The thrill of Fairford was, of course, only a momentary diversion
from his personal situation. After a month of furious correspondence about motives and feelings, Helen sent him money to get
home. Before leaving, he sent off two chapters of his Blake manuscript to Faber and Faber and dropped in to see Geoffrey Keynes
in Hampstead to discuss a possible textual error in Keynes's reader.

Keynes invited Blake biographer, Monica Wilson, and opened his Arabian Nights collection of Blake engravings. A wrenching irony was that on June 8, 1937, just two weeks before Frye was to step on the *Empress of Australia* for Canada, the Board of Regents finally approved a $600 payment for Frye out of an obscure and thinly-funded scholarship called the Susan Treble Trick and the Mary Treble Currelly Travelling Fellowship controlled by C.T. Currelly. It was supposed to help eligible instructors to travel to "Europe and the Near East, especially in Italy, Greece, Palestine and Egypt" to enrich their teaching. Although the administration was stretching the terms with Frye, Brown's tardiness was a likely indication of his ambivalence about Frye.

Unclear, and probably disgusted with what was really going on at Victoria, Frye headed straight up to Gordon Bay from Toronto to see Helen. His prospects were bleaker than they had ever been. He'd now failed at both Oxford and his book. There was the grim outside chance that he might have to return to the Maritimes to become a United Church minister. In gloom, he continued to work on the Blake manuscript. Frye's prospects suddenly brightened, however, when his friend Roy Daniells quit his job in July for a position at the University of Manitoba. The administration had little choice but to hire Frye. In order to discuss the job, Chancellor Wallace suggested that Frye canoe down to his own summer home on Go Home Bay. Frye demurred, suggesting the less hazardous option of taking the train to Toronto and meeting him at Vic. Replacing Daniells who had quit with a recently raised $2,400 salary, Frye was taken on as a "special lecturer" at a salary of just $1,600 "less 5% cut," an obligatory sacrifice to remind staff of the Depression. Because the Board clearly defined his position as a one-year job, they were expecting him to return to Oxford.

Although it was only a tiny opening to a brighter future, Frye and Helen seized the opportunity to get married. Frye surprised his close friend Art Cragg with a request to officiate at a ceremony in the Emmanuel College chapel on Aug. 24. For the Kemps, who had accepted Frye as a *de facto* son-in-law for years, there was little overt excitement or even willingness to come down from the cottage. Mrs. Kemp grumbled genially that the city, after all, was hot and somewhat disagreeable in August. A snapshot of the two taken on the steps of Emmanuel College after the ceremony shows a still very young couple, a bit disoriented in the glare of the morning sun, gazing neither at each other nor at the camera. Frye had his usual flaring thatch of yellow hair. His suit was so lightweight and tight, it exaggerated his thin boyish torso. After the short ceremony, the party went out by streetcar to the Guild of All Arts on the eastern outskirts of Toronto for a wedding "breakfast." From Moncton, Cassie expressed mild surprise at the suddenness of the wedding and the fact there was no formal announcement. The couple headed up to Gordon Bay until the term began. Helen later jokingly insisted that Frye spent their honeymoon furiously working on Blake. Frye confirmed this in all seriousness in a letter to Pelham Edgar in which he confessed he tried to put his unruly project to rest that summer. It took rejection slips from two publishers to make him realize that he "had a lot of growing to do."

In the fall, the Fryes set themselves up in a basement apartment in St. Thomas Apartments just around the corner from Victoria College. Because they had little money to spend on furniture, Helen painted some fruit crates in vibrant colours to fill up space. Until she was invited in, the Fryes were regarded with suspicion by an elderly neighbor. Oddly enough, it was the crates which stilled her doubts. Amiably retreating, she pronounced, "Well, I think you're real arty."

As he headed into the school year, Frye was, for the first time in years, exuberant. He felt that somehow he'd now shed the sour chrysalis of all his past and could now begin life on his own terms. Everything seemed resolved. He had the job he wanted and the wife he wanted. He wondered, "What was everything else about?" The problem, of course, was that he only had one year. After sampling security, Frye would have to unroot himself again and go back to the hated Oxford. The Fryes nevertheless settled into a genial round of parties largely centred on the core of voluntary staff of *Canadian Forum*, which now included Helen as contributing editor, then art editor. The young editor of the *Forum*, Eleanor Godfrey, lived with her parents and sister Ray just around the corner at 78 St. Mary's St. on Frye's short block-long route to Vic. For Ray Godfrey, Frye's tilting, forward posture and his flaming blond hair were crucial to understanding his character. Mrs. Godfrey used to call out, "There goes Norrie, I can see the halo." The Godfrey family constituted a salon of left-wing, often Catholic, intellectuals. For their frequent parties the Godfreys managed to attract a core of the arts-oriented intelligentsia of Toronto which included novelist Morley Callaghan, artist Pegi Nichol and feature writer Mary Lowrey Ross and, of course, the Fryes. Frye conveyed such a sense of gaiety about their partying that Cassie mentioned it to Donald Howard with a hint of ruefulness.

Despite Frye's submersion in arcane literary material at Oxford, he seemed more interested in talking to friends like George Johnston about recent Charlie Chaplin movies than *Beowulf*. In *The Canadian Forum*, in fact, he ranked Charlie Chaplin and Walt Disney as the "two authentic geniuses" of Hollywood: "... it is obvious in their pictures how close we are to ballet and pantomime techniques, and how nearly the music comes to organizing every movement of the dramatic action." It would appear too that he considered himself enough an expert on modern fiction to give an armchair talk in February before a meeting of the University of Toronto Press Club on the "technical trends of modern writing."

Although the club executive requested "a complete turnout of members," there was no explanation for why the club considered Frye an expert. Frye nevertheless expostulated like a *wunderkind* who'd already cranked out a dozen *Tobacco Road* classics. "If you ain't got that swing," he warned, "then you needn't try to write." His advice was that every writer "should find his speed" and look for simplicity and "a certain quality... termed 'guts.'" An inevitable corollary of his own use of slang was that the American language possessed "more scope, more elasticity than the staid language of England," and that beginning authors should take advantage of the genius of the vernacular. Improbably Frye also suggested that newspaper and magazine writing served as an excellent training for the beginning author with columns and criticism as appropriate starting points. Obviously Frye was already toying with the notion of criticism as a First Cause of literary expression. By pointing to

Joyce as an author who has progressed from beginner status to "master rank," he rather considerably damaged his argument. Considering Frye's later championing of the comedic and romantic force in literature and society, it's interesting that he still saw satire as "the coming form of literary expression." He saw that in contemporary satire there was evidence of a "growing American moral consciousness" analogous to Mexican mural painting.

Frye's determined pop cult stance was odd in light of his future development but his Oxford year obviously instigated a Spenglerian feeling that the arts in Britain, Germany and Italy were "in midst of a creative reaction." This realization must have depressed him as he looked ahead to the fall when he had to return to Europe. The administration now sealed his fate by re-awarding him the Trick Travelling Fellowship. At a March 24 meeting of the board, Frye was provided a skimpy $750.

Soon after his appearance at the Press Club, Frye published a story in *Acta*, "Face to Face" which applied his advice-to-young-writers formula. Written in grating slang ("some niggers had told him"), it was, in fact, a satire which ridiculed the all-absorbing Thomist philosophy, then popular among Catholic intellectuals, which seemed to reduce everything to a Beckettian wasteland of greyness. "Grey was the synthesis that contained them both, the stability which stopped all conflicts. God was the supreme greyness, you see." Frye cast the story like a Conrad tale with two salts reminiscing over cigars about the discovery of a South Sea Island where the natives "got rid of all their taboos and superstitions ... They had no idols, no myths I ever heard of, no personal God and no remembrance of a prophet ... They frowned at things in deep shadows and bright lights, and smiled at things that were halfway between ... You see, these people were entirely colour-blind." Venting hostility over depersonalized, bureaucratized faith, Frye injected an extreme Swiftean touch which parodied his own critical concerns: "After I'd been there a while, I began to realize that everything that ails our civilization today is, essentially, colour. Our philosophy, our science, our art, our mortality, all ought to be held together by the living faith of religion. But they aren't, because there's no general principle in our religion to connect them that isn't confused, approximate and badly defined. Not only have we no such general principle, but we haven't even a word for it in our language, our language being as confused as our thinking, and we haven't got it in our language because we haven't got it in our eyesight. We can't *see* that everything is grey, therefore our religion is literally not common sense, therefore everything we try to base on our religion is insane. Oh, if we could only root colour out of our eyes!—or out of our children's eyes—we'd remember ... I thought I was pretty superior too, at first, looking at their images of God—patches of what was only yellowish-brown or blue-green to me. But when I saw the reality and clarity of their vision ... I fought hard to unthink the whole idea of colour—to make myself realize that it was *low* on the evolutionary scale—low and savage compared to their power of seeing grey."

Under the pseudonym, Richard Poor, unwillingly thrust upon him by Eleanor Godfrey, Frye tried fiction again in the June issue of *The Canadian Forum* with "Fable ... In the Nineteenth Century Idiom." A quasi-Biblical tale with allegorical spirits raised by "a daimon" to tempt an innocent young author with the kingdom of literary fame, the short effort is a heavily allegorized joke directed at Frye's own search for a formula of success in writing.

Despite this dabbling in idea-fiction, Frye also kept alive his academic side by trying out a couple of his essays for Blunden on the Graduate English Club. His essay on Chaucer's *Troilus and Cressida* impressed Margaret Roseborough as an intensely Freudian reading. She remembered his attention to the fertilizing rains associated with lovemaking and his own line that "all night it rained." Norman Endicott was so incensed by Frye's paper that he accosted Roseborough afterwards and demanded to know why she hadn't asked certain pointed questions, apparently incapable of it himself.

At the end of term in early May, Frye waded through 107 of his own students' exams and for the first time, suffered penance as an "examiner," an exam monitor, earning the princely sum of $3 a day. In July and early August, after a period up at the cottage, he taught a teacher's course covering the entire 19th century from Romantics to Victorians in six weeks. He lectured for a punishing two hours a day for $480 but the income was crucial for his Oxford year.

In mid-August he landed a critical plum, reviewing the annual art exhibit, which that year featured surrealism, at the Canadian National Exhibition for *The Canadian Forum*. Barely three years after the first surrealist exhibit in London, its excesses were laid before the eyes of the staid denizens of Toronto. Enjoying the role of curmudgeon, Frye used the show primarily to comment on the role of art in a cycle of decadence, war and rebirth. Surrealism through its own evolution could be a redeemer of a dying civilization. André Breton, in fact, had called just three years before for "the building of a new world ... whose evolution opens an unlimited field to human hope."

Frye first outlined three distinct stages of surrealism, the first related to the disaster of the Great War and the second and third to the injection of Freudian, Jungian and anthropological theories into the practice of surrealist painting. The first was mimetic: " ... art in so incoherent a world as ours can only be an art stuck together from odds and ends." In the second stage Dadaists drew on more primitive substance, summoning "the authentic dream image from their midriffs," inheriting "the whole tradition of sadism and the 'romantic agony' of the nineteenth century ... an All Hallows Eve of demoniac horror and obscenity."

In outlining the evolution of a third, constructive stage, Frye revealed for the first time his fundamental allegiance to the notion of a universal and thoroughly hygienic symbolic language. "Painters began to realize that the subconscious speaks a universal and intelligible language, a language of symbols no doubt, but a language from which all existing languages, all myths of all religions, and all the effective imagery of art, are derived. So the destructive anarchism of the Dadaists passes into the synthetic movement of surrealism." This evolution inextricably connoted high purpose, separating false satire from the genuine: "Café intellectualism, pseudo-cultured giggles at bourgeois stupidity, arty remoteness from life, the painting of critical clichés rather than pictures—all these defects of modern art must join the dodo before the ferocious brutality now given carte blanche over most of the world."

Just before going overseas, Helen and Frye once again retreated up to the Kemp cottage, where he suffered a massive debilitating attack of hay fever. As a child he had suffered asthma attacks which his sister Vera had suspected were tripped off by a reaction to his astrakhan coat. Although this would indicate susceptibility to any respiratory allergy, Frye had never before suffered a hay fever reaction, even in the pollen nightmare zone of southern Ontario. Just as he was preparing to leave Helen and Toronto, Frye saw psychosomatic significance in its sudden violent appearance. Frye would continue to suffer hay fever every year thereafter. As soon as he could afford it, he tried to be away from Ontario in the late summer. New drugs in the sixties alleviated the worst effects but it remained a serious problem which adversely affected his work.

## OXFORD

Not surprisingly, Frye was depressed when he set off on the *Empress of Britain*. The food on ship was bad and he had an asthma attack the first night. His ship companions were a little less eccentric this time and Frye got off easy with lectures over breakfast by an amiable Briton who preached the virtues of a bran diet. Over the radio, he heard Chamberlain's ominous pre-Munich speech. While the other passengers seemed "worried, depressed and anxious," he noted "absolutely no smash-the-buggers feeling" and a curious indifference to war itself. He himself seemed to furiously dismiss everything with the basic conspiratorial theory of his age group: "... the violent murder of millions of innocent people to support a stupid blunderer against a bullying lunatic so that a few millionaires can become multi-millionaires doesn't strike me as a moral issue." In a calmer afterthought, he wondered "if war comes, will it be a Marxist or a Spenglerian one?"

As the boat entered the channel, Frye had to confess that war was all around him and even viewed the four-power capitalist pact as possibly "the beginning of a transition from national to international Fascism." At Cherbourg, the steward told him there wasn't much to see when in fact there wasn't much else to see— submarines, massive offshore sea barricades with turrets and anti- aircraft placements in the coastal rocks. At Southampton, the defence forces were practising in the night sky with searchlights, training seven different beams on a single white plane. In London, Frye stayed the first night at a Russell Square hotel, rising the next morning to Chamberlain's empty "peace in our time" declaration. Frye noticed that no one was fooled. The mood was gloomy and despondent and war preparations continued as before. Several subway stations were closed for "structural alterations" and the parks were being dug up for trenches. He considered that the preparations might delay war at best for six months to a year. Because of recurrent rumors that the universities might be closed, he wondered "if they'd close down for any other reason, not involv- ing so much murder?"

When he got up to Oxford he settled into a flat on Polstead Rd. with Rodney Baine and Mike Joseph. Though having to endure a fussy landlady improbably called Mrs. Grylls, the three men settled down to a typical student bachelor life based on stretches of serious study tempered by Frye and Joseph with heavy ale consumption in the nearby Gardiner's Arms. Joseph joked that they suffered alcoholic constipation and couldn't pass a pub without going in. To Charles Bell who'd set up a flat with Mildred Winfree, they represented the modest hazard of underfed and lonely compatriots. Not long after his reunion with them, Bell had the misfortune of being intercepted in the company of a bundle of freshly-bought honeydew melon and cheese by Frye and Baine. Given their ravenous curiosity over his purchases, Bell could hardly escape inviting them over to lunch.

Subsequently the Bell-Winfree household became a *salon* which offered Frye an outlet for company and musical interests. Mildred, who was in the Bach choir, even managed to convince Frye to buy a recorder to fit into the prevailing fad for medieval music. A rare photo of Frye at Oxford shows him playing the piano at the Bells' thin and correct and lonely. It was Mildred particularly who noticed his loneliness and he quietly admitted to her once that his separation from Helen was agonizing. She was both touched and a little amazed at this because she had never seen such devotion in a man.

Blunden seemed pleased to see Frye again and reported that he had been a big hit with Geoffrey Keynes. This astonished Frye because his impression was altogether different. Blunden however ruined the accommodating mood by expressing his admiration of the amount of work some people get done. Hitler, he thought, was a good example. To Helen, Frye wrily reported "the year is going to have its difficulties." Both Blunden and Bryson were eager to push him into preparing for his examinations. Blunden particularly urged Frye to suspend his Blake project. Although initially Frye frittered away much time talking at the Polstead flat, the pressure of work ultimately sent him to his books.

For Helen he ran down to London to review an exhibit of Canadian art at the Tate Gallery. In his letter home, he confessed that it was a generally mediocre show. In the face of the tepid British response, though, he became surprisingly defensive. "There is life and buoyancy in Canadian painting, of a kind not often found outside France, and fading there, a pleasure in bright colour and adventurous outline for its own sake." Once more he posited his extreme view of cultural death in Europe and the role of the creative artist in the coming Armageddon. The survival of art itself would depend "on whether the cause which nearly every genuine artist there is supporting wins or not. If that cause is defeated, Canada will be one of the few pockets of creative activity left."

In London, he looked up Alan Jarvis at University College who'd toured Europe with Douglas Duncan and brought back a catalogue of approved Nazi art: "Mostly portraits of Nazi gangsters, senti- mental evening-on-the-farm pictures intended to illustrate the romance and dignity of the peasantry ... " The catalogue instigated a central observation in his review: "... however bad Naziism may be it cannot be so bad as it is painted." A month later, Frye and Joseph again went down to London to experience a powerful antidote, Picasso's *Guernica*, "the best contemporary work, I've ever seen."

Despite his hard work at Oxford, Frye conveyed little enthusiasm for what he was doing. He complained that the year away had
an unfortunate effect on his writing style and he seemed to have
few good ideas for papers. He was once more dismayed at the poor
lecturing. Nichol Smith was "prolix and dull." Tolkien on *Beowulf*
reminded Frye of his own worst lecturing: "... top speed, unintelli-
gible burble, great complexity of ideas and endless references to
things unknown, mixed in with a lot of Latin and Anglo-Saxon and
a lot of difficult proper names which aren't spelled ..."

The one project which buoyed him was a paper for the Bodley
Club based on ideas set off by a reading in Toronto of Daniel
Defoe's obscure *A Short History of the Devil* which Frye had seen
as a possible influence on Blake. What interested Frye was the
way society threw up huge conspiratorial theories focussed on
putative bogeymen like Jesuits or Jews. Although it took in the
complete range of European history, it had manifest relevance in
an age of Nazis. Frye read it on the last night of term in early
December at breakneck speed because of time-restrictions. He
found most of the Bodley Club members sozzled, but despite
this double hazard, the paper seemed to go over, the audience
surprisingly attentive.

He immediately headed down to London and, stopping at the
Burnetts, had a conversation with a Jewish refugee who had been
incarcerated in Germany and beaten every day by a storm trooper.
Frye got a good sense of their particular brand of humour. "They
asked each day if he were a Communist, and if he said no (he isn't
one) they beat him for lying, if he said yes they beat him for
admitting it, if he said he didn't know they him beat for impudence
and if he didn't answer they beat him for sulkiness." A Jewish
ballet dancer and actress also at the Burnetts escaped beatings but
found she couldn't leave the Thousand Year Reich without an
exceptionally stupid panel of interrogators collecting information
about her "the size of the Oxford Dictionary." One of their more
discerning questions was whether "Ophelia," referring to her role
in a Hamlet production, was a code word.

As they had planned at the beginning of the term, Frye, Baine
and Joseph set off for Paris for the month-long Christmas holiday.

Although Frye laid out plans to attack the Louvre and tour the cathedral towns, the trip was essentially pragmatic. Frye had to stretch every dollar and Paris had the advantage of being close and "incredibly cheap." They stopped in Rouen for a couple of days to see the cathedral and St.-Ouen, noting that the trip was probably going to be diminished by the French caution in packing cathedral glass away during *le moment critique*.

Frye's Left Bank hotel, the Jeanne d'Arc on the Rue de Buci, was so undistinguished that he failed to mention it once to Helen. He settled into a typical, cheap Parisian life, visiting crucial museums and whiling the nights away in cafés such as the Dome. As unattached students, they were inevitably prey to Left Bank pimps and whores. Just after Frye had defended his long blond hair to Joseph and Baine, an ugly tart came over and ran her fingers lovingly through it, suggesting that he should meet her later at the Café des Sports for a private "little trifle." For days after, Joseph and Baine twigged Frye everytime they came near the café. Frye reported it in a letter to Helen and just when she received it, she happened to bump into Chancellor Wallace who asked how Frye was getting along. To the dismay of Wallace whose world view barely acknowledged Paris let alone whores, Helen blurted out the story. Nevertheless, in Paris Frye's hair did continue to have its effect. An awed but polite Parisian man came up and asked, "Ees it real or artificiel, monsieur?" Frye countered any objections by claiming it was a permissible form of exhibitionism, acknowledging that while some people laughed at it, they nevertheless looked.

Unlike the Italian trip of 1937, it seemed to be Joseph who was most energetic in forcing Frye out of his room to tour museums or see movies which included a French version of Disney's *Snow White*. Frye put up with it but seemed to enjoy burying himself in the ten copies of *The New Yorker* he brought along. He did little serious work of any kind. Just before Christmas, Joseph and Frye went out to see a snow-covered Chartres on what turned out to be the coldest day in 60 years. Since the temperature was about 0°F, there was no chance of lingering on the gargoyles outside and Frye spent much of his time hovering around the only warm register inside the northern transept. His thoughts moved inexorably to

Helen. He decided that he had no possible chance for happiness unless she happened to be there and decided that they must see Europe together or at the very least, New York City, if they couldn't afford the former.

If Chartres offered physical agony, it was the overpowering labyrinth of Versailles which stunned him with revulsion: "The Doge's Palace at Venice was perhaps bloodier, but lustier ... [but at Versailles] ... when you get in the dead centre of all the algebra and sit down there the sheer monstrosity of the scheme *does* get you, all right, like Hitler's voice." To offset the numbing algebra, there was St. Denis with its "lovely 12th century glass, with a light blue you don't see much of at Chartres." He was now so fascinated with the medieval image, in fact, he gave both Joseph and Baine a copy of Mâle's book on cathedrals.

On New Year's Eve, Frye and Joseph went to a Montparnasse café and stayed until six in the morning drinking heavily. Because he had barely eaten all day, the alcohol had a particularly potent effect. Although he remained fully conscious he found himself shouting obscenities about Chamberlain. Frye was doing a lot of drinking all year and the cheapness of Parisian cafés wasn't helping his sobriety. He later confessed to Helen: "I've drunk more this last year than I ever expect to do in the next ten years: if I'm ever separated from you again, which God forbid, I shall become a sot."

Before leaving Paris, Frye and Joseph took one more excursion to Bauvais, Amiens and Chantilly. As usual, they visited cathedrals but Frye also tried to touch base with his family's central tragedy in Amiens by attempting to track down the grave of his brother. With no information about the labyrinthine cemeteries, he of course failed, noting to Helen that the grave would be in any case just a cross, since whatever hit Howard would have done the burying.

Amiens was also the home of the great "messianic, prophetic cathedral," heralded by Mâle and Ruskin. It was here that Frye encountered a radiant amalgam of the medieval motifs, the wheel of fortune, the rose window and the Last Judgment—the latter in an elaborate archway bas-relief—which would haunt his own later criticism. In the wheel of fate which bordered the rose window on

the outside, a king with crown and sceptre stood at the twelve
o'clock position with figures rising towards him and then falling
away into decline and deterioration in a clockwise motion.
Although the juxtaposition of the wheel with the rose window is
suggestive, the two weren't necessarily intended to be conceptually
combined. At Notre Dame de Mantes, however, the wheel of
fate, the mandala of Christ *and* the Last Judgment are integrated.
Twelve events of the Judgment are positioned like clock numbers
around the focal point of Christ and his adoring angels. The mouth
of hell is on the exact horizon at three o'clock, the nadir at six, held
by Archangel Michael, the resurrection at the horizon at nine and
the bosom of Abraham at twelve. Although Frye did not see Mantes, synthesizing forms was a natural impulse and his own story
wheel, implied in "The Archetypes of Literature" and outlined in
*Anatomy of Criticism* was similar to Mantes.

When he got back to Paris, he wrote Chancellor Wallace: "There
is something about the enormous completeness and relevance of
the medieval achievement that is overpowering when one sees it
in the plastic arts, however little one may be affected by its philosophy or literature. The Protestant is, I suppose, committed to iconoclasm but when he sees the icon in front of him in all its splendour
he can realize the sacrifice he has made."

## OXFORD AND ITALY 1939

Frye's return to London elicited the simple comment "ugh!" After
a month of Paris and northern France, he had to make jest of his
continued disappointment with Britain. His first meal of steak,
kidney and mushroom pudding "came to a little over two tons—
sorry, I meant two shillings." He popped into St. Paul's but had to
flee under duress because of a "theological speculation" engendered by the tomb of Major-General Mountstuart Elphinstone
"who was somebody big in Bombay." "Speculation: when the last
trumpet shall sound ... will the mouldering skeleton in the tomb

get up and start adjusting its skull, or will the marble statue arise gracefully to heaven ... ?"

Ironically it wasn't Oxford (or England) which beleaguered him so much as the fearful procrastinations of the Victoria College administration about confirming his position for September. Blunden, in fact, was most sensitive to Frye's plight and drew attention to job openings. Two lecturing positions, one in northeastern Romania, in the path of the coming war, and one in Hyderabad, India, were obviously out of the question. There was also the possibility of a fellowship at All Soul's. But Frye wanted to return to Victoria and fumed about the seeming indifference of the Vic administrators. The bursar was delaying his payments. As his worry grew, Frye even suspected that the administration might so much prefer his own replacement, Henry Noyes, they would be willing to write off the money invested in him since he was an undergrad. Once more, the transoceanic mail exacted its toll. Letters were delayed and noncommittal.

Frye had written Wallace in mid-January scorning Blunden's hope that he'd win a first. Once more angrily denouncing the exam system, he proclaimed his future: " ... now that I have discovered that I can make a fairly good teacher I have something tangible to work for." Although this expressed hope and determination, it was hardly an insistent demand that Wallace confirm his job. In answering Frye, Wallace made an observation, which could be read as a veiled criticism of Frye: "... scholarship in a University such as ours, falls short of its full achievement unless the scholar is also a good teacher." Frye's worry blossomed into paranoid fury as he again suspected that Henry Noyes was going to get the job. He felt no comfort in recalling Roy Daniells's warning that Vic's "brass hats" couldn't be trusted. Besides joining the Chinese Army, he said, his only reasonable fall-back position was to become Helen's housekeeper and help out with a baby.

When Helen chastised him for his suspicions, he apologized but noted that Vic had no trouble coming through in 1937. Since the Board of Regents tended to rubber-stamp administration decisions, Frye was not being unreasonably impatient. He was already itchy to get teaching and pictured himself only half-jokingly as a young academic rebel who was going "to make things hum in that hick town of ours": "My lectures next year will be twenty-five times as good as they were last year, and I can lecture on anything from *Beowulf* to Beverley Nichols at a moment's notice ... And then, when I hit a PMLA conference they'll think it's an air raid, or the Martians." At the same time, the delay in confirming his appointment, which lasted well into May, exacted its toll. Frye was once again pondering the *deus ex machina* of a lucrative novel. This would not provide financial freedom, it would permit him, he claimed, to be the satirist who could use his skills in defence of social reform. "I've got the stuff of an unusually good writer in me, and the sooner I get established as one the sooner I can start defending people ... I know how to make fools of people, and I don't want to be absolutely dependent on a sycophantic college ... "

Despite the anxieties, eventually ameliorated by an encouraging letter from Robins and the decision of Henry Noyes to take a job in Manitoba, Frye was determined to bring Helen over to see Italy and possibly Germany. He wanted Mike Joseph to go along but Joseph had been so disgusted with the Italian rape of Albania, he wanted to travel entirely in France. Helen moreover was so wary about war scares that Frye had to implore her to be more decisive: " ... there isn't any danger of war unless somebody loses their head and blunders into it." He felt that the cynical politicians and armament manufacturers on each side would prefer self-preservation to immolation. He was personally incredulous that a war could ever start over an anti-Semitic dictatorship like Poland.

For Blunden, he worked on papers on King Lear and another complicated one on the history of language. Blunden as usual managed to do everything wrong. Although he never seemed to remember what Frye was saying, he claimed to immensely enjoy just hearing Frye talk. He even suggested that Frye might prepare a table-talk book of his commentary on literature. He made a curious gesture by giving Frye a Latin translation of *Hyperion* with the apparent underlying suggestion that reading some Latin would do him some good.

Frye found his stock rise with Blunden and generally among the Merton staff when he became involved with a production of the

Floats, the Merton dramatic society which had been banned the first year he was there because of administrative disapproval. The play was an adaption of a Conan Doyle story about a professor, played by Frye, interested in mesmerism. When the professor works on a student in front of an audience, "they exchange souls." When they go home to the professor's home, everything gets extremely confused when the student and professor's daughter exchange souls. Blunden's wife played the professor's wife and Blunden himself was so excited by Frye's performance that Frye figured that if he could just learn cricket, he would be a hero.

Between June 8 and 12, Frye wrote the last exams he would ever face and as he expected, they were as intimidating, infuriating and sickening as ever. When it came time for the oral exam, the viva, he was called in with a collection of classmates. Each was alphabetically joined with another student and assigned a time for a 15-minute examination. When they came to Frye's name there was an ominous pause and instead of his being teamed with another and given just a 15-minute slot, he was asked to be ready for purgatory from 11:20 to noon. Badly shaken, Frye headed for the library to bone up on Dryden. He failed to write a question on Dryden and suspected that the examiners were sure to probe this weakness. Understanding the futility of this strategy, Jack Mason tracked him down and jerked his thumb to indicate that he should follow him. Mason took Frye to the Bear, a nearby pub which had just opened. Frye downed a double scotch, and promptly felt better. By the time he had to get to the examination, he had downed another double scotch and sailed through the inquisition. As it turned out, the examiners were just a bit leery about an apparent paraphrase of a Middle English passage on one of Frye's exams and requested a literal rendering. He quickly responded to that and a few other minor points and he was dismissed in only about 15 minutes. It's probable that since Frye was a solid candidate for a first, the examiners wanted to be sure of his competence.

Finally at a Board of Regents meeting on June 20, Victoria College made Frye a member of the permanent staff. Chancellor Wallace's confirming letter didn't catch up with Frye until London when he and Helen were already on their way to Italy. He answered it in Paris and affirmed truthfully but coolly that he considered himself so cognizant of the "religious and historical traditions of the college" that he "would rather work there than anywhere else." About his trip to northern Italy, he was more exuberant and suggested that despite the late return date, he would be able to prepare his courses without problems.

The plan for attacking Italy was simply to cover the territory of 1937 without Rome. Frye originally pondered a Paris, Florence, Pisa, Siena, Ravenna, Vienna and Munich route, with priority to those places in Tuscany which he and Joseph had rushed through to get to Rome. From Paris the Fryes headed to Florence to wait up for Mike Joseph. They were sitting at a restaurant eating ice cream when Joseph unexpectedly arrived, plunked himself down and said, "You got a first, you rat." Despite this initial bit of good news, there was little to sustain it in the shadows of war. Nearly all Italians dreaded the Nazi warmongering. They were sour and sometimes openly hostile to foreigners. With his blond teutonic hair, Frye was spat at in Ravenna. Since he had been consistently taken for a German in 1937, Frye interpreted this as a healthy indication of anti-German feeling. When busloads of vacationing Hitler Youth bawling the Horst Wessel song out of the windows passed in the streets, Frye noticed that the Italians openly glared with hatred.

Italian-style Fascism was itself omnipresent: when they travelled up to the isolation of San Gimignano, they discovered that, although it had been designated a national monument, it had been befouled with the absurd stencilled homilies and exhortations of Mussolini: "The olive tree has gentle and soft leaves, but its wood is harsh and rough"; "War is to man what maternity is to a woman"; "The best way to preserve peace is to prepare for war."

Inevitably, they made it to Venice where Frye again complained of the vapidity, the commercialism, the cheating, the bad food, the "caterwauling" gondoliers. Frye relished the old clichés, the "deathless joke" of an American tourist that Venice was the place where every house sits on its piles. When they left Venice for Padua, the railroad station was draped in swastika banners to welcome a Nazi chieftain and they read with great amusement that the gondoliers met him on his arrival. Frye imagined their welcome: " 'You wan' guide? You wan' pos' card? You wan' feelthy peecture?' Sure he wants them. He wants everything he can get."

Throughout this trip and the earlier 1937 expedition, Joseph had been an invaluable companion because of his knowledge of Italian and French. He translated the newspapers and had an intelligence officer's curiosity about the current war scares. In Venice, he talked to a Canadian reporter claiming that Hitler was expected to march on Sept. 1. When they ended the trip in Paris, however, Joseph started talking with unflappable unconcern to a couple of fellow New Zealanders about a suicidally preposterous auto trip about Sept. 1 through east France to the German border, up to Danzig, down through Poland into the Balkan states, around to Vienna, and back to Paris. When the Fryes headed off from Southampton on the *Empress of Britain* on Aug. 12, they were acutely anxious about Joseph, a fear that was not alleviated by their arriving in Montreal on Aug. 23 — the day of the signing of the Hitler-Stalin pact. Of course, a week later the war had started with the lunatic New Zealanders near the German border.

**WAR GOVERNED THE NATIONS**

Back in Toronto, the Fryes rented a walk-up apartment near the corner of Bathurst and St. Clair, a half-hour walk down to the campus. They furnished it simply with pieces made by Helen's father who was then out of work and eager to keep busy. Although their apartment was in a bland section of the city, Frye often walked to the campus through a wealthy district on top of the St. Clair St. escarpment overlooking the downtown and the cool blue lake beyond, a section famous for Sir Henry Pellatt's fantasy castle, Casa Loma. Frye charitably described it in an essay years later as half "bastard French Renaissance" and half "bastard Spanish Renaissance, like Siamese twins born out of wedlock."

Although he established a basic routine, there was now no

obvious chance of "the long-hoped-for year" of Frye's Christmas dreams. The war presented immediate practical problems. His colleague, Joe Fisher, signed up the first day of hostilities and his courses had to be apportioned. Frye took Fisher's 18th century course, about which he was neither prepared nor particularly knowledgeable. For honors students Frye had to cover Milton and Spenser, 17th century prose including Walton and Browne and 19th century prose including Arnold and Newman. He had of course boned up at Oxford, but it was a scramble to keep up. Later in the term, Cassie reported that he "is another one whose duties crowd on him—worries him because he cannot get enough done in his time. He ended off once saying 'and the books I should be reading look reproachfully from the table.' "

The major worry, of course, was the war itself. On campus, there were efforts to soft-pedal its importance. The first issue of *The Varsity* projected a quote of President Cody into a banner headline: "CONTINUE YOUR STUDIES." Many of Frye's friends scorned "the Bore war" which could only degenerate into a blood bath in which elderly politicians and arms manufacturers would butcher another generation of young men. The Fryes had an early indication of another reality when his Oxford classmate, Jack Mason, wrote: "If the business goes any length of time there will not be a whole man left in this bloody continent ...." Along with the appalling death rate, Mason reported the intellectual gloom created by the closed theatres and art galleries.

To their relief, the Fryes also received a letter from the unflappable Joseph who claimed to have sabotaged his zany East European auto expedition by insisting on going into every museum and cathedral on the way to the German border. His strategy stopped the trip just short of the border. Joseph then joined the British artillery, eventually helping to pulverize the Nazis in the Lowlands.

Frye, however, continued to be ambivalent about the war. Although he received automatic dispensation as a clergyman, he felt it immoral to accept such protection. At the same time, he was utterly baffled how, with his clumsiness and incompetence in practical matters, he could ever be a soldier. At best, he would just get in the way and probably end up dead like his brother Howard.

Obviously there was no point in making a brave public gesture along the lines of Karl Barth who did border duty as a Swiss private. One of his friends who became a major in military intelligence later insisted that Frye, safe in a bunker or institute somewhere, would have been superb in analyzing the enemy's codes or strategy but the suggestion was never made. Even Cassie, who had been so traumatized by Howard's death, was curiously noncommittal. She was herself deeply aware of the German and Japanese menace and her own attitude about Frye's joining up didn't seem coloured at all by the family tragedy in 1918.

It is astonishing how well Frye kept hidden his dual anxiety about the war—especially during the dark days of the great Nazi victories of 1940 through to 1942—and his writing, from his students. He presented the persona of a man confidently absorbed in his academic responsibilities. Vic students were from farms or small towns and cities. Seeming to possess a bottomless cultural ignorance, they were not prone to making challenges in class. To these students Frye was alternately baffling and exhilarating. He appeared dogmatic and epigrammatic in his lecturing style, pronouncing, for example, that there were just two choices for an epic. The class—mostly girls—would take the information down slavishly but often grouse among themselves about his ideas. Some even insisted that since he lectured without notes, they were not receiving properly prepared lectures. Yet when a student from 1939, Phyllis Thompson, who would become an English professor in Chicago, reviewed her notes four and a half decades later, she was amazed how clearly they anticipated his later critical formulations. To her, the epigrammatic lecturing style matched Frye's appearance of angelic messenger, with his mound of white-blond hair and delicate, slightly prim, face.

As a lecturer, he did in fact present an idiosyncratic presence in his classes. He was punctual, turning up just as a class was settled. He almost always spoke extemporaneously, bringing along only a primary text to read key passages. Sometimes this was an actual hindrance as he attempted to make books behave to his memory when he tried to find a passage. When he took on an American literature course in 1939-40, he had to write home to tell Cassie to send him his boyhood edition of *Huckleberry Finn* because the pages of his new text refused to turn at the right places. His short, often emotional, recitations of poetry, addressed from memory to a spot above the students' heads, contrasted with the dispassionate analysis. His ideas were delivered with a deep, flat, cool tone which masked the pervasive nervousness he felt in any social gathering. Locking his head, his eyes furtively slipped back and forth as if he were a little afraid of a disturbance breaking out in the classroom. His physical presence too was made disjointed and slightly awkward. Because he could be wobbly, he was never too adventurous or physically demonstrative. He often latched a hand onto the back of a chair and walked one step forward and one back, letting his hand go, then reapplying it. Many years later, Margaret Atwood joked that she was so intrigued by this action that she was tempted to examine the spot where he paced to see if there weren't some magical properties connected with it. He sometimes paced cautiously along the length of the blackboard where he drew huge diagrams and charts to illustrate complexes of symbols, the most famous being his "manic-depressive chart," the serpentine swiggle showing the rise and fall of the fortunes of the Jews in the Bible. Like an old Methodist circuit rider, he seemed totally indifferent to his physical environment and had no need for lectern or raised platform. There just had to be himself, a book and a body of students which could range anywhere from half a dozen to several hundred.

What absolutely distracted students, however, was his penchant for pausing for as much as two minutes and gloomily scanning the class to see if there were questions. His students assiduously kept their heads down towards their notebooks to avoid any sign of life which might indicate an auction bid. Embarrassed by this silence, bolder students made a policy of trying out *any* relevant question, just to relieve the tension. In the late sixties, one student became so concerned with his silences, he raised the question with one of Frye's colleagues, David Blostein. Blostein advised the student not to worry because Frye wrote his books in those silences. There was an element of truth in this. Frye considered each of his lectures so important as a genuine intellectual exercise, he deliberately courted spontaneity of ideas with improvisation. If he came up with an exciting idea or realization, he would write his notes out afterwards when he returned to his office and these would trickle into his writing. In his first year, he took over a section in a drama course for Pratt and in the course of talking about Jonson's *Every Man in his Humor* and *The Alchemist,* the long-pondered shape of comedy, which became a crucial element in all his later thinking, crystallized in his mind. When he was facing retirement nearly four decades later, he was almost plaintive in his lobbying to continue teaching because of this crucial link between his lectures and his writing. Kill one, he implied, and you kill the other.

In handling questions, Frye could sometimes prevaricate. He always responded quickly, but he could answer like a guru with riddles, epigrams or hermetic quotes which could throw an aggressive questioner off balance. He could be abrupt with those who were trying to be smart at the expense of either himself or the subject. If faced with a genuinely dull or befuddled student, however, he was incredibly gentle, trying to elicit and deal with the student's problem. What he most wanted to see in a class was intellectual seriousness, a willingness to be exposed to ideas outside the ordinary range of middle-class thinking. He believed that a student should be thoroughly rattled and upturned by university education, particularly in the freshman year. As a result, he tended to look a bit gloomy if a class' silence was persistent. When his own pauses elicited nothing, he would try out an elementary but key question in a dry, cautious voice, often finding that he had to answer it himself. There was a sadness in this, because it gave him the impression that he wasn't making even a basic imprint on the imaginations of his students.

Nothing could be farther from the truth. His effect, particularly on girls, was legendary. Christina McCall Newman confessed to virtual intellectual rape in her first classes with Frye in 1954: "... he came into a classroom one September afternoon wearing an academic gown that was rusty with age, stood behind the lecturer's podium, looked at us through his rimless glasses and began to speak about John Milton in a voice devoid of passion. By the time he'd finished speaking, 50 minutes later, almost everybody in the room was in the grip of an intellectual excitement we had never known, and that night I wrote in a Commonplace Book I was pretentiously keeping, 'I think my head is coming off.' " This Jovian omniscience, of course, belonged to a later period when Frye saturated himself year after year with primary texts. In 1939 he was really scrambling just to keep one step ahead of his students; he found it nearly impossible to read and deal with anything but required texts.

He did make a point, however, of nibbling whenever he could at two major works which deeply interested him, Joyce's *Finnegans Wake* and Dante's *Divine Comedy*. Despite his public interest and support for *Ulysses* over the censorship issue, Frye was really much more interested in *Finnegans Wake* which seemed to explore a similar territory as Blake's prophecies. He had looked over a copy which Mike Joseph had bought in Oxford when it first came out and his interest was renewed soon after the war started when Helen noticed the original edition for 89¢ at Eaton's College St. store. When Frye rushed over to buy it, the clerk confessed she thought it a bad bargain. Frye became so entranced with the form of the work, he considered writing a book on it after he finished the Blake study. What eventually blocked him was the sense he would have to deal too much with the disagreeable figure of Joyce himself who seemed to have cemented himself into his work.

His interest in Dante belonged inevitably to wider theoretical issues which, along with a deepening interest in Spenser, took him further from modern literature. *The Divine Comedy,* in fact, represented one of Frye's great reading priorities because he recognized how central Dante was to his theoretical concerns. Frye bought an Italian language edition in his first year teaching and started working his way carefully through *Inferno.* Here certainly was an elaborate and quite conscious intertwining of theory (of the four levels explicitly outlined in Dante's *Convivio*) and practice (the geographic shape of symbolism). Like the pattern of Blake's *Job* the "comedy" is a poet-led and utterly encyclopedic quest down into the deepest, icy rings of hell where the journey reverses itself, ending up in a high, supernal realm of love. Like Blake's visions, it explored every dimension and suggested a timeless, Christian resolution.

Once established in a real academic position, Frye was ironically prey to old ambitions to be a creative writer. In fact, his most noteworthy writing published that year consisted of two short stories, "Affable Angels" and "The Resurgent." Like his 1938 story, "Face to Face," they concealed serious philosophical and literary questions behind either vaudevillean dialogue or smirking intellectual ironies. There was now, however, a more serious edge. The stories, in a sense, were personal theatre which dramatized the confusions and simple hopes for art and life during war.

In "Affable Angel" published in *Acta* in January 1940, two Beckettian louts Harry and Augustus are walking down the West India Dock Road in London. While their language is full of un-English ain'ts, their concerns are cosmological. In fact, the very first word of the story is "gyroscope" which Harry quickly expands into the haunting imperative of Frye himself: "Universe is a big gyroscope. It spins and keeps its balance. Nobody knows how it does but it does." Then with Biblical suddenness, an angel appears. "His body gave out a soft glowing golden radiance, his huge wings were silver-tipped and his hair, which hung soft and thick over his shoulders, was a purplish-black." Augustus, who had been expecting some other kind of apparition in the Dickensian dockside, dismissed him as too sentimental. The angel is understandably deflated and confesses he had just wanted to join them for a beer, making himself visible by standing by a factory chimney. After downing an unseemly amount of beer, he stumbles and comments puckishly about "fallen angels." As he flies homewards, he intercepts a Nazi bomber over the Thames. Even with bombs nearly raining down on his head, Harry possesses the soft-headed idiocy of the pro-fascists Frye ran into at Oxford: "Not bad chaps, Nazis. I was in Munich last summer. Always givin' seats to women in trams." The bomber, however, suddenly crashes and "far up in the air came the sound of a whoop."

Published in the quiet of the phoney war, a full seven months before the Battle of Britain, this odd story combined both Frye's anxiety about the war with an almost child-like expectancy that Nazi evil was doomed by avenging, if somewhat beery, angels. Without much effort on their part, Harry and Augustus can assume a superstratum of helpful spirits who not only search *them* out but protect them.

Soon after, Frye published "The Resurgent," a much darker story, in the *The Canadian Forum*. Written as a serious parody of Balzac's "The Unknown Masterpiece," the story is narrated by Hortense, the humorless sister of a recently deceased artist. Her brother Andrew had been a disciple of an abstract artist called William Lomat. The fascistic Hortense scornfully summarizes Lomat's romantic image of the artist: "Of course the sky is blue and grass is green ... But the artist cannot respond to these data: his must be a devious, subtle, even deformed mind: he must twist what he sees out of shape to create his own patterns. The artist *qua* artist is a rebel, a revolutionary, and his genius is a disease which helps to cure the world homeopathically." With the fascist (or Stalinist) Resurgence, Lomat is exiled and his student Andrew Larrabin becomes a social realist, the genius of such works as "Hard Work, that sensitive study of the strength of horses, the unconscious nobility of the peasants and the dignity of honest labour." But Andrew is haunted by the spirit of Lomat. While he works "to design three large murals, depicting Wars Past, Wars Present and Wars Future," apparent insanity overcomes him. He fills a canvas full of meaningless lines, and confesses that "as long as the trance lasted I was sure that I was achieving a supreme symbol of something or other, exactly as our dreams seem so tremendous when we're asleep and so vapid when we wake up." He paints another canvas full of enormous rectangles, painted black and trimmed with red and yellow and called "Prison." Deliriously he hallucinates whiplashings and "sharp pains in the stomach, genitals and kidneys as though kicked with heavy boots." Just as he nearly finishes the War Future sketch and prepares to design a new flag, he utterly collapses.

Andrew now paints "Insanity": " ... I saw that I had covered a canvas with a network of lines, drawn in such a way that wherever one looked one's eye seemed to be on the point of getting some sort of unifying pattern, only to see it dissolve again in chaos. But no: that doesn't give the least idea of the picture's effect. It sent your eye frantically scurrying all over the canvas in search of that missing clue that would bring the whole scheme together: you got into a panic when you couldn't find it and would start over with the same result." The following day, Andrew is dead and his prissy sister destroys the canvas "out of respect for the memory of a great artist." Hortense sees his death as a tidy martyrdom which serves the needs of the state. Andrew died because he had fallen prey to the evil virus of Lomat's unacceptable imagination. His death therefore confirmed the dangers of wandering outside the boundaries of convention.

Although radically different in style and structure, both stories exhibit an anxiety about cosmological coherence. "Affable Angel" has the image of the gyroscope which refuses to give its meaning and "The Resurgent" the chaotically ordered canvas which gives a fleeting sense of meaning only to dissolve and destroy the artist. Both images, of course, were Frye's own nightmares as he struggled with an idea of total coherence within the seeming morass of Blake's prophecies.

Frye's last published story, "Prelude," was published a year later in *The Canadian Forum*. Compared with the intensity of his two previous *Forum* efforts, it was flimsy. The story retells the golden apple myth with an embarrassed but querulous Paris and three naked goddesses quibbling like self-conscious sophomores in a college revue over who is most beautiful or worthy. Paris makes the traditional mistake of accepting Venus's temptation of beauty over knowledge or power, even with the clear vision ahead of a ten-year inferno. Given innocence, Paris rejects easy grace and goes the route of complication and war. There's little sense to the story except that humans will eternally be human and jump off cliffs.

Despite the tentativeness and technical shakiness of the stories, they were an important process for Frye. When he considered the results disappointing, he consulted E.J. Pratt. Pratt, himself a late starter, simply advised Frye to establish his name in critical writing and return to fiction later if he wanted. There was nothing unorthodox about this, of course, since many major critics write fiction or poetry. It is undeniable too that the stories did show promise. While they suffered from excessive density and sophomoric self-consciousness, they showed the kind of conceptual interest that was the trademark of mythic puzzle writers like Jorge Luis Borges, Umberto Eco or Italo Calvino. Interestingly both Eco and Calvino later showed interest in Frye's critical work. Frye acknowledged later in life that he suffered partly from the lack of a model that Borges's work, then quite obscure, would have provided. He later strongly endorsed inclusion of a favorite story by Borges, "The Gospel According to Mark," in a college anthology. Borges's absorption in re-creating the patterns and labyrinths of former literature as well as his overt Christian interests, were in fact ideally suited to Frye's interests. But the ambivalence over "creativity," of criticism vs. "real" creative writing continued to be a source of doubt. Frye's later obstinate equation of criticism and fiction and poetry, which few ever accepted, obviously lay in this unresolved tension.

After the school year, the Fryes went up to the Kemp cottage and gloomily listened to the war situation on a neighbour's radio. They heard Churchill's speeches which attempted to boost the morale of the British when France fell in mid-June. In reaction to his depression over the situation in Europe, Frye wrote one of his most impassioned polemics for the August issue of the *Forum*, "War on the Cultural Front." Gone was the self-conscious Shavian growling of his earlier opinion pieces. Now there was the weight of prophetic conviction.

He approached the question of democracy at war as he would a fundamental literary concern, on the level of terminology: what *was* democracy, he asked. He claimed that it really comprised first and foremost a cultural rather than political or even economic theory. Fuelling its whole existence at the core was an inspired anarchy of "private enterprise in art, scholarship and science." Set off against it were its two implacable enemies fascism and communism which Frye bitterly attacked as "essentially synthetic or religious modes of thought ... efforts of an organized social will to compel human life and science to fit a certain pattern of ideas."

In fact fascism and communism were cultural twins: " ... crude, gaudy realism of painting and pompous broken down classicism of architecture in both countries had been foreshadowing the Soviet-Nazi pact for years." Beside this "Woolworth level" of culture was the highbrow and experimental culture of the democratic laissez-faire. In a sense free culture had a genuinely heroic role which dictators, false heroes manufactured by propaganda, could not tolerate.

What was exceptional about the essay, though, was Frye's vision of the emerging fascist world state: "A world-state would be there-fore a handful of dictators backed up by huge armies of Praetorian guards ready to supply more when they die, ruling over vast slave populations. After criticism has been clubbed, reform machine-gunned, art degraded to the poster and circus, religion to caesar-worship, science to engineering, the surviving slaves would be well-fed and clothed, and nothing could overthrow such a state but an invasion from Mars ... In the present war it is our business to disintegrate and disorganize this world state *whatever else happens.*"

When the Fryes went home to Moncton in July, Frye was confronted with major family problems which left him little able to attain the equilibrium he needed to work on Blake. It was the first time that Helen met Cassie in person and it was stressful because Cassie's health had deteriorated alarmingly. Frye con-fessed in shock to Herm that she seemed more like 90 than 70. Herm alluded to a fear of cancer that Cassie had had since Vera's infancy, but Frye himself couldn't fathom the possibility. Cassie resisted seeing a doctor, claiming that Herm could not pay the bill and a doctor would not like the dirt and disruption of the household to which she hadn't been able to attend. It's probable that she well knew she did have cancer and simply didn't want to face the chilling diagnosis.

After visiting art galleries in the area, Helen left for Toronto as planned. Frye stayed behind, reporting to Helen that Cassie's worst day was the day after she left. He prepared Helen for the possibility of more financial cut-backs to help his parents by hiring a woman to housekeep and care for Cassie. With so many worries around him, he had to admit that he couldn't concentrate on Blake. Instead, he helped Herm out on delivery errands, hauling paint cans and worrying how Herm, at 70, was going to keep up his business.

## HUNTING THE FINAL SYNTHESIS

Because he had now designed his own courses, Frye's teaching load in the second year was more humane. One result of the freer time was a small voluntary study group in Biblical typology he mounted through the auspices of the Student Christian Movement. At the University of Toronto the SCM was a wholesome YMCA-type organization which organized study groups, hikes and teas. Because the SCM received official sanction at Vic, professors were encouraged to give extra-curricular courses with a religious theme relevant to the student's studies.

In choosing Biblical typology, Frye was cautiously resurrecting his own personal interest from graduate school. Frye had started learning typology as a way of understanding how Blake was reading the Bible and had become engrossed at Merton in the two-volume R.H. Charles commentary on Revelation which showed how much it summarized Old and New Testaments. However crucial to his own work, typology had languished for Frye because of a nearly complete lack of contemporary secondary materials. The Old Testament specialist at Emmanuel, A.S. Orton, could only point vaguely to some literature in German. With his weak German, Frye inched into some Goppelt and Bultmann only to find even that material had limited interest. With little to borrow, he developed his own ideas and schema through Blake which were so refreshing, students and colleagues soon urged him to write a book on the Bible. It was such an obvious idea that Frye procrastinated for decades.

Despite its novelty, there was an unassuming Sunday-School atmosphere to his class. The group of six to ten students would meet usually in his office or the Sun Room of Wymilwood in the last afternoon. Frye showed that, although the Bible was a crazy quilt of writings, it had undergone an intensive editing process in which very deliberate connections were made throughout to bind it into one prophetic statement in the Book of Revelation. Bible footnotes and concordances existed precisely to show the reverberations of Old and New Testament. Some students raised in liberal backgrounds, however, parrotted the prevalent view that the Bible was really just a collection of ancient writings of dubious provenence. Since the Bible was starting to be an embarrassment in middle-class culture, Frye's approach was a little unsettling because he was taking the Bible seriously.

More fundamentalist students considered that Frye was potentially heretic because he focussed on the symbolic rather than factual basis of the Bible. In other words, for Frye, like Blake, Biblical symbols like the flood and the ark or Adam and Christ were not absolute facts buttressing faith, but imaginative archetypes which reverberate throughout all literature and which should be internalized or possessed as models of vision and ultimately action. His course did, however, provide an intellectual halfway house for students raised in fundamentalist backgrounds who wished to see meaning, both religious and literary, in the Bible without the constraints of dogmatic, moralistic faith.

It is obvious from D.H. Lawrence's abusive, Nietzschean view of Revelation as resentment in *Apocalypse*, that for anyone raised in a strict non-conformist home Revelation can be a source of great anguish. Rather than a victorious synthesis of the Christian vision, Lawrence saw it as the apotheosis of Christian hatred, in which everyone, except for some white-robed prudes who sail up to a silly "jeweller's paradise of a New Jerusalem," gets thrown into an endlessly burning lake of fire. Unlike Lawrence's, Frye's own religious background did not emphasize Revelation and so he did not have such grim personal associations.

As his course developed, Frye would use a similar methodological approach to Revelation as Lawrence, identifying recurrent symbols in opposed manifest or demonic aspects. While Frye accepted the cyclical aspects of symbolism, he latched firmly onto the penultimate comedic view of the New Jerusalem, in which all things are made anew. Like the Puritans and Blake, he saw the New Jerusalem vision suffusing life, not replacing it with a childish fantasy of afterlife. As a result, he was always hostile to Lawrence's near-fascist cycle of life vision elaborated by such earthy Revelation symbols as the hero on the white horse and the supposedly magnificent red and green dragons. What is curious is that two thinkers, using similar symbolic techniques came up with completely antithetical readings.

Frye carried on the discussion group for four years under the aegis of the SCM and each year changed its name and presumed focus. Starting in 1940 as "Mythology and Symbolism of the Bible," it supposedly became more focussed on Revelation in 1941. In 1942, the course was announced as "Comparative Religion" and in 1943 "Symbolism in the Book of Revelation." Despite the chameleon change in name, Frye's course revolved on much the same issues each year.

Ironically enough, in 1944, Frye was drummed out of the SCM because both he and his students seemed indifferent to the wider range of SCM affairs. Frye briefly continued it alone until just after the war. When he complained that his students were having trouble understanding *Paradise Lost*, John Robins confirmed simply that students didn't know the Bible. As a result, Frye set up his course as an official religious knowledge course which was soon mobbed and eventually celebrated as one of the best courses ever offered on campus.

In late November 1940 less than four months after seeing his mother, Frye received a telegram from Herm summoning him home. Cassie was so ill in fact that she died just hours after Herm sent the cable. It was the weekend and Frye had to borrow money from John Robins to pay for his ticket to Moncton. Frye took over the arrangements, self-consciously choosing "one of the less hideous caskets and a floral 'pillow.' " When Vera arrived from Chicago the day after, they held the funeral in the undertaker's parlor, where Cassie's body lay in an open casket, her face artificially made-up. They spent the next few days cleaning up the flat and disposing of Cassie's property and destroying much of the family papers and correspondence. While the death of Cassie was sad, there was an inevitable sense of relief that she had been delivered from the lonely poverty and illness she had never deserved. They agreed to meet for Christmas in Montreal to boost family morale.

Although Montreal was chosen primarily as a convenient meeting place, it was the Layhews who put them up and turned the visit into a proper family occasion. Helen and Frye, who came for only a few days, stayed with his boisterous cousin Lew and his wife of two years, Jane. Lew, who had always suffered from the Howard Methodist hauteur, was anxious about Frye's status as an ordained minister. When offered a drink at a party Lew was throwing for his cousin, Frye asked for Scotch, downed a shot neat with one throw and immediately asked for another. The gesture exhilarated Lew and nearly made him whoop in relief, "He's one of us!" Frye did not exactly spend the rest of the evening dancing on the tables but he loosened up enough that Vera confessed to Lew it was good to see him relax. Vera thought that her brother was prone to excessive work and was a little afraid of its effect.

This was an unhappy time for Frye. The war situation kept deteriorating and he hadn't the time—or the nerve—to touch the one project which meant so much to him: the Blake book. For a long time through the war, there remained the fear that his ideas would remain in an inchoate pile of manuscript which would never be published or recognized.

Helen herself was suffering problems of morale. McCullough and Lismer had left the gallery in 1938, and the staff lecturers had to run the department themselves without help. Because of the war, Helen and the other lecturers found it increasingly difficult to attract audiences for lectures and tours. The education committee reported a 50% drop-off in attendance between July 1939 and July 1940. On top of it, the committee set its priority on the Saturday morning children's art classes. Nevertheless, Helen soldiered on, keeping up a respectable attendance in her Members' Study Group where she continued her eclectic mix of topics from the History of Ornaments to Design in Films in early 1941.

She resigned, nevertheless, in the spring and became for the first time, a dependent wife. To fill time and earn much-needed spare cash, she painted decorative trays with magnolias. Her senior partner in this cottage industry, Harold King, who was an art teacher at Northern Technical, showed her how to minimize the work with a few deft strokes of the brush. After nearly six years of intense work at the gallery, it was hardly a work of destiny but when Helen complained of it at a party to a British sculptor in Toronto, Jacobine Jones, she consoled her by cheerfully confessing that her own income, cut off by the war, was currently being buttressed by her painting roses on babys' chamber pots. A *Toronto Star* editor, George Gillespie, who lived in an adjacent apartment in their building, then suggested Helen take a job on the *Star Weekly* as a reprint editor who scanned the North American press for articles to reprint. Her major standard of comparison, apparently, was the *Reader's Digest*. Nevertheless with her on-going duties with the *Forum* and her continued ties with the art community, art remained central to her life and this inevitably spilled over to Frye.

In conjunction with an oddly combined Toronto Art Gallery show of the wealthy 19th century genre painter, Horatio Walker, and the leading preceptor of the Group of Seven, Tom Thomson, Frye heard a talk by Arthur Lismer on January 10, 1941, which engendered his own article in the March *Forum*, "Canadian and Colonial Painting." It was an important review not only as a germ of Frye's famous "garrison mentality" thesis but as an expression of a deep personal root in all honest art. The title itself suggested that there are two kinds of art, and therefore tradition, which can assist or betray the contemporary artist. Walker, who painted an English-looking Canada for Europeans, totally missed the obligation to look at the real land. He was not creating art but merely a satisfying dream image. Real art, therefore, must have a foundation in anxiety, which in Canada was the artist's fear of the unanswering wilderness. Around this apperception, he built a structure of symbolism, components of which easily derive from the past but which are made anew by their adaptation to an actual environment. What this meant was that a new Canadian art could not be instantly created by copying old styles. Canadian artists had first to feel primeval fears then heroically work against the nihilism.

In late June the Fryes headed up to an SCM conference at Chaffey's Locks on the Trent Canal and then headed back down to Kingston for the Conference of Canadian Artists, which was a serious effort to drag the Canadian art world out of its parochialism. Although Frye himself was just a casual participant, Helen became the first secretary of the new organization in Toronto. From Kingston, the Fryes travelled down to Moncton to join Vera and Herm. Although he was now in his seventies, Herm carried on his hardware business as before and was even beset by determined widows eager to marry him. The Fryes stayed for nearly two months and it was here for the first time in two years that Frye started moving again with his Blake book. He wrote little but came to a realization that all he had done so far was inconsequential.

He had the gift of two major breakthroughs which helped revitalize the book. When Helen went away briefly with a friend for a weekend, Frye enjoyed another epiphany. What instigated it was an ordinary caffeine fix. He had downed sufficient coffee in the evening that he couldn't get to sleep. Suddenly he realized that what he really wanted to do with the book was to write an encyclopedic overview of all he knew about literature at that time which would parallel the line of Blake's works themselves. Considering the way he had filled himself since late childhood with encyclopedic overviews of human culture, it is not surprising that he should have eventually applied the idea to himself. In a sense he had already realized that Blake's work encapsulated the core elements, genres and spirit of western literature and would therefore represent a projection of a much deeper unified tradition.

He scribbled a few notes about his idea but remained illusive about its nature in his writing. There was only one hint in the conclusion to an article on prose fiction he completed at that time: "The only synthesis of experience that makes no claim to be anything more than one out of infinite possibilities is the work of art. But that too has its own canons, rules, and methods of structure, and this final synthesis must be hunted out of its lair." The idea stayed with him and Frye intrepidly called Part Three of *Fearful Symmetry* "The Final Synthesis." What the phrase really anticipated for Frye in technical, structural terms, of course, was the

*Anatomy of Criticism* itself. Frye was clearly set to undertake a grand cultural sweep to show "... how all cultural products of a given age, medieval or Baroque or contemporary, form a unity that can be felt or intuited, though not demonstrated, a sense of unity that approximates the feeling that human culture is a single larger body, a giant immersed in time." Although this was written decades later specifically about Spengler and hobbled by the phrase "though not demonstrated," it was a faithful expression of his own animating vision as he looked at Blake. He realized late in life that the exhilaration from such a vision could only belong to a younger man since it would demoralize and possibly silence an experienced scholar.

This was a tremendous step but the new objective effectively opened a Pandora's box which would threaten precisely the book which had engendered it. Since 1934, Frye had been writing the Blake book as an introduction to the works of England's most impenetrable poet. A surviving fragment from an early version shows that Frye's eagerness to be an easy guide and proselytizer for the work of a poet who remained unread, he considered, only because of some troublesome but ultimately surmountable problems. Frye's new "expanding eyes" treatment now meant a shift from accommodation to a complexity which at times could surpass Blake's own.

In terms of the actual form of the book, Frye had to wait for another decisive breakthrough which put a Blakean image at the core of his analysis, the notion of Orc-Urizen cycle in the books five to seven of *The Four Zoas* which had eluded him for eight years. As with his caffeine-induced vision, Frye was hit by the notion in absurdly mundane circumstances. He was accompanying Helen on a Saturday morning shopping trip and while sitting in the bored husband's seat in a women's wear shop on Yonge St. just below Bloor, he figured out the cycle. While he recognized that this finally was the key to his book, he knew that a huge amount of work lay before him. Essentially the second half of the book had to be torn apart and reconstructed around this image. It was ultimately concentrated in Chapters Seven to Ten of *Fearful Symmetry* but, because of its implications, permeates much of the book.

It became so central, in fact, *Fearful Symmetry* is close to being a book about *The Four Zoas*, which depicts the work as a failed epic serving as a symbolic code book linking Blake's earlier and later work. The crucial supposition was that Blake, as Frye showed for the surrealists, was refining his symbolism and coming to terms with creating his own final synthesis, the apocalyptic *Jerusalem*.

Quite simply, the image of the rebellious Orc overthrowing the senile Urizen was not enough because it suggested an ever-repeating natural cycle in which the youthful, rebellious Orc himself becomes the geriatric Urizen tyrant who was to be overthrown by another new Orc. St. George, in other words, always became the dragon. There had to be a new figure who took mankind off the natural cycle. According to Frye, Blake found his hero in the figure of Los, "the genius of civilized life." Although never stated, the distinction had a profound tie with the war. While any fascist could be a rebellious Orc, only a builder and artist could be a Christly Los. This had some urgency since he felt the romantic Nazi myth of Rosenberg's *Myth of the Twentieth Century* might have a clear, if demonic, attraction for people.

## SATIRE BEGINS AGAIN

Although the easy-going atmosphere of Vic militated against a strict publish or perish policy, Frye still knew he had to make some appearance in the journals. When Frye's old friend Roy Daniells started *The Manitoba Arts Review* in 1938, he knew that *any* essay from Frye would not only be good for the journal but professionally important for Frye. After some genial pressuring from Daniells, Frye finally worked up a paper he wrote for Blunden called "The Anatomy in Prose Fiction."

In this work, Frye complained of confusion of terminology. To liberate works like Montaigne's *Essays* and Browne's *Urn Burial* from the "purlieus" of literature, he suggested that the term "fiction" should refer to all "prose which is literature." Against "the

old Ptolemaic view of prose literature as made up of novels, bad
novels, formless fiction and Examples of Prose Style," Frye
sketched out his own four forms of prose fiction, the romance,
the menippean satire (or anatomy) with the sub-category of the
encyclopedic farrago, the novel, and the imaginative biography,
the confession. Taking up nearly three quarters of the piece, the
hero of fiction was obviously menippean satire, which just happened to be Frye's favorite. He dismissed romance in a single
paragraph, observing that novels like *Wuthering Heights* and *Heart
of Darkness* had more to do with the romance and ballad forms
than the work of Austen and Meredith. Discussion of the novel
disappeared after a single curt, and horrendously arrogant, statement that "Bunyan ... is the only one who contributed anything of
importance to the novel."

In prose satire he obviously found his own image: "The satirist
is an observer of man thinking: he seeks ideas and their spokesmen
as sedulously as the trained novelist avoids them." An anarchic
bad boy, the satirist uses his work to protect art from the control
of procrustean philosophical ideas. Frye was clearly suggesting
that literature was an infinite imaginative realm, free of moral
and philosophical invasion: "Not only does the Menippean satire
defend art against all attack from without but ensures that there
shall be no shirking of the infinite novelty and variety of the work
to be done within." Frye was more graphic about a subdivision of
the anatomy, the encyclopedic farrago. Once more he was seeing
his own intellectual, though still anti-academic, impulses residing
in a single prose form: "Dusty learning has an appeal only for a
certain type of mind: what we get here is a thick cloud of dust
blown out of a library by a cyclone." Frye was in fact presenting
himself with an ominous mandate which would lead to another
work with the anatomy title.

Against the bruising polemics and stylistic sprawl of his anatomy
essay, Frye then produced a lean analysis of rhythm in poetry,
"Music in Poetry" which he placed with *The University of Toronto
Quarterly*. It grew ultimately out of his fourth-year essay for Pel-
ham Edgar on the poetry of Browning in which he examined
Tennyson's claim that Browning had music in him but couldn't get

it out. Frye thought that Tennyson's consideration of "musical" was incompetent. Frye, in fact, compared the two poets to contrast the vacuous sing-song pattern usually considered musical with the authentic energy of a "cumulative rhythm." "When a poet who obviously knows what he is doing produces a harsh, rugged, dissonant poem, music is probably the cause of it ... when we find a careful balancing of vowels and consonants and dreamy sensuous flow of sound, we are probably dealing with an unmusical poet." Unlike the militancy in the anatomy piece, Frye demonstrated an almost Buddhist calm as he peered into poetry precisely to find the qualities of poetry. In a sense, the essays represented the two contending sides of Frye: the rebel and the mandarin.

"Music in Poetry," was really quixotic. Frye's activist view of the giant-killing aspect of creative endeavor quickly reemerged with the deepening war crisis. Until Montgomery's great victories at El Alamein in early November, in fact, the Allies had done little in three years to reverse the Nazi onslaught. Many of Frye's friends including Earle Birney, Ernest Sirluck and Claude Bissell were now beginning to sign up for service. Canadian artists under the direction of Charles Comfort were enlisting in a new war art program. The Canadian Federation of Artists, now only a year old, promulgated a leftist National War Effort Petition and War Policy Statement in July 1942 which called for "mobilizing Canadian artists and craftsmen in a total effort for victory."

While equally militant, Frye's own response was idiosyncratic and personal. In the October 1942 issue of *The Canadian Forum*, he lambasted *Our Lady Peace and Other War Poems* by Mark van Doren and *Poems* by John Berryman for failure of nerve. While spending only one paragraph of five to actually review the books, Frye provides a clear explanation of his negligence: "The similarity of all these lyrics in tone, mood, subject and form is so oppressive that the strain of trying to find something new to say ... is getting me down." He attacked contemporary poets who complain about rather than act against the evil of war. Frye identified a further sin which revealed a key personal prejudice: "For the average poet has no God and no coherent ideas behind his symbols ... His

symbolism and imagery are therefore disjointed and shot out at
random into the blue ... "

Frye finished with an ostensibly irrelevant reference to Shelley,
whose work, even when ridiculous, appeared refreshing beside
the contemporary complainers. "Shelley also deprecated war and
Fascism, or what meant Fascism in his time. He yelled and
screamed and got hysterical about it; he blithered and spluttered
his way through huge sloppy poems with enough bad lines to
torpedo an epic; he hawked absurd pamphlets around the streets
of Dublin ... he fought for pacificism, atheism, revolution, free love,
vegetarianism—anything rather than the hopeless complaint and
constipated elegance. I should like to go and read some Shelley
now, if it's all right with everyone." The last line would be peevishly
adolescent, except for the fact that the moment it was written was
the darkest hour of the war.

In a letter to A.J.M. Smith about Canadian poetry, he kept up
the attack, complaining that the work of Alan Creighton suggested
an age "of the statue's feet, of iron mixed with miry clay and
a certain amount of horseshit." In quite explicit contrast, Frye
mentioned his own exhilaration at hearing the first reading of E.J.
Pratt's "The Truant," at Earle Birney's apartment.

To contemporary taste, "The Truant" is a rather curious effort,
a gritty mishmash of romantic clichés, which dramatizes the Promethean struggle of a "bucking truant with a stiff backbone,"
("Third cousin to the family of worms") who dares to be truculent
before the Awful Presence, the Great Panjandrum. The truant
ultimately shows that the Panjandrum has no qualities except those
provided by human culture: "Before we came/You had no name."
Restive about the decrepitude of the Awful Presence, humanity
has a day of revolt and defines the Panjandrum as merely "a rain/
Of dull Lucretian atoms crowding space."

The final defiance echoes the war:


We who have learned to clench
Our fists and raise our lightless sockets
To morning skies after the midnight raids,

> Yet cocked our ears to bugles on the barricades,
> And in the cathedral rubble found a way to quench
> A dying thirst within a Galilean valley—
> No! by the Rood, we will not join your ballet.

Frye was so excited by the poem that he eagerly pronounced on its importance. He bluntly told Smith that "it would be calamity not to have it" for his new anthology of Canadian poetry. He called it Pratt's best poem yet: "It's Blake's conflict of Orc and Urizen, the Prometheus-Jesus agent of humanity revolting against the God of universal machinery. It's the subtlest and maturest piece of symbolism he's done, and he always has been a symbolic poet rather than a chronicler or ballad-spinner. Furthermore, it's the keystone of all his earlier symbolism, and it's the target the earlier best things were pointing to." Not surprisingly the poem quickly turned up in the December 1942 issue of *The Canadian Forum*. After finishing the *Anatomy of Criticism*, he called it "the greatest poem in Canadian literature." Two decades later, he still raved about it: "[When] I heard Ned read *The Truant*, [I] felt, not simply that I had heard the greatest of all Canadian poems, but that the voice of humanity had spoken once more, with the kind of authority it reserves for such moments as the bombing of London, when the powers of darkness test the soul and find once more that 'The stuff is not amenable to fire'." In 1965, he added another angle: " 'The Truant' ... foreshadows the poetry of the future, when physical nature has retreated to outer space and only the individual and society are left as effective factors in the imagination." Frye even went so far as to claim that the poem had an "important influence" on his work on Blake.

Like his interest in Shelley's polemics, Frye's response to the poem was exaggerated by his own thirst for Blakean heroic imagery. At this blackest of times, Frye's instincts were closer to the obdurately sunny perspectives of his Methodist background. Even his image of satire was influenced by an evangelical kill-the-dragon approach.

In a paper he delivered on English satire on Feb. 17, 1943, as part of a Victoria College series, "Satire: Theory and Practice," he personified satire as a prophetic rebel in the bleak underground of human vision. Unlike tragedy which took one "into a hell of narrowing circles, a blasted world of repulsiveness and idiocy," it was satire alone which led one out again. Frye quite deliberately used the image of the questing Dante who reaches the dead centre of evil and simply passes through, leaving the behemoth Devil stuck in ice "bottom side up." Frye had actually ended his paper with a line from Skelton's "Colin Clout" that the devil was dead. When he showed it to John Robins, Robins audaciously told him that the ending should have more punch. In walking down to campus one morning, Frye thought of the Dante image of the questing poets making it through "the arse" of the devil to the shores of Purgatory and he added a new last paragraph. The devil wasn't merely dead. His loathsome presence merely demarcated the last stage before a new world unfolds. It was a central and decidedly evangelical image which Frye used repeatedly in his writing. By contrast, that low cousin, irony, was a kind of "intellectual tear-gas that breaks the nerves and paralyses the muscles of everyone in its vicinity, an acid that will corrode healthy as well as decayed tissues."

Frye was now taking whole areas of literary expression—irony, comedy, tragedy and satire—and suggesting how they operated against each other. Tragedy took the hero (and the reader) grandly down into a hellish sinkhole and left him there. Irony created the diseased fantasy that monsters were vanquished simply by ignoring them. The fall of the anti-hero was necessarily less spectacular but the destination was similar, a pus-filled pit which happened in this case to be self-dug. Only in satire was there a suggestion of the victorious hero. For Frye satire represented the initial stages of a romance which took a hero though repulsive monster-filled caverns to brighter vistas. As a function of literature itself, satire was the Theseus of culture battling odious language, propaganda, advertising, bureaucratic dissimulation, restoring the world by killing the dragon and releasing the youths. If tied to the image of the Last Judgment, satire belonged to the animating force that sweeps trapped souls out of the underworld. Even at this early stage, then, there was a notion of narrative integrity, of territories of verbal expressions bordering on each other in a wider scheme which had an evangelical as well as mnemonic intent. By suggesting strange alchemical admixtures of expression—irony and tragedy melding in Gloucester's suicide attempt in *King Lear*, for example—Frye was playing with a somewhat amorphous prototype for his celebrated narrative story-wheel in the *Anatomy of Criticism* with its bewildering, overlapping phases.

Frye also offered glimpses of his expanding theoretical concerns in his reviews of new poetry in the back pages of the *Forum*. Even with a tiny sample base, Frye positively strained to pronounce on the visionary health of opposing poetic expressions. After savagely eviscerating Berryman and van Doren in 1942, for example, Frye confidently blessed a trend towards the craftsmanship and impersonality he saw in a British anthology of poetry and prose of servicemen, *New Writing and Daylight*. What this meant was that "the cult of the politically-inspired romantic melancholy, which was getting so sterile and impotent, is on its way out."

He confessed, though, that what he really liked were the essays and critical articles. This left poetry in the middle ground of passible interest, with fiction, only two years after his last published story, clearly in the dog-house. Because Frye never altered this hierarchy, his taste for new creative work, always uncertain, was terribly blighted by an innate preference for discursive writing. Some of this engendered an extraordinary self-consciousness. In trying to review *Voices, A Quarterly of Poetry*, and Delmore Schwartz's *Genesis, Book One*, he really wrestled with himself over the task of criticism. With a mixed metaphor, he decided, "The critic's job is to operate the turbines by which this creative Niagara of creative energy can be brought into people's homes, to pick the one or two seeds out the millions which are predestined by nature to live." Like Eliot, he saw no point in impressionistic historicism of the sort which would, for example, pronounce "a languorous and effulgent charm that is worthy of comparison with Keats." On the other hand, the opposing curmudgeon tendency of harsh, negative comparisons between contemporary poets and the greats was equally wrong. The obvious stance for the popular critic was just to relax, avoid invidious comparisons and try to enjoy poetry for its own sake and let the good-bad sorting process do most of the work by itself.

In the fall of 1943 when he was promoted to assistant professor, Frye effected one crucial and distinctly audacious step up the academic ladder. He suggested, and landed, his first graduate course, not on Blake, who was still in the academic basement, but on Spenser. He managed to sign up three students, Fredelle Bruser, Rosemarie Schawlow and Mildred Shanas. Given his typological interests and uncomplicated professional ambitions, it wasn't surprising that he would attempt such a course. What is surprising is that the graduate secretary, A.S.P. Woodhouse, allowed it. Woodhouse, whose own interest in Spenser fascinated Frye, was clearly indulging his junior colleague. He even told Bruser, his own student, that she was foolish to spend her time over at Vic with Frye. To Bruser, Frye was a completely obscure academic with little visibility even on his own campus. She had been attracted to him purely on the advice of her professor at the University of Manitoba, Roy Daniells, who insisted she study at Vic with a young man he knew "with a mind like a razor blade." Certainly the three students received an intense first-time exposure to Frye's wind-tunnel approach of accelerated learning. Forty years later, Mildred Shanas remembered both "the stretch and pull on the intellectual muscles which a Frye seminar demanded — and about the all-too-frequent blanks, when a neophyte mind could not keep up. From time to time, as you were attentively working through some concept with Frye, you became aware that for the past ten minutes or so you had understood nothing, and you simply had to wait until he surfaced again and you could grab the thread."

In contrast to the historical approach of A.E. Barker and Woodhouse, Frye spoke about Spenser almost exclusively in mythological terms. Bruser remembers no references to other scholars, no intense consideration of influences. When she attempted to write her MA thesis with Frye, Woodhouse wouldn't allow it. Under the direction of Barker and Woodhouse, she wrote a thesis called "The Theme of Chastity in Non-Dramatic Literature of the English Renaissance," slipping only a few of Frye's ideas past her examiners. Rosemarie Schawlow, whose brother Arthur later won a Nobel prize in physics, was officially stationed at Vic and closer to the orbit of Frye. But even her own thesis, "Spenser and Renaissance Platonism," which was signed by Frye and Barker, was closer to the University College historical approach, and was made distinctive only for the odd reference, for example, to Osiris from *The Golden Bough*. Frye's very nearly total obscurity and professional powerlessness was coincidentally underlined when he attempted to sponsor her for a Harvard doctoral fellowship to study under Douglas Bush. When her application was turned down, both she and Frye were shattered.

Even though he socialized and dined with his graduate students and kept an anxious eye on their welfare, it is remarkable how well hidden Frye kept his turmoil over his Blake manuscript. He rarely mentioned it and didn't even draw much attention to Blake's work itself. Mildred Shanas remembers one exception when Frye, barely suppressing a grin, announced to his little class that he had just had a baby. "He let us flounder over that one for a well-timed moment, and then explained: *Fearful Symmetry* was finished. No more details." Otherwise Frye remained private, launching into seminar discussions without anecdotes or topical comments.

Frye in fact was almost leading a double life. At Vic he was a popular, dedicated junior professor who was an adviser to the *Acta* staff, and who was nearly in as much demand as honorary president of graduating classes as John Robins. He gave talks to a liberal arts club on *The Golden Bough* and music appreciation. While he was known as a United Church minister who arranged music and delivered sermons for the Christmas service in the college chapel, he was easily recognized as someone who refused to take the traditional Methodist values too seriously. Weeks before his major paper on satire, he allowed himself to be judge of "the most typical co-ed," a rather innocuous ersatz beauty contest at Vic about which some older staff were known to grumble. He once quipped that he regretted being head judge because he wished he could judge the other parts. He was also agreeable to being shanghaied for judging entries in the annual *Varsity* literary contest, and he criticized the annual Undergraduate Art Exhibit at Hart House. In the Feb. 1943 exhibit, Frye showed himself unapologetically evaluative, criticizing one Wilfred (Roloff) Beny, later photographer, "for a lack of underlying unity in his use of color, which turned his 'Symphony' into a cacaphony."

At home, of course, with his interminable, unruly project facing him, it was a radically different situation. In early 1943, he had already worked nine years on a manuscript which no one seemed to want and which chronically displeased him. Following his new ideas for the scope of the book, he had launched a full new version in the spring and summer of 1942, completing half by the start of the term. He then fussed over the ideas of the last half and started back slogging at it in the spring, only to find he had to rework the first half again. By the end of the summer of 1943, he had halted once more in the middle of his old nemesis, *The Four Zoas*, but kept on working until he finished a new version in February 1944. He then sent it off to a new Canadian subsidiary of Random House which rejected it. He was so unhappy with the book that he started rewriting it before receiving a rejection note. Even then, Ambassador House took a very long time to report on it, and Frye fell into a depressed mood. Helen noted it was the first time she had ever heard him sound bitter.

A major problem was Frye's intense isolation. He had worked so long on the book, that he no longer understood the problems people would have with Blake. This was reinforced, of course, by the odd circumstance that he had never had to present Blake to either students or fellow scholars. The only inkling he had of difficulties was the book's length. When he numbered page 658, he realized that most people would no longer consider it a short book. But he had learned Blakean symbolic shorthand so well, that there was now no obvious separation of Frye and Blake.

He was directly confronted with these problems only once when he gave the manuscript to his colleague, Kay Coburn. Although Coburn was then unpublished, she was already ten years into a massive lifelong job of editing the notebooks of Coleridge. She was naturally oriented towards a conservative textual approach which would become a Victoria College trademark. Although noting an immaculately typed and prepared manuscript, Coburn was disturbed that the text was replete with unsupported statements which seemed far too audacious for a young scholar with no established credentials. She was impatient for footnotes, authorities and a more obvious separation of Frye and Blake. She thought he was mismanaging some very exciting ideas with critical weakness. Nevertheless, before meeting with Frye over lunch at one of the Bloor St. restaurants near Vic, she went through the entire manuscript. She tried to be as gentle and supportive as she could but when she sensed that Frye intended to have no footnotes at all, the matter became closed for her. Coburn sensed her opinion was very unwelcome to Frye who was impatient and agitated, but she had to give it.

Frye's sour mood was not helped by the war itself. While it was now more obvious that the Allies were going to defeat the Nazis, the period from the autumn of 1942 saw the beginning of heavy enlistment among students and friends. Eventually all male students were required to enlist into the officer training corps and train with artillery and vehicles on the weekends. Starting with the Italian and Normandy campaigns, *The Varsity* and *Acta* listed the names of dead students and alumni. The daily papers grimly published numbered casualty notices from Ottawa divided into the three forces and subdivided by categories of confirmed dead, missing, and missing and presumed dead. As the casualties mounted with no sight in end, Frye began to fear and hate the appearance of the lists. Helen's favorite brother, Harold, who had published an impassioned anti-Nazi letter in *The Canadian Forum* in Oct. 1939, dropped out of Vic, joined the RCAF and served on the notoriously dangerous bombing raids over Germany. In February 1944 on a raid over Schweinfurt, the vital ball-bearing centre of the Reich, his plane was reported missing. Like the Fryes in the previous war, the Kemps had to contend with the slaughter of a bright, adored child. Helen herself was so shaken, she never lost her uncomprehending sense of loss at Harold's death. For the rest of her life, she cherished a framed photo of Harold in his air force uniform.

# PART THREE

Despite all his reverses, Frye completed yet another version of the Blake book in March. He intrepidly wrote "the manager" of Princeton University Press, announcing that he had finished a manuscript tentatively called "*Fearful Symmetry: A Study of William Blake* ... a complete and systematic interpretation of Blake's poetry and symbolism." While he said his study focussed on the prophecies, he emphasized that it dealt with Blake as poet rather than mystic or occultist, and attempted to make Blake relevant to the contemporary world. When the Princeton publisher, Datus C. Smith, Jr., replied that he would indeed like to see it, Frye sent off the large 658-page manuscript with another note bumptiously pronouncing the book "complete and ready to print" except for footnotes which he hoped to make mercilessly compact and unreadable.

Frye had been attracted to Princeton by a rumor that the press enjoyed a wartime hoard of paper. Because Princeton printed its own books, it did have a legal right to own paper but possessed no particularly large stockpile. While quixotic, Frye's choice proved fortunate for quite another reason. Datus Smith set a policy of inspecting all new manuscripts himself and either quickly rejected them personally or passed them on to his editors and readers. This policy prevented manuscripts circulating interminably around the house and wasting time, and also allowed Smith to develop an instinctive feel for them and watch over their progress. But Smith was an Asian scholar and and so he passed Frye's difficult manuscript to his literary editor, Jean MacLachlan.

MacLachlan looked it over and strongly recommended that it be sent to an academic reader for evaluation. Her outline of the manuscript is valuable because that version no longer exists. She repeated Frye's stated objective of first trying "to provide a compact grammar of Blake's symbolism" only to see this grow into a huge detailed study on Blake's poetry "with side excursions into the nature of satire, the romantic poet, the historic cycle, the epic, etc." It appears that at this stage, *Fearful Symmetry* started with a 200-page outline of Blake's thinking, probably similar to the published version. This was followed by a shorter 75-page analysis of how Blake's poetry fit into the broader perspective of English poetry. Much of the rest of the manuscript was a commentary on his works, most prominently of course the prophecies, in order of composition. The conclusion evaluated Blake's achievement and evaluated him in relation to the twentieth century.

Because of Smith's instinct for readers, Frye was again lucky. In the Princeton area, Smith greatly admired Richard Blackmur, but had no faith in his ability to identify a commercially viable manuscript. Carlos Baker, on the other hand, whose interests took in both Hemingway and the then-wildly-unpopular Shelley, had a good record for spotting winners. Smith sent Frye's manuscript to Baker.

Baker wrote a mixed four-page report, raving about the manuscript's strengths and bludgeoning it for its weaknesses. Baker wrote: "Mr. Frye appears to know more about Blake than any other living critic; his book is full of the most acute perceptions and insights; he has gaiety and humor, aggressive wit, and a kind of gamy truculence ... He brings to the book a close and reasonably reverent knowledge of several arts—poetry, music, painting—a knowledge required, it seems, for the proper study and explication of Blake; he knows the Bible as few scholars do; and he appreciates the fact that the attack on Leviathan Blake cannot be successful without the application of a many-sided strategy."

But his criticisms were equally harsh. Baker bluntly doubted that the "seemingly interminable book will materially aid the cause of Blake after all. It requires as much of the reader as Blake's Prophetic Books themselves do." He felt it completely inappropriate for the general reader, calling it "super-intellectual and on the whole a somewhat eccentric book." Like Coburn, he complained that it was impossible to distinguish between Frye's commentary and his paraphrasing of Blake. He resented Frye's interpreting other poets in Blakean terms which distorted the intention of the individual poets, "in effect telling them that what they really meant was not at all what they thought they meant, because what they thought they meant doesn't square with the total pattern." He concluded that Frye was creating his own tragedy in the book by knowing and seeing so much. He saw the book as a "diffuse epic in prose" which actually consisted of three books, "a treatise on the unity of western poetry; a treatise on Blake's critical opinions; and a dictionary of Blakean symbolism." Interestingly he made no negative comment about its oddity as a specifically scholarly book.

While the reports for Frye's book ominously went into a rejects file, Smith wrote an upbeat letter which balanced genuine enthusiasm with the bad news that Princeton could not publish his manuscript as it was. He quoted four major excerpts from Baker's report, balancing the positive and negative comments. Unfortunately, he left out Baker's barb about the "super-intellectual" difficulty and Frye continued to possess a curiously naive belief that he'd produced an elementary handbook. Smith suggested the awful possibility of a rewrite. He wasn't bluffing. Frye's book represented just one of the many borderline manuscripts the press rejected every year with a clear conscience, despite initial enthusiasm.

Frye answered with a surprisingly mild letter which reflected his own sense of defeat over the manuscript. He defended the complexity of the book, insisting that "all of the book is about Blake; it is not a fantasia on Blakean themes." He agreed with Baker that the book was really three books but didn't see them as separable. He claimed that he had no objection in principle to cutting or revising the manuscript but didn't know how. Baker provided one decisive idea, that Frye divide the book into three parts instead of two. In Baker's plan, theory about the unity of western literature would be placed in a grand conclusion. Passing along Baker's suggestion, Smith still expressed firm interest in the manuscript.

Frye was not at all devastated by the thought of another major rewrite. He already sensed that the book was too long and bloated. Another rewrite for the most promising chance of publication so far was not, he felt, going to be onerous. Towards the end of May he reported to Smith that he was at work on it again and confessed his gratitude to Smith and the unknown (to him) reader: "So personal a book as mine is unusually vulnerable to unsympathetic criticism, of the sort that would interpret its cultural high blood pressure as a desire to show off."

Frye's upswing in mood and sense of purpose perfectly matched the Viconian *ricorso* everywhere, of birth following the terrible disaster of the war. For Frye there was an uncanny literal truth to this. On the night of the VE victory celebrations on May 8, when Helen and their neighbours, the Gillespies went out, Frye stayed at home to babysit George Gillespie's pregnant sister-in-law, Edna Fulford, who had just started to go into labor. Very quietly and anxiously, Frye remained on guard until the Gillespies arrived home to take Edna to the hospital where she gave birth to her daughter, Nancy, shortly after midnight.

Frye's rewrite that summer largely consisted of bridging loose material or excising it altogether. He removed his Blakean analysis of other Romantic poets. As he remembered it, his biggest task was to cut the tangential theoretical material which obstructed the view of Blake's own work. Much of this later reappeared in the *Anatomy of Criticism*. He did follow Baker's suggestions to turn it into a three-part book, realizing when he finished he'd produced a concerto form. But he failed to make a grand conclusion on the unification of western art, making a few suggestions in the last few pages.

Frye also cut the material on Blake's relevance to the modern world, leaving the suggestion implied throughout rather than boldly stated. Despite this, his fundamental intention was still very clear. In a deliberately self-conscious statement for the promotion of the book, he wrote: " ... Blake is not only the great genius of English poetry and painting that he is now generally admitted to be, but a thinker of an insight that will amaze and fascinate the modern reader, who may readily see in him one of the few really accurate modern 'prophets', with ideas that suggest extraordinary possibilities of expansion and development in our day ... His poetry is 'obscure' only because he is trying to discourage the lazy reader and attract the energetic one. He thus suggests that all great poets demand a similar effort of response, that immense reserves of meaning in all great poetry are still untapped, that the major task of critics is still to be done, and that only by accomplishing this task will poetry, and the other arts with it, be able to make its full contribution to civilization."

In trying to re-create rather than explain Blake, however, Frye failed to attend to the chronic complaint of all readers before or since that there was no easy separation of Frye and Blake. In the text, they seem to merge and produce a coordinated statement. Although he bridged material with parenthetical phrases and explanations, he failed to make it much easier for the general reader by providing a glossary or dictionary of symbolic forms and figures. There was an attitude at once arrogant and naive that everyone had spent every minute of the last 15 years pondering the significance of William Blake's most difficult work. Since Frye posited a cathode-anode theory of Biblical re-creation, that diffi- culty itself induced an active "spark of illumination," any problems of this sort arguably lay with the lazy reader who did not want to understand. More than "a clear and complete solution," this suggested the brain-twisting regime of a Zen master.

At the end of August, Frye sent off his revised manuscript, reporting to Smith that most of it was rewritten and a total of 170 pages removed. On reviewing the new version, Baker was genuinely enthusiastic. Although nearly all his former criticism could still be applied to the new manuscript, there seems to have been no Machiavellian misrepresentation on Baker's part to slip an eccentric but obviously important book past gullible editors.

MacLachlan herself had a go at it and noted that there was no longer an "impression of diffuseness." She again cautioned

Princeton about the book's difficulty: " ... I doubt whether the good old 'general reader' who happens to 'love Blake' will have the fortitude to endure the rigors of Mr. Frye's argument." Three weeks later, Smith wired Frye that his manuscript was accepted for publication and hoped to produce it in a year. On Oct. 28 with E.J. Pratt as witness, Frye signed a contract which finally put to rest his troublesome 11-year quest. When he first received Smith's telegram, Frye had a day of ecstasy, but he was so busy with the start of the term and the move from the apartment into a new home, that there was little time left to really celebrate.

The home in the upper-middle-class district of Moore Park in North Toronto was Frye's first real material luxury, accomplished only by means of a stiff mortgage which left the Fryes, like most couples of the time, in transfixed penury. Although the down payment came from Helen's wartime salary at the *Star Weekly* she quit her job in the summer of 1946 to become a housewife. As a *Forum* stalwart, she naturally felt the overnight changeover from comparatively serious wartime content to the *Star Weekly*'s old pipe and slippers formula too jarring for comfort.

Helen kept up her ties with the *Forum* and the art world, and wrote the occasional freelance assignment on art, but became much less publicly active. While helping Frye maintain the old Victoria College ideal of entertaining students for dinner at home, she didn't turn into the invisible, uncomplaining academic's wife who typed and edited her husband's manuscripts. In fact, she read his work so little it became a well-established family joke—used to calm people's nerves—that she too had never read *Fearful Symmetry*. With no sense of sacrifice, she gardened and sewed, supervised renovations and tradesmen and fielded phone calls so Frye could get on with his writing. Her zealotry in this was usually quite well justified. Frye got easily trapped into unnecessary obligations. When Helen was out once, a lady phoned up to have him read over a simplified version of the Bible for mentally defective girls. When she offered to pay, he "wrote her that as there was no precedent for such a service he would charge her at the rate his plumber, an honest man, charges, that is $2.50 per hour—2 hours it took him." Frye then ruefully discovered that plumbers' rates were $5.00 an hour. It was, Helen needlessly reported, an imposition she would have blocked.

They bought their house from Frye's undergraduate professor of aesthetics, Reid MacCallum, for what was then a hefty $8,000. A basic two-and-a-half storey home, it would serve them permanently. The bleak rocky backyard would be transformed by Helen's energetic gardening. Frye himself had no illusions, though, about his role as a Norman Rockwell *pater familias*. He joked about arriving in pouring rain on their first day to find MacCallum alone in the empty house with his cat. "Reid had a watermelon grin on his face because he loves moving; the cat didn't, and glowered at me like a reincarnation of Heathcliff, which from what I've heard of her she could be. I think she put a spell on me in all matters connected with household management." This latter included the assembly of a backyard laundry tree which left Frye, Helen and a later boarder defeated in an exasperated but amused quandary. Frye managed to cut grass and shovel coal into a balky furnace but otherwise left the household management to the greater wisdom of Helen. A student who visited a couple of years later, however, claimed that the household was really set up for Frye's needs. There were enough chaotic stacks of books to beleaguer a bibliophile.

The Fryes initially let out the attic bedroom—which would eventually become Frye's permanent workroom—and a small living room to Edna Fulford and her baby, Nancy, who had been living in the summer at the Gillespie cottage. As a result, their first taste of home living was not dominated by astringent cerebral pursuit but the complications of an infant. The Fryes welcomed the disruption. Edna and Helen shared the housework and both families dined together. Edna and her daughter stayed for a year until Edna moved back to an old job at the Lakehead. To Edna, the Fryes had a child-like enthusiasm for their house and every new possession in it including a small Lismer painting which the artist gave them.

This was the period too when Helen, now in her late thirties, most seriously considered having children. The Fryes had been baffled when for year after year, Helen did not get pregnant. In an era which possessed no fertility clinics, gynecologists could do little more than console bruised feelings with sexist fatuities like "It's difficult to get an intelligent woman pregnant." There were small consolations: the Fryes did not idolize children as did the slightly younger couples who created the Baby Boom. While Helen could crow with joy over the safe birth of a friend's baby, she could also burst into angry imprecations in letters to her parents, about neighborhood children who damaged her shrubbery and flower-beds. There was also the convenient rationalization, for Helen, that Frye would not have written all his books with the noise and disruption of a family. Yet while he considered himself a poor role model for boys, Frye himself continued to possess yearnings for children. And Helen, rationalizations notwithstanding, never really came to terms with the situation. Her barrenness later became a festering psychological wound.

**GREAT TEACHER**

All through the war Frye taught small, cloistered, mostly female classes. The hordes of returning veterans, eager to catch up on their lives, now changed all that and propelled him into a cross-campus celebrity. There couldn't have been a wider gulf between themselves—battle-seasoned, pragmatic, sometimes cynical and brutalized—and this pale, thin blond whose sole observable strength was the power of words. One veteran was a behemoth from northern Ontario called Douglas Fisher who'd worked as a hardrock miner in his teens and was an armored car operator in the Canadian Army Lowlands sweep. Fisher had little idea about university. When he took a summer course for veterans, he coincidentally encountered Frye in a section on Shavian comedy and was so electrified he figured that if this was university, he had to have more. He nearly reversed his decision when Frye's colleague in the course shambled incompetently through the next section. When Fisher decided on taking the honors English courses with

Frye, he went to him for advice. Towering over Frye, who sat on the window ledge like a boyish wraith obscured in a blur of light, Fisher got so tongue-tied that Frye kindly asked him to sit down. Frye reworked Fisher's query in the baldest terms: "Do you think you can handle the honors course?" When Fisher replied he could, Frye who would always show an uncanny judgment about students merely affirmed, "Yes, I think you can." Fisher thereafter thrived. As a freshman candidate he became a giant-killer in the 1957 federal elections by defeating one of the country's most powerful politicians, C.D. Howe.

There was also the return of more senior students whom Frye had known from years before, like Peter Fisher (no relation to Douglas) and Gordon Wood who'd been army officers, and his old friend George Johnston, who'd been an RCAF pilot. Fisher had once sought out Frye to talk about Blake in the thirties. He was once spotted meditating on the *Tibetan Book of the Dead* on the rifle range in New Toronto. By the end of the war, he was an infantry major, veteran of the ferocious Italian campaign. He was one of the very few people Frye knew who operated on his own intellectual level and could feed his own imagination. They were often together, downing beer in the pubs just off campus and talking for hours. Fisher was deeply interested in Oriental philosophy. He not only opened that area for Frye, but also instigated many of the Oriental references in Frye's writing. In a later memoir of Fisher, Frye gave tribute to Fisher's herculean mental command which could even humiliate him: " ... [Fisher] walked into my office and announced that he wanted to to do an M.A. thesis on 'Blake's method, in the Cartesian sense.' He nearly walked out again when he discovered that I had not read the *Bhagavadgita* in Sanskrit, which he believed any serious student of Blake would have done as a matter of course."

Fisher had an excess of post-wartime energy which was both voracious and infectious. After downing several lethal drinks called Zombies in the Frye's backyard one evening, he and Gordon Wood roared down Avenue Rd. in his car at twice the legal speed, and talked all through the rest of the night in his flat on Huron St. He was also prone to mystical thought which, besides Mahayana and

Zen Buddhism, took him into some bizarre areas of western mythology like the Egyptian *Book of the Dead*, and occultism like Yeats's *A Vision*. Frye himself had always, of course, been fascinated with structural analogies of occult thought and poetry. He ultimately considered, however, that a zany, overripe work like *A Vision* would invariably provide false leads which would propel him away from the core of poetry. It was Fisher nevertheless who kept the interest simmering and, as a result, Frye's first academic paper after finishing *Fearful Symmetry*, "Yeats and the Language of Symbolism," was focussed on the relationship between occultism and poetry.

These veterans all had their stories from the war which Frye could only absorb with a vicarious unsettled comprehension. Douglas Fisher took four years to reveal he'd seen a Churchill tank which had suffered a rare direct artillery hit at a crossroad near Carpiquet. When Fisher looked inside the still-hot Churchill shell hours later, he saw four skulls reduced to smudges with four rows of teeth leering in the dark. When Wood entered Venice, he was so sickened with the brutality he'd seen up the spine of Italy, he could bear neither to enter nor approach St. Mark's cathedral. As for Peter Fisher, he told Helen and Frye about a German who had fallen into the hands of a British Gurkha unit. The Gurkhas thought it a good joke to decapitate some of his friends and put the heads in a circle around where he lay unconscious. When the German roused himself, he looked around at the heads, then at the grinning collection of Gurkhas behind, and went insane.

Considering what Frye had intended with *Fearful Symmetry*, it was not totally surprising that these veterans would have been drawn to Frye for their studies. Conscious of the brutalizing effects of the war, Frye insisted on hard academic discipline partly to redirect their attention. He drove both Fisher and Johnston with a sense of urgency which was immensely ironic in terms of his own failure at the comparatively simple task of an MA thesis. Frye succeeded beautifully. Both had their theses finished, accepted and signed on May 27, 1946.

On the eve of the publication of *Fearful Symmetry*, Frye was for the first time exerting influence on the thinking of his graduate students. Both Johnston and Fisher wrote on Blake and both showed a proclivity to delving into the wider symbolic, rather than intellectual, aspects of literature. While Johnston actually cited the unpublished manuscript of *Fearful Symmetry* and was obviously guided by Frye, Fisher was typically independent in his own approach, writing more on the level of an accomplished colleague. Yet Fisher's thesis was called "The Method of William Blake" and reflected many of Frye's own concerns.

Only three years after seriously doubting Frye's capabilities, Woodhouse was now confident enough about him that he directed graduate students his way. As well as the Spenser, Frye gave a course on Blake heavily embroidered with Joyce's *Finnegans Wake*, which attracted a brilliant graduate student, Hugh Kenner. Kenner had been soured by four years of Woodhouse's paternalism at University College. While he knew his own interests and thinking were quite different from Frye, he was fascinated by Frye's own rebellion against the arid historicism that prevailed at Toronto. To Kenner, Frye was a dazzling, somewhat arrogant, figure who was bursting with the conviction that he'd actually found the key to western literature.

After Kenner took Marshall McLuhan's former job at Assumption College in Windsor, he often returned to Toronto and lunched with Frye. He remembered Frye's telling him after the publication of *Fearful Symmetry*, "If Joyce or Yeats had read it, it would have saved them so much time." Another time, Kenner asked Frye about a seemingly inconsequential detail in *The Waste Land* and Frye replied, "I haven't had the time to figure that out yet." To Kenner, who'd always acknowledged the mysteries and paradoxes of the creative process, Frye's attitude indicated an insistence that poetry yielded "to method, like a word puzzle or a safe."

Kenner's memories aren't distorted. In his sketch for the promotion of *Fearful Symmetry*, Frye pointed to the common view of the prophecies as "mysterious cryptograms whose claims to be important works of art could not be seriously considered until they had at least been clearly and completely solved. This book provides such a clear and complete solution ..." Once the model was revealed by critics, moreover, the way was clear for creative writers to surge ahead with clarified, purposeful symbolism. With *Fearful Symmetry*, he realized the potential of such a grammar and reported that "the testimony of many complete strangers, some of them well-known writers, leaves me no doubt about its value to practising artists." Much of the confusion in poetry, in fact, he thought was the result of confusion over the function of criticism: "We shall never fully understand the 19th century until we realize how hampered its poets were by the lack of a coherent tradition of criticism which would have organized the language of poetic symbolism for them."

**GOD**

When Frye received his six free copies of *Fearful Symmetry* from Princeton in the Saturday mail in March 1947, he confessed to Smith that he "spent the weekend purring and stretching myself. I had every reason to suppose that after all that work, the actual sight of the book would be an anticlimax, instead of which it was a bewilderingly delightful surprise. But then I knew nothing about your plans for that superb title page, with the lovely upward swirling movement of the Dante sketch, or for the dust cover with its ingenious adaptation of *The Book of Los* frontispiece ...or for the handsome spine with its flame design, a design which suggests with perfect accuracy of what the 'fearful symmetry' is about." Of course, it wasn't just appearance which impressed him. It was the relief that after 13 years the book was no longer the embattled project of an eccentric young scholar.

For Frye, this was a literary event as important as any major new novel or poetry book. He was just as interested in its popular impact as its academic importance. He was electrified to hear that *Time* was planning a review. Even before publication, he urged MacLachlan to interest Edmund Wilson in using the book as a lead for a review article in *The New Yorker*. This was not entirely opportunistic. In 1944 Wilson had very favorably reviewed *A Skele-*

*ton Key to Finnegans Wake* by Joseph Campbell and Henry Morton Robinson which he commended as a puzzle-solving manual which revealed difficult but important literature. MacLachlan simply advised that Wilson was notoriously resilient to direct pleas.

Frye also tried to make abundantly clear to his publisher that he had the inside track in Canada to help promote it. Certainly around Vic there was a great deal of excitement. Students put in advance orders and when stock arrived in early April, the books quickly disappeared. Like a star, Frye obligingly signed copies for his students. Frye's graduate students in his Blake seminar feverishly studied it in the few days before their exam.

Except for skimpy, positive notices in *The New Yorker* and *Newsweek* shortly after publication, the local Toronto reviews were the first to appear. On May 17 in *The Globe and Mail*, William Arthur Deacon reviewed it as a "Masterly Interpretation of William Blake's Poems." Calling it "one of the finest pieces of interpretative criticism in the language," he insisted that "all lovers of poetry will rejoice that Blake can now be understood easily by the many, who have always believed these prophecies must contain noble ideas artistically expressed in cryptic form..." Deacon even insisted it was "fun to read." On the same day, *The Toronto Star* published another breezy review "Sanity of Genius Found in Blake."

Another of the older Toronto critics, B.K. Sandwell, also wrote a long glowing review in the July 19 *Saturday Night* with the headline "Student of Pelham Edgar's Writes Epoch-Marking Volume on Blake," which seemed to balance a supposedly dependent past with a limitless future. The photo in the review showed Frye with short blond hair, stern face and set jaw, looking up slightly to the left where a source of light shone down. He had the wholesome look of a Youth for Christ campaigner. Although writing in a popular journal, Sandwell also insisted on its case: "...the whole body of thought of William Blake ... Mr. Frye with an amazing degree of success exhibits as completely coherent, richly illuminating, and not too difficult to follow when one has grasped certain essentials of Blake's literary method." This insistence reinforced Frye's own opinion that the book was perhaps stuck between popular and academic worlds. To Earle Birney, he wrote, "The reviews ... are slow in coming out—I suspect that the book is too academic a subject for the large circulation magazines and too popular for the *Wissenschaft* journals."

He only began to see the real problems when students and faculty began to complain about it. After a formidable struggle, one student insisted that for as long as she lived she would not be able to understand the book but since it was so obviously important, she would sit on it and absorb it by osmosis. In time, Frye would confront the serious problems of the book and in his preface to a paperback edition in 1962, he grudgingly confessed, " ... if I were to write it again I should probably write a more conventional book, more concerned with the reader's superficial difficulties with the text and designs, less concerned with recreating Blake's thought and attitude in my own words."

The difficulty, moreover, led to precisely the kind of cabalistic response which Frye came to fear. Some of Frye's better under-graduates became obsessed in figuring out Frye's cosmologies. James Reaney, poet and graduate student of Frye in the fifties, parrotted Frye's own *Fearful Symmetry* statement about students staying up overnight to read the book. Over coffee at Murray's Restaurant, they assumed self-induced Brahminical proportions, which at first tremendously annoyed Reaney before he himself became a convert. The group, known to others as the Fryedolators (and much worse), plainly developed the dimensions of a cult. They gossiped feverishly about Frye as a person. They culled college legend for often inaccurate stories about his social and sexual attitudes, even about the length of his penis. If the latter suggested Adonis, what mattered most, of course, was the Jupiter-sized brain. Frye saw and knew everything. His students reported a gallery of doors like that in Hesse's *Steppenwolf* suddenly revealing a pleth-ora of new vistas. With only a faint sense of irony, they would try to keep up with his latest pronouncements by anxiously prodding each other, "Well, what did God say today?"

The girls who belonged to the group later realized they were in the grip of a primitive groupie reaction. They were more like fans of Sinatra. On the pretext of *Acta* business, they tried to hang around his office as much as possible to be near *him*. It appears that Frye did nothing to encourage this kind of response; his behaviour was neutral. Because he so much believed in the old John Robins tradition of socializing with students, he couldn't easily drop his *Acta* obligations or stop asking students up to the house for dinner. But he was badly annoyed by the adulation, and the overdone student response precipitated an increasing restlessness about his place at Vic.

Certainly for a difficult academic book, there were very strong North American sales which amounted to 1,100 copies in just the first half-year. While Frye expressed surprise, telling Smith he had expected "it would sleep like Rip Van Winkle, and possibly for about the same length of time," he busied himself auditing and trying to maximize sales and exposure. He passed on complaints he'd received to Smith about its lack of availability in Canada in the summer, the result of Princeton's shutting its warehouse for vacation. He fussed over the failure of *The New York Times* to review it, and a book embargo in Britain which effectively banned *Fearful Symmetry* overseas. Datus Smith reported, however, that even if their British co-publisher, Oxford University Press, could print their own edition, they would face very difficult paper shortages and binding problems.

While international reviews continued to come in slowly, none had quite the impact on Frye than that of Edith Sitwell in the Oct. 10 issue of *The Spectator*. Here was a well-recognized literary figure outside academe who was prepared to say: "The book is of extraordinary importance, not only for the light it throws on Blake, but also philosophically and religiously ... It is a book of great wisdom, and every page opens fresh doors on to the universe of reality and that universe of the transfusion of reality which is called art."

Coming at the start of a very heavy teaching year with three times the students of the war years, Frye took until January to write Sitwell a simple thank-you note. Sitwell reciprocated with a copy of her recently published collection, *The Shadow of Cain*, its title poem a Blake-like prophecy. Frye quickly inserted a flattering

one-paragraph review of it in the January *The Canadian Forum,*
pronouncing it as "beautiful and erudite proof" that Sitwell was
now a major poet.

He gave a much more detailed accolade in a personal letter
towards the term's end, calling the poem "a very lovely, haunting,
and almost unbelievably suggestive poem. The apparently effortless way in which a contemporary situation expands, by way of
certain human archetypes, into its ultimate values of primeval cold
and unquenchable life, makes the poem a kind of miniature epic."
Displaying a presumption of omniscience, he added, "I know by
this time what to look for in major poetry, and I always find it.
Reversing the axiom, when I find what satisfies me in a poem I
know that it is major, and *The Shadow of Cain* belongs to the
restricted canon of major poetry."

Flattered by his generous words, Sitwell replied in kind. Reporting Maurice Bowra's own enthusiasm for the book, she proffered
the mantle of authority: "Really, it is most exciting to me to know
that at last we have the critic we have been waiting for. But it goes
further than that. I think you will also prove to be the religious
teacher we have been waiting for."

If Sitwell's accolade was precisely what Frye had dreamed, it
was not a universal reaction. One of the most perceptive critics of
the book was Edward Bostetter writing in an obscure Seattle
journal, *Interim,* who gave vent to the major problems most people
were having with *Fearful Symmetry.* Bostetter was one of the
very few reviewers of the book who immediately understood and
sympathized with Frye's mythic approach which otherwise looked
so unconventional in North American critical circles. While admiring, for example, the way Frye sliced wonderfully through the
symbolic obscurities of *Jerusalem,* which bedevilled Mark Schorer,
author of another recent book on Blake, Bostetter nevertheless had
a major *caveat,* Frye's propensity for artful symbol-mongering:
"Unfortunately in his zeal to clarify Mr. Frye often turns obscurity
into confusion. In probing to the last meaning of a symbol, he
sometimes destroys its identity by pushing it so close to another
that the distinction between the two is lost ... The result is an
eerie kind of double talk ... Mr. Frye seems to find a symbol in

everything ... in the piling of symbol upon symbol he bewilders and exhausts the readers ... the unwary reader may get hopelessly lost and never find the golden thread that will guide him into and through the poems themselves."

While Frye carefully watched all the responses, good and bad, there was an oddly personal dimension to his book which he saw as Jungian father-swallowing. Frye in fact sent copies to all his early mentors, Blunden, Edgar, Davis and Keynes who had all had to contend with earlier versions of the book. Almost on cue, three out of four made their responses polite but cautious. Blunden received his copy as he was packing up for Japan and said with possible relief he'd have to wait until he returned to Britain to read it properly. But he was effusive about Frye's constancy: " ... I still recall vividly your devotion to Blake at Oxford and I rejoice in the spectacle of such constancy of imaginative endeavour ..." Suffering from serious thrombosis in his left leg, Edgar related part of "a long symbolic dream involving you and Milton and William Blake." Edgar personified his severe pains as jokingly as he could as "some uninvited celestial adventurer [who] had followed Milton's track through the spheres, but had selected *my* left foot in [?] ... as his terrestrial point of entrance." He nevertheless was eager to add a chapter on Frye for a memoir he was working on and asked for some data to help him. His request instigated one of Frye's very few spontaneous autobiographical writings, later published in Edgar's *Across My Path*. Pressured by work, Davis handed his copy over to a junior colleague at Smith College, Helen Randall, to review for the U of T *Quarterly*. Keynes was by far the most generous of the mentors and reviewed the book at the end of the year in *Time and Tide* in Britain. Coming on top of a spate of Blake books, Keynes claimed that "with the force of an Atlantic roller," Frye's book carried "our understanding of Blake's message well into the inland of our consciousness..." Despite this generosity, Frye never lost a suspicion that Keynes did not regard his approach as central: just one more critic to note.

Despite a harrowing academic year and the ups and downs occasioned by the reviews of his book, Frye took a break to attend his first MLA conference in Detroit in December. He went purely to experience the wider world of English scholars which after nearly a decade was still a mystery to him. It was one of the very few times he went to a conference without actually delivering a paper. In fact his desire to go was considered eccentric at Vic and John Robins wondered if he didn't want to sniff out a job. Robins may have been ignorant of Frye's doubts about Victoria. Certainly on the basis of his growing reputation, he was offered a couple of jobs. The chief qualification for one opening in the South seemed to be more a taste for raccoon hunting than knowledge of English. Another, offered by Merrit Hughes at the University of Wisconsin, was more serious, but involved teaching such a horde of freshmen that Frye was only tepidly interested. Frye's roommate at the convention, Barker Fairley, told Frye the obvious, that he would get many more offers and should be patient if he wanted to leave Toronto.

**THE ARGUMENT OF COMEDY**

Rather than the MLA, Frye's career was soon to be taken up by its schismatic offspring, the English Institute. There was an eerie casualness to Frye's investiture. When Philip Wheelwright began looking for papers for an English Institute session on comedy, Frye's former graduate student, Rosemarie Schawlow, directed Wheelwright to Frye. In the summer of 1948, Frye so completely fussed over the "The Argument of Comedy" up at the Kemp cottage, that Mrs. Kemp protested. A half-hour paper hardly needed that kind of effort. Frye responded that one can make a fool of himself in considerably less than half an hour. If any case, he had a gut feeling that his paper would be a crucial statement. Although he made no conscious effort to tighten the unruly style of his Blake book or his Yeats essay, there was a dramatic shift to the clearer, leaner style of his later writing.

Unlike the carnival grab-bag of discussions at MLA conventions in the conference halls of big-city hotels, the English Institute met

in early September in a single ordinary classroom in Philosophy
Hall at Columbia University in New York and required just one
other room down the hall to serve up coffee and doughnuts. It
seemed almost quaint but nearly all the important literary theoreti-
cians participated. When Frye gave his talk, Helen and Rosemarie
sat at the back trying to beam assurance at him but he was so
terrified at giving his first major paper to a scholarly gathering,
that the occasion was totally lost on him. There were no wild
accolades or stormy denunciations but a quiet acceptance of
another scholar taking his place. Frye's own place was so quickly
acknowledged that he was soon on the supervising committee of
the Institute and by 1953 was chairman. As he hoped, the comedy
paper was important, and it became the one most reprinted over
the years.

Fundamentally for Frye, comedy represented a potential tragedy with hero and heroine frustrated in love and carried down by
social forces often represented by an ugly old grouch. All ends
well. The hero and heroine are married but, just as important, the
old man and all he represents is integrated into the new happy
social unit on stage. What initiates the social healing is the magical
"green world," really a dialectic full of symbolic overtures, where
everything first comes apart then rejoins to create a new vision of
life where no one is excluded. In this sense, comedy is the completed movement of all literature. Reflecting an idea in *Fearful
Symmetry,* Frye quite explicitly said that tragedy is uncompleted
comedy, thereby suggesting the cyclical nature of literature.

Frye's rather visionary affirmation of "fairies, dreams, disembodied souls, and pastoral lovers" would occupy him for much of his
subsequent career. He obviously suffered no embarrassment from
this unfashionable interest in a world obsessed with twisted ironies.
He even anticipated negative criticism by insisting that his fantasy
world was no more illusory than "the stumbling and blinded follies
of the 'normal' world ..."

When one of the young co-founders of the recently established
*The Hudson Review,* Frederick Morgan, wrote Frye about publishing the paper, Frye replied that while the paper was called for, he
just happened to have a "just completed" article which "like the

Shakespeare paper, contains a good many new ideas ..." It had a ponderous title, "The Four Forms of Prose Fiction," and turned out to be a piece of astute self-plagiarism, an expanded, reworked version of "The Anatomy of Prose Fiction" published six years before in *The Manitoba Arts Review*. It did not appear for nearly a year, but it was the start of Frye's exposure in the celebrated American literary journals.

Although tighter in style and better organized, the new version followed much the same ideas as the original, except to add a fifth "quintessential" form seen in the Bible and *Finnegans Wake* encompassing "the fall and awakening of the human soul and the creation and apocalypse of nature." Frye dealt with the novel largely in opposition to the anatomy and romance forms. He sniffed that the novel was only *one* form of fiction and not the epitome. It was meaningless to call romances bad novels: they are not novels at all. He dismissed the contention that as an older form, the romance was "something to be outgrown, a juvenile and undeveloped form."

Frye recast many of his ideas about fictional forms in terms which could be regarded as Jungian. Defining the novel as extroverted and personal, the romance as introverted and intellectualized, he completed the circle with the anatomy which he defined as extroverted and intellectual and the confession which was introverted and intellectual. For the first time, in facing the problems of categorizing and defining genres, Frye created new sub-categories, divisions of divisions. While there are four chief strands in fiction, there were also "six possible combinations of these forms." For example, *Moby Dick* was a romance-anatomy which combines the "romantic theme of the wild hunt" with the "encyclopedic anatomy of the whale." *Sartor Resartus* united the confession and anatomy. Despite all his propagandist efforts in the name of a separate anatomy category, he later continued to find such contemporary anatomies as *Zen and the Art of Motorcycle Maintenance* infallibly listed and sold as non-fiction. One clear victory was the anatomy section in Cuddon's *A Dictionary of Literary Terms* which acknowledged Frye's thinking.

Frye's academic interests, which looked so distantly gnostic, were reinforced constantly by the surrounding world. His interest in comedy and ritual led to a series of four *Forum* editorials from 1946 to 1948 on the unlikely topic of Christmas. Clearly there were no fairyland solutions for the real world. Yet in the midst of a deteriorating political situation there was hope: " ... no matter how often man is knocked down, he will always pick himself up, punch-drunk and sick and morbidly aware of his open guard, spit out some more teeth and start slugging again." And no matter how bleak the world looked with its starving refugees and war fevers, Frye bravely insisted " ... we can offset our helplessness by affirming Christmas, by returning once more to the symbol of what human life should be, a society raised by kindliness into a community of continuous joy." Spurning Christian chauvinism, he saw Christmas as a universally recognizable winter solstice festival, like the Roman Saturnalia, which can engender a recognition of "a power of life which is both the perfect form of human effort and all we know of God, and which it is our privilege to work with as it spreads from race to race, from nation to nation, from class to class, until there is no one shut out from the great invisible communion of the Christmas feast." But there was a Christian perspective, an advancement of thought. The Roman Saturnalia, after all, was a fantasy of slaves for a Golden Age, "a dumb, helpless ritual which said symbolically that the structure of Roman society was all wrong." By contrast, the original, unsentimental idea of celebrating Christ's birth involved a realization of visionary plan: "Christianity speaks of making the earth resemble the kingdom of heaven, and teaches that the kingdom of heaven is within man."

In fact Frye was daily reminded of the opposite, the post-war world of destroyed cities and armies of refugee children. When an Army social worker friend of Ray Godfrey's, Margaret Newton, was having trouble finding a place to board, the Fryes let her rent the attic rooms and a small living room on the second floor. Newton had worked finding homes for war orphans in Europe and was emotionally burnt out. The Fryes offered the right kind of quiet emotional support which enabled Newton to restore herself. Helen in particular kept an anxious eye on her. When a trunk of Newton's returned from Europe had been soaked in a flooded hold, its sour sea-smell permeated the side entranceway of the house. Helen joked that when the smell dissipated, Newton would be back to her old self. Newton entered into their life, sharing breakfast with them and, if either of their budgets allowed, sometimes beer in the late evening. Over breakfast, both Newton and Helen enjoyed Frye's reading of *The Globe and Mail* which was an energetic performance of amiable growling at the stupidity of politicians and dictators.

## ACTIVE AND SELF-COORDINATING

As he entered 1949, Frye was alarmed at a void of "dithering time" which clouded his sense of energy and purpose. It was, after all, over three years since he finished *Fearful Symmetry* and "as a means of systematizing my life," he decided to keep a diary. "Inertia," he advised himself, "was the chief enemy of the soul." His summary of the day would tell him, he considered, whether he'd wasted the day or not and give him an opportunity to analyse his dreams, lectures and conversations. The analysis of dreams in particular he saw as "field work in anagogic interpretation." The irony was that between the New Year and the end of May, his will to overcome his supposed sloth led to a tireless, all-consuming, encyclopedic account of his life in some 129 pages of tiny cramped writing. The teenage obsession with personal discipline would now also emerge in a mission to cure the flabbiness of literary theory, theology, and educational and social theory.

Mercilessly self-flagellant, Frye loaded up the first pages with a fantastic web of New Year's resolutions. He expected to start early morning piano practice and memorize a bewildering collection of eighteenth-century music. He would work daily on "this unending nightmare of languages" with a regime of German, Italian and Latin. In the next few weeks, he would concoct an array of writing projects, including a couple of novels on university life. Intrigued by the commercial success of novels on Jesus like *Quo Vadis, Ben*

*Hur,* and *The Robe,* Frye thought he could try one himself as a way of expressing his own ideas of the actual crucifixion. There was the idea of a manual on writing for students and a continuation of "a dozen papers" ambition to be fulfilled for the year. Nearly everything got lost in the rush of a new academic term. Frye was soon condemning himself for "buggering around" if he lost so much as an afternoon without significant work. But there were two suggestions he formulated with enormous implications.

The first was a "short and simple book on Spenser" which he later demoted to "a tiny handbook." He went so far as sketching out a skimpy preface for the book which pointed to a central theme of his real work for the next few years, the eradication of evaluation in literary criticism. He also proposed a book "on the geometry of vision, which will analyze the diagrammatic patterns present in thought which emerge unconsciously in the metaphors of speech, particularly prepositions (up, down, beside and the like)." Explicitly related to this was the need to "explore mandalas" which in itself was a reflection of his deep interest in Jungian psychology.

Ironically one of the books he adamantly refused to consider was a study of T.S. Eliot, which a graduate student David Hoeniger had suggested. "I said no: I could write only about people who were open at the top, and he was sealed off at the top. I had no idea what I meant, but he understood. People who enter into religious systems as he has done deny the integrity of the verbal universe ..."

Haunting all these schemes was his adolescent dream of co-ordinated masterpieces. After he finished *Fearful Symmetry* he developed the idea of a Pentateuch. "Blake was the Genesis; a study of drama, especially Shakespearian comedy, was the Exodus; Leviticus was to be philosophical (a dream of a 'Summa' of modern thought had got into my skull very early), Numbers was to be a study of Romanticism and its after effects, and Deuteronomy was to deal with general aesthetic problems." Suddenly he started redefining these projects in terms of his adolescent dream of the seven masterpieces and in his diary even applied simplified alphabetic symbols to them. With a touch of sarcasm, he now called them "the seven pillars" and finally came to realize that the categories represented themes and not actual books. Only now at age 37, could he be delivered from his boyhood obsession.

Because of the intensity of his writing plans, he felt increasing doubts about the "corniness" of Victoria College, of the weak guidance of the now gravely ill Brown and Bennett, his replacement, in college affairs. There was the added irritation of an hysterical Board of Regents which still stood like the Methodist Inquisition over student affairs, particularly *Acta* of which Frye remained staff adviser. The year before there had been a tremendous blow-up over a poem by Peter Grant, "Concrete Conception" published in *Acta* about a latter-day virgin birth. It had won a student literary contest judged by Marshall McLuhan.

When *Acta* editor, Douglas Fisher, took the poems to Frye, he readily agreed that McLuhan had made the right choice. He confessed that he was personally disturbed: if a liberal arts college was going to censor a parody of the immaculate conception, then something was seriously wrong. It was at this point that student rumors spread wildly, casting Frye into the hero's role. According to the legend, Frye went in to see the Principal. Quoting relevant passages from Milton's *Areopagitica* he threatened to resign. In the view of one *Acta* sub-editor, this was an act of consummate courage since Frye had not yet established a reputation and he would have been thrown out penniless into the street.

The reality, of course, was much less romantic. For one thing, Frye had already published and been celebrated for his Blake book. He found the administration weak-kneed with fears of board reaction, sincerely wanting the whole incident just to blow over. This is in fact what happened. A little later, Frye had to beat back a revolt from college lowbrows who traditionally eyed *Acta's* budget whenever the magazine was in political trouble.

On top of these parochial irritations, the future didn't seem too promising either. His new graduate students had so little spirit and maturity, they could not come up with their own thesis topics. Only a decade after his own Laocoön struggle with Blake, he was dismayed to find few "seekers." The problem was fundamental and pervasive: " ... in education we can no longer distinguish interest, which leads to the passive receptivity of being entertained, from concentration, which is active and self-coordinating." There were as well the hazards of would-be disciples who seemed to return to school "because they didn't want to grow up, and are busy looking for splendid and inspiring leadership in a community fit for culture-heroes." He admitted his total embarrassment with disciples and their need to be dominated. He secretly blessed Eleanor Godfrey and Bill Graham as two individuals who did not expect him "to take off for the sky at a moment's notice."

His success as star lecturer, however, spread across campus and was most obvious in his Bible course which he taught in 1948-9 to both first and fourth year students. It drew such crowds from across the campus, students who failed to get seats stood at the back or sat on the radiator covers on the sides of the largest room at Vic. Despite his popularity, Frye could be deliberately harsh and unaccommodating on the principle that an undergraduate should be intellectually turned upside down. He once asked, "If I were to look for the Kingdom of God, where would I look?" After some vague answers by other students, a freshman, Hope Arnott, who'd been frantically waving her hand for attention, got her chance. "Why, sir, I would look within." Although Arnott's answer was basic dogma from Luke 17:21, which Frye shared, Frye mauled her by saying, "Then you'd be cross-eyed." Arnott, of course, went back to residence and cried for a week.

Because of the theological implications of Frye's ideas, his lectures drew the attention of campus fundamentalists. One student, June Clark, chose one of Frye's Bible classes to read an open letter criticizing Frye's view of Jesus as a mythic as opposed to historical figure. As Clark read her statement, Frye lost all color in his face and seemed to be rigidly controlling himself. Frye answered Clark's concerns with a directness but gentleness which impressed one student, Douglas Fisher, who knew that Frye had the intellectual equipment, social support and probably the inclination, to savage Clark. His own defence was so good that there was an impulse among Frye loyalists to applaud at the end but they remained silent out of fear of Frye's opprobrium. Yet Frye privately stewed about the incident so much that it became yet another factor in his growing doubts about Toronto.

Frye's one exceptional student, Peter Fisher, continued a once-weekly intellectual free-for-all with Frye in the bar of the Park Plaza Hotel, as part of his PhD preparation. Their concerns were almost entirely cosmological, focussed on analysis of great themes such as the *bardo* cycle of afterlife of Tibetan Buddhism and Yeats's Great Wheel, with which they played by slotting figures into phases: "Fisher's only idea was that the fool at the end of Yeats' phases is regarded by the world as a comic hero in a tragic context, whereas the point that stops the wheel turning is the point at which he becomes the tragic hero in the comic context: the ambiguity of Samson, Jesus and Lear."

Despite his peculiar New Year's characterization of sloth, Frye kept up a blistering pace of giving undergraduate lectures, supervising his graduate Blake seminar, editing *The Canadian Forum*, speaking to community groups, doing a talk on Kafka for CBC, attending meetings of a culture commission, helping to proofread and edit *Acta*, supervising the student Writers Group and helping out in the annual literary contest. In fact, by Jan. 23, he was already complaining of being tired. "I don't much care to be busy: one side of me pulls away from activity on the plea of wanting to write, and urges me to a real psychosomatic blowout, catching flu and going to bed and being coddled for a week."

Although Frye later resisted, and resists to this day, the supposition that his theories were closely influenced by Jung, the Jungian influence was surprisingly pervasive in his notes. It affected his analysis of his dreams. One dream in particular gave Frye one of "the first of the autonomous breakthroughs Jung talks about." It concerned a delayed visit of Roy Daniells and "some unknown stranger" who nightmarishly seeped into Frye himself. He recognized the Daniells presence from a conversation he'd had with Helen that day but the stranger seemed to represent a plethora of forbidding presences, all the way from an abstraction of Frye's neglected music to the ghosts of his dead brothers, Howard and Northrop. If this was a first breakthrough, there were few advancements. Frye nevertheless detailed his dreams and sniffed out every connotation and reference from the day's activities and conversation. One more mysterious dream which could easily represent the fragility of his own theories was that of his inhabiting a huge crystal palace with an array of doors and windows he was desperately trying to keep "shut and locked against intruders." A key problem of interpreting dreams he soon realized was that while it was easy to sort out the sources of images, it was difficult to remember the *narrative* sequence of episodes.

While references to Jung were ubiquitous, Frye was on the point of spurning him. After spending an afternoon reading Jung's *The Secret of the Golden Flower,* he seemed to downgrade Jungian psychology to the level of a mental exercise: "I think I've pretty well got the hang of Jung, and should start serious work on Freud now." He complained that Jung "jumped over the libido Orc-hero to his archetypes without incorporating him." There was already a seed of doubt as well in his realization that because literary criticism was so weak it could be invaded by any stronger discipline with coordinated theory. If literary criticism could develop its own core of theory, it could ward off such bad or distorting influences.

He was able to give vent to this in a paper eventually published as "The Function of Literary Criticism at the Present Time" for the Toronto Colloquium which was the basis of the famous polemical introduction to *Anatomy of Criticism.* Frye casually called it "ye next thynge" in his diary and intended it simply "to boil down my L ideas." He worked on it on the weekends and, oblivious to its importance, complained in his diary that it took too long. Everything guaranteed its obscurity. The Toronto Colloquium was very much a staff affair which received no publicity or coverage in either student or city newspapers. When he read the paper on Feb. 28, Frye glumly noted he pulled only the usual English department cabal and just a handful of undergraduates. The reaction was decidedly mixed. In giving the summation, Fulton Anderson said he liked it and then ominously departed. Marshall McLuhan, rumored by one mutual friend to be out to get Frye, talked about "essences" in a prophetically obtuse manner.

The title, a deliberate steal from Matthew Arnold, drew attention to the fact while there was no real function at present, there ought to be one. Although reasonable in tone, he is quite devastating in suggesting that critics really didn't know what they were doing.

Frye identified a crucial deficiency: the presumption that literature could be captured inside linear history, "a bald chronicle of names and dates and works and influences, deprived of all the real historical interest that a real historian would give it..." In opposition to this was Eliot's expansive notion that "the whole tradition of Western poetry from Homer down ought to exit simultaneously in the poet's mind..."

To illustrate how primitive contemporary criticism was in fact (as opposed to ancient rhetoric), he pulled his old chestnut, the sloppy classification of prose forms which failed to deal with prose like *Gulliver's Travels*. More broadly he complained that criticism had failed to make "any serious effort to determine what literature is" or "whether there are different levels of meaning in literature, whether they can be defined and classified." Quite bruising in all this was the explicit assumption that literary criticism was a scientifically rigorous discipline which should now be separated from the activity of "critical readers."

Given Frye's cosmological concerns, it was certainly not untoward to raise James Jeans' astronomical concerns in his *Mysterious Universe* about a universe defined and contained by mathematics. Frye suggested the literary corollary, that "literature exists in a verbal universe, which is not a commentary on life or reality, but contains life and reality in a system of verbal relationships." Yet for all the scientific talk, Frye flirted with outright mysticism, suggesting a "higher unity," a precious, inviolable, supernal zone of significance which, like the postulated but unknown "God" of theology, must be approached with care along a special path: " ...if we assert this final unity too quickly we may injure the integrity of the different means of approaching it. It does not help a poet to tell him that the function of literature is to empty itself into an ocean of superverbal significance, when the nature of that significance is unknown." Implicit in all of this was the image of a literary Jerusalem which stands at the end of literary effort and was protected from the intrusions of dull literary historians, misdirected moralists and picky aesthetes who inevitably get lost on the snarled pathways below. The force which would show the way, of course, was an awakened science of criticism which would integrate the "huge aggregate or miscellaneous pile of creative efforts" of literature "within a total form."

Precisely when the diary came to an end in late May, Frye started working seriously on his Spenser book. He tried a new approach to composition by hiring a former student, Betty Mihalko, a stenography expert. Two and three times a week, he had two-hour dictating sessions with her. One day, he dictated so much, Mihalko seized up with writer's cramp. Although general theoretical considerations of this new book spilled over into new work, the manuscript never reached a finished stage.

Despite this furious sense of direction and productivity, Frye still seemed curiously naive about his place in professional academia. This was dispelled by a visit from Herbert Davis who stopped off in Toronto on his way home to a readership job at Oxford. He told Frye he'd sat on an appointments committee at Harvard and Frye's name had come up but had been eliminated because of a desire to appoint a Harvard graduate, Archibald MacLeish. Irrespective of prospects at Harvard, he told Frye he *had* to apply for a Guggenheim fellowship. Davis's suggestion was forcefully followed up by the classics scholar, Eric Havelock, who had taught at Vic from 1929 to 1946. Havelock's own insistent interest seems to have lain behind a trip by the Fryes in early September to Moncton, Cambridge and New York. Havelock entertained the Fryes at the Harvard Faculty Club, introduced him to some faculty admirers of *Fearful Symmetry* and bluntly told Frye he'd "been in Toronto long enough." He seemed to have no new job to offer but had been behind an attempt to get Frye into the General Education faculty which included I.A. Richards.

While the temptations were great, both the Fryes felt lingering "British" sympathies directly blocked the way. In a letter to her parents, Helen described a curious barroom encounter with another couple in New York. While hardly decisive, the meeting did reveal the unquestioned depths of their loyalty to Canada, which would be hard to displace. "We feel that we've had enough travelling and are ready to settle to work where the dollar doesn't figure quite so much. One guy we met was squiffed, had a blonde Jewish floozy with him, asked us if we didn't think it was true

America stopped supporting England, did we think we'd be with the US in a war with Russia, had we any children, were we the sort of people that made the French Canadians outstrip the English-speaking in Canada, had Norrie ever done me dirt with other dames, admitted we looked happy as hell, wouldn't believe we'd been married twelve years. Poor Norrie's hayfever left him rather deaf and he didn't hear all of this nonsense so I had to counter with jovial but firm and ladylike remarks."

## SCHOLARLY PROSPECTUS

In November Frye did follow Davis's advice and focussed all his writing plans on an application to the Guggenheim Memorial Foundation, the usual source of funding for major arts scholars. Like many writers applying for a grant, he conveyed the impression that with a year off he was facing a modest bit of clean-up work when, in fact, he was outlining the labour of the next four decades. In a newspaper interview in March, he more realistically acknowledged that his plans might occupy the next ten or 15 years.

In his application he claimed that "the only critical methods that would work on Blake were those that had been explicitly recommended for allegorical poetry in general by medieval and Renaissance criticism. Thus Blake proved to be, not a special kind of poet, but a typical allegorical poet." The last four years had seen him, he said, "collecting and sorting out material for a comprehensive study of Renaissance symbolism." Since his notes fell into three main categories: epic, drama and prose fiction, he breezily suggested that "the total project is thus a three-volume study." He said he'd finished a draft of the first book "a study of Renaissance epic based mainly on Spenser's *Faerie Queene*," and merely needed some time for footnoting and documentation. The second work would be on Shakespeare's comedy and as he saw the background research for both Spenser and Shakespeare as "inseparable," he wanted to do them simultaneously.

For the epic volume, he planned "to trace the evolution of the primitive elements of the epic ... not only in the ancient epics themselves but in romance, ballad and myth." Another stage involved examination of the ancient heroic epic which led to the Bible which Frye said had grown out of "epic materials." In a half sentence which would give him a 40-year headache, he identified the need of illustrating "the place of scripture in literature, specifically of course of the Bible in Western literature, as a kind of definitive epic or 'monomyth' ..." After consideration of medieval allegory and fourfold meaning from theology and Biblical commentary, poor Spenser got squeezed in at the end "to weave all these strands together."

Even then Spenser is not really good enough, and Frye threw in a hint of his Los-Orc argument to explain that there is "a developing central argument in the epic tradition" in which the bald muscle-flexing heroism in Homer is replaced by a kind of revisionism, partly from Christian influence which forces "later poets to consider more carefully what a heroic act really is." Since Spenser "failed to solve the problems in this," he would have to discard him for Milton who as an epic poet provided "a clear, consistent and complete analysis of the heroic act in his two epics. The book ends in a careful study of *Paradise Regained*."

Even before Frye started, it was obvious that it was theoretical concerns that were chiefly animating him. "My present project contains, first, a theory of verbal meaning which tries to unite traditional theories of meaning, such as Dante's scheme of four levels, with modern ideas about symbolism. Second, a theory of literary symbolism which will present all the essential possibilities of literary symbolism in a single form, in other words a kind of grammar of symbolism. I have already produced one of these grammars in *Fearful Symmetry* ..."

Not surprisingly, the Guggenheim Foundation displayed a touch of caution in the face of this expansive application. One adviser wanted to know how Frye was going to contribute to scholarship. Frye quickly sent off a two-page, single-spaced defence. Barely suppressing his anger, he attacked the fact-monger school of historical scholarship, bluntly accusing scholars of "failure of nerve" in moving from the necessary, but only elementary and peripheral, background research into the foreground of the total patterns of the art itself. He demanded a synoptic study of *The Faerie Queene*'s symbolism and outlined steps in considering the epic as a unified structure rather than a basket of influences.

In particular Frye wanted to study Spenser's use of nature myths which, Frye insisted, "form so many of the major structural principles in his allegory." Although he observed that scholars tended to underplay details like the Garden of Adonis reverberations in the third and fourth books, much of this mythic reflection was quite explicit in the mythological handbooks and allegorical commentaries on Homer, Virgil and Ovid, which were contemporary with Spenser. In other words, a key to Spenser's poetry was the criticism of his own time. It would then be only a small step towards a mythological handbook which would hold true for any poet. The strongly-stated letter worked marvels with the Guggenheim administration and he soon received a letter requesting his financial needs during his sabbatical.

True to the Guggenheim outline, he first undertook a consideration of Dante's four levels of meaning in an essay he sold soon after to *The Kenyon Review*. Placing it in this most imperial of literary magazines was easy. One of his Vic colleagues who knew one of the editors suggested he try them out. Frye entered into correspondence with Philip Blair Rice who was excited by the published essays which Frye sent him. When Frye sent off "Levels of Meaning," *Kenyon Review* quickly accepted it. Although the *Review*, edited by John Crowe Ransom, was primarily an organ of New Criticism, Rice managed to slip through three of his theoretical essays in just a year and half from early 1950 through the following year. But Rice then died, and *The Kenyon Review* interest faded away.

"Levels of Meaning" briefly listed a "precise scheme" of meaning from the Middle Ages: the literal, allegorical, tropological or moral and anagogic. While John Danby also suggested applying the four levels of meaning to literary criticism in his *Shakespeare's Doctrine of Nature* in 1949, Frye proposed a "modern restatement" of the theory. By-passing philosophical consideration, he reiterated his familiar dictum that "the obvious place to start looking for a theory of literary meaning is in literature."

This was a four-part exercise for climbing the mountain of literature and human potential. The first, basic literal understanding, was taken for granted. The second level of allegory, where most critics got off, was basic criticism. The third moral level was more idiosyncratic, adapted to weld Frye's own notions of morality and liberal education to a process of archetypal recognition and consolidation, ideally informed and shaped by the inclusive structure of the Bible. Education was extremely important as a releasing mechanism for "the powers of words." The recognition that archetypes fit together into a vast verbal universe led to the top of Everest, the potentially theological and non-critical apperception of "the surrounding fields of cultivation."

Another glimpse of his vast Guggenheim plan, related to his ideas on the epic, coincidentally made an appearance in an introduction to a collection of poetry and prose by Milton which Frye completed just before going away to Harvard. Although Frye outlined his ideas about the epic, it was clear too that foremost in his mind was the romantic conception of the release of the power of words: "Milton, the agent of the Word of God, is trying to awaken with his words a vision in us ... If we surrender to his charming and magical spell, and seize his fables of hell and Paradise, they will become realities of earth, and the stories of Adam and Samson our own story."

At precisely the same time that he was finishing off his Milton introduction, he broadcast a popular radio series for the CBC, advertised after the first talk as "an important series ... *The Writer as Prophet.*" Important or not, the CBC didn't appear to have any real confidence in the series. The 7:45 time slot for the first broadcast on June 16 listed only "Literary Talk." CBC folklore has it, in fact, that the series was a quick fill-in for another failed series. Frye himself was so far past his deadline that his producer nervously phoned him up. Frye soothed her by saying, "I'm a former typing champion and I am now rolling the first page into the typewriter and I will soon have the script."

Effortlessly written for an intelligent radio listener, the scripts were astonishing. Here was a writer who was bedevilling his own colleagues with dense, difficult theory, but could suddenly turn around and write for a popular audience. Just after his abuse of centrifugal approaches among scholars, Frye intrepidly wrote about his writer-prophets, Milton, Swift, Blake and Shaw largely with simple historical detail but just enough analysis to justify the theme of writer as prophet. Through the easy scripts, there was, however, a more crucial hint of Frye's magical, reformist, conception of literary power. Frye pointed out that even the misanthropic Swift managed to understand the fairytale magic of his Gulliver tales: " ... they are admirable things, and will wonderfully mend the world." In the next talk on Blake, Frye repeated Blake's insistence that no matter how depraved or ugly the world, we have to keep "the vision of that simple and child-like world ... a model to work by ... So Blake, as he looks at London, sees the New Jerusalem in it with a child's innocent eye ... What the poet sees now are the 'dark Satanic mills', the hideous sweatshops that starve women and murder children, but it is the poet's business to point out that a clean and free world is hidden behind them."

## ON THE EDGE OF HARVARD

In Cambridge, the Fryes first settled in a room, which Douglas Bush's wife, Hazel, found in a high school teacher's house on a dead-end, Kenway St. Ensconced in the centre of the upper-middle-class area, they were surrounded by Cambridge's mouldering ambience of dense flowering bushes, vines and immense wooden Cape Cod houses. For once, Frye found the leisure to take time off and attend concerts. There was an almost Mozartean combination of culture and locale which Frye would always remember with fondness, particularly when faced with the dystopian nightmares that most American cities would become in the sixties. The Fryes enjoyed themselves so much in fact, that they agreed that if there was one place to be after Toronto, this was it.

Eric Havelock, who saw a lot of them that year, continued to hint at Harvard's interest in him.

Frye naturally fell in with the English department young bloods including Richard Ellmann, a great admirer of *Fearful Symmetry*. Ellmann, who was teaching a graduate course in Blake and Yeats, made it a required text in his course. He and graduate student, Robert O'Clair, studied the book paragraph by paragraph. Frye's friendship with Ellmann and O'Clair led to their suggestion that Frye become an honorary member of Kirkland House which meant the occasional house dinners and cocktail parties. This was mostly socializing but Frye did involve himself in the Kirkland House Forum and the following spring gave a general talk on Blake.

Early in the fall Frye went down to New York to give his paper, "Blake's Treatment of the Archetype," in an all-Blake session of the English Institute. This is one of Frye's most obscure papers and has only been reprinted once. It is also one of his most important, representing a key link between his thinking on Blake and the ostensibly un-Blakean *Anatomy*. Although admitting that the study of Blake could be "a long and torturous blind alley," Blake's symbols for those inclined could be "a calculus for all their criticism." He provided four moods or states in which art is created, Eden, Beulah, Generation and Ulro into which "every poem of his regularly resolves." He laid down a chart dividing the demonic symbolism of experience and apocalyptic symbolism of innocence. The point, however, was not categorization but the acquisition of an apocalyptic sense in the student. Essential to this was the casting off of the traditional notions of heroism, the romantic *macho* Orc for the Christian figure of Los: "The true hero is the man who, whether as thinker, fighter, artist, martyr, or ordinary worker, helps in achieving the apocalyptic vision of art..."

Frye showed signs of modulating his extremism. For one thing, he chose to write in a simple style to minimize misunderstanding. For another, Frye played with the notion that criticism was not, after all, crucial to the creation of new art. He conceded that "theories of poetry and of archetypes seem to belong to criticism rather than to poetry itself." The reason Blake made such an effort to drag everything "up to consciousness, and to do deliberately what most poets prefer to do instinctively" was "the breakdown of a tradition of criticism." While Frye was letting poets off the hook, he was now telling critics their job: to sort out the mythology of the age, to realize "the comic vision of the apocalypse or work of Los, the clarification of the mind which enables one to grasp the human form of the world."

Frye was therefore just as aggressive as ever in the name of Blake. Just as the Bible was the great code of art, "Blake seems to provide something of a code of modern art ..." Fundamentally, though, Blake's work itself was solidly anchored in the Bible with his two tragicomic visions of Orc and Los, of Genesis (which leaves Israel in bondage) and Exodus (which leaves it in the Promised Land). Besides ransacking Blake, there was another crucial job ahead, mining the minerals of the Bible for the sake of modern criticism. As often before, Frye was really announcing his own agenda.

After the session, both Frye and Philip Wheelwright were eager to go down to Princeton to see a production of Eliot's *The Family Reunion,* and Wheelwright offered to drive the Fryes down in his own car. Halfway down the New Jersey Turnpike in the midst of an intense dispute over Spinoza, Wheelwright collided with a truck which cut him off from the left. Frye was thrown against the windshield. His right arm was broken, his glasses were smashed and his forehead was split open. The ambulance took him into nearby New Brunswick, N.J., for a week's hospitalization. Ostensibly Frye's arm healed quickly but it remained stiff and in later years, arthritic. In classroom lectures, the arm hung down like that of an injured war veteran.

When the Fryes returned to Harvard, they moved into the Brattle Inn on Story St. which was a glorified boarding house where they ate on a card table and washed their dishes in the bathtub. With great plans to write a couple of books, Frye could not write a single word. His right arm was disabled by a forearm cast and sling, and his right eye patched over. He had to depend on Helen as secretary to handle correspondence and take dictation. He was faithful to his Guggenheim grant plans and dictated notes for the Spenser book from a large rocking chair.

Able to start typing a bit in November, he managed to finish up a long article for *The Hudson Review* about a rather motley collection of recent novels. Frye squirmed in discomfort over contemporary, ironic literature. He was troubled, for example, by "some rather nagging irony" which muddied the polarized narrative in Marcel Ayme's *The Barkeep of Ble'mont*. Gheorghiu's apocalyptic novel, *The Twenty-Fifth Hour*, likewise garnered a smirk about despair: "not even a Messiah can save us now." Frye's one genuine moment of enthusiasm was in recounting the story of Luca, in Moravia's *Two Adolescents*. This story, noted Frye, "is a humble but genuine example of what the great religions are talking about: of losing one's life to find it, of gaining charity through renunciation, of becoming free by cutting oneself loose from everything that attaches and motivates."

In sending the review in to Morgan, Frye was a bit apologetic, and hinted he might work more fruitfully on other material. Morgan next sent him *Boswell's London Journal* to review and again, Frye turned in an adequate but uninspired effort. After a little bit of civilized hemming and hawing, Frye and Morgan consolidated on a more productive course, and Frye subsequently reviewed the growing output of theoretical criticism which included the newly published work of Cassirer, Susanne Langer, Allen Tate and Hugh Kenner.

General theoretical considerations were now utterly crucial. When Frye was still in a sling, Helen wrote a worried note to John Crowe Ransom about "a provisionally accepted" article for *The Kenyon Review* called "The Shape of Literary Criticism." Frye had sent an only copy of a revision shortly after coming back to Cambridge from a short holiday in Maine and hadn't received any acknowledgement. It was, in fact, to appear shortly in the Winter issue as "The Archetypes of Literature" as part of the series "My Credo: A Symposium of Critics," a collection really of dogmatic soliloquies. One former student called it the "mini-*Anatomy*," the essay which provided the core elements of the book to come.

In announcing his own new branch of literary criticism—the archetypal—Frye naturally condemned other approaches. He was unkind about commentators in "brightening the corner where they are" and downright abusive about evaluative critics who play "an imaginary stock exchange." Frye's own suggestion for an inductive, centripetal approach was fundamentally cosmological: " ... whereas the profound masterpiece seems to draw us to a point at which we can see an enormous number of converging patterns of significance. Here we begin to wonder if we cannot see literature, not only as complicating itself in time, but as spread out in conceptual space from some unseen center." What Frye implicitly suggested was a vast mandala of literary archetypes, sectioned into four parts and animated at the core by emotional dynamics of wish-fulfillment, the human desire for a better world.

Frye also inevitably drew on his early experiences with Spengler by arranging the literary "archetypes" of romance, comedy, tragedy and elegy and satire into the four seasons of spring, summer, autumn and winter. There was, among other associations, the corresponding life pattern of the hero: birth, marriage, isolation and defeat. The hero also is projected into the collective image of the symposium, and communion in the comic vision, and tyranny and anarchy in the tragic. At this stage, the pattern was close to the traditional Last Judgment or Harrowing of Hell form with a luminous communion at the top and loathsome hell-hole at the bottom. Biblical scholar Austin Farrer had in fact published a detailed symbolic analysis of Revelation in 1949, *The Rebirth of Images* which included a diamond-shaped diagram encompassing the seasons, Biblical figures, compass points, gems, the four elements, and ritual celebrations. Frye had absorbed it but what differentiated his own effort was his assumption that such a pattern could extend to *all* literature.

The importance of religion in all this was absolutely central because of its tendency to soak up a "definitive body of myth." The critic steeped in sacred scriptures could then "descend from archetypes to genres, and see how the drama emerges from the ritual side of myth and lyric from the epiphanic or fragmented side, while the epic carries on the central encyclopedic structure."

When this came out, it was received with cautionary awe among some of the Harvard graduate students including Robert O'Clair. Although O'Clair considered the essay a bit wacky, he nevertheless endeavored to apply its proto-*Anatomy* categories to Ben Jonson's *Bartholomew Fair* for an assignment. Frye remembered O'Clair, fortified by whiskey, coming into a Kirkland House dinner with exasperation on his face, sitting down and asking him to figure it out. With finesse, Frye slotted the figures into the schema.

Although Frye's presence on campus was unofficial, the English department asked him to give a lecture as part of a series on Shakespeare which included Alfred Harbage and Gerald Bentley, Sr. It was an ill-disguised secret that the series was intended to sniff people out for a major Shakespeare appointment. Frye gave his paper, "Shakespeare's Comedy of Humors," at Radcliffe College on Nov. 30. As before, Frye called for the establishment of fundamental definitions to clear up theoretical muddiness which he saw in Shakespearean criticism particularly comedy. In an effective dig, he flatly declared that "the most recent dramatic critic to be primarily interested in the structure and categories of drama appears to be Aristotle who did not say much about comedy." Concerning the latter, he pointed out a "dry bald little summary" of Aristotelian origin called *Tractatus Coislinianus*. With examples and clarifications of three recurring character types, the pompous hypocrite (alazon), the humble figure (eiron) who deflates the alazon's pretensions and the buffoon (bomolochos), the paper reflected its source. Frye played with a fourth category, the snob or prig (agroikos) but uncertainly appended it to the alazon. Unfortunately with its arid list of "polar" types and sub-types, the essay style hardly sent a rush of springwater along the "dry bald" riverbed of Aristotelian criticism.

If the published version was even halfway faithful to the original talk, Frye was clearly putting himself out of a Harvard job. According to Jackson Bate, then a junior staff member, the conservatives in the department were looking for a conventional scholar to lecture in Shakespeare and direct doctoral theses in Elizabethan literature generally. Certainly with his obdurately anti-historical bias, Frye would have looked like a grenade-bristling terrorist beside the winner, Harbage. Even though the conservative faction won, they placated the Frye supporters with the reasonable idea that Harvard would hire him in few years when a more general appointment opened. Everyone seemed to expect that Frye would jump at a Harvard appointment. While Helen enjoyed titillating her parents with the news, she warned them not to talk about it in Toronto because rumors of Frye's restlessness were rife there.

As Frye flirted with non-Canadian ambitions, he was faced with a bruising irony: writing *The University of Toronto Quarterly* annual review of Canadian poetry from the heart of Cambridge, Massachusetts. While he was directing fierce polemics against evaluation in academic studies, he quickly and inevitably fell into the role of evaluative critic. His first effort involved reviewing just two books, *Of Time and the Lover* by *Forum* alumnus James Wreford and *The Tight-Rope Walker* by Norman Levine. Frye bluntly concluded, "This is clearly not a banner year for Canadian poetry ... One looks hopefully and constantly, in reading through this material, for some signs of an ability to express the simple rather than the commonplace emotion, to use traditional metres without unenterprising monotony, to make the art of writing a poem a fresh experience instead of a conditioned reflex of nostalgia." In 1950 Frye's likes and dislikes were inconsequential but it was precisely in the early 1950s that Canadian poetry blossomed, putting Frye into a central position which surprised him. By the end of the decade, his reviews not only ballooned nearly tenfold in size, they coincidentally thrust Frye into the unappetizing role of the critic who poets loved to excoriate.

Although Frye had expected to lecture in Britain in the summer, Robert Heilman at the University of Washington in Seattle asked Frye to teach a quarter-session on the Romantic period just when his British sponsors failed to confirm his trip. Impressed by the uncomplicated promise of money when he was nearly broke, Frye accepted immediately. In late May, the Fryes flew to Chicago to see Vera and other friends like Ernest Sirluck, then moved on to Madison, Wisconsin, where Merrit Hughes, Ruth Wallerstein, Helen White and Jerome Buckley pulled out the red carpet with considerably more than sociable motives.

Flying from Minneapolis to Seattle in a stratocruiser at the then dizzy altitude of 15,000 feet, they settled into a domestic luxury which mocked their former Brattle Inn existence: a ten-room, four-bathroom house on 10th Ave. near the university. The house overlooked a yacht club on Portage Bay, on the outlet to the ocean from the inland Lake Washington which lay along the eastern edge of the city. Helen, stunned by "grass like Persian carpet and roses four and five inches across," was in a gardener's paradise.

The whole social environment was open and generous. They were quickly befriended by the staff, most particularly William Bostetter and his wife Betty. Bostetter, who had reviewed *Fearful Symmetry*, had suggested Frye's coming to Seattle for the summer. Frye coopted their ancient piano and received the dubious attentions of the Bostetter cats including Figaro who curled up around Frye's non-pedal foot as he played Mozart concerti.

After the intense Harvard year, the summer in Seattle appeared almost frivolous at first. The Bostetters took the Fryes out on a drive around the Olympic Peninsula and, over beers on a beach, Frye relaxed with tales of his summer mission in 1934 which was now a polished performance hiding once-painful experiences. The Fryes also did the rounds of the department parties, cleverly attaching themselves to a scholar with a heart condition who invariably insisted he had to leave at midnight. Frye was impressed that the atmosphere before midnight was one of high spirits but afterwards, if they stayed, deteriorated into quite different confessions of the intellectual isolation created by the implacable mountains closing off most of North America. The question of Seattle's ambience was more than academic. Robert Heilman was eager to replace a departing scholar with Frye.

What really impressed Heilman, however, was that of the number of young stars he got out to Seattle to teach, Frye was a conscientious lecturer who was not looking to get paid to lap up some mountain scenery. In fact, the return to the classroom started to generate such a spill of ideas, he was "reduced to scribbling notes furtively in little books in the corners of parties." Frye's seminar in the old Parrington Hall was noteworthy for its eccentricity and baffling conceptual difficulties. One of his students, Herbert Lindenberger, found Frye's class at first bizarre, yet so full of revelations they stayed with him throughout his own career. Lindenberger noted that Frye did not lecture so much as try out

theoretical ideas: "The class was supposedly on Romanticism, but
if Mr. Frye ever intended it to be this was never entirely clear. He
suggested we read certain Romantic poems for particular class
sessions, but the particular poems never occupied more than a few
minutes of class time. Indeed, they usually served as a jumping-
off point for larger assertions that moved far away from Romantic
literature to places like the Bible, Dante, T.S. Eliot and the like.
Usually at the beginning of each class session Mr. Frye put a chart
on the board based on Blake's map of the psyche. It looked like
this:

> Eden
> Beulah
> Generation
> Ulro

In the course of the session he would fill in each of those categories
with concrete matter—images, titles of poems or parts of poems,
names of authors, all manner of things. I had never seen anything
of the like before. He never explained directly what he was up to."

Like most graduate students of the time, Lindenberger had been
heavily influenced by the work-by-work approach of New Criticism
and at first spurned Frye's ideas, obdurately debating Frye in class.
Finally he realized that what he had been taught himself was *one*
approach not *the* approach. What surprised Lindenberger was that
instead of being "a flaming Orc" figure who imposed his view, Frye
was always remarkably patient in class in hearing out objections.
Because Frye had published only a few articles it wasn't obvious
that his ideas fit into a broader scheme. Although his efforts to be
understood usually resulted in bafflement, there was one hilarious
misunderstanding. Frye put a pattern of concentric circles on
the blackboard. Explaining that one of the circles "enclosed the
unconscious in Wordsworth, another, the unconscious in Coleridge" he pointed to the center of the circles and asked what that
represented. After a long silence, the poet Richard Selig (then in
his senior year) who always sat in quiet intensity beside Frye,
blurted out, "The genitalia!" The class erupted in helpless laughter

Frye's parents, Herm and Cassie, with brother Howard, around 1899.
(PHOTO COURTESY OF JANE LAYHEW)

Northrop at about three years old.
(PHOTO COURTESY OF NORTHROP FRYE)

Northrop with his mother around 1919. (PHOTO COURTESY OF NORTHROP FRYE)

WINS SECOND PLACE

The typing champion, 1929.
(PHOTO COURTESY OF JANE LAYHEW)

High school graduate, the notorious pink blotter picture: on the upper left corner Frye scribbled, "Me, God save us."
(PHOTO COURTESY OF NORTHROP FRYE)

A source of nightmares for Frye as a child. Faithful "Burned to ashes at the stake." From *Pilgrim's Progress* by John Bunyan, 1885. (COURTESY OF THE OSBORNE COLLECTION OF EARLY CHILDRENS' BOOKS, TORONTO PUBLIC LIBRARY.)

College graduate, 1933.
(PHOTO COURTESY OF NORTHROP FRYE)

Frye as freshman in Charles House, 1929.
(PHOTO COURTESY OF NORTHROP FRYE.)

Playing William Byrd at Oxford, 1938.
From the left: Mildred Winfree, Frye, and
Charles Bell. (PHOTO COURTESY OF NORTHROP FRYE)

Norrie and Helen on the south steps of
Emmanuel College on their wedding day,
August 24, 1937.
(PHOTO COURTESY OF NORTHROP FRYE)

Frye relaxing with the Kemps at the Gordon Bay cottage, 1941. Top row from left: Roy
Kemp, Mrs. Kemp, Helen. Bottom row: Harold, Mr. Kemp, Frye.
(PHOTO COURTESY OF NORTHROP FRYE)

"Old Vic" The Victoria
College Building.
(COURTESY OF THE ARCHIVES OF THE
UNITED CHURCH OF CANADA,
VICTORIA UNIVERSITY, TORONTO)

The weary travellers on their 25th
wedding anniversary. (COURTESY OF THE ARCHIVES
OF THE UNITED CHURCH OF CANADA, VICTORIA UNIVERSITY,
TORONTO)

The author of *Fearful Symmetry*, 1947.
(PHOTO BY JOHN STEELE, TORONTO)

Frye as Chancellor of Victoria College, 1980. From the left: Kenneth R. Thompson, Rev. Richard Maurice Boyd, Frye.

Frye receiving an honorary degree from Dartmouth College, 1967.

Northrop Frye as Moses. This caricature appeared in an 1982 edition of the *New York Review of Books*.

Frye in his study, 1977.

Northrop Frye as Yoda taken from a cartoon in University of Toronto's *the newspaper*, 1982.

(DRAWING BY PHILIP STREET)

Frye with author B.W. Powe,
April 1988.
(PHOTO COURTESY OF B.W. POWE)

Northrop Frye with Margaret Atwood on the occasion of her receiving an honorary
degree from the University of Toronto, 1983. (PHOTO BY ROBERT LANSDALE PHOTOGRAPHY)

for five minutes. Frye who had turned beet-red laughed just as hard but the force of the class's explosive reaction was a clear indication of how much tension he had built up with his confusing structures.

## PERMANENT AFFECTIONS

After 14 months away, Frye was delighted to get home. He quickly settled into his old involvements with *The Canadian Forum* and even became literary scoutmaster again for *Acta*. Aware of the rumors about job offers he'd received in the States, he took pains to soften his image by presenting a whimsical face in interviews. In *Acta Victoriana*, he drew the comic contrast between his digs in Cambridge and his palace in Seattle. In *The Varsity*, he emphasized his shaky credentials with an admission that in public school he resided "comfortably near the bottom of the class." As for his writing plans, he only puckishly suggested that he wanted to write a whole shelf of books, "a flexible shelf with bookends to accommodate any number." Helen handled the new anxieties about Frye in a similar fashion. When the wife of the new President of Victoria, Margaret Moore, admitted to nervousness about meeting the author of such a formidable book as *Fearful Symmetry*, Helen quickly scoffed, "Oh, you should see his baby pictures."

Much of this, of course, was purely for show and mixed badly with his continued doubts about the university. Compared with the glory days of the late forties, the academic atmosphere was increasingly corroded by a sports-addled student population. In *The Varsity* interview, he expressed alarm over illiteracy. With a dig at the prevailing vapidity on campus, he suggested a worse problem, "the lack of ideas, and of the will to say anything." This melancholy observation provided one justification for spending less time with students. He soon liberated himself, in fact, from the job as staff adviser to *Acta* and coincidentally, the editorship of *The Canadian Forum* a little later. While this freed more writing time, his statement showed how much the whole question of education continued to trouble him. It was in this period too that Frye developed his image as distant and formidable. It was a tribute to his apparent coolness in class, that students in his 1953-4 Milton class were stunned and disbelieving when Frye lost emotional control of himself and nearly wept reading a passage out loud from Milton.

Frye was well planted in Toronto in particular and Canada in general. In *The Varsity* interview he jokingly designated Toronto an excellent place to carry on important work: "There's security in a place that leaves you alone. I could jump on a table in a crowded restaurant and begin to sing, and nobody would pay any attention." When Robert Heilman cautiously prodded him about the state of him "permanent affections," Frye now seemed eager to affirm his loyalty. "I look around my desk and see it piled high with Royal Commission reports on Canadian culture, Canadian magazines and books, letters about jobs in Canada, Royal Society and Canadian Humanities Research bulletins and I realize how deeply intertwined I am with this community."

There was now the further factor of Herm who left Moncton for good to live in Toronto with his son. He'd always been a frequent visitor to both Toronto and Chicago but now Helen thought he would be better cared for at their own home. Herm's dream for retirement seemed always to be modelled on his own father's: to settle down on a family farm and lazily scan the countryside through the haze of a cigar. Now lame, he couldn't go for long walks in Toronto and had to resort to observing and commenting on whatever small activities were transpiring on the decidedly unstimulating street. His life was hardly empty. He was an upbeat man who considered that the best place to be was precisely where he was at any time. Like Vera, he visited the Kemps' Lake Joseph cottage in the summers and for years he'd been pursued by a couple of determined Moncton widows, one of whom had a way of turning up wherever he was and resolutely dating him. After a year, though, he went to Vera's in Chicago where Vera's teacher friends called him "Pop," took him for car rides and more easily bantered with him than his son's academic friends.

While Frye was unquestionably reaffirming his place in Canada, he still groused about one of the less attractive obligations, making a "critical survey of Canadian poetry, which means that I have to read every god-damned jingle published in this country ..." Although his new review for *The University of Toronto Quarterly* was twice the size as the previous year, there was, in fact, a duty-bound earnestness to it. The only quiver of excitement was his ostensibly peevish attack on Irving Layton's *The Black Huntsman*, the work he said of "a noisy hot-gospeller who has no real respect for poetry." Layton had by this time identified himself as a sensualist who loved to excoriate Presbyterian Canada. Claiming Layton was as fettered as the society he attacked, he deflated the poet with a celebrated one-liner for which he would pay dearly: "One can get as tired of buttocks in Mr. Layton as of buttercups in the *Canadian Poetry Magazine...*"

While Layton had merely twigged Frye before in a little squib about a "Mr. Butchevo Phrye/was born to pry/Among old bones/ And cemetery stones," he now launched into a decade-long hate campaign of quite disgusting polemics which were astonishingly reprinted years later in *Engagements*. It was obvious that Layton couldn't stand any critic who failed to recognize the pure genius of each and every one of his poems. The difference was fiercely ideological as well. Layton believed as dogmatically in the inspirational power of real experience as Frye believed in the power of literary convention. By refusing to be drawn into debate with Layton, Frye handled the conflict better than Layton's later victims. In time, even Layton got tired of his campaign and eventually admitted that Frye was a titan of literary criticism.

Despite his ambivalence about Canadian literature, he quietly plugged away to raise its profile. He was the first professor at Vic to offer a Canadian Literature course in 1954 as a one-hour Religious Knowledge option. At the time, this was a decidedly thankless task. Other than a few standard texts like the A.J.M. Smith poetry anthology and Susanna Moodie's *Roughing It in the Bush,* there was little of the cornucopia of reprinted material available 15 years later. One of his most fascinating essays on CanLit, his 1956 "Preface to an Uncollected Anthology" simply outlined what he thought essential but was not easily available. In class he repressed his own feelings about CanLit and tried to counter the disdain among students for it. One student from his second year remembers how earnest Frye was in trying to engender interest, even inviting the small class up for dinner at his house. She was embarrassed by how little enthusiasm even a great critic elicited from students.

This, of course, was only a sideline to his theoretical work. His Princeton publisher, Datus Smith, had been up to Toronto in the summer of 1951 for a conference and had missed Frye. He did pick up the scintillating rumor that his new book was "coming along before too long," and naturally expressed strong interest. The letter had not been forwarded to Frye in Seattle and he took three months to reply: " ... my approach to Spenser ... involved me in so many questions of general critical theory that an entirely new book forced its way across my line of vision and demanded to be written instead. This is [a] book dealing with the sorts of issues raised at the end of *Fearful Symmetry:* whether 'literature' means an order of words or simply an aggregate of literary works; whether criticism is an empiric technique or a discipline founded on general principles; what can be done with such words as archetype, genre, symbol, etc. It all sounds very vague and windy, but it isn't really: it's just an unorganized jig-saw puzzle. But I think all the pieces are there, and, after a lot of hard thinking, I feel able to start fitting them together."

What Frye was trying to firm up, of course, was the outline of *Anatomy of Criticism,* but he was still lost in preliminary stages. It was a sometimes relentless quest. When Lester Pearson was installed as the new Chancellor of Vic on Feb. 4, 1952, Frye impiously used the blank spaces of his engraved luncheon invitation to scribble out an outline of chapter three, called Structural Archetypes, of his book. Number eight of his list became the basis of a major essay published the following summer, "Towards a Theory of Cultural History" and the "First Essay" in the *Anatomy:*

1. Dreaming and waking. Desire and reality.
2. The world & its human transformation by work.

3. The limited (natural) and the unlimited goals of work.
4. The function of art in hypothesizing and so making infinite the goal of work.
5. Apocalypse interpreted as the transformation of all experience into a dream form.
6. Opposite pole the frustration of action, or the anxiety dream.
7. Hence the logic of the god, usually ironic when not human; heroic when human.
8. The human protagonist or hero:
   a) as god (mythical phase) over man and nature.
   b) as hero (romantic phase) human but partly supernatural.
   c) as leader (high mimetic phase) human and natural but exceptional.
   d) as one of us (low mimetic phase); realistic, descriptive, recognition forms.
   e) as inferior to us (ironic phase) [his status is *not* moral but in terms of the amount of freedom of action allowed him].
9. Every phase has its anagnorisis or recognition: that's the tonality or mode which defines the phase.
10. [left blank]

Underneath this he noted three "Symbol Chapters": Perseus, Hercules, Theseus. In a schema redolent of an outline in Lord Raglan's *The Hero*, Frye numbered nine crucial "stations" in the blank space inside the invitation which showed parallels between the stories of "Eden" (an elaboration of Christ's life), "Beulah-Ulro," and the specific myths of Perseus, Hercules and Theseus. Eden was the fullest column and provided the pattern for the others. The nine stations of Eden were nativity, baptism-epiphany, ministry, crucifixion as spectacle, God's disappearance from the world, escape of soul-dove from hell, resurrection, fixing of shadow and apocalypse. There were often uncertain or missing parallels among the five columns. The fourth station of crucifixion was fullest and most comprehensive across the five columns. Under Eden, Frye noted: "Crucifixion as spectacle. Mourning mother. Betrayal by disciple." Under Beulah-Ulro: "Agon with dragon and pathos or death in conflict. Fixing of pharmakos. Betrayal by woman (second)." Under Perseus: "Killing of Andromeda's dragon." Under Hercules: "descent to hell foreshortened with second death." Under Theseus: "Minotaur quest." It's clear that the subsequent abstraction of the *Anatomy* was fundamentally based on an inductive hash of concrete narrative details.

## CHAIRMAN (1952-1953)

Frye was very determined in the summer of 1952 to push ahead with his book and confessed to Frederick Morgan that his effort to fight his way "out of a very complicated book" was so engrossing, it was depriving him "even of the faculty of reading." Through a new editor, Benjamin Houston, Princeton University Press kept an eager eye on his progress. When Houston seized an incorrect note in *The Kenyon Review* that Frye was preparing "a forthcoming book on literary genres," this flushed out a correction from Frye that his book, now called "Essay on Poetics," was really to be based "on a theory of symbolism which divides into five sections, of which one, the middle, is concerned with form and theory of genres. It's into this middle section that my work on dramatic and fictional genres will go. The article you like of the levels of meaning is much closer to the real basis of the book."

Yet there was nothing burdensome in this. Helen in fact reported him "terribly happy." On the last day of July, he had "six chapters laid out and three more to write—he's doing damn well." Ominously and correctly, she added, he "has interruptions coming up." The most serious was the college's effort to replace John Robins as English Chairman. The Vic administration thought that most logically Joe Fisher should be appointed, leaving Frye to plug along unhindered with his work. Fisher, though, suddenly sickened and deteriorated with cancer soon after his appointment in July 1952. When Fisher knew he was dying, he called in Frye to brief him on what he'd learned about the administration of the department. Frye didn't quite believe that Fisher would soon die but realized at least he would have to act as *de facto* chairman. Before the year started, Fisher did die and Frye found himself in charge.

Because the department was still so small, his new job didn't impinge excessively on his work. In a short dull letter to George Johnston at the end of November, he reported that most of the work was "getting papers written." Frye felt confident, moreover, that he could fall back on the advice of John Robins. Just before Christmas, Robins walked out of the senior common room roaring with laughter only to collapse of a heart attack and die shortly afterwards. Frye confessed to the recently hired David Knight that even if nothing else happened, the department could just barely manage. Ruth Jenking then went into hospital with a serious illness. Feeling like the Ancient Mariner, Frye confessed to Johnston: "This has been a hell of a year: one begins to hate it, in that irrational way one looks at a year as a contained 'thing.' " Hugh Kenner sensed that with the deaths of his mentors Edgar and Robins and the retirement of Pratt, Frye, the acolyte, was suddenly and uncomfortably required to fill the void with his own eminence.

Despite the setbacks, he nevertheless suddenly became more active as a reviewer for *Hudson Review*, and Morgan let Frye review an anthology of unpublished work on Coleridge, *Inquiring Spirit*, edited by his colleague, Kay Coburn. Despite generous comments, there was a strand of severe criticism directed at both Coleridge and Coburn. Frye groused back across a century about Coleridge's own value judgments, "his careless denigration of everything French." After his exertions in the name of Blake, he had an odd complaint: that Coburn was too eager to make Coleridge "relevant" to modernity; that he was, for example, Freudian before Freud, when his ideas did not need such a contrived boost. Frye implied that everyone, including Coburn, had it wrong and then proceeded to outline Coleridge's Blake-like conception of imagination as "the power that unifies ... not the thing which is unified, the real coordinating principle" or Logos. Frye saw this Logos as absolutely central to Coleridge. "It leads him, in criticism, to the conception of all literature as contained within an order of words identical with one personal Word—perhaps his greatest legacy to modern thought, and one still unexplored. It leads him, even in science, to a type of speculation aimed at restoring the system of analogies and correspondences on which medieval symbolism is based." Once more, Frye was talking about his own work-in-progress.

Pleading with Morgan that he was "frantically busy" and "knocking himself out to get a book finished," Frye passed on reviewing other books—including one by Richard Blackmur—and suggested that new works by Susanne Langer and Auerbach were closer to his concerns.

In fact, he continued to review nothing but literary criticism and works of symbolic philosophy and psychology. As a freelance Aristotelian himself who was ransacking Aristotle for ideas, he showed interest in examining the school forming under R.S. Crane at the University of Chicago. Despite the promise of a scrappy outsider either pummeling or swearing allegiance to the Chicago school, Frye's two amiably negative considerations of their books were largely shadow boxing.

His view of New Criticism arising out of a review of Allen Tate's *The Forlorn Demon* had considerably more bite and anticipated his devastating attack on T.S. Eliot a decade later. As a leftist, Frye naturally abused the school's reactionary lament about cultural decline, "the Great Western Butterslide, the doctrine of a coordinated synthesis in medieval culture, giving place, at the Renaissance to a splitting and specialized schizophrenia which has got steadily worse until it has finally landed all in that Pretty Pass in which we are today." Frye identified this nostalgia as just that, a neurotic and impossible search for the Fountain of Youth in the past. The argument would be trivial except that the middle ages, "like the moon in Ariosto, a vast repository of all cultural acquisitions," had always been a very important repository for Frye himself.

But for him, as with Austin Farrer, there was need of re-creating and transforming the images of the past, not of making an impossible return. In an accompanying review of Herbert Read's *The True Voice of Feeling*, Frye made the unquestionably cabalistic point that romanticism in poetry was "an attempt, not to know essences like Mr. Tate's angels, but to create them, or rather to liberate them." In a conveniently placed consideration, in the same review article, of Francis Fergusson's *Dante's Drama of the Mind*, Frye pointed out, through Dante's quest, the personal angle of "imaginative" reading: "the central process of freeing the will through a series of progressive rebirths, until the pilgrim reaches the original unfallen childhood of the Golden Age."

Critical theory intruded everywhere now and even lay its claim to the distant future. In early March 1953 he took Helen down to London, Ont., where he was to give a talk on the symbolism of the Bible to a church conference organized by his Emmanuel College classmate, George Birtch. Still feeling depression and even cynicism from a gruelling school year, he complained in a diary fragment of the dullness of the trip which was aggravated by the frosted windows blocking off even the small diversion of the winter landscape. He gave Helen Henry James's *The Other House* to read, reminding himself that he must check Rose Arminger for the significance of her red dress and white parasol. Then Frye "diddled at" his archetypes, noting, "The city of destruction and the dangerous Acrasia garden need more pairing."

By entering into a specifically church-organized affair he seemed to have every unappetizing aspect of his past religious life thrown at him. Even the Birtches' manse was designed in poor taste by his arch-persecutor at Emmanuel, Alfred Johnston. He bemoaned the evening service and its intense association in his mind with the dreary piety of his worst minister in Moncton which led him to equate church services and wasted time.

According to Frye's account, the next morning's meeting was farcical. Frye played the piano for the hymn. When he played a wrong note, he cringed and secretly wanted to kick himself. A brouhaha erupted over the presence of a reporter. Other wrangles pushed his talk back so far that Birtch had to intervene to let him speak. He found safety in the blackboard where he wrote down a table of apocalyptic symbols but he inwardly cursed the waste of his time and the church's money to bring him down to London. Some of the questions were eccentric and irrelevant. Frye quipped to himself that "if I had a full hour and a half I might have converted some of them to Christianity." On the way to the train station, however, Birtch urged Frye to write up his ideas on the symbolism of the Bible and once more feeling the claustrophobia of the frosted windows, Frye wrote out an outline for a book on the Bible he might be able to start after "EP," his *Essay on Poetics*, cynically noting that if he finished *that* in the way he wanted, he could write potboilers out of it for the rest of his life. The whole trip was a strain, ending with a potluck meal at home of baked beans and "ancient" meat which severely wrenched his stomach.

Barely two weeks later, Frye's spirits were considerably lifted by a completely unexpected letter from E.D.H. Johnson of the Special Program in the Humanities at Princeton. Johnson offered Frye a new lectureship financed by the Princeton 1932 class. The position required a major lecturer to teach a seminar for twelve or so upperclassmen for one term each year and deliver four or five public lectures. Otherwise he could keep working on research and writing. Johnson, who did not know Frye, informed him that the committee chose his name unanimously as their first incumbent. Johnson suggested a somewhat obvious theme for Frye's seminars, literature and myth, but left it to Frye to exactly determine his subject if he accepted. Frye was delighted by the appointment and considered it a "real break." After a term of working with Jay Macpherson, his only regret was that she could not continue with him right away because there would be no place for her at the all-male Princeton.

## PRINCETON

Frye continued to procrastinate on writing his formal lectures for Princeton and by the end of 1933 was beginning to worry seriously about them. He rationalized his procrastination by telling himself he should feel out Princeton to determine how to shape the lectures. There was also confusion over whether the lectures constituted the book or whether Frye would expand them into a larger, more complicated book.

Soon after he arrived in Princeton in early February, he had a conference with Benjamin Houston to try to clear up his plans. In a fit of optimism Frye assured Houston that he hoped to have a manuscript ready in June. He seemed quite serious about this and established a regime to push vigorously ahead. His sponsor, E.D.H. Johnson, arranged a carrel with typewriter for him just outside his own office in the Firestone Library. Johnson later reported: "No sooner would he arrive in the morning than his typewriter would simply explode, and with virtually no interruption would proceed for two or three hours while the pages of manuscript accumulated, seemingly without revision." This sufficiently depressed the department typist that she felt that the only honourable course was to submit her resignation. Her anxieties were relieved only when she inspected Frye's typing and discovered that he was committing the cardinal business-school sin of x-ing out his errors. His legend was set for all time, however. Johnson incorrectly remembered that Frye's ability was so prodigious that Frye merely worked out what he wanted to say each evening in his head and simply typed it out non-stop the next morning. Actually Frye could only have been copying previous material since his early drafts were always composed in longhand.

Johnson also managed to arrange accommodation for the Fryes on Prospect Ave. The owner, an economist on leave, painted Tamayo and Klee-style canvases and insisted on violent decor, green-grey walls against two of brilliant cerise in the dining room. "The two smaller bedrooms he wanted spattered, one blue on white, the other red on white. Princeton's painters watched him in horror while he demonstrated what he wanted, then they packed their apparatus and walked off home in high dudgeon."

Although Frye settled into a routine quickly, it wasn't until two weeks before his actual formal lectures that the Special Program in the Humanities could pry titles out of Frye for the talks sched- uled at 5 pm on Tuesdays and Thursdays from March 2 to 11 in McCosh Hall. Frye was almost assiduously bland and literal in the titles he offered. The series itself was a lame "Some New Uses of

Criticism." The lectures themselves were "The Critic and His Public," "Symbols of Fact and Fiction," "The Language of Poetry," and "Myth and Society." Despite the unpromising fare, Frye drew a capacity crowd of between 150 and 200 people, mostly under-graduates, and unlike most other academic lecturers, maintained the crowd throughout the series. In *Anatomy of Criticism* Frye noted that the book is based on his lectures at Princeton. One critic, Robert Martin Adams, expressed scornful disbelief that a human audience could ever absorb such a dense argument.

Frye belatedly acknowledged that there was an exhilarating confusion about the direction that he was going because of the novelty of his ideas but seemed that somehow people would under-stand. But E.D.H. Johnson later reported: " ... I had the impression that only a minority of those present were able to follow with much comprehension his dense and complex argument. His manner did not aid easy comprehension, since he spoke at great speed, adher-ing to his manuscript which certainly had not been prepared with the skills of the lecturer in mind. I well remember the expressions of incomprehension which one heard from many of the auditors following each lecture, though we all realized that a work of great originality and high distinction was in the making." After the final lecture, Frye was in an ebullient mood, but almost immediately came down with flu. He "sank a dinner and two martinis, went home, lost the dinner, and fell into bed." But he could also report a "big ovation at the end, everything declared to be unprecedented in the recent history of Princeton, so I feel very relaxed about it."

Unlike his Cambridge and Seattle year, Frye often seemed a business-like figure who was impatiently absorbed in his work. People now seemed increasingly incapable of discriminating between Frye's self-absorption and the supposedly remote worka-holism which would color his image in the next couple of decades. Frye was evidently a man on the march and, as a result, rather formidable. As a social figure at Princeton he was not well remem-bered. Helen stood out more clearly because of her accessibility and off-color language. Yet the presiding genius of Princeton's literary community, Richard Blackmur, took a liking to Frye and they often lunched with a music professor, Ed Cone, in Princeton's

single decent restaurant. Blackmur usually prepared himself for
lunch with a couple of stiff martinis. Blackmur's drinking was not
atypical and although not shy to drink themselves, both the Fryes
were rather beleaguered by the tippling at Princeton. In letters to
friends he joked that they had drunk so much alcohol, their clothes
didn't fit anymore. "Helen says if anyone would ask her in for a
saucer of milk she'd jump at it."

Frye was quick to project some of the deficiencies of Princeton
into a broader critique of America: "One young mother reported
to us that her little girl had come from kindergarten with an A plus
in Facing Reality. American students go on from there. The little
girls grow up to be beautiful big girls of the kind my students go
with and have been bringing lately to show me. One of them got
Helen into the women's washroom and asked her what it was like
being married to a real intellectual type, and did she try to read
everything I read." He added: "I'll be glad to get out of this country,
although I think that fundamentally it's trustworthy enough. That
is, when American democracy decides, in its confused, lumbering,
dithering way that it really can't get along any further with Senator
McCarthy, it sticks him into a damn soap opera, and lets the
housewives decide whether he's hero or villain ... they did the
same kind of thing with MacArthur the last time we were here."

By the end of their stay at Princeton, Frye admitted his exhaustion, more from the taxing social involvements than academic
responsibilities. He looked forward to a long vacation in Britain
and Europe, hoping to read "nothing but timetables." In late
August when he thought it would be hot, he contemplated a side
trip to Scandinavia which he perceived as "cool, comfortable,
middle-class, and not too damn educational." Precisely when they
were wondering about accommodations in London, A.S. Roe visited Frye to thank him for supporting his book on Blake's illustrations of Dante. Roe said they were welcome to use his wife's flat
on Marloes Road near the Kensington Infirmary.

It was the first time since the beginning of the war that the
Fryes were overseas and they were discomfited that the effects of
the Nazi air raids in London were still so evident. The bombed out
sections of Oxford St. had the appearance of a carnival midway

with temporary sheds. Although rationing had just been lifted, there were still shortages. Their own adjustment to Britain took longer than expected and, except for the conventional side trips to Stonehenge, Oxford, Cambridge and cathedral towns like Salisbury and Rochester, they stayed in London. Frye violated his resolution about work. Because Houston had made it clear that he would wait for a manuscript of the longer book rather than just his lectures, Frye spent much time scribbling notes and mentally rearranging the pieces of the "unorganized jig-saw puzzle."

In his introduction to *Anatomy of Criticism* Frye gave the definite impression that the book was really the result of merely working up his public lectures at Princeton and doing a scissors-and-paste job on his previous theoretical articles. But even a cursory glance at the articles and the final text show that the borrowings amount to only a few paragraphs at a time. His final manuscript was a complete reworking of the earlier material.

# PART FOUR

After coming home from Britain, Frye worked on his manuscript so completely that, except for a TV program on Blake, he barely touched other work. He made good progress through the school year and two weeks before he was due out in British Columbia to teach a summer session on Milton, Frye sent off his typescript on June 13 to Benjamin Houston. In a dry little note he said that the book, which he now called *Structural Poetics*, had best be out of sight so he could get caught up on overdue assignments. He explained that he could either drop or amplify the two primitive illustrations sent with the manuscript; one of them showed the circle of Apocalyptic Imagery with an appended chart of cyclical symbols, and the other circular scheme represented the relationship of the forms of drama. Princeton, worried about the book's excessive schematization as well as the extra cost, exploited Frye's own anxieties and axed them. Despite the lessons of *Fearful Symmetry*, Frye—once more hoping for "as wide a reading public as possible"—opposed defacing the text "by the sequential scrofula of footnote numbers."

Houston sent the manuscript to Douglas Bush to evaluate. Bush was a well-known humanist critic who believed that literature provided moral nourishment, and therefore this choice appeared eccentric. But Bush had the reputation of being a fair reader who could quickly discern a book's marketability. In his official report sent on July 28 from his summer home in Norwich, Connecticut, Bush gave *Structural Poetics* high marks. He understood the magnitude of the book but identified it strictly as "high-brow." "There have been many essays and a few books, but nothing approaching this in scope, and its method is largely original." In an appended letter, however, Bush admitted he was "a dubious guinea pig, since I have very limited sympathy with the fashionable 'mythic' approach to literature." He groused about Frye's idea that the critic was "monarch of all he surveys." Soon after this he published a well-known cut-up of myth criticism, "Mrs. Bennet and the Dark Gods: The Truth about Jane Austen."

He further quoted a passage from the manuscript where Frye's analysis appeared to go wild in "IBM manner" with categories of romance, its six phases parallelling three of tragedy and three of comedy. He continued: "My chief complaint has to do with the total conception of literature that is everywhere implied and sometimes half-stated, namely, that literature is a series of patterns constituting a verbal universe which exists to provide materials for the super-sophisticated critic's solitary games but has no relation to life, no 'meaning' for the mass of cultivated people who, for some 2,500 years, have thought they were being nourished by it. This verbal universe seems to me inhuman and stifling." Because Bush felt that pigeon-holing was the obvious consequence of Frye's approach, he suggested a conclusion to "make clearer the purpose and utility of his analysis. Otherwise, in spite of the constant cerebration that has gone on, the book may seem to be more inert than dynamic."

While Bush was reporting on the manuscript, the Fryes were ensconced through July and early August in a "temporary" division of WW II army houses called Acadia Camp, just off the University of British Columbia campus in Vancouver. Frye had talked for years about coming out to teach a Milton course for Roy Daniells and the job was partly a favor to him. The UBC campus is notoriously isolated from Vancouver and, with no car, the Fryes had to depend on Laurenda Daniells to ferry them around on errands. The Fryes spent a lot of time over at the Daniells's house two blocks away. They settled comfortably in the midst of a young family, where the loss of a baby tooth was an event of cosmic importance. In retrospect, Laurenda was amazed at the Fryes' ability to handle these domestic episodes with unaffected brightness. Invariably, however, Frye submersed himself in shoptalk with Daniells who always remained one of his enthusiasts.

He had few priorities for writing. To handle the nagging obligation of Charles Currelly's memoirs, the Fryes brought along Currelly's mass of dictated notes on long foolscap pages. In spare moments, either Frye or Helen attacked them, trying to knock them into some shape. Their efforts, which received little support and no money from Ryerson Press and a few tut-tuts for a misspelled name from a museum martinet, was the rambling memoir *I Brought the Ages Home*.

A more congenial task was writing "Towards Defining an Age of Sensibility" about how "reptilian Classicism, all cold and dry reason," moved to "a mammalian Romanticism, all warm and wet feeling." Just weeks after finishing the *Anatomy*, Frye was already noting, "I do not care about terminology, only about appreciation for an extraordinarily interesting period of English literature ..." Frye emphasized a return to imaginative primitiveness which was reflected in the use of metaphor "as part of an oracular and half-ecstatic process." Frye placed a similar, very significant discussion of the metaphor in the *Anatomy*, showing how the metaphor is an irrational technique of creating a direct link of identity between subjects and objects. A man is not *like* a lion, he *is* a lion.

While Frye hardly invented the lion-man discussion of simile and metaphor, it was he who appropriated it for a personal mission which ran like a golden thread through his work of the next 30 years. His intent was to spread imaginative poetic thought throughout society to soften and cancel the effects of procrustean logic and ideology. In a sense, it was a stand-in brother for his earlier literary guardian angel, satire. Without ever denying, along with Jung, the importance of rational thought, Frye would be unwavering in supporting a submersion in poetic experience.

Despite the congenial summer in British Columbia, the Fryes found themselves in a web of anxieties when they got home.

Because doctors discovered fibroids in Helen's uterus, she was hospitalized for a hysterectomy in mid-September. The night Helen entered the hospital, Frye tried to relieve his own fears by playing through 25 Clementi sonatas without stopping. Although there were no complications, she took three weeks to convalesce. Emotionally unsettling at the best of times, the hysterectomy possesses an especially dreadful ring of finality for any woman who wanted but had failed to produce children. Still depressed the following spring, Helen never managed to put her infertility to rest. To help iron out the household complications, Helen's friend writer Blodwen Davies moved in for a couple of weeks.

With the pressure to finish off the Currelly memoir, Frye retreated to his attic to bash out some more of the manuscript. Fussing over a CBC radio talk on Oswald Spengler and a review of Canadian literature which the Canadian legation improbably planted in an Argentine magazine, Frye still hadn't the solace of any news from Princeton about his manuscript. The very day he wrote David Erdman to sniff out the situation, the Princeton board met and accepted the book. Almost exactly ten years after that of *Fearful Symmetry*, the acceptance meant little to Frye while his editor Houston was full of praise and confident it would sell as well as *Fearful Symmetry*. This was not a unanimous opinion and while Princeton was keen about the book, they projected such low sales they appealed to the trustees of the class of 1932 for a $1000 subsidy to help with the publication. For such a complicated book, the press made few requests for changes in the text. They agreed with Bush's insistence on a grand conclusion but didn't categorically demand it. Since this had been Frye's original idea, it was just a matter of restoring his former format.

The biggest problem, however, which dragged out for a year, was the question of Frye's title, *Structural Poetics: Four Essays*. At Princeton, there was opposition to both "poetics" and "essays." Houston reported that the board felt that readers would associate poetics with prosody, the formal study of poetic form, particularly metre and rhyme. Houston also confessed that the word "essay" would imply "a disjointedness in what is really a well-organized book." Reporting one board member's suggestion of *A Grammar of*

*Archetypes,* he offered the possible solution of retaining *Structural Poetics* if it were buttressed by a more descriptive subtitle. Frye's immediate idea for a title change was *Principles of Literary Symbolism* but thought it too close to I.A. Richards's *Principles of Literary Criticism.*

The problem raised a flurry of consultation both at Princeton and Toronto. Frye was dimly amused by a colleague's droll suggestion, *Myth Is the Pith.* While both he and Princeton maintained a new working title of *Criticism as Structure,* he still hung on to the hope of using "poetics," even recalling the book's earliest working title *A Defence of Poetics.* He insisted, probably correctly, that poetics itself would not be misunderstood at a time when literary theory was increasingly fashionable. If he had a problem himself, it was "structural." Houston sent him a long list of plausible alternatives:

A DISCIPLINE FOR CRITICISM

A DEFENSE OF CRITICISM (but not the status quo)

AN ARCHITECTURE FOR CRITICISM

AN ANATOMY OF (or FOR) CRITICISM

CRITICISM AS KNOWLEDGE

SYSTEMATIC CRITICISM

LITERARY CRITICISM: MODES, SYMBOLS, MYTHS, GENRES

A CONCEPTUAL FRAMEWORK FOR CRITICISM

A NEW GROUND FOR CRITICISM (Bacon's inductive leap)

SOME NEW USES OF CRITICISM (your lecture title)

A GRAMMAR OF CRITICISM (too close to Burke)

LITERARY CRITICISM: A THEORY OF KNOWLEDGE

AIMS AND METHODS OF LITERARY CRITICISM

Interestingly, Frye scribbled another quixotic but revealing suggestion, *A Fable for Critics,* at the bottom of the list but didn't pursue it. He responded immediately that if the double "an" of the fourth suggestion were chopped out, he much preferred *Anatomy of Criticism* because of its association with Burton's *Anatomy of Melancholy.* Burton's approach "with all its parts, sections, members, and sub-sections" would presumably touch "lightly on" and thereby offset "the schematization of my book which will probably get a lot of people down." As usual, Frye was expecting too much of his readers and critics. If there was any general association with "anatomy" it was an unfortunate one with cold dissected corpses which gave Frye's enemies great satisfaction. He had himself used "anatomized cadaver" in *Fearful Symmetry*. Frye in fact still resisted "anatomy" enough to try to slip in "Criticism as Structure" at the end of his letter. Houston prevailed by reporting "a great wave of enthusiasm" for *Anatomy of Criticism*. Despite his basic satisfaction with that title (with retained subtitle, Four Essays), Frye liked to be reminded that *Structural Poetics* was his original preference.

While he was racing to finish revisions, Frye had little breathing space. He had to swear off assignments. Understandably insisting to Frederick Morgan that "the book I'm writing is a tough one" he could only make a vague promise to review Robert Graves's *Collected Poems*. He somehow found the time and on the eve of finishing his final *Anatomy* manuscript he was prepared to admit a split between "an objective or systematic mythology" and Graves's leading us "towards the mythical use of poetic language, where we invent our own myths and apply them to an indefinite number of human themes."

As he hurried towards completion of the *Anatomy*, sending off a final revision of 340 tightly crammed pages to Houston on Dec. 22, he faced a mind-shattering set of five speeches just after Christmas. At least two of them, "Quest and Cycle in *Finnegans Wake*" about Joyce and Blake, and the paper he completed in the summer "Towards Defining an Age of Sensibility" he delivered at the MLA convention in Chicago. Nevertheless Frye put on such a dazzling performance in Chicago that Hazard Adams wrote him into his novel *Horses of Instruction*. Dizzy with Frye's exposition of cycles, Adams's protagonist goes to bed and dreams of a conversation between Blake and Charles II.

Frye was now so busy he felt compelled to decline a fellowship sponsored by John Crowe Ransom. His "production line during the last few months," he joked, "has resembled the opening scene of *Modern Times*." His first priority naturally was to settle down to routine and repair "some of the breaks in my teaching and lecturing." Ransom did compel Frye, however, to come out to the School of Letters summer session at the University of Indiana where he was to teach a somewhat obvious course, "The Poetry and Symbolism of William Blake" in July. Expecting that it was going to be "meteorologically close to the mouth of hell," Frye was not disappointed. Set up in a house in a bleak prefabricated suburb, they were so isolated from the campus, Helen had a good morning's hike just to come for lunch.

Frye's immediate priority, interestingly enough, was an essay on Wallace Stevens. He had always been fascinated by Stevens but what provided the impetus was Stevens's *Collected Poems* published in the fall of 1954. After an orgy of commentary on critical trends in the past years, Frye finally looked as if he were shifting to practical criticism. The odd thing was that he was determined to keep the *Anatomy* apparatus *out* of his analysis. He even patted himself on the back for this, later claiming, quite incorrectly, that he didn't do "any systematic work on Stevens until the *Anatomy* was in proof." He hesitated, he said, "because of the number of people who say that I am a deductive critic reading my own system into everybody whether it is there or not." He did in fact raid Stevens for more primitive associations: "At the end of autumn come the terrors of winter, the sense of a world disintegrating into chaos which we feel socially when we see the annihilation wars of our time ..." At the outset of winter, Stevens showed "the auroras of a vanished heroism flicker over the sky ..."

Frye was really drawn to Stevens for a complex of reasons. He was a poet "for whom the theory and the practice of poetry were inseparable." He was a poet "centrally in the Romantic tradition," a New Englander besides who interested Frye as much as Emily Dickinson. There was even a religious dimension. Although Stevens saw the need for renewing the earth over "surrender to heaven," he had "no interest in turning to some cellophane-wrapped version of neo-paganism." But Stevens, the supreme symbolist of symbolists, fed Frye precisely when Frye himself wanted a motive for metaphor. Frye worked through his metaphor ideas again which had appeared in the *Anatomy* manuscript and in "Towards Defining an Age of Sensibility." He corrected Stevens on the meaning of metaphor over simile and suggested "a world of total metaphor, where everything is identified as itself and with everything else, would be a world where subject and object, reality and mental organization of reality, are one. Such a world of total metaphor is the formal cause of poetry." This involved an imaginative act which "breaks down the separation between subject and object ..."

All through this period Frye came alive with suggestions of how to locate and recover the primitive power of poetry. In a speech he delivered in Indiana, "Literature as a Mode of Thought," he virtually repeated his claim from his promotion sketch for *Fearful Symmetry:* "The essential patterns of action and thought in literature are reservoirs yet untapped of present and future knowledge." There was a lingering question of how literature creates action. In a review of René Char's *Hypnos Waking,* he saw the utility and explosive power of the aphorism which operated on "the principle of the Bloody Mary: it has to be swallowed at a gulp and allowed to explode from inside." This hearkened back to the image of God's presence. When incarnate in man, He spoke as Jesus in parables, "aphorisms to be re-created in action," not deductive propositions. In an English Institute session that year, "Sound and Poetry," Frye also suggested that poetry liberated from the book might rediscover "its primitive gift of charm," which he later claimed would engender a magical "involuntary physical response."

**ANATOMY OF CRITICISM**

Just before heading off to Harvard for a spring teaching term in 1957, Frye cleared away all the various "foul" galley and page proofs. Houston had high hopes for the book and was proud to be involved in it. Frye replied that he hoped "the book will be treated as a distinguished one: I very much fear that it's a work of genius, which usually gets a much lower rating." This was a trademark Frye quip: joking but accurate.

It was clear that Princeton didn't really know what they had. They cautiously ordered a first printing of 2,100. While this was over the usual run of 1,500, they thought the supply would last three to five years. Although Frye was not displeased with the book's design, its baldly-lettered dust jacket and plain text design jarred badly with the efforts undertaken for *Fearful Symmetry*.

Although close to the publication of a major book, Frye's summer appointment at Harvard had little significance. Almost to underline the tenuousness of his stay, his "furnished" apartment across the Charles River in Boston was virtually empty. The apartment was sandwiched between the brutalizing noise of Beacon St. at the front and Highway 1 at the back which ran along the nearby river embankment. Frye joked that his sleep was cruelly disturbed by a half-hour of dead silence at 3:30 am between the finish of one day and the start of the next.

Some students knew of Frye through his Blake book or his journal articles but he was not generally well-known. He taught history of criticism in a large lecture hall in Harvard Hall at ten in the morning and then a literature and myth course directly afterwards in the Fogg Art Museum in a funereal room normally used for slide showings where the windows were covered with black drapes. The only lighting was a little lectern lamp shining on his chest and face. In navigating the wide stage, he was troubled on rainy days by a roof leak which dripped water onto the stage invariably missing a bucket.

In the course of the usual shopping-around in the first two weeks of courses, students quickly passed the word about Frye's prodigious interest and his official enrollment of about 90 exploded with auditors. By then, it was too late to stop. A crocodile line of enthusiasts travelled across Harvard Yard from the first to second lecture. One student, Helen Vendler, found it exhilarating to hear the *Anatomy* before it was published. When it came out at the end of the term, she, like other students, bought it primarily as a way of getting a fix on a conception that was so grand, it was difficult to properly absorb in lectures. When it was published in mid-April, there was an excited groupie reaction similar to the one at Vic ten years before. Students snatched up copies and asked Frye to sign them.

In the year of the *Anatomy*'s publication, it was, ironically enough, Blake which most absorbed Frye. All over the United States, universities and art galleries were caught up with Blake bicentennial celebrations and in his role as specialist, Frye was run ragged making appearances. By the end of the year, he confessed his consternation at "falling in and out of planes," being "a sixty-year-old smiling public man at forty-five." He wasn't totally consistent with smiles. At Skidmore in November, a *Saratogian* photographer caught Frye looking harassed in front of a skimpy bulletin board covered with a thumbtacked Blake exhibit. But advocacy of Blake was hardly uncongenial and he put out his missionary best. At Cincinnati not long after Skidmore, he amazed his former graduate student, Hugh Maclean, by bounding up to the podium and talking in pure prose on Blake for a solid 50 minutes without notes.

Despite increasing doubts about the drift in Blake studies, Frye had never, of course, lost his enthusiasm for Blake. He energetically attacked Blake in every conceivable direction. He produced a bibliographic essay for a special MLA book, an unusual extended commentary on a single poem, " Blake's Introduction to Experience," and a breathtaking symbolic breakdown of Blake's *Milton*, a part of which appeared in a non-Blakean context in the *Anatomy*.

Frye also delivered a bracingly populist essay, "William Blake after Two Hundred Years" at Vassar and Wellesley in which he indulgently proclaimed a new era of popularity for Blake. While Frye was correct, he suggested all the wrong reasons. Although Blake did become wildly popular for the next 15 years, it was most often for reasons of obscurantism and anti-modern mysticism and not, as Frye insisted, that Blake's poetry lacked sentimentality or irony or that it was easy or that "his prophecies are among the best possible introductions to the grammar and structure of literary mythology." As in his Stevens essay, Frye returned to the centrality of metaphor in opposition to rational thinking; he insisted on its utility in "giving people an immediate form of imaginative experience."

Beyond a continued interest in metaphor, however, there was little to indicate any organic development out of the *Anatomy*. Logically, there was a whole universe spreading out from his overt confession that as a work of "pure critical theory," it needed a practical volume. Since he called this necessary new volume morphological in nature, Frye was returning to ground zero with the *Anatomy*. The meaning of the book with all its categories would not be revealed to literary critics until applied.

Even before the *Anatomy* was published, Frye appeared to retreat from this wearying prospect. Although it would take a quarter-century to explicitly articulate his feeling, he possessed a niggling doubt that despite his own disclaimers, the book's approach was too ironic; it didn't represent a statement of social commitment or faith or genuine literary experience beyond purely technical concerns. Frye was in fact immediately taken up with the wider social and educational utility of his ideas, and was now stepping out once more as a Blakean evangelist. While still at Harvard, he blocked off much of May to prepare for a speech, "Culture and the National Will" at Carleton University in Ottawa where he was going to receive the first of the 36 honorary degrees that he would go on to accumulate.

His speech was the precursor of dozens of speeches he would give to buttress the role of culture and, in particular, the university in society. Frye had now come full circle from the querulous graduate student who scorned the role of professor to a fully convinced academic who considered the "real world" the university. "Here," he said to the Carleton graduates, "you are in contact with reality at every point: this is the engine room; this is where the great ideas and forces and symbols that shape human behaviour take their start. Soon you will be in the ivory towers of business, in the escapist retreats of the suburbs, in the charmless magic of teaching, or in the schizophrenic fantasies of government. Wherever you are, you will be in a labyrinth, and only four years at Carleton will give you the clue to it."

Literature, in all its forms, was utterly central to the educational experience, providing "the keys to nearly all the imaginative experience that it is possible for us to have in life. The central part of this training consists of the Bible, the Classics, and the great heritage of our mother tongue." For the first time, Frye fiercely emphasized the Bible as a central element of education. A grade eight student who didn't know the story of the prodigal son, he pronounced, "has been deprived of one of the keys to the whole imagination and thought of western culture, no less than if he had been deprived of the multiplication table. An educational theory which does not recognize this is not just a mistaken theory: it is criminally negligent."

Frye was in Ottawa just a month later at the University of Ottawa to boost the newly-created Association of Canadian University Teachers of English (ACUTE). There, a sensational headline had Frye brutally pronouncing OLD SCHOLARS ON WAY OUT. "Scholars are on the way out, a Toronto university professor said Saturday, and they are giving way to 'intellectuals'." He listed an awesome agenda for the New Scholar, which as usual reflected his own personal priorities: " ...the role of metaphor in conceptual thought; the social and political uses of poetic myth; the relation of symbolism and imagery to faith and conduct, are a few of the questions that are likely to engross us in the near future." It's not surprising that it was at the ACUTE conference that Frye first felt vulnerable and isolated, as if, after the *Anatomy*, he'd walked right out of mainstream academia into an area no one seemed to understand or much care about. Since Frye now had the aura of scholarly giant, it's interesting that his graduate student, Jay Macpherson, published a poem about Frye, "The Anagogic Man," in the July 1957 *Canadian Forum*, which caught the vulnerable side. The Anagogic Man, Noah, captain of the Ark, carries "a golden bubble round and rare":

> Its gently shimmering sides surround
> All us and our worlds, and bound
> Art and life, and wit and sense,
> Innocence and experience.

Forbear to startle him, lest some
Poor soul to its destruction come,
Slipped out of mind and past recall
As if it never was at all.

While Frye was preparing to barnstorm again for Blake in the
fall of 1957, he wrote Benjamin Houston announcing that he had
a book of essays he might consider. He received an odd reply
which was more absent-minded than cool. While keener later,
Houston at first expressed an interest in the essays only as a
basis for Frye's promised practical volume. Parenthetically he also
announced that Princeton was allowing *Fearful Symmetry* to go
out of print in hardback. Frye had expressed some interest in
getting the book into paperback possibly through Indiana University Press. While Princeton was eager to prevent Indiana's poaching, it hardly moved fast. It took a month and half to announce the
decision that it would come out with its own limited paperback
and that in itself took another year to produce. That edition in turn
went out of print in December 1960 and it wasn't until August of
the following year that Princeton leased it to Beacon Press for
reprint.

Since both Blake and Frye on Blake were developing a substantial readership in the universities which would explode in the 60s,
this fumbling at the dawn of the golden age of cheap academic
paperbacks was astonishing. But while Princeton appeared to be
hemming and hawing to Frye on the question of their paperback
program, they were enthusiastically approaching at least one other
author for a new paperback list. One addled manager approached
Frye himself for *Shakespeare and Christian Doctrine,* a book actually written by his distant cousin, Roland Mushat Frye, which did
in fact appear high on the new list as #4. By contrast, after very
healthy sales with Beacon Press, *Fearful Symmetry* made it back
to Princeton only in the late sixties as #165. Frye of course did
not see this confusion as a ringing endorsement.

Unlike the speedy Toronto loyalist reaction to *Fearful Symmetry,*
there was a clammy silence around the *Anatomy.* Not a single
Toronto paper reviewed it. Since the *Anatomy* was a complicated

theoretical book, that was not totally surprising but there were so few books then produced internationally by Canadian authors, that there should have been some attention. Accepting the view of Princeton that the book would be a sleeper, Frye was no longer anxiously scanning the horizon for every review, planned or published. The lack of comments about the book in his correspondence indicated quite clearly that from the very start, he was prepared to let the book go its own way. A quarter century later, he even joked, "I have a tendency to behave like a puppy that's just smashed some crockery. I walk away as quickly as possible. After I finished the *Anatomy of Criticism*, I realized there was going to be a great to-do about the theory of criticism, but that wasn't my affair."

The first important positive review, interestingly enough, was by a 27-year-old Blake enthusiast at Yale, Harold Bloom, who as a freshman had found *Fearful Symmetry* "the best book I'd ever read about anything." Bloom's review of the *Anatomy* in the *Yale Review* was prophetic in defining Frye's potential force: "His very great book, which will be widely read and used, but mostly by critics under forty, will not much affect the dogmatism of the now Middle-aged Criticism." Bloom's attitude was backed up by Frederick McDowell in *Western Review* who pronounced that the *Anatomy* "may become as seminal for the next decade as the pronouncements of Eliot, Pound, and Richards were for the 1920's and 1930's ..."

For the most part, however, the academic reaction, which dribbled in over the next *two* years was negative, nervous or wary. Considering that the book would sell over 100,000 copies over the next 25 years and would be one of the most quoted academic books of its time, the attention given to it was often sparse and disappointing. At best, critics amiably shook their head and chuckled at Frye's personal audacity and perverse artfulness. In the *Hudson Review,* Robert Martin Adams wrote, "Professor Frye's is one of the strangest and most interesting literary minds in existence; like a whirling dervish, he incorporates somehow a Thomistic rigor, a prophetic vigor, and the diabolical persuasiveness of the Ancient Mariner." Eerily echoing Frye's own doubts, George Whalley went farther to suggest an underlining futility of purpose:

"Yet so much of it is perverse, ingenious, desolate; at a crucial point gaining rhetorical speed and assuming a sharp edge to seek safety in irony, as though desire were in perpetual conflict with vision."

There were inevitable concerns about how Frye's archetypal approach seemed to violate the idiosyncrasy and integrity of literary works. In *The Canadian Forum*, Eli Mandel was awed at Frye's equation of Tom Sawyer's cave with Theseus's labyrinth, and Jonah's whale with the Christ-harrowed hell and Eliot's "toothed gullet of an ancient shark." It was precisely this insensitivity to individuality which infuriated Frye's graduate school friend, Margaret Stobie: "If ...Tom Sawyer's cave is at the same time the belly of Leviathan and symbolic of the fallen world; and if any pole becomes the Cross, then all sense of proportion is lost and meaning becomes meaningless. The mind is not freed, but trapped."

Frye rarely had a chance to debate the issues personally. Before he arrived at Cornell to deliver an unrelated paper, "Homer and Nature," in April 1958, however, a senior professor alerted the secretary of the Graduate English Club at Cornell, Robert Scholes, about the possibility of a debate between Frye and Mike Abrams who was dismayed by the excessive systematization of the *Anatomy*. In a classic debate which thrilled students, Frye and Abrams squared off in a small amphitheatre classroom in the Statler Hotel. Abrams complained of the book's "fearful symmetry" and quoted Pope's "Epistle to Burlington" about Timon's maze garden:

> On ev'ry side you look, behold the Wall!
> No pleasing Intricacies intervene,
> No artful wildness to perplex the scene;
> Grove nods at grove, each Alley has a brother,
> And half the platform just reflects the other.

Abrams extended his criticism in a commissioned *University of Toronto Quarterly* review of the *Anatomy* which didn't appear until an astonishing two years after the *Anatomy*'s publication. He was skeptical about its complexity and sarcastically pondered the lack of "an appendix that will open out into a square yard of tabular diagram." Like Bostetter over a decade before, he wondered " ... to what extent are the inevitable sequences of repetitions, variations, parallels, and antitypes genuine discoveries and to what extent are they artefacts of the conceptual scheme?" He continued: "Any extended and complex literary work can, by the omission of unsuitable elements, be made to resemble almost any archetypal shape."

Abrams then admitted that while he could never find four-leaf clovers, his wife casually plucked them out of the grass. Until he read Browne, he never imagined the world full of quincunxes. Now he saw them but "they are not there in the way that four-leaf clovers are there, but only in the way that circles, triangles, and dodecagons can also be there, given the prepossession and the will." Frye retaliated with a joke. He wrote Abrams thanking him for his review but adding that he would now never be able to remember the face of Abram's wife, Ruthie, without a frame (presumably pentagonal) of four-leaf clovers. Abrams's review raised the difficult question that if one of Frye's intellectual peers was confused and dismayed by the *Anatomy* set-up, how was this book ever going to be communicable to *anybody* but a half-dozen all-knowing disciples and colleagues.

With his light-hearted talk about quincunxes and "medieval encyclopedic tables designed to comprehend the *omne scibile*," Abrams partly stumbled on the answer. When Frye himself read Francis Yates's 1966 book *The Art of Memory* which outlined the old "hermetic science" of mnemonic wheels and patterns used in the middle ages and Renaissance to encompass all knowledge, he realized that with the *Anatomy* he had designed his own memory system to contain all he knew. He had, as a result, fulfilled one of his chief outstanding ambitions left over from both *Fearful Symmetry* which reiterated his graduate school quest for an "alphabet of forms" and his Guggenheim plan of presenting "all the essential possibilities of literary symbolism in a single form."

When his old friend George Johnston dropped into his Toronto office some months after the *Anatomy* appeared, Johnston quite coincidentally opened the book at the circle of fifths section which unified the phases of romance, comedy, irony and tragedy. Johnston told him that if he could establish that, "the book is made." Frye later confessed, "At that point, I realized that that really was the centre of the book. And that at the centre was what Jung and his cohorts called the mandala, a circular diagram that anybody at any age could be exposed to. The difficulty from there is in trying to circumvent the lazy teacher who wants to present this as a substitute for the experience of literature, and to try to reach the teacher who realizes that this is more like the lens of field glasses, so that you see what you're experiencing."

He certainly was very cautious about the schema himself. Although he continued to use categories and "polar" concepts, Frye almost never identified works of literature by his own *Anatomy* terminology, least of all with the numbing array of phases in his Great Wheel. He even once used one of his technical terms, "fairy tales in the low mimetic displacement," with a virtual smirk. This was unfortunate because theory free of application is simply unscientific. One of Frye's most astute critics, Frank Kermode, complained that Frye "has not yet allowed himself to study, in terms of his diagram, one single work of art."

Inevitably, however, the *Anatomy*'s narrative circle was central to any consideration of the book's utility. When one of Frye's doctoral students, Alvin Lee, was preparing for the extremely difficult comprehensive exams at Toronto, he seized on the *Anatomy* terminology to help summarize literary works on 5x8 file cards. He did so well in his orals he received a rare first. While he had some doubts about the story wheel, he managed to test it years later when he was helping his wife Hope devise a major reader series, *Literature: The Uses of the Imagination*, based on Frye's theories. The closets in their old stone house in Dundas had been chaotically stuffed with Xeroxes of stories, poems and plays for the project. To organize the mess one weekend, Lee decided to see if he could slot the material without forcing into the phases of the story wheel and found the schema surprisingly accurate. Wayne Booth on the other hand suggested chaos if "the five most respectful readers of the *Anatomy*" categorized one single work.

As Douglas Bush initially feared, however, there was always a lively interest in the wheel itself as an object of super-intellectual veneration. Certainly after suggesting it, Frye himself had no reason to complain about efforts to visualize it. Over the next couple of decades, he would receive elaborate diamond or circle-shaped *Anatomy* schema from enthusiasts and erstwhile disciples which were in fact very suggestive of memory theatre charts. As early as 1963, Memye Curtis Tucker was laying out charts for a PhD outlining the *Anatomy* schema. As part of his own PhD, Robert Denham fiddled with Frye's schema and published an array of diagrams in his 1978 book, *Northrop Frye and Critical Method*. Everett C. Frost and Sydney Feshbach each devised their own variegated elaborations. Although he once quipped that they some-times looked like molecular protein diagrams, Frye was always friendly about these attempts and refused to condemn anyone for anomalies: " ...my version of that vision also has a subjective pole: it is a model only, colored by my preferences and limited by my ignorance. Others will have different versions, and as they continue to put them forth the objective reality will emerge more clearly." He was even grateful that his disciples proved more ingenious than himself, particularly in trying to figure out how the four stories with their six phases fit together.

Simply because of Frye's explicit ordering in the *Anatomy* text, however, there was an inevitable cookie-cutter approach to the various individual schema. Almost everyone, for example, showed a counter-clockwise rotation through romance at the zenith, trag-edy on the horizon, irony and satire at the nadir, and comedy on the opposite horizon. In her original diagram Memye Tucker had a clockwise direction which Frye corrected. Many critics like Wil-liam Wimsatt have noted that Frye contradicted his own 1951 schema which, coincidentally, was closer to the traditional Last Judgment layout. Frye's earlier schema has an apparent clockwise movement from comedy to tragedy to satire to romance which reflects a summer, autumn, winter, spring cycle. While embar-rassed about this contradiction, Frye later claimed he made the change because "it was easier to work with as my conceptions grew more elaborate and complex."

If academe remained leery about Frye's fathomless scheme, a major New York educational publisher, Harcourt Brace and World, immediately scouted Frye. Like all major textbook publishers,

Harcourt editors wanted strong new names to formulate or contribute to new projects. The *Anatomy* attracted the interest of Harcourt's Bill Goodman who tried to involve Frye in a revision of a college text, *Major British Writers*. Frye was determined to sell Harcourt on the idea of Blake as a major British writer but received a tepid response. As an alternative, Harcourt offered Frye an essay on Shelley at which the original contributor, Ivor Richards, had balked. When Richards unexpectedly decided to complete it, Harcourt offered Byron to Frye as consolation and signed a contract for a long 8,000 word essay, thus offering Frye a crucial entré into the world of mainstream publishing.

After ripping the historical approach apart in the *Anatomy*, Frye's acceptance and completion of this Byron assignment was astonishing. It showed Frye incongruously sifting through gossip about Byron with the clarity and zest of his CBC series, "The Poet as Prophet." Frye seemed to recall his own younger self in "the Byron type, who continues to be baffled by unanswered questions and simple anomalies, to make irresponsible jokes, to set his face against society, to respect the authority of his own mood ..."

## PRINCIPAL

Despite the fact the *Anatomy* was doing so well that it had to be reprinted in Jan. 1958, Frye was still in the eye of the storm. Both his work projects and travelling seemed amiably diffuse. He easily found the time to edit a new edition of E.J. Pratt's poetry which publisher John Gray casually requested by phone. He quickly sensed that, unlike his books for his other mentors, Edgar and Currelly, this assignment was going to be easy and enjoyable. After consulting with Pratt himself, he was ready to go only a month later and chirped to Gray about some of Pratt's new poems such as "Myth and Fact." In a bruising irony however Frye casually insisted on a designer who would make the book "look like what it is, one of the essential books in Canadian literature and a definitive collection of Canada's biggest poet, and not like a rebound copy of the Ford Salesman's Handbook." Frye had such distaste for the designer's typesetting ideas, he nearly withdrew his introduction. While not quite as bad as the manual he feared, the book bore a startling resemblance to the blandly designed high school textbooks of the period.

Through the spring and summer, Frye seemed so laid back, that he appeared almost to be treading water. He was hardly chasing fame. Although he was a star of the "Program in Criticism at Texas" which included Robert Graves, W.H. Auden and T.S. Eliot, his presence was more benign than momentous. Likewise he passed up a chance to go to a celebrated Harvard myth conference in June for the annual gathering of Canadian scholarly organizations, the Learneds. His summer, spent at the highly regarded summer school of Columbia University, was equally inconsequential. Unlike the Boston apartment the year before, he was set up in the comparative splendor of an apartment overlooking Riverside Dr. with its wooded bank falling to the hazy Hudson River. Frye regularly lunched with Fred Johnston and Bill Nelson in the Faculty Club, luxuriating in Renaissance shoptalk. Frye's presence had no connotations. He was there simply to teach. In his free time, he worked on the Byron essay for Harcourt.

The autumn back in Toronto began with a brutal shock. On Labour Day weekend, his friend Peter Fisher took three friends sailing on Sunday afternoon near Kingston. Caught by a line squall with blinding rain and 65-mile-an-hour winds, the sloop sank killing Fisher and two others. Frye had always possessed a sense that Fisher was the luckiest of men who could, and did, walk like a protected angel through battlefields. Badly shaken, Frye confessed to their mutual friend, George Johnston, that he kept dreaming Fisher was still alive.

In a freakish coincidence, Frye was soon on a plane to North Carolina to deliver a paper on "Lycidas" about Milton's drowned friend, Edward King. If ever there was a test of Frye's theoretical resolution of convention over reality, this was it: "One may burst into tears at the news of a friend's death, but one can never spontaneously burst into song, however doleful a lay. *Lycidas* is a passionately sincere poem, because Milton was deeply interested in the structure and symbolism of funeral elegies, and had been practicing since adolescence on every fresh corpse in sight ..." As he had done for Edgar and Currelly, Frye gathered up Fisher's writings, publishing them as *The Valley of Vision.* He said goodbye by dedicating an anthology of Blake criticism to Fisher with lines from "The Introduction" to *The Songs of Experience:* "The starry floor, /The wat'ry shore, /Is giv'n thee till the break of day."

Though he had recently had it easy at Vic, Frye soon faced a serious problem which would affect all his plans for years, the request that he become the college's academic head, the Principal. The President of Victoria, Art Moore, had to replace Harold Bennett, who was approaching 70 and had already stretched the pension rules. As the college faced a great deal of expansion and upgrading of staff, Moore and many of the staff wanted a high-profile academic for the job. Frye's name came up repeatedly. When Moore approached Frye, Frye tried to put Moore off by throwing him three names of academics who might do instead of himself. None, however, was available when Moore investigated. When a board member started pressuring for another candidate who was unacceptable to both Frye and the rest of the staff, Frye very reluctantly agreed to take the job.

Moore tried to make the job as painless as possible by agreeing to cover much of the irritating paperwork. He also promised Frye the sabbatical he was eagerly anticipating. When Moore and the Chairman of the Appointments Committee, Ralph Mills, went before the Board of Regents on Jan. 15, to recommend Frye, Mills made explicit their desire to alter the Principal's role sufficiently to allow Frye to continue "the work which had engaged so much of his attention through recent years." Frye was alarmed by the obvious hazards of the job and accepted partly "on the grit-and-oyster theory that if one had something to annoy one, one might become more productive." This was Frye's call to duty—something that his Methodist conscientiousness could not ignore. The one positive argument which made most sense to him was that of Roy

Daniells who told him that his writing would reflect what he was. That turned out to be truer than either Frye or Daniells may have imagined.

Inevitably there was dismay that Frye would take an administrative position when his career logically indicated serious writing. Even an undergraduate sat down in gloom in front of Frye and blurted out, "Are you going to be *happy* as Principal?" He wasn't and was never going to be. He at least had a short window of freedom and remained optimistic that, despite the job, he could plow ahead with a major book. Just that fall, Frye offered Princeton the intelligence that, rather than his practical *Anatomy* sequel, he wanted to land a sabbatical leave to tackle "another big study, heading in the general direction of a kind of theory of narrative, and rising out of a comparative study of epic-romance structure which was one of the by-products of the Spenser interest ..." Five months later, he was still confident about a book on "continuous prose forms" and even managed to send an outline to Houston.

A curious result of his elevated social status was a request that he go to NATO's 10th anniversary convention in London, the Atlantic Conference. He was to attend both as a Canadian representative and as *rapporteur general*, as well, responsible for finalizing a list of recommendations at the end. At the instigation partly of MP Henry Jackman, Frye was flown up to Ottawa to be enlisted by John Diefenbaker himself. In June 1959, Helen and Frye found themselves ensconced in the stuffy Piccadilly Hotel with 56 other Canadian delegates, 36 of whom were considered "distinguished." Despite the opening by the Queen and the potential for unadulterated pomp and circumstance, the conference did have quite a serious side. Picking up an idea from Dana Wilgress, Frye's declarations committee recommended a "Studies Centre for the Atlantic Community ... to serve as a clearing house and intellectual focus," to help "combat Soviet ideological warfare." It sounded like a silly bureaucratic idea, except that within the context of the times, western values were constantly being abused everywhere in the developing world. The press, however, never took it too seriously. It garnered spotty attention even in right-wing London papers.

Feeling like Jonah escaping the whale, Frye and Helen fled the

Piccadilly for the less pretentious Whitehall Hotel on Montague St. and stayed on in London for several more weeks. On an unusually hot day, Frye received an invitation to deliver the Page-Barbour lectures at the University of Virginia. He was immediately intrigued by the possibility of balancing Eliot's odious *After Strange Gods* with his own lectures and answered he would be "very deeply honored" to deliver the lectures.

Returning to Toronto, he prepared to become Principal of Victoria College. Almost to cover its improbability, Victoria College staged an *event* in the 1,750-seat Convocation Hall which freely combined student dadaism with a medieval procession. With streaming toilet paper rolls lobbed down from the upper balconies, it was an event just short of pandemonium. Gate House undergraduates marched in with bagpipes and signs proclaiming that "Gate House Conceives Another Principal," and "The Truth Shall Make you Frye." After a prayer by his old teacher Kenneth Cousland, Frye was sworn in and robed like royalty in a scarlet gown.

Frye then gave probably his most eloquent speech in the defence of education. Unlike the funereal speeches delivered by most administrators, this was a fiery religious sermon. The university was so important it carried, he said "a weight of authority far greater than the authority of state or government or even social custom. It derives this authority, not from itself, but from its cloud of witnesses, the communion of wisdom, of the thinkers, artists, and statesmen whose work it studies and carries on." This in turn served to break up social complacency and revitalize society: " ... there must be a continuous current of mental energy flowing into the world from the university, which is the powerhouse of freedom. The university stands for what humanity can do, and for what the rest of society is free to do if it tries." He suggested that even an exam-harried, benzedrine-zonked student can hazily recognize "that something of which his own mind formed part was much more deeply involved in the nature of things than he had ever dreamed." Once this has happened, "in some mysterious way, his mind continues to revolve around the vision at its heart: the vision of what the poet Yeats calls the sages standing in God's holy fire." Frye unapologetically underlined the religious connotations of this vision: "The sources of creative power in the human mind are inexhaustible. If we could realize that they are infinite and eternal as well, and that the human mind is therefore linked in its nature and destiny with a divine mind, that would be the final motive for learning and the final guarantee of its value."

Frye of course knew that the whole educational apparatus was really set up to homogenize students rather than to create maladjusted Davids. He excoriated educators: "Who watered the stock of ideas, drained the content out of learning, cheated their children of the pleasures of the intellect, crippled them for life in the arts of words and numbers, and then seized all the positions of power and influence to impose their miserable follies on future ages?" Frye discerned that the devil did not reside in teachers' colleges or bureaucracies but in the complacency of everyone's minds: "The root of all the nonsense in our education is our stupified satisfaction with what we call our way of life."

The speech created enough excitement that Clarke, Irwin, agreed to publish it as a booklet. In preparing the manuscript, the senior editor, R.W.W. Robertson, heard about Frye's Bible course, and asked Frye to think about working up his notes. Frye replied that while he might free some time the following summer for such a project, "the future of this particular part of my work is a bit vague." Frye of course would take two more decades to wrestle this bogey to the ground.

If he inhabited the exhilarating role of prophet defending educational honesty, he was hardly finding the practical principal's job congenial. He hadn't even been in his office two months before he was expressing private dismay: " ...I'm joining committees at the average of one a day, and am getting the illusion of making policy while learning about the relative merits of travertine and terrazzo tile, statistical predictions of staff-student ratios in 1968, property values on Bloor Street, and the proper number of formal parties to allow the residences. One banks one's fires, and hopes that one is also adding more fuel, in some mysterious way."

This mishmash of the serious and trivial was an accurate representation of his job. As faculty head, Frye was able to impose many of his own values simply by hiring as many of the top young scholars he knew, including David Hoeniger and John Robson neither of whom were Fryedolators. He helped supervise the construction of the new Pratt library, trying to humanize its blocky international-style coldness by insisting on a concrete, instead of glass, wall over the reading room on the west so that students wouldn't fry to grease spots in the afternoon. He supported the renovation of the college chapel from a dingy unpopular place to one of the brightest chapels in downtown Toronto.

But it was this "nightmare of irrelevant ritual" which beleaguered him. For his friend King Joblin who later temporarily became his replacement, he itemized the alarming round of college rituals: supervising and speaking at the Freshman Weekend, the First Class Honour Dinner, Charter Day, even reading out names at convocation. He inevitably got stuck with curious administrative tasks. Robert Heilman, who was passing through Toronto, visited Frye and was stunned to find him preoccupied with touring and listing the college toilets which were disabled by the excavations of the new subway along Bloor St. Frye usually bore such duties with stoicism but his anger could erupt murderously. When a graduate student was talking with him, Art Moore brought in some papers for him to review and to the consternation of the student who had enjoyed Frye's generosity, Frye was curt, even rude, in telling Moore he had already read them. Among staff, Frye sometimes seemed so disinterested, there was the suspicion of an open book hidden on his lap. Even worse, some staff members became aware that Frye was not a determined fighter. Whenever there was a serious controversy even on an administrative issue directly involving himself, his support was not necessarily guaranteed.

Very early on, Frye knew the trivialities could overwhelm him and complained to Johnston, " ... I rather miss the freedom with which I could drop everything and hike out along Bloor Street trying to solve *ambulando* some problem about prose form or verse rhythm." But he recognized the key to his own position which precisely matched what Art Moore most wanted out of Frye: "A university community doesn't want a leader ... [rather] a kind of focus of articulateness and it seems almost pathetically grateful to have anyone try to be that."

His glum mood was certainly not helped by the tragic death of his father at age 89 on Dec. 11, 1959, in Vera's Chicago apartment. Although the details are unclear, he seems to have accidentally started a fire. Helen had been alarmed years before when he was living with them in Toronto that he'd turned up a stove burner to full heat and left it, thinking he'd turned it off. Also, Herm was a smoker, and could have been careless. Because of his lameness, he was unable to get out in time to save himself. An inquest found no foul play, only a freakish and sad misfortune. Frye read scripture at the funeral.

Not long afterward, Frye experienced a curiously radiant personal vision which seemed to eradicate any harsh view of death. Art Moore called for a lock-up of senior administrators at the Guild Inn to consider directions for the college. Frye remembers waking up and opening the curtains to find a blazing vision of snow and ice. Icicles hung down on two branches outside. On one sat a cardinal and on the other, a blue jay. It was perfect balance but had no particular meaning. Frye confessed, "If I could have died then, I would have died a happy man."

### EXECUTIVE RHYTHM

Frye was now entering "an executive rhythm of life," and even allowed himself the odd cynical sniff about the explosion of academic criticism. He attacked "pseudo-theses that do not prove anything" and suggested that "all commentary on Joyce, Eliot and Yeats ought to be suspended for a little while—say about five hundred years." He was, on the other hand, just a year away from agreeing to write a little book on Eliot for a new Scottish critical series, Writers and Critics. He also undertook an "exciting" assignment to review Samuel Beckett's fiction for The Hudson Review.

Rather than seeing something new, however, Frye happily found himself in the hall of mirrors: Beckett reflecting Joyce, Eliot, Yeats, Proust and Dante.

When it came to contemporary Canadian literature Frye continued to be unmoved. A student reporter, John Robert Colombo, even captured a glum judgement from him at a student gathering, "Canadian writers the worst" which Colombo's mischievous editors turned into a front page headline. Since 1941, Frye only acknowledged a little progress against this glowering Canadian incubus. "Approaching early Canada was like being a tiny Jonah entering an immense whale. However, recent writers have succeeded somewhat in reducing this to an imaginatively manageable shape." As before, there was just cause for the tardiness: "Unfortunately Canada has no ghosts or cycles to help the writer. Canada lacks the indefinable look of a lived-in country."

Nevertheless, he continued to force himself on CanLit with no great relish. He'd finished off a decade of poetry reviews for *The University of Toronto Quarterly* only to slide into the jury system of Governor General's Literary Awards, becoming head of the English section from 1958-1960 and overall chairman from 1961-1963. This meant receiving a great pile of books each year to evaluate for fiction, non-fiction and poetry awards. As a chairman, he had a few agonies. He had to cross off four of his own books as ineligible in 1963. Although he was usually liberal and consensus-oriented, he locked himself up with Frank Watt and Mary Winspear in an Ottawa hotel room for half an hour until they agreed to give the non-fiction prize to Marshall McLuhan's *The Gutenberg Galaxy*. No one, including Frye, was keen on it from a literary point of view but Frye simply felt that their committee would look ridiculous if they failed to choose it.

By now he was a literary force with a definable Frye-adoring cabal. His own graduate students included poets James Reaney and Jay Macpherson. James Reaney had so accepted Frye's ideas that in a 1959 *Poetry* review, Reaney reflected Frye's hopes about *Fearful Symmetry*. Calling the *Anatomy* a time-saving "poet's handbook that T.S. Eliot's criticism failed to produce," he saw poets pondering "literally hundreds of designs for poems, all from literature itself." CanLit now had "a giant critical focus with some mythopoeic poets trying to live up to it." Reaney himself experimented with patterns, most notably in *One Man Masque*, which has a circular action "through life, then death, and back into life once more": "Since my thesis was on Yeats and Spenser I was using them, but I was also using Frye's mandala and the ruthlessness with which I planned the shape of the play comes from his views that you should adapt a convention and let it carry you where it may." He was intrigued by the notion of displacement and as an exercise with his own writing students would suggest taking, say, a traditional Robber Bridegroom scenario and setting it in modern Winnipeg. With Macpherson, Daryl Hine, Richard Stingle and Colleen Thibaudeau, Reaney put out a new journal in September 1960, *Alphabet*, focussed on myth-oriented criticism and new creative writing. It reflected an extravagant desire to build a New Jerusalem through art.

If Frye was supposed to be a Field Marshal coordinating a literary movement, he was the world's worst. Except for Jay Macpherson, who was hired by Kenneth Maclean at Vic in 1959, he had no lieutenants even close enough to talk to. To a junior member of the group, Margaret Atwood, he was an *eminence grise* who wafted "from one mysterious point to another, surrounded by a nimbus of eminence." Frye's sole literary advice to Atwood seems to have consisted of the somewhat less than monumental admonition that getting a graduate degree and teaching college English might be more valuable than running off to Britain and becoming a waitress. Atwood's first work outside of college was a cycle of poems based on classical myths, which was published in *Alphabet*. While her fiction belongs to the underbelly of vision, Reaney notes that her symbolism unquestionably breaks down into distinct levels "below the ground and above the ground."

The weight of his own literary reputation simply meant that in Canada Frye was becoming a living ikon who was expected to pronounce on each and every practical literary issue. For Frye himself this was often just an extension of the kind of student discussions he'd run around Vic and Hart House for a quarter-century. But it developed national repercussions when, for example, he talked on practical writing at two conferences in the early 60s. Frye had continued to insist so brazenly on the equivalence of critical and creative endeavor that he audaciously told insecure poets and writers to buck up their courage and enter a new world arm in arm with the tough boys on the block, the critics. His nemesis, Irving Layton, countered Frye's ideas with the proclamation "poetry is celebration not cerebration." Writing a little later, Layton was less delicate: "The critical achievement of Northrop Frye is a myth carefully nurtured in Canadian universities by fartless pipsqueaks. Actually he's a sterile ideologue." Despite the bombast, Layton had a genuine anxiety about "young, impressionable writers" coming under the influence of too much self-conscious academicism.

Frye handled this abuse simply by ignoring it. He continued to regard Layton as a loose cannon on the deck and did everything he could to keep out of his way, even frustrating efforts to get them together. When Layton saw that Jericho's wall was not crumbling, he ultimately gave up. Nevertheless he felt compelled to sound Frye out about the effect of his polemics. Blandly but beautifully, Frye replied that he "never worried much about your comments on me, because I never have felt there was anything personal in them."

More than ever there was a separation of image: the abused—even demonic—Canadian cultural figure, and the international scholar who quietly slipped away for conferences. The substance of his career had always belonged to the latter and would continue to do so. In April 1960 he shared a conference on myth with such fashionable luminaries as Alan Watts, Joseph Campbell and Mircea Eliade at Harvard and another in mid-July on "The Dramatic Focus" with Kenneth Burke at Georgetown University.

He tended some old gardens too, turning out a brilliant typological essay, "The Structure and Imagery in *The Faerie Queene*" for a renaissance conference at the University of Western Ontario and essays on Shakespeare's *The Winter's Tale* and *Love's Labour's Lost* for seminars at Stratford. His fame moreover provided tempting opportunities in the States to influence academic publishing trends. In 1960, Karl Miller, who was a virtual one-man operation managing Beacon Press paperbacks in Boston, put Frye on his editorial board to tap his knowledge. As a result, Frye managed to make accessible such ostensibly unpromising items as Austin Farrer's *A Rebirth of Images*, Mircea Eliade's *Patterns of Comparative Religion*, Gaston Bachelard's *The Psychoanalysis of Fire* and Hans Jonas's *The Gnostic Religion*.

But increasingly his attention turned towards education. If literature was the direct means of liberating creative power in society, education provided the stage. This had been clear in his general speeches since the *Anatomy* but now his interest took a concrete turn. Certainly the times were right for it. American educators in particular went into a panic over the Sputnik launch in Oct. 1957, which seemed to indicate that the communist system was far ahead, especially in the sciences. Suddenly attempts to rethink curriculum approaches, which had languished before, were actively promoted. Both in Canada and United States there was an orgy of conferences backed by an ominous array of scholarly associations. Probably the most influential was the Woods Hole conference in Massachusetts in Sept. 1959, which psychologist Jerome Bruner organized and then recorded in his extravagantly influential *The Process of Education*, "a manifesto for those out to improve the intellectual quality of our schools," which drew attention from John Kennedy's White House mandarins. Bruner favoured an approach "of 'models in the head' based on general understanding, from which hypotheses about the particulars could be generated and then tested against experience." His "most controversial statement"—which deeply influenced Frye—was that "any subject can be taught to anybody at any age in some form that is honest."

Bruner's book was barely out when Frye was in Ottawa speaking at a Royal Society conference with the theme of "The Responsibilities of Canadian Universities." In his speech, "The Critical Discipline," Frye wandered off topic and broadly considered education as an evolution of phases, from primary, to secondary and university levels. Directly citing Bruner, Frye wanted a scientific adaption for literature centred in early education on "the study of the myths and folk tales, the stories of the Bible and of Classical legend, which organize the whole of one's later literary and imaginative

experience and yet make sense to the youthful mind." The ultimate
point, as ever, was to dislodge the student from the "lotus land" of
"ordinary social environment ... and prod him into further voyages
of discovery."

All of this attention to early education was new. Even in the
*Anatomy*, Frye was content to see reform stop at the 19-year-old.
A major factor in Frye's wider interest was that the chairman of
the Board of Education of Toronto, Roy Sharp, had approached
him earlier in the year with a vague but insistent desire to break
down the barriers between the Board of Education and the University of Toronto. At first Frye didn't quite know what Sharp was
trying to get at but the vision of a properly coordinated educational
stream began to haunt him. After his Royal Society speech, he
participated in *ad hoc* meetings during the summer to thrash out
ideas. These were so successful that a joint committee was formed
with representatives of the board and the university, including
Frye, in September 1960. This soon led in November to a Joint
University-Board Committee with five sub-committees to consider
English, foreign languages, mathematics, science and social science with representatives from all three levels of education.

While these studies all ended up in *Design for Learning*, the
whole apparatus generated enough interest that the Ontario Teachers' Federation put up a then very impressive $50,000 grant estab-
lishing an Ontario Curriculum Institute to keep the ideas moving.
The creation of the institute in Nov. 1962, suggested by Jerome
Bruner himself, was entirely spontaneous and so independent of
official channels that it created political jitters. Liberal Party leader
John Wintermeyer sometimes saw a dark teacher conspiracy in it
and wanted "an educational research institute" run by the government. While at first slow to react, the governing Conservatives
stole the idea and set up the Ontario Institute for Studies in
Education, or OISE, in 1965, which developed into a ten-floor
monument on Bloor Street staffed quite substantially with Americans. Because the original Institute was quickly outmanoeuvered,
Frye was unforgiving and became a bitter opponent of OISE,
which he called an "avuncular avalanche ... which completely
obliterated ... a grass roots movement."

Frye's increasing focus on education was obvious in his Page-Barbour lectures, "The Well-Tempered Critic" in mid-March 1961 at the University of Virginia. For the first time outside of broadcasting, Frye was trying to be the populist but the earnest theorist kept getting in the way. He was juggling so many themes, they tended to fall over each other. They were not, as Frye claimed, "like the boxes of Silenus" fitting snugly into each other. Two friendly critics, Bill Blissett and George P. Elliott, openly complained of losing the thread of the argument.

There was the ghost of an original theme, possession, which Frye had used for a speech at Kenyon College in Nov. 1959, "Literature as Possession." This became the original title of his Virginia lectures and provided the basis of his second talk. The question of possession was broached by a long preamble of poetic and prose styles which fell neatly along the line of hieratic and demotic lines. Presumably the more authentic the form, the more it would sink into the core of the individual. Poetry was "always the central powerhouse of a literary education." A quarter century later, Frye would call poetry "a holy of holies in the middle" of the Jerusalem of language. This was the first thing to expose a child to.

If literary education involved an Aristotelian awareness about form and style, its effect was almost surreptitious. With the "rhythm and leisure [of poetry] slowly soaking into the body and its wit and concreteness into the mind, [literary education] can do something to develop a speaking and writing prose style that comes out of the depths of personality and is a genuine expression of it." In turn, it would regenerate itself through articulated speech: "Good writing must be based on good speech ..." There was a sense that if a student could just see and know the varieties of good and bad speech and writing, which Frye took pains to itemize, there would be a great expurgation of verbal and intellectual junk residing in the brain: "The study of literature purifies our experience of the private and irrelevant associations of stock response."

Because Frye had just agreed to write a short book on T.S. Eliot for the popular Writers and Critics series, he had an unusual opportunity to see if stock response would easily lift like a poisonous vapor from the work of a great writer. Frye was deeply interested in how great writers produce enduring work while remaining ideological screwballs. In *Fearful Symmetry*, he had an early notion that criticism had to "isolate what is poetic and imaginative and annihilate what is legal and historical." This implied that the writer could easily become alienated from the positive meaning of his own work. As a result, the inspired critic had a prophetic, purifying role. Blake did this for Milton, and now Frye for Eliot. This was not inconsequential. As an imaginative force, the poet visualized the Promised Land: "on the historical level, he may often be a lost leader, a Moses floundering in a legal desert."

The assignment was attractive as an experiment and looked easy. Frye had absorbed Eliot since his student years and stuffed his poetry into his teaching and writing wherever it would fit. The assignment was discharged quickly and efficiently. In late January 1961 he not only agreed to produce a short 128-page manuscript by December of the same year, he made such good progress, he sent off his manuscript a month and a half early in late October.

Following publisher notes, Frye produced a scrawny biographical first chapter and then headed into the second, "Antique Drum," to eviscerate Eliot's social and political attitudes, which took a "myth of decline" form. There was the "bob sled or 'down we went' theory" that viewed the middle ages as the height of western civilization. It was the Puritan Revolution which wrecked the splendid medieval consensus. Frye quoted Eliot's contention in 1947 that the British Civil War of the 1600s had not ended. These were Frye's "clichés of hostility" intended to lay bare the "permanent achievement" of a monumental corpus of literature. Unfortunately hostile readers, including Eliot himself, never seemed to get beyond the first two chapters.

Irrespective of the controversy, the book was an important one for Frye because it represented the only extended practical criticism he ever wrote about modern literature. Coming directly after the *Anatomy*, it showed that Frye was not about to use his vast *Anatomy* structure as a meat-grinder, shearing poetry into bits. Nevertheless, he made it clear that the symbolism of Eliot, like that of most major writers, is easily revealed by a simple diagrammatic approach. Because of space problems, for example, Frye said he couldn't comment in detail on *Four Quartets* so he simply instructed the reader like a student: first draw a cross, then a circle on the outside and one closer to the centre. The horizontal line was clock time, the vertical the holy dimension of God's presence descending into time. The big hemisphere was divided between an upper plenitude and lower vacancy; the small hemisphere between the rose garden and the subway, or "innocence and experience." This was not quite the Last Judgment because there was no purgatorial element. Nevertheless, Frye saw the *Four Quartets* as forming "a single vision that begins and ends at the same point," inevitably adding that "the archetype of this cycle is the Bible, which begins with the story of a man in the garden." Paradise was lost and regained with a bejewelled city added to the garden. Frye might shrug off detailed commentary but he was determined to show how the readers of both Eliot's later poetry and drama could climb and descend the apparatus of time and salvation with its compartments of symbolism, through the round of seasons and underground and underwater quests.

Although *T.S. Eliot* was not exceptionally easy to write, Frye managed to finish both it and *The Well-Tempered Critic* by October. The editor Robin Lorimer at Oliver and Boyd was delighted but then concerned when he discovered it was 30% too long. With Jeffares he explored the possibility of having Frye expand it to fit another series but decided to ask Frye to make a cut on the pretext that an extra half-signature would spoil the profitability of the book. Frye was miffed but accommodating. Disenchanted, he predicted that the book "may be a bust." It must have nevertheless given some satisfaction in knocking the last nail into the coffin of New Criticism. The following year, he brazenly declared "the Mythopoeic school ... is dominant in criticism at present having superceded the orthodox new criticism."

A bruising irony was that two days after Lorimer rejected *T.S. Eliot* as too long, Julian Muller of Harcourt rejected *The Well-Tempered Critic* as too short. Muller claimed that "the economics of publishing present an almost insurmountable problem." This was an exaggeration. Scribner's, after all, made a small fortune from a 99-page lecture book by Étienne Gilson, *Reason and Revelation in the Middle Ages*. But Harcourt was sincere in its belief that it should go to a university press and so Frye had it sent to Indiana which accepted it. Even then Indiana's director, Bernard Perry, wondered if couldn't be expanded. It was nevertheless published in emaciated form with large print and wide margins. Despite the embarrassment, Harcourt left the door wide open to Frye. Obviously reacting to the educational theme of *The Well-Tempered Critic*, Harcourt's president William Jovanovich, who had become deeply interested in Frye's ideas, offered an advance for a book on education.

At the start of 1962, Frye felt so overworked, he had to admit, "The way I feel now, I shall probably be spending the entire month of June horizontal in a darkened room." He complained to George Johnston that his dream of a year off didn't seem terribly bright. In the Laocoön of "hands clutching and grabbing, and the dialectics of decision," there were "crude" temptations to pack it all in and become the President of Mount Allison University or general editor of "an unending series of books." Then, curiously, Frye quite unplaintively mentioned to the awed Johnston that starting the following week, he would be travelling to Haverford, Brown, Harvard, Nebraska, Rochester, back to Toronto to speak to 3,000 psychiatrists in Convocation Hall and on to Mount Allison. His voluminous lecture papers now almost always appeared as essays and by June he had a staggering commitment to turn out 15 articles by the year's end, as well as several books to finish and edit. The latter included the T.S. Eliot book which was turning into an albatross. Frye cut his manuscript so severely that Robin Lorimer now wanted him to expand it again, perhaps with the relatively easy device of a full bibliography. Frye sat on it for most of the summer and then sent off a new version in mid-October.

Frye now had so many tempting offers, he seemed incapable of refusing. In the spring of 1963 he agreed to do the Centennial Lectures at the University of Western Ontario. On top of that Columbia University wrote in April to ask him to deliver the Bampton Lectures in 1963. Because of a somewhat eccentric bequest, the prepackaged themes were theology, science, art and hygiene. It took Frye nearly a month to accept. Focussing on the theology topic, he saw a chance to make a run at an unshakeable theme, "the typology of the Bible and some consideration of the role which the symbolism of the Bible has played in literature, more particularly English Literature." All this determined Wesleyan activity unfortunately blocked work on an *Anatomy* successor which, Frye claimed, was very much on his mind. Frye still viewed many of his articles as "bits and pieces" of the book and wanted time off to attempt to synthesize them as he'd done for the *Anatomy* itself.

He soon gave this up, though, because Bill Goodman of Harcourt thought it opportune for a general collection of previously published work. Frye produced a simple manuscript of essays dating back to his 1947 Yeats's essay, none of which he altered because of *Anatomy* concerns. He seemed so little concerned about the *Anatomy* schema that he published his famous "The Archetypes of Literature" essay with its spring-romance, summer-comedy equations which contracted his later formulation. Only the title proved to be a complication. Bill Goodman's suggestion, which Frye immediately approved, was *Spiritus Mundi* from Yeats' poem, "Second Coming" ("when a vast image out of *Spiritus Mundi*/Troubles my sight ..."). There was strong opposition to it from the sales department which thought that with an esoteric Latin title, the book would be incorrectly buried in the religion section of bookstores. Neither Frye nor Goodman were impressed with this argument and the decision was delayed so late that the title page was designed and set in proof. When the sales department persisted, Frye came up with *Fables of Identity* from E.J. Pratt's *Towards the Last Spike*, a title which recalled Frye's suggestion of *A Fable for Critics* for the *Anatomy*. Goodman nevertheless framed the title page proof and put it up like a trophy on his apartment wall.

Helen, who'd taken the brunt of all this industry at home, insisted on a proper holiday for their twenty-fifth wedding anniversary in August, and they headed off to Copenhagen in August.

He was immediately back in harness in early September as chairman of an English Institute session on Romanticism with speakers M.H. Abrams, Lionel Trilling and René Welleck. Because he was so busy, he hadn't wanted to do the session but it gave him a vicarious pleasure to announce that the anti-Romantic attitudes of Hulme, Eliot and Pound in the 20s belonged on the junk heap of history. He produced a somewhat bland essay which barely suggested the importance of Romanticism in his thinking. There was no indication, for example, of his interest in its continuity through contemporary science fiction and murder mysteries. It did, however, reveal a crucial cosmological approach which sometimes seemed more essential to Frye than terminology. Working like C.S. Lewis, Frye marked the location of a key symbolical element like the Garden of Adonis. Viewed as up and beyond in Spenser and Milton, it was down and inside in Keats. It was Blake of course who saw Jerusalem as something inside. Mankind had failed to see it "because he has been looking in the wrong direction, outside." If he thought he could simply discharge any obligation in those days without further complication, he was sadly mistaken. A former student from the 1957 Harvard year, David Dushkin, attended the session and immediately started pressing Frye for a small book on Romanticism for a new Random House paperback series. Frye threw his hands up in horror at yet another assignment. He vainly tried to put Dushkin off for three years but the persistent editor finally won a contract for *A Study of English Romanticism.*

An almost freakishly casual complication in this wild period was a phoned request from the Canadian Broadcasting Corporation to write and broadcast the Massey Lectures for 1962. Based on the idea of the BBC Reith series in which high-powered intellectuals tried to approach a general audience, the Massey series had been inaugurated the year before with British economist Barbara Ward. Frye would note acidly that the CBC could never be so audacious as to start a Canadian series with a Canadian.

Nevertheless, Frye was intrigued with the idea of producing a poor-man's guide to his thinking. Faced with the difficulty of his two major books, few might have expected that Frye could handle the needs of a popular audience. CBC producers, however, still remembered his radio scripts through the 40s and 50s. The remarkable aspect of the series was that its production was so utterly unremarkable. Even the "contract" was a typed letter with a few basic agreements, including a $4,000 fee.

Frye wrote this series so quickly and effortlessly he couldn't remember much about it except that he continued working in his usual fashion right up to broadcast date. In the fall he went down to the CBC Radio headquarters, a rodent-infested red-brick former girls' school on Jarvis St., and simply read his scripts into a microphone. The producer, Robert McCormack, a Trinity College graduate who was nearly as shy and reticent as Frye, hovered over him with a stopwatch. Familiar with the constraints of both lecturing and preaching, Frye timed each lecture perfectly.

The CBC was not overwhelmed by Frye's six talks. In the Nov. 3-9 issue of the *CBC Times*, it featured "Behan at Home with Louis MacNeice" on the cover and placed a short article on Frye's series on page ten with no photo or illustration. Starting on Nov. 9, the CBC started broadcasting the talks at the apologetic hour of 10:30 pm.

The CBC also followed the pattern of the Reith Lectures by publishing the scripts. In a slightly stern letter to CBC publications department, Frye announced, "The lectures have been written in a deliberately conversational style, and the printed version will be carefully edited by me, and not by anyone else, to conform with the rhythm of the spoken word."

Except for the white cover which featured a large orange calligraphic design, the 68-page published lectures possessed a rather ungainly design of small print, cramped line spacing and narrow margins. It fitted into the standard format which the CBC started the year before and maintained throughout the series. Peculiar to all the series' titles, *The Educated Imagination* was extravagantly successful. Published in 1963, it sold out its 4,000 printing and had to be reprinted the same year. By 1970, it was in its seventh impression and by 1983, its 18th, with an accumulated Canadian sale of 88,000. By contrast, few titles in the series made it much beyond a second printing. Some of this success was artificial because it later became required reading on grade 13 English curriculum in Ontario.

There was, however, some talk of its publication by the popular producer of intellectual titles, Mentor Books which published intellectuals like Alan Watts, Marshall McLuhan and John Kenneth Galbraith, but nothing came of this, and Indiana University Press eventually published its own edition the following year. Unfortunately the failure of the Mentor Books edition had serious repercussions in banishing Frye and his ideas, unlike those of McLuhan and Galbraith, to the perimeter of public recognition in the States. Nevertheless, *The Educated Imagination* would remain Frye's basic entry point for popular audiences. He relinquished all desire to unload the technical aspects of literary study and let himself go about the First Cause of literature itself, the imaginative vision.

Considering he'd just written a long bland essay "The Developing Imagination," it's astonishing how energetic was this companion piece. Frye managed to enliven all his old themes with zest and immediacy. Literature was focussed on itself not life, he said. It followed its own conventions so thoroughly that to read a popular romance or thriller was to reread the simple tales of Cinderella or Bluebeard. To be real, literature had to be literature-like, not life-like. Far from being trapped by its own mirror reflection, literature regenerated life by reversing the process of "ideals and great visions ... becoming shoddy and squalid in practical life." Although there was the promise of magical transformation, this was not a woolly gnostic process leading to the stars. The romantic wish-dream had in fact to be solidly weighted with the anxiety dream to get a proper vision of the here and now. And no matter how far the reader got into poetic vision, like Dante, he had to return to life with that vision.

In response to the clichéd equation of art and unbridled emotion, Frye had his usual warning. Emotion was crucial but dangerous. Pure unadulterated emotion, after all, was a Hitlerian temper tantrum. It had to be contained by reason but there were limitations to that too. Literature released emotion, made sense of it and used it constructively.

Because it presented visions not dogma, literature was fundamentally amoral. Its ultimate effect, though, could be thoroughly moral. Seeing horror in literature was exhilarating because it is "full of the energy of repudiation." The more exposure to horror, "the less likely we are to find an unthinking pleasure in cruel or evil things."

Behind it all was a structuralist notion that the human mind constructs because it is already constructed. The whole point of literary studies was to understand and explore the symbolic layout, which was already there, and reject dysfunctional aspects which could range from wild emotion to procrustean logic. At the centre of the process was the exploratory power of imagination, "the constructive power of the mind set free to work on pure construction, construction for its own sake."

MILTON, ELIOT, SHAKESPEARE

Frye was so busy he now talked of "the black pall of commitments" hanging over him. In February he had to clear page proofs for *T.S. Eliot* and ponder its impact. After rewriting it three times, he confessed, "I got very browned-off with it and can hardly read it now." He also had to deal with his book of essays for Harcourt and a collection of critical essays on Blake for a Prentice-Hall series he'd agreed to do two years before. Admitting he was dawdling on it, he thought it appropriate to his own "assessment of the contemporary state of Blake scholarship." Besides his Beacon Press work which involved an introduction to Bachelard's *The Psychoanalysis of Fire* that year, he was also coordinating a new college reader series for the Canadian market, which drew in some younger scholars who impressed him.

Somehow he managed to collect his wits for his Centennial Lectures in early March, "A Tetrachordon for Milton," at Huron College at the University of Western Ontario. Because Frye had absorbed Milton into his very bones from his teens, he was able to deliver his four talks nearly impromptu to large audiences of 350. His old graduate student, William Blissett, who chaired the lectures, sat behind Frye and watched in quiet amazement as he marched through his complex lectures with just a handful of index cards. Frye was nevertheless under such overt strain that a student reporter was compelled to note that "his brows never seemed to unknit." Although tape recorders were not *de rigueur* then, someone had the inspiration to record the lectures, donating the tapes to a grateful Frye for transcription.

When he worked them up into a manuscript in the summers of 1963 and 1964, he admitted they were "a distillation of undergraduate lectures" with some borrowings from earlier material, including his 1950 Milton reader. They also appear to contain some of the ideas on the epic which once belonged to the abandoned Spenser-Milton book. To a very real degree, they were disappointing. The lack of narrative drive and intensity in the published lectures, which had animated his 1950 introduction, didn't fully reveal the magnitude of importance that Milton had in Frye's life, second only to Blake.

Not surprisingly Frye treated Milton's poetry as a mythic entity with a quite overt cosmology. More important, Frye entered his own Protestant landscape, particularly in identifying the philosophical vision shared by Milton's Galileo and Blake's Newton that "thinks it is more important to study the world than change it." Opposed to this, of course, was the action of the Word: "The vision of liberty pulls away from the world and attaches itself to the total human body within, the Word that reveals the Eden in the redeemable human soul, and so releases the power that leads to a new heaven and a new earth." Divine power "symbolized by music and poetry and called in the Bible the Word," releases energy "by creating form." Protestants generally emphasized the re-creation of the Word of God in sermons, as opposed to the body of Christ in the Eucharist. It was Milton who took this farther from the pulpit into life through the agency of "verbal liberty, the power to know and utter ..."

When they were published in 1965, the lectures captured mixed reviews and disappointing sales. By 1975 the University of Toronto Press suggested that it may have come to the end of its usefulness and an employee even had the temerity to read a negative review to Frye over the phone by someone in the Milton establishment.

Frye was of course furious and insisted it be kept in print. He sensed early on that the book was a sleeper and wouldn't come into its own until the current generation of Miltonists died off.

Frye was now due for a rush of books. *The Well-Tempered Critic* came out on April 4, 1963. Barely a few weeks later, Oliver and Boyd came out with Frye's 106-page *T.S. Eliot*. Unlike *The Well-Tempered Critic* which moved slowly through the usual academic channels, there was an immediate explosion over the Eliot book. While Frye possessed anxieties about the book, nothing could have prepared him for the outraged response from Eliot's bastion, Faber and Faber. The first reaction was a frosty letter from the Faber and Faber Vice-President Peter du Sautoy which was followed up by increasingly angry letters from du Sautoy and eventually Eliot himself. Du Sautoy seriously expressed distress at Frye's saying Eliot joined Faber and Faber as director in 1923 instead of 1925. Pointing out the triviality of such a fact in a book of criticism, the editor Robin Lorimer alluded to a perhaps more obvious source of irritation, Frye's excoriation of Eliot's ultra-conservative political and religious beliefs. He recalled Eliot's petulant demand that a publisher recall an encyclopedia for suggesting Eliot's fascist sympathies. Lorimer then wrote Frye explaining the situation, adding that if du Sautoy hadn't earlier been so uncooperative in providing copyright permissions for the book, he would have attempted to have Eliot himself read the introduction for accuracy. Given the hostility of Faber and Faber, Lorimer offered to publish a corrigendum.

But that wasn't the end of it. Eliot himself wrote Oliver and Boyd on June 12, saying that a corrigendum would be inadequate because it suggested that there were no other mistakes, and primly noted "other curious errors" in the same chapter. He concluded by insisting that Oliver and Boyd's explanation of Frye's heavy workload underlying the factual slip-ups was inadequate and that Frye shouldn't have bothered undertaking the book. Eliot felt so strongly that he made it clear he had read his letter to the board of Faber and Faber before sending it off.

Eliot then undertook to write a two-page memo regarding the other mistakes. It is a common reflex of offended subjects, particularly of journalism, to use factual errors as an attempt to undermine the entire argument. It's interesting that a major critic of the 20th century should show such an obsession with minuscule and highly debatable errors of fact in a small introduction, when, presumably, the whole book lay open to him. As a result, we have no clear indication of the source of his irritation. In his memo, all we have is trivia. Eliot pointed out that his primary interest was originally not philosophy but literature, that there was no widespread interest in Oriental philosophy at Harvard, that Ste. Beuve was not a psychological critic, that Bradley was not a leading philosophical opponent of pragmatism. He stated that he discovered the French poets in 1909 when an undergraduate and that Baudelaire was not a *symboliste* but a forerunner of that movement. Finally he insisted that Anglo-Catholicism was an interest which developed in him after he joined the Church of England, concluding with an exclamation mark that one does not *join* the Anglo-Catholic wing.

How any of this could have entered smoothly into a corrigendum is questionable and Oliver and Boyd resisted Eliot's attack. Characteristically Frye himself sat out the storm without a word. He received the occasional update from Oliver and Boyd with process-blackened photocopies of Faber and Faber missives.

Compared to this, even the negative reviews were positively genteel. Considering it "a martini too dry for mere human taste," F.W. Watt levelled a fair complaint that despite Frye's own "elementary handbook" description, it didn't "provide a simplified exposition of Eliot's life and works for beginners." Curiously, years later Francis Sparshott called it "the closest Frye has come to a potboiler." For all the outrage and curiosity in correspondence to Frye over his apparently rude attack on Eliot's ideology, even British reviewers tended either to avoid the question or chuckle amiably over it. William Blissett saw Frye avenging Eliot's anti-Blake bias as Leavis had done with Eliot's anti-Lawrence bias. Unlike Leavis's "knobby instruments," however, Frye's were sharp. Despite the controversy and rather thin attention in the review press, the book was an academic bestseller which outsold the other titles of the Writer and Critic series. When the series died, it went into an American reprint edition, finding its way into a University of Chicago Press Phoenix edition in 1983, which acknowledged its position as a classic of criticism.

Besides juggling a scary number of commitments, Frye spent the summer working on the Milton book and preparing material for his Bampton lectures in November. Although he attempted a holiday in Ireland for a month from mid-August to mid-September, work tended to find him whether he wanted it or not. An essay by David Erdman for the Blake reader reached him in Dublin. There was ongoing anxiety over his Bampton lectures. Although he initially suggested Biblical typology and its influence on English literature the previous year, he reported in February that he rejected the theme, and wondered if he could combine the Random House idea of romanticism with the Bampton obligation. Perhaps because of personal compulsion, he mentioned the typology theme again in June, rejecting it, he claimed because of his ignorance of Hebrew. This had the look of a joke but genuine fears about Hebrew would haunt him for 20 years more as he struggled with his manuscript of *The Great Code*.

Finally, as late as mid-June, he settled on what he considered an easily available subject, "The Development of Shakespearean Romance." The theme would be "the elements in Shakespeare's early plays that lead in the direction of the four Romances of his final period." There was a strong suggestion of his *Anatomy* circle of stories. His talks would each focus on one play of primitive or ancient setting, leading through tragedy and irony to comic restoration:

1. Prelude to History (*Troilus and Cressida*)
2. Nature and Nothing (*King Lear*)
3. Fool's Gold (*Timon of Athens*)
4. The Return from the Sea (*Comedy of Errors*)

A Shakespeare theme would be ostensibly easy. It would effectively resurrect the third part of his old Guggenheim project and help amplify his famous 1948 English Institute essay and its *Anatomy* permutations. But there were dangers. Frye was always mindful of the threatening scope of Shakespeare which might stymie

even "the most heroic effort of criticism." Intrepidly announcing
his topic didn't in itself do anything to resolve any of the major
questions. One thing he didn't realize was that he would also be
delivering his lectures on the eve of the 400th anniversary of
Shakespeare's birth, a year in which there would be close scrutiny
of Shakespearean subjects. His hesitancy seemed odd but until
recently he had never lectured so much as a full course on Shakespeare at Vic and was unhappy with that. Certainly the obstacles
of his own work schedule meant that Frye really didn't intensively
work on his lectures until quite late. While he promised material
on three lectures beforehand, he arrived in New York with only
two roughly completed. This certainly wouldn't imperil Frye's
performance but it may have been a factor in endangering structural control of the manuscript.

In terms of pageantry, his lectures received high priority.
Although he planned to slip into New York and stay at the amiably
grungy King Crown's Hotel, Columbia assigned a personal chauf-
feur to pick him and Helen up at Idlewild and deliver them to a
suite in the Waldorf-Astoria. Before his lectures Frye was even
driven in a limousine right on to campus to the outside steps of
the Low Library auditorium where vehicles are normally forbid-
den. Frye was surprised and delighted to see a Canadian Ensign
put up behind the lectern. Frye was now a star and as he made his
way to the front with what seemed extravagantly long curly hair,
there was a touch of bobby-sox excitement among the graduate
students. Memye Tucker Curtis, the first to formulate a doctoral
thesis on Frye, travelled all the way from Georgia and lined up an
hour in advance.

Despite his plan to focus on one play to show an aspect of a
romantic cycle, Frye's lectures turned into an extended exposition
on comedy. Right from the start, there was a curiously un-Fryean
confusion about terminology and focus. Categories of romance,
comedy, an all inclusive "comic framework" like the Bible all
juggled with each other uncertainly. The basic concern expressed
in the very first sentence of examining "principles of criticism and
with the enjoyment of Shakespeare's comedies" was related to
"a logical evolution toward romance in Shakespeare's work, and

consequently no anticlimax ... in passing from *King Lear* through *Pericles* to *The Tempest*." The subtitle of the lecture book nevertheless became an ambiguous "The Development of Shakespearean Comedy and Romance." Ignoring his predominant enthusiasm for satire in the 1930s, Frye claimed he has "always been temperamentally an Odyssean critic ... attracted to comedy and romance." Part of the confusion over terminology seemed to lie in his efforts to escape his own announced topic headings.

While he repeated many of the points of his previous work on comedy, Frye was especially eager to tie the comedic to the primitive. It was through the channel of archaic comedy, with a stripped down, culturally exotic landscape that modern sophisticated man found a spiritual lodestone. This was a fundamental human legacy. While Minoan or Mayan drama "may not have plays like *King Lear* or *The Alchemist*, it will almost certainly have plays like *Pericles*." A play like *Pericles* in short had an especial importance. It's here that Frye started explicitly promulgating a Magian aspect which would carry him for the next two decades. Frye was always predisposed to the magical "green world" solutions of comedy but now laid greater emphasis on the potency of magical solutions. He said that "drama is born in the renunciation of magic, and in *The Tempest* and elsewhere it remembers its inheritance." He spoke unequivocally. "Magic attempts to repeat, on a human level and in a human context, the kind of power ascribed to God in Hebrew religion and elsewhere. God speaks, and the forms of creation are called into being: the magician utters spells or recites names, and the spirits of nature are compelled to obey." But while this pointed to a direct link between spell and action, Frye fudged on how this principle worked in the apparently analogous metaphorical structure of literature.

At the end of the second lecture on Wednesday evening, November 20, things were going very well. Although his last two lectures were in rough form, he expected to use the weekend to polish them up. He enjoyed a lunch with a young Harcourt editor, Ron Campbell, who would soon become associated with a number of new projects. Then on Friday afternoon, President Kennedy was assassinated. There couldn't have been a more brutal irony for someone lecturing in evangelical terms about comedy in an age of irony. Frye was shocked and depressed, and was unable to make much progress on his last lectures. He could not escape the events. When he met Angus Fletcher and Memye Tucker for lunch on Monday, their table was coincidentally beneath a television set up so customers could see the funeral. They had to shout at each other through the loud drum roll of the cortège.

The following week, Frye managed to get through his talks without giving the impression of failing quality. In the published version of his lectures, there is no mention or reflection of the assassination, but it affected Frye deeply. In a speech a month later, he showed a militant quality: "A world in which the presidency of the United States can be changed by one psychotic with a rifle is not real enough for an intelligent person to want to live in it." During the next decade, Frye steadily darkened the imagery of his social criticism. In *The Modern Century*, he talked of "the world of the tiger ... never created or seen to be good ... the subhuman world of nature, a world of law and of power but not of intelligence or design." By the early 70s he was even using the phrase "this neo-fascist age."

## SABBATICAL

After two crushing years, Frye was desperate for a sabbatical. While he knew he needed physical and emotional rest, he also sensed the more insidious danger of intellectual attrition. He had to admit that because he hadn't had the time to read very much since 1950, he was "beginning to feel like a spider trying to spin a web in the desert." He was still very eager about an *Anatomy* successor and felt that despite the administrative complications which exhausted him, "a very large idea is gradually taking possession of me for a third book." In March 1964, the board finally approved a sabbatical so that Frye could make some unhindered progress on his work.

Fame, however, threatened the sanctity of a year off. While Frye set himself up with an unlisted number, this only cut off a psychotic's crank calls which had recently bedevilled him. The world itself did not go away. The *Anatomy* was now in fact an unassailable presence in the universities. Going into its seventh hardback edition, it was being leased out to Atheneum for paperback release. Its author was portentously identified as "a critic who now looms like a ghostly colossus over the whole world of modern academic literary criticism." In an unprecedented step, the English Institute board designed a special session for September 1965 to consider Frye's place in literary studies. According to the Institute chairman, R.W.B. Lewis, Frye was simply "the most powerful critical force in English-language critical activity today." The session chairman, Murray Krieger, went further, admitting that Frye "has had an influence—indeed an absolute hold—on a generation of developing literary critics greater and more exclusive than that of any one theorist in recent critical history." Educational organizations and publishers continued to try to plug into his apparently fathomless wisdom. Delivering a speech "Criticism, Visible and Invisible," Frye acted as presiding guru in mid-April for a "Sequence and Change in the English Trivium" conference at Trinity College, Hartford, Connecticut.

The publishers Harcourt Brace, previously interested only in Frye's essays, now opened up cathedral doors of temptation. With the baby boom soon to force massive university expansion, publishers saw a huge market for standardized reader anthologies. The 1962 Norton Anthology was already so successful in English departments that Harcourt decided to chase it with a Frye-designed series. Conceiving it as a gargantuan 3,500 page "Survey of British Literature" covering six historical periods, Harcourt lavished enormous amounts of time and money on the project. Frye acted as editor and, with the advice of Ron Campbell, assigned five of the strongest younger scholars in America, John Leyerle, Angus Fletcher, Paul Fussell, Geoffrey Hartman and Hillis Miller to sections on the Middle Ages, the Renaissance, the Restoration and 18th Century, the Pre-Romantics, the Victorian Period. He himself planned to put together a Modern Age volume. For major meetings in New York, Frye's lieutenants were put up in style in the Waldorf-Astoria. Known to Campbell as the "chrestomathy gang," they coined their project "Burnt Norton" as a back-handed tribute to their competition. They socialized among themselves after hours but never with Frye. Rarely intimate at the best of times, Frye was now a bit of a conundrum. In another context, Angus Fletcher noted that Frye was sometimes known "locally" as the Wizard of the North. At meetings Frye sat at the head of the table with corporate secretaries scribbling down his golden words.

Yet despite Harcourt's attention and the collection of sterling talent, the project fizzled close to completion ten years later. Both Frye and his supervising editors at Harcourt became preoccupied and failed to enforce deadlines. There was one twitch of panic in 1971 when Ron Campbell picked up a rumor of a similar series being designed by Oxford University Press to catch the Norton. Everyone got busy and in 1972 Frye spent months working on an immense, but unfinished, "General Introduction" of some 184 pages emphasizing "the particular gimmick of our anthology, that English literature is a linguistic and typological unity from the beginning to the present ..." Three more years went by, however, when the project, facing a shrunken college market and the indomitable Norton, sputtered out.

A more fragile Harcourt project, Literature: The Uses of the Imagination, an English reader series for grades seven to twelve was begun more cautiously. Facing indifference and even opposition inside Harcourt, it nevertheless managed to make it into print. Its epigenesis lay in an evaluation of Harcourt's Adventures series for grades seven to twelve. The series had once held a phenomenal 70% of its American market and had started to slip to a still very impressive 50%. Because this slippage was inevitable, there was hardly any corporate panic, just interest in newer, revitalizing approaches. Jovanovich had asked Henry Steele Commager and his own Harvard teacher, Howard Mumford Jones, to evaluate textbooks before with little success. Knowing Frye's involvement with the Ontario Curriculum Institute, Jovanovich expected a more positive result and sent Paul Corbett up to Toronto for a backyard conference with Frye about examining *Adventures*.

Although Frye was reluctant, he did turn in a highly readable 16-page evaluation which he himself coined "the blitz," a term which became its in-house nickname at Harcourt. Intended for senior executives, it was considered so devastating that it was felt it should be kept away from lower level editors who might be demoralized in the midst of their revisions. Contraband copies nevertheless percolated down to the "pit" and often the effects *were* upsetting.

Frye immediately perceived that *Adventures* had little to do with literature but with the inculcation of progressivist Americanism obsessed with social integration. Even 15 years later in a speech, "The Beginning of the Word," he could barely modulate his distaste: "[The readers] showed no interest in literature, but a great deal of interest in the stereotypes of middle-class Americanism. They presented some of these with legendary names attached, like Washington and Lincoln and Franklin, others as types, like the pioneer and the inventor; but their greatest object of reverence was Helen Keller, to whom all the volumes recurred, because she represented so triumphant an adjustment to the normal. They were called the 'Adventures' series, and the frontispiece of the first one was a picture of a little girl staring into a mirror. That is, what they pretended to suggest was mental adventure; what they actually suggested was narcissism."

Frye was especially upset because he had firmly established the antithesis to this frozen self-regard years before in an article on education in *The Canadian Forum*: "... the purpose of liberal education today is to achieve a neurotic maladjustment in the student, to twist him into a critical and carping intellectual, very dissatisfied with the world, very finicky about accepting what it offers him, and yet unable to leave it alone." Just "one real dose of culture," he predicted, and the "chronically irritated man" would never again be tempted by the world of popular culture.

Unfortunately, he didn't see many pungent doses at all of "real culture" in *Adventures*. For one thing, he felt the editions he

examined suffered a paucity of substantive literature. Poetry selec-
tions were often limericks and doggerel and seldom got more
rarified than the reassuringly anti-intellectual verse of Kipling.
There was too, he felt, a methodological thinness. There was little
attention, for example, to discovering the generic qualities of characters and plots. He concluded his report with an outline of a quite
different approach. He asked for a literature-based series offering
material to interest even the brightest of students. As often before,
he was really remembering himself and the glorious mistake of
Palgrave's *Golden Treasury* which had so thrilled him in high
school. He now wanted to give that experience to others.

William Jovanovich saw no reason to dismantle *Adventures*,
which in fact was extensively revised through the years. He did,
however, perceive a niche for a series which would reflect Frye's
ideas. Although Frye had little time to supervise a major new
project, he was prey to the temptation. Along with the developing
college readers, a new junior high and secondary school series
would reflect his ideas right down to grade seven. He later confessed he didn't believe his own theories until he could see them
implemented. There was the danger too of hypocrisy. In an MLA
speech in December 1963, he reminded his audience of his complaint in the *Anatomy* of "the absence of a coherent teaching
program for English" which had obviously not been rectified.

Jovanovich flew up to Toronto to wine and dine him and generally play on Frye's obvious personal desire for an innovative series.
Jovanovich, who had a reputation of backing new ideas, was convinced enough himself to spend up to $2 million on it. Frye agreed
so long as he remained a figurehead. Only a couple of weeks after
he sent his report in, one editor was writing to a friend that the
series was not only certain, it could expand into a grade one to
twelve concept with a series of anthologies for advanced readers.
It nevertheless took over two years before Harcourt and Frye
reached an agreement on Frye's overseeing a 17-paperback anthology series with six teacher's manuals for the central junior high
and high school years. It was another year more before the vast
series started towards production.

For the crucial junior high texts, Frye roped in two former

students, Hope and Alvin Lee. Hope Lee was a former school teacher and *Alphabet* editor and consistently injected the reality principle into some of the woollier notions flying around the series. Alvin Lee, who was a PhD student of Frye's and a senior English professor at McMaster, provided theoretical consistency. Despite being mired with the complications of five young girls, including twin babies, Hope Lee developed a modest obsession with getting the first volume, *Wish and Nightmare*, produced to force the completion of the rest of the series. She developed an in-house conspiracy with a junior editor, Kathleen Daniel, and enlisted Jay Macpherson. She ransacked the local Dundas, Ont., public library and photocopied enough stories and poems to fill up closets in their rambling stone house.

Early in his sabbatical, Frye also became involved in another million-dollar application of theory: the National Film Board's film for the Montreal World's Fair, *Labyrinthe*. Some senior film people, including Roman Kroitor, Tom Daly, Colin Low, Wolf Koening, Hugh O'Connor, met on May 14, 1964, at a St. Jovite ski lodge above Montreal to discuss their pavilion for the upcoming World's Exposition at Montreal in 1967, budgeted at $1.4 million. Despite the easy, bucolic setting, the group sweated through a day of practical and theoretical discussions. As impromptu secretary, one of the producers, Tom Daly, filled an astonishing 58 pages of notes. The ideas of the group led to a film pavilion which was to be viewed by over 1.3 million people at Expo '67. It was so popular that lineups of five and six hours were common.

Despite the legend of Frye-as-mighty-guru which has grown up around the *Labyrinthe* success, Frye really wasn't all that crucial to the final form of the movie although he had a great deal to do with its background structure. It was clear from Daly's notes that plans were already advanced for a cinematic palace that would sketch out the stages of life. This might possibly involve leading the audience through as many as seven chambers to see a short film about each stage. Although this was quickly seen as impractical, the seven stages were still a basic pattern animating the project. The NFB people, in fact, showed persistent interest in Frye's formulation of a sevenfold Mosaic cycle which Daly sketched out diagramatically in his notes. Although Frye talked about an Exodus cycle in the *Anatomy*, he never fully outlined such a pattern in his writing:

1. arrival, air and water, floating
2. pastoral garden of innocence
3. youth, city, building
4. desert, turn of cycle
5. agon, conflict
6. death, metamorphosis and dissolution
7. celebration, dance of nature

The last three steps had an Easter parallel, the *agon* of Good Friday, the *pathos* of the Saturday and the *anognorisis* or recognition of Easter Sunday. By the end of the session, the group had settled on a final pavilion form, two cinematic chambers separated by a dark maze of glimmering lights and odd sounds through which the audience had to walk.

The intensity of interest in an articulated cycle ending in deliverance was probably exacerbated by the increasingly bleak social climate of the sixties. When Roman Kroitor asked what stage society was in now, Frye immediately answered "We're [in] the desert, the waste land. We can stay there forever." As the desert was typologically equal to the sterile threatening dragon, Frye's remedy was simple and unequivocal: don't hesitate, "attack the monster." In suggesting the theme of a book he'd write 20 years later, *The Secular Scripture*, Frye emphasized that such mythic superstructure wasn't fantastic but personal: "There's only one story, the story of your life." Monsters, after all, were projections of internal psychological states.

Despite Frye's role as Grand Theorist, he turned out to be the populist spokesman, warning the NFB crew of portentousness and even, surprisingly, of using classical or Biblical imagery which a popular audience would not follow. He was intrigued by Wolf Koenig's idea of an overhead labyrinth device which would lift over the audience when all seemed darkest and generate both surprise and, Frye hoped, a burst of laughter. Frye also cautioned against a too-literal translation of his pattern, saying that "the purpose of discussing the central myth is not to dress up this story but to have it in your mind in presenting the film sequences."

The producers didn't in fact hold to any plodding scheme and the crucial last segment, now known as *In the Labyrinthe*, was impressionistic and structurally flexible. Desert and winter scenes were followed by an African crocodile hunt in which the river monster was killed. In one scene, a middle-aged woman rubbed her face in evident stress and then there was a lifting of mood with brighter scenes of adolescent girls in ballet class and a christening of a baby. But there was a continued oscillation of bright and sombre images, suggesting the intertwining of life and death.

Despite his suggestion of "a very large idea" for an *Anatomy* successor Frye really spent much of his sabbatical year cleaning house. In a state of optimism, he dated his preface September 1964 for *The Return of Eden*, but didn't send in a final manuscript until the following May. In the summer of 1964, he also finished off the manuscript of his Bampton Lectures. Memye Curtis Tucker remembers the editor's insistence of their being tightened but, given the diffuse quality of the final work, Frye largely ignored the objection. He had the usual, though amusing, wrangle with the title. While he wanted to entitle them either *The Bottomless Dream* from *Midsummer Night's Dream* or *Offered Fallacy*, Columbia University Press considered them both obscene, so he had to go with a bland alternative *A Natural Perspective* from *Twelfth Night*. As he did with *Spiritus Mundi*, he resolutely stole *The Bottomless Dream* for a chapter title in *The Secular Scripture*.

In the fall of 1965 the Fryes headed off to Britain, to take up residence at 42 Gordon Square as guests of the University of London. Still pondering comedy, he made a speaking tour of universities to Leeds, Keele, Liverpool, Newcastle and Edinburgh. By coincidence, he received an invitation to deliver the Alexander lectures at the University of Toronto for March 1966. Although he had just signed for a lecture series at Western Reserve on English Romanticism in mid-October, the manifold temptations of another Shakespeare topic seemed too much to resist and he decided to explore the dark-half of vision, the tragedies.

When Frye got back from Britain, he was faced with two quite stunning job offers from Princeton and New York University. The New York offer in particular was so tempting it rattled even Frye's intensely rooted nature. While the salary was a handsome $30,000, the real attraction was a support staff of personal secretary, two half-time research associates, plus two part-time "readerships," or graduate students. He also had a conference and library fund of $5,000 each. His teaching load was light and there would be *no* administrative duties.

The offer came, of course, when Frye was utterly fatigued and bored with the principalship at Victoria and wanted greater liberty to write. He approached his old friend, Ernest Sirluck, then Dean of Graduate Studies, after a Senate meeting, showed him the letter and told him it would be difficult to reject. To Sirluck, Frye did not sound bitter so much as eager to enter a new stage of his career. Sensing the emergency, Sirluck quickly consulted with Claude Bissell and Art Moore and with a bit of tetchy haggling, they came up with the idea of establishing several university professorships and giving one to Frye. As an immediate offer, however, Bissell promised to match the salary and benefits of NYU. Frye would be set up with a personal secretary and a research assistant at the new graduate residence, Massey College, and would be relieved of administrative duties.

In the meantime, Frye was flat on his back with flu and ruefully joked about an apparent correlation between sabbaticals and illness. To Winchester Stone, who was behind the NYU negotiations, he wrote that there was nothing wrong with the New York end, and that "all my difficulties are with leaving here." This was not entirely true because Frye was a bit leery of NYU's tacit assumption that he would attract other big name scholars for conferences. Helen in particular felt that Frye should be giving speeches rather than introducing them.

As he headed into the spring with an overwhelmingly strengthened position, Frye was unaccountably blocked in his work. While he enjoyed the ability to read without guilt, he began to fear that he had only managed to catch up on old work and had after a year, effectively fallen behind. There were strong personal reasons for his lack of focus. Although he hadn't kept in close touch with

Richard Blackmur, Frye found himself very depressed by Blackmur's death in February. His sister Vera was also now seriously ill with a rare and poorly understood spinal cord condition called adhesive and calcific arachnoiditis. In April Frye flew down to Los Angeles to visit her for two weeks. Although Vera had managed to live with the condition for four years, it was becoming so aggravated, and she suffered such severe chest and abdominal pains that she required surgery. She walked with canes but even so, she was prone to falls. Later in the year, her neurosurgeon suggested nursing care. Although Frye tried to have her come back to Canada, Vera wanted to stay in California and found a place in a North Vermont Ave. convalescent hotel.

Frye stayed home all summer to work. From a distance he watched the jostling around the approaching English Institute session on his theories in early September. He was quite eager to hear the discussion, maintaining that "no writer who is not completely paranoid wants his house to be either a fortress or a prison."

The session chairman, Murray Kreiger, was an ideological adversary of Frye, but he showed no malice in designing the session. By choosing two important young scholars, Angus Fletcher and Geoffrey Hartman, he in fact showed courage by allowing the question of Frye to pass out of the hands of older critics who might have axes to grind. Unfortunately, both Fletcher and Hartman may have been too respectful. Their contributions were cautious and failed to reveal much of their reservations about Frye's ideas. Nevertheless, they spoke for their own young constituency. Fletcher saw Frye's system in terms of Haussmann's redesign of Paris: opening up large boulevards through old clogged neighbourhoods to let in air and light. What appealed to young scholars in Frye, said Fletcher, was not the ostensible recidivism of Frye's numerology and typology but "the openness of his system, the freedom with which he catapults himself and his readers from one *arrondissement* to another." Using Copernicus's arresting image of a "virile man standing in the sun ... overlooking the planets," Hartman likewise pointed to the liberating expansiveness of Frye's approach. He approved Frye's neo-Romanticism and roundly dismissed the notion of Frye as weird occultist. Yet only five years later Hartman was to call Frye and McLuhan "these optimistic Magi of the North" who were out of sorts with "the darker insights" of certain modern critics and philosophers.

Wimsatt, on the other hand, was the heavy, the well-known enemy who gnashed his teeth at myth criticism. Frank McConnell, a student of Wimsatt at Yale, reported that the *Anatomy* was then "virtually contraband in the graduate school—or at least compromising." In Wimsatt's history of criticism course, the *Anatomy* was the clear Enemy throughout. After the promise of a searing apocalyptic exposition, however, he only took one day, the last, to discuss it.

Acknowledging his English Institute critique was "rude," Wimsatt nevertheless confidentially proclaimed it "fundamentally faithful and correct." He saw himself as the devil's advocate called in at the last moment of a canonization hearing. Wimsatt took full advantage of the fact that in broad outline, Frye's theories were easily satirized. He aimed at some easy targets. He described the exceptional complexity of the *Anatomy* circle pattern as "superimposed fourth-of-July pinwheels, with a reversing sequence of rocket engines." He drew attention to Frye's inconsistent use of spring and summer for comedy and romance. Like a dentist he insistently drilled away at Frye's conception of primitivism, snorting out Frye's phrase a "primitive response [is] demanded of us" no fewer than three times. He also coined the term "gnostic mythopoeia" which assumed an anagogic escape through layers of grime towards pure light: "Myth, like a dome of many-coloured glass, stains the white radiance of anagogy."

While Wimsatt's attack was engaging, he didn't develop much of a coherent argument beyond amiable invective. There was an obvious underlying personal element. As a leading proponent of New Criticism, Wimsatt snarled at the view of "the verbal critics, the New Critics, groveling in the wintry cellar of verbal irony, and at the other end of things the heroes on the high sunlit plains of myth and romance lift their gaze to the apocalyptic windows of the morning." While such a hope, ironically, was mythic, it didn't elevate the wintry cellar an inch. In a further attack which wasn't published, he reportedly ended his talk with a pronouncement that "the wave of his direct influence upon graduate students is now over the crest" and that "Frye is a neo-Ricardian ... Everything good he got from someone else." With that, he left the platform and led his entourage out.

A Frye loyalist, Memye Curtis Tucker, wrote out some notes on what was said and done. Tucker was so fiercely loyal she went to the length of seeing Wimsatt's wrinkled shirt as a sign of disrespect. Frye would have none of it and defended Wimsatt. He sensed there were extenuating circumstances why Wimsatt sounded so irritable.

Ultimately the whole exercise may have been most valuable for flushing out an eloquent statement from Frye of his own essential visionary purpose which derived from study: "The mythical structure of literature is not this vision, but it is the only way of getting into it. Literature is not ultimately objective: it is not simply there, like nature: it is there to serve mankind." Unfortunately there were always social forces standing in the way and the critic had to be revolutionary. "The immense pressure toward conformity in thought and imagination is society's anxious response to mythopoeia ... No one person, certainly not one critic, can kill this dragon who guards our word-hoard, but for some of us, at any rate, there can be no question of going back to our secluded Georgian quarters, from which serenity has since disappeared."

The conflict, such it was, was almost a fluttering of hankies. Only a year later in October, an ostensibly innocuous symposium on French structuralism at Johns Hopkins drew such luminaries as Jacques Lacan, Roland Barthes, Jacques Derrida and Tzvetan Todorov. They ushered in a bruising new era of criticism in America which made the Frye session look positively quaint. Here was the seed in North America for the dastardly schools of semiology, post-structuralism and deconstructionism. All of them were more oriented to concerns of linguistics, communications and a gruesome starwars of clashing texts and subtexts. Ironically they managed to draw the attentions and loyalties of such erstwhile Frye lieutenants as Geoffrey Hartman, Harold Bloom and Hillis Miller.

## MYTH OF CONCERN

As he came out of a disappointing sabbatical year, Frye showed some urgency in trying to firm up a new direction. While his two major books possessed concrete objectives, to redeem Blake and reform criticism, all he had now was a complex of ideas searching for a context. He was more clear about his objective—an exodus from the labyrinth of ironic perception—than how to resurrect the means, a revitalized poetry-centred imagination. In the mid-60s he started calling this imaginative process the Myth of Concern. This was a return with relish to the apocalyptic circle which separated the world into desirable visions of romance and comedy and the repudiated visions of tragedy and irony.

While this imagery was easy to chart objectively on a blackboard, Frye now emphasized it was fundamentally a projection of desire, in which a person accepts one and rejects the other. There was nothing intrinsically moral or complicated in it. In the simplest terms, Frye once claimed, "I think there has to be an assumption that life is better than death, freedom better than slavery, happiness better than misery, equality better than exploitation, for all men everywhere without exception." In a 1961 speech, "Academy without Walls," he said, "All genuine art leads up to this separation and that is why it is an educating force." The vision was rather like a buoy which infallibly stays upright in the worst storm. In this sense Frye was merely repackaging the evangelical optimism of the typological and mythopoeic traditions. When Tolkien "converted" C.S. Lewis to mythopoeia in 1931, he posited the notion that only through myth-making "can man aspire to the state of perfection that he knew before the Fall." Another aspect of separation was the cleansing of ideological and moral anxieties. In passing from the study to the possession of poems, "a dialectical separation of permanent imaginative structure from a mass of historical anxieties takes place." This obviously was a personal variant of the delousing Frye attempted with Eliot.

In three papers from Oct. 1965 to Oct. 1966, "Speculation and Concern," "Knowledge Worth Having" and "The Knowledge of Good and Evil," he thrashed out his ideas. In the process he showed signs of stripping off some of his own ironic distance. Though not speaking as strongly as in his wartime polemics, Frye sniffed at the predominant ironic expression which he called "detachment from detachment ... self-hatred reflected in the torment of and humiliation of others." Speaking through Blake and Lawrence, he noted that man had lost "his nerve about taking charge of his own world." There's even the happy ghost of Methodism in his utterly unscientific statement, "We notice that what we feel like identifying ourselves with in literature tends to be social rather than purely individual, a festive group rather than an isolated figure." These attitudes quite simply opened the future again to Frye by returning Frye to his own past. Associated with this process was a language which had forgotten its own mythopoeic resources, to arouse constructive action. All through this period he talked about the baneful "cult of objectivity," "the prestige of the subject-object relationship" and the presumptions of a "demythologized" religion. The ogre was the flat, uninspiring object connected to the flat uninspiring fact. The word "God" meant nothing more than the "dead word" ether; however as a metaphor which tied the reader into a relation of creative power which extinguished the subject-object distinction, it connoted verb-like strength.

With this kind of agenda it was logical that Frye would want to focus his lecture series for Western Reserve University on the mythopoeic aspects of Romantic poetry. But his first major piece of business was oddly antithetical: elucidating the vision of tragedy for his Alexander Lectures on Shakespeare in March 1966. Since he saw the wish-fulfillment and anxiety dream fitting together into "a fully conscious vision," there was a purely coincidental opportunity to outline aspects of two visions in less than two months.

As an exponent of comedy and romance, Frye couldn't of course avoid taking a veiled swipe at the aristocratic presumptions of tragedy. "The Greek heroes," he said, "belong to a leisure class remote from our ordinary preoccupations; this gives them more time not for enjoying life, but for doing what the unheroic cannot do: looking steadily and constantly into the abyss of death and nothingness." Simply there was a futility to tragedy. Tragedy starts as a revolt against irony, "the independence of the way things are from the way we want them to be." It ends catastrophically, forcing an accommodation with ironic reality: " ... we then come to terms with irony by reducing our wants." There were inevitable limitations: "expressions of despair" are "the only kind of philosophical reflexion that we are likely to get from a tragedy ..." Whatever tragedy pronounces on poor dead Hamlet, Lear or Othello, or their distraught survivors, however, it acts differently on the audience: "The end of a tragedy leaves [the spectator] alone in a waste and void chaos [sic] of experience with a world to remake out of it. It is partly because of this insistent challenge to the spectator's re-creative powers that the great tragedies are so endlessly fascinating to critics: merely to experience them seems to demand commentary as part of one's response."

Frye admitted he had as much trouble with *Fools of Time* as any he'd done of that "fantastically difficult genre," the public lecture. Whatever his apparent insecurity, he fell so much into a schematic pattern of thinking, he produced observations like, "We may now apply our principles of isolation to the three-fold structure of the tragedy of order ... These three types tend to be attracted to two opposite poles." This schematization, which recalled the outline of "Eccentricity," started from a fundamental view that there were three types of Shakespearean tragedy: order (fall of princes: Julius Caesar, Macbeth, Hamlet), passion (separation of lovers: Romeo and Juliet, Antony and Cleopatra, Troilus and Cressida) and isolation (loss of identity: King Lear, Othello, Timon of Athens). Cautiously forestalling criticism that "these are not pigeon-holes, only different areas of emphasis," he piled on a three-fold pattern of characterization for social, or order, tragedies, the order figure, rebel figure and nemesis figure.

There were even organizing principles in the background, the order of nature and the wheel of fortune. The latter alarmed one reviewer who incorrectly insisted it was a motif of the middle ages and not of the renaissance. In separate plays too there were schematic outlines. In the total action of *Hamlet*, Frye saw "three concentric tragic spheres, each with a murdered father and a nemesis." There were external patterns, in the skein of related archetypes. Frye told his audience of the worlds of Tantalus and Sisyphus, of Prince Henry as "the emerging sun-king," of Cleopatra as Venus, Isis, Circe, Omphale, whore of Babylon. Not surprisingly, British reviewer Christopher Ricks jumped on Frye's own pigeon-hole denial, saying that "any pigeon-holer has to say that ... Here are 78 small drawers—very handy, except that we don't need 78 small drawers."

In another of those dark ironies which had a way of corresponding with Frye's thought, Frye had to attend to the cremation of Vera following her death in early April in Los Angeles. The previous October her neurosurgeon had been optimistic she could live a productive life for several years, but her decline had been rapid. Although Frye was very attached to Vera, her death was especially painful because it represented the end of his immediate family. Over the next couple of years, Frye tried to settle her estate. Corresponding in impotent fury with faceless court bureaucrats on the other side of the continent, he attempted to track down some jewelry which had disappeared after Vera's death. Compared with this unhappy Californian finality, Evergreen Park in Chicago remembered Vera to the point of veneration, spontaneously starting a memorial fund and naming a school library after her, complete with oil portrait.

In his lectures in May for Western Reserve University in Cleveland, Frye returned to the myth of concern and mythopoeia. Absolutely central in western culture before Romanticism was the prominence given "to the subject-object relationship ... the rational in contrast to the empirical attitude to nature." Romanticism changed this, becoming "the first phase in an imaginative revolution which has carried on until our own day, and has by no means completed itself yet ... the anti-Romantic movements in France and England of fifty to sixty years ago, [are] best understood as post-Romantic." This echoed Frye's almost apocalyptic expectancy of the late 30s, that a burst of new romantic energy could bring Nehemiah back to rebuild Jerusalem's walls.

There was again a three-fold evolutionary pattern in his Romance lectures. The decadence of Beddoes led to the Promethean struggle of Shelley to the epiphanies of Keats. In his study of

Beddoes, Frye had a lot of fun pursuing personal interests, like ghosts and the bardo-world between death and rebirth. He touched base with the morbid side of Romanticism which Frye considered a first step towards a view of absurdity, the corrosive nothingness or death-in-life which haunts so much modern literature and philosophy. As such, the vision rather begged an answer, a *creative* response which he conveniently found in Shelley.

His absorption in Shelley's cosmology was strikingly vibrant right from the first paragraphs. Because Frye almost never wrote about Shelley, except as a straight man to Peacock in *The Educated Imagination*, he was always a hidden factor, lying behind the precursor Blake. Suddenly Shelley became the Dante in Purgatory leading the critic Frye so completely that the Shelley chapter summed up what Frye had been talking about in his recent essays. The agency of man's recovery of his myth-making powers, of course, was poetry, which revealed the myth of concern: "Poetry speaks, not the language of fact or reason, but the language of concern, of hopes and fears and desires and hatreds and dreams." Against the "one-dimensional progress toward death," "dreams and inspiration, and poetry" work in a reviving counter movement. Poetic thought had the power to counter the "great parade of stubborn facts and 'hard and fast' distinctions." Abstraction, after all, was "the product of a repetition of experience without fresh thought." "In the world of time and space" God too was dead: "he was of course never alive there, but any God who can die is much better dead."

Keats's world was ostensibly antithetical, more hallucinatory than bold. There was confusion in "the imprisoning, paralyzing world of dream." Endymion's world "has the fragility that goes with something that is only potentially alive." Endymion *has* to go on a quest "to strike these roots into experience." As Dante, Endymion must descend to the depths to a lower labyrinthine world which is more subjective and cut off from the natural world. There is a route back not as clear as in Dante but one which conditions both extreme subjectivity and objectivity. The point is not the ultimate abandonment of dream, but its clarification and realisation: "He does not awaken *from* his dream into a different world: he awakens the dream *into* his world, and releases it from its subjective prison."

Frye wrote *A Study of English Romanticism* almost reflexively. He managed to write up his lectures in the summer and after a furious rewrite of the last 20 pages, sent them off in mid-August, fleeing to Europe for a vacation. Random House sent it to a reader who complained about hasty writing and Frye's failure to approach a wider audience. While the reader thought it "a fine book," he was disappointed that Frye had not attempted "*the* eminent book defining romanticism." Frye made few changes and deliberately suggested a bland descriptive title which his editor, David Dushkin, accepted. Following the format of the series in which it was published, it went immediately into a pocketbook-size paperback. It sold well enough to justify a second printing in Oct. 1968, but received negligible critical attention: a grand total of two reviews in all of North America, including one by Frye's former graduate student, Ross Woodman. Like a drugstore paperback it then sank into oblivion until the University of Chicago Phoenix editions picked it up in 1982. Its initial fate was ignominious and unjustified. The book turned out to be the key to everything Frye was to think about in the next two decades.

## THE MODERN CENTURY

Although Frye was now supposed to enter higher office, he had to wait over a year before the idea of his university professorship even went before the University of Toronto Board of Governors in May 1966. It wasn't until Jan. 1, 1967, that he received his official appointment. In the fall of 1966, moreover, he had to occupy two offices, Principal and President of Victoria College, the latter because Art Moore took a leave of absence. Theoretically he should have sat very quietly in Moore's office until Moore reappeared but he somehow got dragged into complicated financial negotiations with the Ontario government. When he finally moved into Massey

College in April, he bitterly complained to an unfortunate graduate student who desperately needed his thesis evaluated. He said he'd "moved through five offices and three secretaries in the last three months; everything has got mislaid or put in the wrong place ... However, this nightmare should be over for a while."

He wasn't fully established at Massey College until he acquired a new and permanent secretary, Jane Welch, early the following year. A Nottingham native who'd recently immigrated to Canada, Jane improbably won her job through the government employment agency, Canada Manpower. Apparently unable to formulate questions, Frye sat for the greater part of the interview in embarrassed silence. Unaware of Frye's ability to type nearly twice her own speed, Jane then departed to the Personnel Dept. for a standard typing test. Though she got the job, Frye maintained such distance, it took three or four years before he would communicate even the smallest details about his many trips or personal life. Jane kept his once chaotic files tidy, and fielded the ever growing demands on him for appearances and writing assignments. Conscious of his inability to say no to honest requests, Frye once quipped, "It's all very well to have a yes-man, but a no-woman is much more useful."

One of the great ironies of escaping practical administration was that Simcoe Hall bureaucracy was conspiring at precisely the same time to destroy his beloved honours system. This had been so effective that the University of Toronto often ranked near the top in North America in producing the highly prestigious Woodrow Wilson fellowships. Just by itself Victoria College produced six Woodrow Wilson fellows among graduates of 1961, including Margaret Atwood. In a Macpherson Commission hearing, Frye railed against lowering entry standards, calling it "lunatic and suicidal." Unfortunately the university proceeded, wrecked the system, then paid bitterly for the decline in standards. Frye was unforgiving and two years later even chewed out his gentle American protégé, James Nohrnberg, who casually questioned the inflexibility of Toronto's honours system.

Although he saw the year as a disappointing scramble, he somehow managed to put together and deliver his strongest public talks ever, the Whidden Lectures in January at McMaster University, which were published as *The Modern Century*. The dark symbolism of his recent *The Fools of Time* seemed to have leaked into the new lectures. The symbolism of his first talk, "City of the End of Things," was full of wintery, despairing twentieth-century images, of progressive philosophies running amuck in rationalized genocide, of brazenly deceptive advertising and propaganda, of chronically broken social promises. The modern City of Destruction was a concatenation of egos, "ants in the body of a dying dragon, breathing its polluted air and passing its polluted water." Frye added the brutal image of the medieval Wild Hunt, the souls of the dead marching at top speed to prevent themselves from collapsing in dust. Even the active mind saw only a frozen reflection of itself in the mirror. Although it could not "move on its own initiative," it could shatter a frozen Narcissus impulse by recognizing its own ugliness and forcing the mind out and away toward "a genuine human destiny." As always, the only honest pathway was the arts which are "almost entirely on the active side."

A clearly dishonest pathway was the fruitless pop-prophecy of McLuhanism which played over the surface of things, seeing cosmic significance in such fads as white lipstick. Because there was so much feverish attention to McLuhan at the time, Frye's comments tended to console the beseiged liberal constituency in North America, starting to suffer the depradations of the youth culture and its zany gurus.

Frye set up bleak images which demanded resolution, but he was not so good at providing a remedy. In his second talk he wandered off into an analysis of the role of nationalism in the arts, painting and the conception of modernism. Although Frye was speaking in 1967 on Canada's centenary, he blundered politically. A vigorous brand of cultural nationalism was appearing, led in part by such recent students as Dennis Lee and Margaret Atwood, yet Frye was still insisting: "Complete immersion in the international style is a primary cultural requirement ..."

Frye raised the awful question of whether the arts were *really* effective in encouraging an active response, but he slithered away from the issue by calling it the question of the accuser. Inevitably he came back to his long-standing and more comforting theorem that "the whole structure of society itself, is an anti-art, an old and worn-out creation that needs to be created anew." While that promised apocalypse, Frye was not about to present a typical late 60s agenda. In the third talk, he sounded absolutely Puritan, complaining of the distraction "one sees on highways and beaches at holiday weekends ... a refusal to face the test of one's inner resources that spare time poses." He nevertheless flirted as much as any hippie polemicist with the notion of primitiveness: "with its immediate connexion with magic," it could regenerate "a long and tired tradition of Western art." Frye was looking as ever for the apocalypse, but only if he could see it rise from the safe shores of academicism. He reiterated his long-standing observation, and presumed contentment, that creative artists were firmly in place in teaching positions in the university. While he acknowledged this pattern is less common in Europe, he suspected Europe would eventually follow along.

*The Modern Century* was really Frye's most thoroughly autobiographical work: so reflecting his personal attitudes, he sometimes seemed trapped in the very Narcissistic reflection about which he warned. Nevertheless, he was very satisfied with the lectures and sensed that he had been more articulate than usual. Despite the anachronisms, the all too frequent references to earlier literature, the lectures were exceptionally well-written. Because of the usual Whidden arrangements, the lectures went to Oxford University Press in Toronto where they were quickly set and published by September.

More than he could ever have suspected, Frye got caught up in his own images of "the world of the tiger," of mankind "like an iceberg ... submerged in a destructive element." In returning from a summer institute of the NDEA in Appleton, Wisconsin, at the end of July, Frye got trapped in Ypsilanti, Michigan, unable to get through Detroit because of the savage race riots which put a hundred square blocks under seige. A section of the city was on fire. He got home by a complicated route through Buffalo but, like the Kennedy assassination, it reinforced the image of black, even fascist, times. In an essay on Dickens for the English Institute in the fall, he reversed the gloom a bit with more familiar imagery.

In Dickens he saw "that the hidden world, though most of its more direct expressions are destructive and terrible, contains within itself an irresistible power of renewing life." It was Dickens's fairy tale logic which ultimately made sense: in the chess game, "black can never ultimately win."

Frye's lectures sold so well they had to be reprinted twice very quickly carrying a very annoying, and politically embarrassing misprint, through to the third printing, "to be colonial means to be mature" rather than "immature." This was Frye's first book to be predominantly reviewed in the newspaper press and was perceived as a healthy reaction against late sixties' counterculture. While never abjuring McLuhan himself, Frye had attacked "nitwitted McLuhanism" enough that some reviewers including his old Princeton friend, Ed Cone, saw the book as an "antidote."

# PART FIVE

At the start of 1968, Frye—for once—had no lecture series or book deadline facing him. While he was eager to get moving on a major book, he seemed unable to get a handle on a major sustaining theme, including the much vaunted myth of concern. He did enjoy a spurt of concentrated effort in February, reporting he couldn't go to a conference in May because he was simply too preoccupied in "trying to unify the subject of mythology, considered in relation to all the subjects, including religion, psychology, anthropology, and literary criticism ..." This was the high water of his confidence that in "the laboratory of myths," literature represented the key to "the mythological subjects: they include large areas of history, political theory, religion, philosophy, psychology, anthropology and sociology." This was Frye's own revenge for the view that literature was a cultural wallflower.

But the force of this idea sputtered out and by May he had to confess he had made so little progress on major new work, "... it is a matter of looking at some very barren scenery to see if I can descry a small cloud that might some day begin a downpour." This pessimism at least didn't impede the completion of two very impressive symbolic analyses of Milton, "The Revelation to Eve" and of Yeats, "The Top of the Tower," the latter of which he delivered at Sligo, Ireland, in the summer. When he published

319

them in a new collection of essays, *The Stubborn Structure* a year later, he saw them as "preliminary studies for ... a long and intricate book on patterns of imagery in literature." Particularly in the Yeats essay Frye used an imperiously wide sweep, linking Yeats's imagery right back to that of Blake, Dante and the Bible, showing common Eros-Thanatos visions, and the repetition of a basic four-level cosmology.

No matter how impressive these essays were, they didn't manage to fire him up for sustained work. Rather he kept his attention on frustrating, and possibly unanswerable, problems of literary purpose. It was easier, in short, to demonstrate a what than prove a why. Still addressing the lingering puritanical questions from his own background about the utility of literature, particularly poetry, he confessed in an unpublished speech, "Literature and Society" that he possessed " ... the steadily growing suspicion that a big cultural change was going on around me ... it looked as though the old unquestioned domination of myth by logic was going." In a longish paper in the summer for the Indiana School of Letters, "Mythos and Logos," he suggested the importance of this for society: "The mythical confronts the logical, evaluates it and assimilates it to the concerns of human existence."

The irony was that in the new and ominous counterculture of the late sixties, the mythical habit of mind *was* establishing itself. Everywhere now, there were groups of university radicals fired up by a sense of apocalyptic purpose to vaporize the Vietnam war and the corruption and stagnation of the North American middle-class life. There was a social sourness everywhere which indicated a pressing need either for Revolution or flight into bucolic backwoods communes. Martin Luther King was gunned down in April. In May, Columbia University was closed down by violent student radicals. At Berkeley, students entered into persistent, open conflict with the university and California governor Ronald Reagan.

While the situation at the University of Toronto was not chaotic, there was potential for trouble. Leaders of a leading New Left group, the Toronto Student Movement, hung around the basement cafeteria of University College in denim jackets and Red Guard armbands, in earnest, conspiratorial knots. They partook of the usual rituals of touring lecture halls and harassing professors. For several years they controlled *The Varsity,* an editor of which later married an heiress of the Lord Thomson of Fleet fortune. Nothing, however, seemed *really* to be happening and there was corresponding desperation when two leaders, Andy Wernick and Phillip Resnick, jumped onstage on Feb. 9, 1969, at the Royal Ontario Museum theatre to interrupt a speech by Clark Kerr, the visiting president of the University of California. They captured the stage and some exceedingly bad publicity. Their "movement" crumbled.

The traditional chasm between University College and Victoria College obviated infection. While there were three or four "radical" students at Vic, they were demoralized. No one listened to them or cared about what they said. Victoria College was not so much right-wing as conventionally middle-class. Certainly any invading militant who would choose to interrupt a Northrop Frye lecture would have been bodily removed by students and indelicately dumped on the other side of Queen's Park Crescent. It never happened.

Almost to emphasize his distance from the zaniness of the prevailing counterculture pantheon of Timothy Leary, Edgar Friedenberg or Paul Goodman, Frye maintained an old-fashioned personal style, keeping his once-flaming blond locks closely clipped in the style of the 50s. His glasses were still Methodist wire-rim and peculiar to himself, his suits tended to be better cut and maintained than his usual thrown-on apparel. He presented the appearance of the old-style school inspector, right down to the appropriate glower of opprobrium for a world which was rejecting everything he treasured.

Inadvertently he was fulfilling the role of prophet, a man out of step, railing against the mindless, mob-like *conventionality* of the erstwhile student rebels. In September 1968, he correctly predicted that the movement has "rather shallow social roots, and does not have a very long-time career ahead of it." In November, he considered the counterculture's belief in the "moral superiority" of social withdrawal an illusion corresponding to his own generation's faith in the Soviet Union. He saw their desperation: "Society does not hate them enough: they have not the prophetic authority to strike at our deepest fears, and are themselves involved in the panic they create." In a speech in December he was damning and prophetic: "Like the beatniks, who have gone, the hippies, who are on the skids, and the LSD cults, which are breaking up, student unrest is not so much social as an aggregate of individual bewilderments, frustrations, disillusionments, and egotisms." Because their quest was fundamentally religious, "the university *qua* university" was unable to answer their needs.

Correct analysis, however, did not stop the plague. Almost a comic parody of more serious politics, a band of New Left English professors perpetrated the "Little Bourgeois Cultural Revolution of MLA 1968." One of their leaders, Louis Kampf, wrote up a puerile account of the business. A radical "caucus" led by Kampf set up a literature table and handed out Mother Language Association buttons. They put up posters of Black Panther Elridge Cleaver, and another of Blake's phrase "The Tygers of Wrath are Wiser than the Horses of Instruction." The posters were torn down and some people arrested. Finally, however, the radicals were placated and even Louis Kampf became a second vice-president, in line to lead the mighty MLA itself. While Frye, unlike the English department at Harvard, did not resign his membership, he stayed away from the MLA for two years, complaining that "the noise makers" had taken over. Yet he was still an enticing target. Even though he was uncomfortable about it, the redoubtable Kampf published anti-Frye polemics in his anthology, *The Politics of Literature*.

Frye was hardly walking away from radicalism when he headed off to Berkeley for the spring term in 1969. Besides teaching an undergraduate course of about 200 students in literary symbolism, he was to deliver the Beckman Lecture series which he called "The Critical Path." Frye was relieved that just two radicals turned up at an early lecture to sniff him out, only to ostentatiously stomp out when they decided there was more interesting game on campus. His stay at Berkeley was in fact remarkably civil. In the last week of May, however, Berkeley erupted in the notorious People's Park Crisis which brought the usual police phalanges into the campus area to battle students who were trying to prevent the university takeover of a vacant lot which students and local hippies had turned into a park. Overhead helicopters shot down a choking pepper gas to disperse crowds. The truculent governor, Ronald Reagan, visited the campus and cajoled and condemned staff and administrators. To Frye the whole affair was extraordinarily hysterical. No one managed to look good. He later confessed in *The Critical Path* it was a sleep-walking ritual in which the conflict was more theatre than substance. He immediately saw the Biblical archetypes that the radicals unknowingly resurrected. The virginal vacant lot fenced off by the students was the Garden of Eden. The students were clearly reliving the old pastoral story of the democracy fighting expulsion by the nasty oligarchy. Because of the slaughter of the Indians, the land was now covered in the blood of Abel. The expelling angels were the police who with their bayonets and gas masks represented "the demonic in its popular science fiction form, of robots or bug-eyed monsters from outer space."

Unlike Mircea Eliade or Alan Watts, Frye was uninterested in, even thoroughly hostile to the wider implications of the counter-culture. While Frye kept insisting that the prime function of education was to liberate students from "a Narcissus mirror of our own experience and social and moral prejudice," this was not to be done extramurally through a mind-altering drug or a quest into Mexico or India. It was to be accomplished, as he had done himself, within the context of books and the disciplined ideas of the university. Ignoring his own *real* Odyssean impulses of wide travel and exploration, Frye seemed to be trying to make a virtue of plain old middle-class coziness with attendant soft bed and personal library. Spurning Byronic impulses, he later admitted he fully understood how Emily Dickinson could create a literary universe with just a Bible and hymnary. Obviously he was never going to accede to the kind of spiritual experiment of Eliade in the 30s who lived in Hindu robes in a Himalayan ashram under the tutelage of a guru. Nor was he going to haunt a primitive lakeside castle like Jung in fur-lined robe and skull cap, sculpting, painting and free-associating with alchemical western thought.

As an advocate of primitivism in thought, this put Frye into a bind. His notion of primitivism was certainly set, even dogmatic: "Poetry which is not primitive is of no use to anybody: every genuine work of the imagination comes out of the most primitive depths of human concern." What he really liked to see, though, was myth orientation in the audiences at poetry readings or in literature students steeped in contemporary cinema. Hairy radicals and hippies reenacting Land of Cockaigne myths apparently had it all wrong. But this tended to put primitivism in Saran Wrap. In speaking from the exact opposite end of the scale from William Wimsatt, poet George Bowering attacked Frye's idea of "a poetry of impersonal nexus, the poem as dance removed from the dancer."

Yet Frye did share the counterculture distaste for the exhaustion and materialism of the middle class. His solution for regeneration, though, was a curious, even absurd, return to the values of his student years: " ... I think what we are in for today is a gigantic Methodist movement. In the 18th century the Church of England got frozen into its real estate and the local squire presented the living to a parson who, of course, had to keep in with him. The Methodists went out into the fields and the big cities that were developing and I think that something like that is happening now."

No matter how many bulwarks Frye threw up around him, he nevertheless gained the patina of a McLuhanesque guru. Although the New Left was suspicious of Frye, most Vic students regarded him as household god. Even the acid freaks of Wymilwood primly abandoned their basement cafeteria seats to take in Frye's Bible symbolism course. Frye's admiring graduate students produced a limited run of Northrop Frye sweat shirts showing Frye's head surrounded by mythological figures. He was even the subject of an interview film by his graduate student, Jon Slan, who'd mixed UCLA film studies with conventional work on Yeats. Budgeted at a heady $4,000, the film *Fearful Symmetry* was full of clichéd stock shots of Vietnam warfare and urban desolation with commentary by Frye.

As the New Left at Toronto collapsed as a credible force, there was a very disturbing attack against Frye from the zany and violent Maoists, the Canadian Student Movement, which operated out of multiple front groups. Like the Weathermen in the States, the

Maoists in Canada were loathed and feared by even the New Left for their fanaticism. It was commonly agreed that because they were so irrational and mysterious, they were funded by the CIA because their wild and impotent actions brought disrepute to all factions of the student left. In January 1969, one of Frye's graduate students, Frank Carner, picked up a copy on campus of an anonymously and odiously written pamphlet, *Objective Idealism is Fascism: A Denunciation of Northrop Frye's "Literary Criticism"* published "under the direction" of a newly created "Necessity for Change Institute of Ideological Studies" and available for $.35 or 1 shilling from addresses in Montreal, Dublin and London. Carner wrote "a message from Ulro," Blake's hell, and indeed it was. Its introduction proclaimed inspiration from the People's Republic of China and Albania and specific authority from numerous Maoist student groups in Canada, Ireland and Britain.

"The case in question" was poor Northrop Frye's thought, otherwise known as "Objective Idealism which is fascism." The purpose of the denunciation was "to mobilize revolutionary intellectuals against him." The Ideological Forum ominously wanted to know all about "the steps you are taking to expose Northrop Frye, and suggests that you organise discussion groups, seminars, and lectures, or form anti-Northrop Frye Clubs." The analysis of Frye's writing was almost irrelevant after this. It was demonology for fanatics and it had a comparatively long life. The pamphlet reappeared in April 1969 rewritten under the name of Pauline Kogan. It was reprinted as late as May 1975 in an issue of *Alive* featuring cover illustrations of Maoist saint, Norman Bethune and a screaming headline, "A Time of Realignment and Qualitative Change!!" Even then, the polemic sneaked into serious academic criticism when cited in John Fekete's *The Critical Twilight*.

Although he made frequent statements on student unrest all through 1968, this didn't totally explain Frye's lack of progress on his own work. At the end of the Christmas holidays, he had to admit yet again that he was feeling "growing pressure from within to settle down and do a long piece of sustained writing." To Harold Bloom, he confessed that he'd done nothing of interest since a paper he gave at Cornell, an early version of "Mythos and Logos."

He hadn't even written up the Sligo Yeats paper. While he talked in a letter of a "large complicated design" for a successor to the *Anatomy* gradually taking him over, he was vague about its nature except to suggest that the myth of concern was to be "a central part of it." There also were his Berkeley lectures approaching in April in which he hoped to interrelate "literary criticism and comparative religion, which seems to me the first subject to tackle in trying to relate literary criticism to other subjects."

It was clear that Frye had returned to the confusions of the 1949 period when he was spilling ideas but quite nervous about concrete work. While he talked about "a study of very wide range, which ... may run into three volumes" at the end of the summer of 1969, he gave no details. As he hashed out his ideas, however, it was obvious that the Bible once more preoccupied his thinking. In his "Literature and Society" paper of early 1968, he saw the Bible in the same mythic sphere as poetry, insisting that "such a book must be read with a mythical attitude of mind rather than with a logical attitude of mind." As a result, he thought scholars like Bultmann should have been talking about remythologizing the Bible instead of "demythologizing."

The Bible now became more firmly tied to his quest to reveal a symbolic universe animated by concern. In a sermon at Vic in November, called "Symbols," he stated, " ... Jesus does not use philosophical language: he uses the language of symbol, example and parable that religion speaks in common with poetry ...." While the language of reason is "implicitly aggressive," "it is only the language of symbol that can express a faith which is pure vision, and has no wish to attack or improve on anyone else's faith. In short, the language of symbols is the language of love, and that, as Paul reminds us, will last longer than any other form of human communication."

When Frye went to a *Daedalus*-sponsored gathering at the Villa Serbelloni in Bellagio on Lake Como in Italy the following September, he worked a complex of ideas about the Bible into his long essay derived from his Cornell and Berkeley lectures, "The Critical Path." A sprawling list of themes projected towards *The Great Code*, some 12 years away. Frye threw them all down in just a few pages in Sections II and IV as possibilities for integrated thought: Vico's three stages of language, the Deuteronomic reform, pericopes, the anxious editing of Bible content, the Bible as a revolutionary product of a defeated nation, the literal belief in God and the Bible, the mythic nature of Jesus in the Gospels, the literary shape of the Bible as comic romance, the Bible as the Great Code of art.

This seemed to indicate finally that Frye had hit a subject which was worth pursuing. By December he confessed that the influence of religion in his own work was not only "getting clearer to me all the time," he was "steadily moving in the direction of some kind of book on the typology of the Bible." His interest received a powerful boost when the Dean of the Faculty of Divinity at McGill, Eric Jay, sent a letter to him the exact same day about delivering the Birk's Lectures for the fall of 1971. Jay conveyed the hope of the faculty that a figure such as Frye would be able to write a *popular* series that would relate theology to a humanities subject such as English literature. Jay did not know Frye, but he'd probably been tipped off by Frye's former colleague at Emmanuel, Rev. George Johnston, about Frye's increasing interest in tackling the Bible.

While quite positive, Frye's answer to Jay was unusual for its secretiveness and caution. He confirmed he would be "around" in the fall of 1971 and could deliver lectures on typology of the Bible but insisted that there be no publication obligation or "any reproduction by tape recorder or the like" which hadn't been cleared with him in advance. He sketched out his particular literary interest of the time: " ... the distinction between continuous prose of the modern kind, and what I have taken to calling 'concerned prose,' the more detached sequences of proverbs, oracles or pericopes that one finds in sacred books."

For his own purposes, he quickly scribbled out a list of ideas, some of which derived from "The Critical Path" essay:

I.
Background: myth as statement about form and language
Depends on written language. Deuteronomy.

Yet close to oral trdn. [tradition] The circle of kernels vs. hours
Parallelism and then narrative.
Comminution of Bible into verses.
Yet unity and symmetry.
The Bible as comic romance.
Editors vs. authorship.
Subjective vs. objective art.

II.
Shift from eye to ear. Monument to papyrus.
Conception of idolatry and of false gods. Essence vs. existence.
History vs. story. Wg. [distinction] makes no sense.
Every event dialectic, polarizing into apoc. [apocalyptic] and dem.
[demonic]
Nature and society deified through the eye. Plotinus vs. the
Gnostics.

III.
Xy [Christianity] and translation
Paradox of translation
Sounds; concepts; images
Milton on analogy of faith
Vision as internal: eventually may "fit" externality.

The strength of Frye's renewed interest in the Bible was clear
when an English schoolmaster wrote him soon after about the
books of Judith and Tobit. Frye groused about the lack of "literary
sense" in scholars like Bultmann who seemed hostile to literary
criticism of the Bible and felt that interest in the form of the Bible
ought logically to lead to genuine literary criticism. Incongrously
he failed to promise the remedy and in fact described his own
typology course in almost self-deprecating terms. "I have been
teaching a course on the typology of the Bible for many years,
largely because I cannot do anything else for my students, and
some day I shall write out my lecture notes." With a little more
assurance, he outlined his own current, quite technical, interests:
" ... the way in which the form of the collection of proverbs or

maxims handed on down to the next generation develops into the post-Pauline pastoral epistles seems to me a possible line of investigation, and of course there is the whole apocalyptic development that except for Daniel got mostly squeezed out of the Old Testament. If one only had world enough and time, to say nothing of erudition, to write the history of literary forms!"

While Frye was supposedly gearing up for major work, he found himself saddled with another public service job which threatened the isolation and concentration he so logically required. When he taught at Cornell for a spring term in 1968, he was phoned from Ottawa and asked to be a part-time commissioner for the new broadcast regulatory commission, the Canadian Radio-Television Commission, which was replacing the Board of Broadcast Governors. The new chairman, Pierre Juneau, wanted an intellectual on the board. Juneau's idea of Frye was received enthusiastically by Lester Pearson himself and it was largely Pearson's endorsement that compelled Frye to join up. As a part-time chairman, he had to attend important policy meetings. It was hoped that Frye could plug into the research department to justify his involvement with the CRTC. Quite simply, he was supposed to be the resident genius generating perceptions about the nature and effects of television.

Of course most everyone at the CRTC was guilty about using Frye's time. Frye himself was early disgruntled with the time and energy the hearings took up. He once pointed at an African mask with drooping eyelids and told research director Rod Chiasson that the mask resembled a commissioner after a day of hearings. Nevertheless, almost everyone noted that Frye seemed reasonably happy on the road. While not garrulous, he did actually become one of the boys who could relax after hours. His relaxation was enhanced by the fact that fellow commissioners included writer Harry Boyle and intellectual Roy Faibish who had a taste for Vico and other types of arcane myth criticism. Frye seemed to enjoy flying off to Ottawa or other cities submerging himself in a practical world. Though usually quiet in hearings, he became known as a bit of a cut-up, and, when faced with an involved plan to split the CBC into BBC-like cultural channels, he joked, "I thought that when you split an amoeba, all you got was two amoebas." He chewed out one prominent executive for quoting Junius as a great Roman philosopher.

His involvement with the Research Department was slow to get off the ground. In a taped discussion with André Martin, Rod Chiasson and Patrick Gossage, all of whom spilled nearly incoherent techno-babble, Frye impatiently asked, "Tell me what to do and I will do it; when you want it done." Chiasson ultimately coaxed Frye into actually viewing television and writing reports. In 1973, he even had a Sony Trinitron glaring down from a shelf behind his desk at Vic. Since it was agreed that the effort of consuming shows was going to be onorous, Chiasson agreed to a strictly limited regime which became known in the CRTC as "the Frye Diet." For two years Frye produced the occasional one- or two-page review. Naturally they showed the swing of his ideas. A show called *Pandora's Box* revealed Frye the Spenglerian: " ... there is in our society a powerful will towards cultural decline ... the brutality of some of our sports ...the fetishism in the cult of the body ... show very disturbing Roman analogies." Similarly the Miss Canada Show was a paganistic throwback: "The function is that of the idols in a polytheistic religion, which project a society's idealized image of itself: thus the Barberini Juno is an image of a well-to-do Roman matron ..." He could even be grouchy about *Sesame Street* which showed him wildly off base. He complained of its "Walt Disneyish cuteness and condescension to children." Impatiently he launched into a phenomenological discussion of masks and persona: "... for me there is never anything under any persona except another persona."

While he hated the shock for shock's sake which permeated a show like *Pandora's Box*, he saw TV finding strength in recapturing the farcical "knockabout spirit." He picked up resonances of Mack Sennett and Larry Semon in a Carol Burnett skit. He sensed television was anti-ritualistic and humanizing.

Yet this humanizing aspect was also overshadowed by an alienating other-world effect too, created by the very coldness of the medium. TV images could impart the sense of disembodied spirits, ghosts in a modern house. In another context, he complained of television's socially alienating effect which included "a decline in the sense of festivity, the sense of pleasure in belonging to a community."

For Rod Chiasson, he produced a small essay on Canadian identity and separatism. Chiasson reminded him, though, that a central theme in earlier discussions was the question of the regenerated image. Acknowledging this as "central," Frye knew he was avoiding it but nevertheless tried to inch towards it in another sketch on icons and iconoclasm. For Frye, of course, this was a way of tying together the totally incongruous worlds of television and the Bible: "Hebrew culture was iconoclastic ... it shifted the emphasis from the eye to the ear, from god as the sun to god as the Word." This linked with the iconoclastic sense of the young: "the present visual foci of American life that television presents ... represent a form of idolatry." Needless to say, while this set off no explosion in the minds of the CRTC bureaucracy, it did show how obsessive the theme of internalization of the word was for Frye. In an essay the same year on Milton's *Samson Agonistes*, "Agon and Logos", Frye launched into a long discussion of the Bible, insisting, "The Word not only causes all images of gods to shrivel into nothingness, but continues to operate in society as an iconoclastic force, in other words a revolutionary force, demolishing everything to which man is tempted to offer false homage."

## THE CRITICAL PATH

Through the Christmas holidays and January, Frye hid before beginning work on expanding "The Critical Path" essay into book length for the Indiana University Press. Its length doubled to 170 pages and he was still dissatisfied with it when he wrote to his publisher Bernard Perry at the end of February. In fact, he suggested he might revise the last two sections. He was so insecure about it that for the first time, he used the provisional manuscript as fodder to scare up a contract to reassure himself that further work was worthwhile. There was a certain unnecessary mystery to this. Perry simply wrote he was delighted with the manuscript and just wanted to publish it for the spring 1971 season.

At the end of March, he managed to get to Oxford and settled with Helen into a suburban home on Headington Rd. His usual away-from-home irritation, noise, insinuated itself very directly in the form of a loud water heater in the closet of his bedroom. The house too was near the highway out of Oxford and the roar of trucks tore at the silence of the early morning. He occupied a large office in Fellow's Quad and savored the irony of returning as a fellow to a place he had once detested.

His teaching load was light, involving just one undergraduate seminar on 20th century poetic imagery, restricted to one student from each college. He also delivered a series of lectures on Blake to relatively small audiences of about 60 accomplishing the feat of operating the slide projector himself. He'd brought along the manuscript of *The Critical Path* and, perhaps trying to soothe Perry and himself, early reported "there won't be any material changes." But he continued to fuss with it and structurally re-formed it. Shuffling large blocks of text around, he added another 30 pages. He claimed that unlike McLuhan who was "all discontinuity and mosaic," he was obsessed with sequence. This was a bit curious because in terms of style the original *Daedalus* version is less gnarled. Perhaps only coincidentally in a sermon in the Merton Chapel, he darkly commented that the real task of creating a book is to get rid of it and "come around to the point at which we can begin again."

Frye later admitted that *The Critical Path* was a "transitional book" which had to be written before anything else. He even made a joke in the preface of its being "a farce ... a fifty-minute lecture stuffed with its own implications ..." As usual, the levity masked hesitancy and even confusion of direction. He started off rehashing his objections to the critical methods with which he'd struggled and presumably settled. Considering it the most personal book he'd written, it made him feel "vulnerable on all fronts."

With so much effort expended on *The Critical Path*, it was odd that during his Oxford stay, Frye was suddenly animated by his ambitious, wider scheme, "a major work of criticism" on "the typical clusters and patterns of imagery in literature," which Frye thought would take several volumes to complete. The outline of the project was so clear, that he was "compelled" to spend an entire month when he got home in late July going over his notes and marginalia to flesh out his ideas. He claimed the book was "taking definite shape." He was determined enough to dig himself in for major work; he proclaimed a moratorium on long-distance travelling, a feeble attempt at isolation which was broken in less than a year with a three-week trip to London and Ankara.

In October he was compelled to return to the Bible by a lecture series at Vic on hermeneutics which included papers by Hans Jonas, Paul Ricoeur and himself. On Oct. 29, he gave his own talk with the spendidly unhelpful title of "Mythology and Revelation." As the student press was obsessed then with the Vietnam War and "the military-industrial complex," there was not so much as a notice in *The Varsity*. When a visiting professor from Virginia, Ralph Cohen, queried Frye about it, Frye laconically told him that it was just the "starting point for a series of three lectures that I have to give at McGill next year."

Paul Corbett, who was now president of Harcourt Brace Jovanovich, picked up a hint (possibly from Ron Campbell or Bill Goodman) that a book on the Bible was now a priority for Frye. Corbett was immediately excited by the sheer commercial possibilities of the idea. Without so much as an outline or letter of intent, he sent Frye a contract dated April 29, 1971, which simply referred to a "work tentatively entitled The Bible and Literature." Although Frye and Harcourt originally saw the book as a manual based on Frye's Bible course which might be appended to *Literature: The Uses of the Imagination*, Corbett did not take the suggestion too seriously and opened the contract to allow for anything. He wrote in a liberal word count of 125,000 words, which works out to an average-sized book of about 400 manuscript pages. The contract set a wildly optimistic Oct. 1 as a deadline, allowing Frye only five months to write it. Although this sort of speculative contract was quite common with major commercial authors, it was almost unheard of in academic publishing. When the publisher of Princeton University Press heard of the arrangement, he openly expressed shock and exasperation.

Frye himself had never signed such a contract without a manu- script to offer and he was anxious himself about its implications. He warned Corbett that the book might turn out longer than he originally expected and that it might not work out as a companion to the reader series. He was even concerned about religious bigots who would be incensed by his heresies: " ... no book by me on the Bible is going to capture much of the red neck vote in Tennessee ... I would not make an issue of my legal rights if you find the book in any way embarrassing." Corbett quickly soothed Frye with a short letter, insisting that "the length of the book you write will be the right length." Neither Corbett nor Frye understood what this would really mean.

Frye nevertheless blocked off the summer of 1971 to work. In early July, he was still loyal to the original concept and described his work simply as writing out the notes of his Bible course "in the form of a handbook." Seeing it expand in complex directions, he realized he would never meet his official deadline but was neither anxious nor depressed about it. He was still positively motivated by the "stupidity of biblical scholars as literary critics." What he simply wanted to do was to apply "elementary" literary criticism to the Bible. The effect would be break a century-long logjam of historicism: " ... biblical criticism is stuck like the Ancient Mariner. It doesn't know any more about historical sources than it did a hundred years ago, no matter how much Ugaritic may have been learned in the meantime. As a result we can only get more and more guesswork on the thinnest possible structure of established facts." As early as August, he was starting to confess that the presumed handbook was in fact going to be a "big book." Needless to say, he finished the summer without anything to send off to Corbett. Unconcerned, he headed off to a conference in Turkey where he read a new paper "Wallace Stevens and the Variation Form."

Few people sensed Frye's new direction. Even when *The Critical Path* came out in the spring of 1971 with new material about the Bible solidly imbedded in a couple of the chapters, no reviewer drew serious attention to it. The book in fact only received a smattering of reviews, mostly in newspapers and left-wing journals like *The Nation* and *The New Leader* but not, interestingly, *The Canadian Forum*. Up to 1979, its total international sales in both paperback and hardback amounted to just over 9,000. It was so obscure in Canada, that a major reviewer and strong Frye enthusiast, Robert Fulford, didn't know of it until several months after its publication. This eventually drove Fulford into a fit of exasperation over the poor promotion and distribution of Frye's books in Canada by American university presses. But Frye continued to spurn agents, publicity or even the rudimentary device of cementing ties with one publisher.

Frye's collection of his writings on Canadian literature, *The Bush Garden*, coincidentally came out at the same time. In contrast to *The Critical Path*, *The Bush Garden* reaction was widespread in Canada and for the most part unusually warm. *Time* (Canada) devoted a whole page to a review and a sampler of quotes. Malcolm Ross in *The University of Toronto Quarterly* ignored the patchiness of the book by wondering what "'specialist' in Canadian Lit has published a volume to surpass—or even equal—*The Bush Garden?*"

From the very start, Frye had watched the book with nervous bafflement. He went so far as confessing "a strong feeling of emptying out the barrel about the reprinting of such ancient articles, and I felt rather diffident about its possible usefulness." This wasn't helped by its original discount-house appearance. The book itself was crudely printed in spiky photoset copy on rough, fast-yellowing stock. The binders managed to cut it with wider margins on the inside than outside.

The idea for the book had originally came from his old student, Dennis Lee, co-founder and editor of the struggling little House of Anansi. A prominent cultural nationalist, Lee thought it opportune to feed a package of Frye's old articles into a newly awakened literary constituency. When Frye was in Oxford, Jane typed up anything of possible interest including the full bulk of his *University of Toronto Quarterly* reviews from the 50s. Lee knocked a manuscript out of what Frye called a "mass of rubble" and rushed the book into print for early March 1971. The only editorial problem was the selection of a title which almost turned into a playful parlor game between Lee and Frye. Lee's favourite was *Dim and Involved* from one of Jay Macpherson's poems. He also listed *This Particular Sun, Inflected Weather, Heavier than Real* and *An Ordered Absence*. Frye listed his own choices as *American Attic* which was too close to Robertson Davies's, *A Voice from the Attic*, then *Solemn Land*. Admitting he liked *Inflected Weather*, he landed on *The Bush Garden* from Susanna Moodie. He thought this appropriate for a book of essays written "when Canadian literature was trying to get out of the bush."

Although both *The Bush Garden* and *The Critical Path* were up for the Governor General's Award for 1971, a friendly insider reported his personal disgust to Frye that "kippers carried the day." Pierre Berton's railroad history, *The Last Spike*, won the nonfiction award. As usual, Frye shrugged it off and consoled his informant with the intelligence that when he was chairman of the committee years before, he had to strike off four or five books of his own as ineligible.

In early October, three days after the official delivery date of *The Bible and Literature*, Frye delivered his three lectures for the McGill Divinity School, "The City of the Sun," "The Burning Bush" and "The Postponed Vision." The series had long been planned before his agreement with Harcourt for the Bible book but it inevitably became tied to the book. So many people turned up that the audience had to be shifted to the student union. Although it was not apparent to the enthusiastic, Frye disliked his own performance. He thought he should have made more progress in his thinking by then and felt so demoralized, he pondered giving up the project. He nevertheless went to the University of Minnesota in October to deliver a couple of lectures, "The Ear and the Eye in Literature" and "The Spoken and the Written Word."

## FACES OF THE BIBLE

All through the first half of 1972, Frye persistently tried out his Bible ideas. Still shy and insecure about his ideas, he managed to slip through a half-year of speaking engagements with barely a trace. A visit to Acadia University in early February to deliver "The Rivers of Eden" did yield one meagre college press report in which Frye identified the Old Testment as a folk epic whose style indicated a "suppression of continuous argumentative prose." A month and half later, he delivered a major series of four talks at Cornell which suggested a basic typological pattern, *The Faces of the Bible*, The Ox: Foreground Imagery, The Man: Foreground Narrative, The Lion: Background Imagery, The Eagle: Background Narrative. But the talk somehow escaped an official tape recording. Grit pushed him through a circuit of Scandinavian universities where he took on new audiences in different cities virtually every day. Between Apr. 19 and 29, he visited Goteborg, Lund, Uppsala, Stockholm in Sweden, Oslo in Norway, and Aarhus, Odense and Copenhagen in Denmark. A little later, he tried out another "Rivers of Eden" talk at the University of Cincinnati, again leaving only the title of his talk for the official record.

When he gave a talk "Pistis and Mythos" at McGill in early June for an obscure scholarly group, The Canadian Society for the Study of Religion, Frye finally produced a document for the society's proceedings, mimeographed in splotchy purple ink. The bald five-page tract of Frye's speech was published like a Puritan sermon with numbered statements. Number one unequivocally set the personal dimension to Frye's whole Bible project, his recognition in teaching his own Bible course that the "crisis of faith" was really "a crisis in understanding the nature of the language of faith." Abandoning this at first, he came back to it repeatedly. The elaboration of this would in fact lead to the crucial history of language section in *The Great Code*.

As literary critic, Frye quickly went on in point three to define the narrative of the Bible as a comic romance with polarized heroes and villains, "a story of a divine hero killing a dragon." Because the Bible was fundamentally mythic, the use of rational concepts of literal truthfulness were irrelevant and distorting: "The effort to treat the Gospels as roughly credible narratives with mythical accretions is dismally futile. The Gospels were myths and any attempt to 'demytholgize' them will disintegrate them to nothing." A word like "God" had simply no basis in the rational language of science or philosophy. To go on "believing" facts which were really metaphors like the trinity was obsessional. In opposition to this kind of knee-jerk faith was the faith defined in Hebrews 11:1-3 "as the *hypostasis* of the hoped-for, the *elenchos* of the unseen." To Frye this was "the realization of human hopes, the dialectic of the invisible." The ultimate goal of spiritual alchemy, however, was to return to life or "making things visible." The vehicle, as always, was the reader: " ... the uniquely dramatic element in the narrative of the Bible affords the possibility of an imaginative response in which the story of Israel and the life of Christ offer a narrative model for one's own experience ...." As a result the Bible was not just a literary work but a kind of practical manual showing the social function of literature through the possession of stories. Underlining the Blakean dimensions of his "argument," Frye ended his outline with Blake's definition of the Bible as "The Great Code of Art," the as yet undetermined title of his new book.

What Frye didn't approach was the crucial question of *how* it should work, how the mythopoeic should be mythopoeic, how the force of the Logos in "releasing power by creating form" should actually work. This was a difficult question and Frye continued to flirt with the anthropological conception of "one of the most primitive and central forms of aural message ... the command, the starting point of action." Essentially, this slotted poetry in the *social* class of the chant of the Trobriand Island magician coaxing plump yams out of the soil for the village larder. He remembered his own excitement in the Christmas eve moon shot of 1968, when for the first time in history human beings lost sight of the earth. As if on cue, the astronauts took turns reading the first verses of the creation hymn of Genesis. In total inhuman darkness, there was a fundamental impulse to restart existence by poetry and symbol. This evolved into a corollary interest in the ancient New Year hymn, the Sumerian *Enuma Elish* with its "magical energy" being released.

Right from the start, then, Frye had a much grander notion of what he was going to do with his Bible book. Rather than just elaborate his own typological analysis, he would integrate all the concerns about literary function which had haunted him since the *Anatomy*. In order to indicate the Bible's source of imaginative power, he had to reverse the effects of Plato's poisonously rationalistic attack on the metaphorical state of mind, the source of some very basic religious problems. This of course returned Frye to Blake, who wanted the world to see the sun as a company of angels and not as a flat, bald coin.

Frye's ideas seemed so well formulated, it was plausible that the summer would see a major breakthrough but it didn't transpire. Since Biblical studies still often demanded crucial linguistic interpretations, Frye was genuinely terrified of his ignorance of Hebrew and Greek. He confessed "... I am so ignorant of all the primary fields of scholarship in that vast area that I am going to have to devote my full time and energy to trying to conceal that ignorance." In mid-August, he was on the edge of panic. Although he had joined the editorial board of *Daedalus* in June, he categorically refused to go to its upcoming conference in Paris: " ... the gigantic book I have undertaken is still in quite a chaos, and the physical, mental and social effort required to attend the conference would really be prohibitive." The same day, he insisted to another correspondent that he had "to shut everything out of my mind and refuse all other commitments until I see whether or not I am barking up a tree that isn't there." A day later he also wrote to Harry Levin to thank him for sending his new book of collected essays, *Grounds for Comparison* and to decline the possibility to contribute to a book on fiction theory because of his Bible book.

The astounding irony was that two days later, Harry Levin was writing out an informal letter to Frye sounding him out about his desire to become the Charles Eliot Norton Lecturer for 1974-5. Because the Norton chair was *the* most important humanities lecture series in North America, Frye was now in line to be crowned as a major arts figure of the twentieth century beside T.S. Eliot and Jorge Luis Borges. Despite the implications for the Bible book, this was an invitation that almost no one could refuse. He accepted, calling it an "enormous honour." Even before he announced plans for his lectures, he saw the utility of Harvard to further his Bible interests. On the basis of having "a lot of John Wesley blood in me" he suggested that he undertake a large undergraduate course on the Bible. He even added the idea of a graduate-level colloquium on typology.

On the edge of a great honour, though, Frye continued to be insecure and edgy. In a letter he sounded a bit envious of Levin's 60th birthday tribute, *Grounds for Comparison*, when the Toronto Maoists chose *his* 60th birthday for an Orwellian hate-Frye session. He was curiously wary and enervated by a biographical essay he was writing for *Daedalus* to the extent he wanted to suppress it. The *Daedalus* editor nursed him along and finally won the essay "Search for Acceptable Words." Although it contained autobiographical material, there was no real injurious fact in it and his squeamishness merely pointed to his preference for snail-like anonymity. Once again, he insisted on banality: "I notice that, at the age of sixty, I have unconsciously arranged my life so that nothing has ever happened to me, and no biographer could possibly take the smallest interest in me."

No matter what personal tensions haunted him, however, Frye always had the security that he was at least alone in his work. In October, Frye's brilliant former graduate student, Jim Nohrnberg, innocently wrote Frye asking him to be a reference for a grant for a book on the relation of the Bible to English literature. Since Nohrnberg had taught a graduate seminar at Harvard in 1967-8 on the re-creation of biblical symbolism in such decidedly Fryeish territory of Langland, Spenser, Milton and Blake, he was no idle threat. Frye supported his application but not without nervously mentioning his own project and the problems of two similar books coming out at the same time.

Through his Bible struggles in the spring and summer, he managed to squeeze out a manual, *On Teaching Literature*, to go with his Harcourt series, *Literature: The Uses of the Imagination*, which after seven years was finally emerging. The series had had a difficult incubation. A senior supervising editor at Harcourt developed an early dislike for it and didn't encourage its development. There was a perception at Harcourt that because the series put intellectual demands on students, it was elitist, a word of high impropriety as educators started abandoning middle-class children for those of the ghetto. As a result, the editors, Ron Campbell and Kathy Daniel, were a bit besieged in their own territory. It was the publisher William Jovanovich himself who tried to boost Campbell's morale, telling him that if he didn't persevere, it wouldn't come to fruition. The project benefited from the obduracy of Hope Lee and Kathy Daniel who quietly labored to produce the first volumes, *Wish and Nightmare*, to squeeze the door open for the rest of the series.

The problems at Harcourt mirrored outside reaction; teachers seemed to be suspicious of any approach which involved theory. For one thing, this connoted learning on *their* part. The teacher manuals were, in themselves, relatively sophisticated expositions of Frye's theories. At the centre were basic outlines and diagrams of apocalyptic imagery divided into "heavenly" and "demonic" categories. Arranged in a circle, these constituted a "circle of stories," a simplification of Frye's complex mandala. Underlying the symbolic pattern was the Bible itself. The series in fact fully intended to dislodge the central role of classical mythology for Biblical mythology on the junior high level. There was an alarming double hazard in this. In the Bible Belt, the series could be seen as blasphemous because of its mythic angle and in the Liberal Belt, as a religious conspiracy.

In his pamphlet which was sent out to 55,000 high school teachers in the United States, Frye addressed all the basic anticipated anxieties which had faced him with the *Anatomy*. While he stated his opposition to rote memory of categories and to pigeon-holing, form did matter because literature unlocked and gave shape to an "imaginative world that remains within us, hidden and mysterious." The purpose of the study of literature was to "preserve a child's own metaphorical processes not distort them in the interests of a false notion of reality."

In a morning-long discussion panel put on for a large NCTE convention audience in a hotel ballroom in Minneapolis, Frye and his project associates tried to draw attention to Frye's approach to literature. Even though it was tied into the launch of the new HBJ reading series, with the head table set up like a war cabinet, it wasn't a controlled or unambiguous occasion. For one thing, the audience was a wild card. One panel member who adored Frye's work, Juanita Abernathy, unfortunately played tapes of young children in schools in Georgia reciting the mythoi by rote memory. Frye himself cringed and the teachers in the audience were clearly upset.

Although many in the audience continued to show overt hostility, there was, amusingly enough, an undignified scramble at the end when it was announced that free copies of *On Teaching Literature* would be available at the back of the hall. The reader series itself went on to a lacklustre future. It sold well enough to stay in print but it set few fires. One of the most brutal ironies was that although the junior high levels books had a heavy Canadian content, they couldn't be sold in Canada's biggest market, Ontario, because they weren't manufactured there. Another irony was that the effort to supplant classical with biblical myth failed and indeed the only reader which went into a second edition was the classical myth reader, *Man the Mythmaker*.

For Frye, the Lees and the Harcourt editors, this was the end of a long haul. Before Frye's flight back to Toronto, they drank too much and satirized hostile attitudes. Frye even called Hope Lee "darling." It was a tribute to Frye's image of obdurate impersonality that James Reaney later obstinately refused to believe that Frye could ever have done such a thing.

With the weight of the Norton lectures now hanging over him, Frye worked hard on his Bible book for much of late 1972 and 1973. Over the course of the Christmas holidays, he managed to complete a draft of 147 pages with the working title of *The Bible and Literature*. He surprised Jane by plunking down the first 75 pages on her desk for retyping. After she was away for a couple of weeks on sick leave, he produced another 72 pages. Like a bookkeeper, Jane duly noted receipt in the back of her business diary but that was all for the entire year.

Frye already had a bit of a seige mentality. He announced in his correspondence that he was "attached to a heavy and unportable typewriter." Without giving details, he talked ominously of "a Four Last Things atmosphere" to his turning 60. He even insisted that, with such a monkey on his back, he had to spurn personal vacations. He thought that "if I were on a sea beach on Antigua I'd go clicking along so I might as well have a typewriter anyway." Inevitably distractions intruded which included both his "academic bad debts" and what looked to be the seed of the Norton lectures, obviously one of the Four, a "return to the subject of Romance, and to see what it is trying to say through all its variants and displacements." For all the bold talk he found himself by mid-April in a muddle, trying to arrange and stuff his many notes into logical themes. He admitted darkly to an editor that "if this sounds confused, dithery and demoralized, it is."

One surprise which perversely threw him further off balance was an attempt by Sydney Feshbach to start a new journal which Feshbach announced would "serve as a revision of the *Anatomy*." It was to bear the acronym of the apostles *MAMALUJO* (Mark, Matthew, Luke, John) from *Finnegans Wake*. For Frye, this merely drew attention to the urgency of another major work to offset the enduring and, for him, baneful Frye-*Anatomy* equation and of course he made every effort to put Feshbach off. A group of Frye enthusiasts including Feshbach, Angus Fletcher and Robert Denham nevertheless gathered in Boston at a Northeast MLA convention in April to discuss their idol. Frye kept a nervous eye on this activity, darkly suspecting that the real interest of the group was in him personally. When Feshbach persisted with the idea, Frye continued to be negative: "I simply have to go my own way, and leave it to others to make what sense they can of it. The *Anatomy* does not seem to be a reviseable book ... a product of its time ... the man who wrote it is dead ..."

A more congenial intrusion was the idea of CBC producer Vincent Tovell to do a one-hour idea program on the development of

Canadian consciousness. Tovell met with Frye over lunch several
times and suggested a three-act program. Frye immediately saw
the utility of the structure which would allow examination of the
Baroque, Romantic and Twentieth Century periods. Although he
was taken with the conception, he knew that his Norton obligations
would make it difficult. Tovell tried to reassure him by saying that
the CBC could take care of the visuals. These would naturally flow
out of the ideas in any case. When Frye agreed, Tovell had journalist Barbara Moon interview him on his ideas about the Canadian
land and mentality; Frye himself wrote up some notes. Tovell and
Moon then knocked out a script which was a splendid bricolage of
ideas and memories. Filming and taping at different periods in
1974 and 1975, the result was *Journey Without Arrival*, one of the
most successful TV documentaries made in Canada.

Despite his adjuring an Antiguan beach, Helen did force a two-
week holiday without typewriter to Iceland in late August, only
weeks after the end of the spectacular Helgafell volcanic eruptions.
Weary of Frye's usual practice of seeing the world by accepting
lecture appointments, she wanted a holiday purely for a holiday's
sake. While Iceland was chosen on impulse, it did have the advantage of no ragweed or late summer heat. Based in Reykjavik,
which Helen particularly liked, they took bus tours through the
romantically bleak volcanic landscape which had so obsessed William Morris. They took in Thingmot, the *real* birth place of modern
democracy. And, Frye being Frye, he read the Palsson translation
of King Harald's sagas *in situ* which directly fed into his Norton
lectures.

Although Frye felt it was probably the best vacation they had
together, the unburnished happiness was only temporary. Helen
had been suffering from enough anxiety and insomnia the past
couple of years that she had started to see a psychiatrist. Her
anxieties continued to increase, however, and she began to display
resentments and hostility at home. While some of this could be
tied to an accumulation of lonely years with a man who worked
so hard under tremendous pressure, her moods became more
irrational. Helen had, for example, always been a keen organizer
of their overseas trips and extended stays at American universities.

With the impending move to Harvard for eight months which involved few real complications, she now seemed uninterested and resentful. Her mood continued to deteriorate and by 1979 when the Fryes went on a lecture tour of Italy, she was frequently disorganized, fretful and forgetful about details. Eventually an encephalograph test provided an indication of Alzheimer's disease. Like many sufferers of the condition, Helen did not much like being reminded of her failing memory and capabilities. Frye had to work around it delicately at home where he sometimes had to fill in as an impromptu cook when Helen simply sat down, unable to function. But the denial had a healthy aspect too. It meant that Helen refused to hide at home and she continued to socialize and travel with a surprising spirit and zest. Frye quite rightly fostered their travel as a mental stimulus.

Although he enjoyed it too, the Iceland vacation had little lasting restorative effect for Frye. In a sermon, he was soon repeating a point he made at Oxford three years before that "the bankruptcy of knowledge is one of the most genuine and tangible rewards for knowledge." Even death—and he'd already called an aspect of himself dead in the spring—was coming "around to the beginning again, the beginning of life within the power that can make all things new,"

If this had a Magian ring to it, not unlike the formula for re-creation he saw in the *Enuma Elish*, there was still the inevitable plodding labor. Because he soon had to firm up his Norton plans for his Harvard organizers, he announced his theme, "the structure of prose romance, stretching from Heliodorus and Achilles Fabius to modern science fiction. It is a large chunk of a general critical perspective which takes off from a book on the Bible and its relation to the imagery of English literature. This latter book is getting so big that I have to try to separate it from other things."

Mixed in with basic correspondence about arrangements for Harvard, there was also an involved conspiracy to keep Frye in Harvard once he came. In a series of letters, Dean Henry Rosovsky and Jackson Bate used every temptation to interest him in a major position. When Bate offered a vice-regal University Professorship, Frye clearly indicated that he was very flattered, claiming that the offer was "the greatest honour" he had received in his life. But Frye was not shy in making clear why he could not accept. He now recognized himself as a major cultural figure in Canada. If he accepted in the current climate of nationalism, "there would be such a feeling of outrage and betrayal so widespread that I should lose nearly all the leadership (if that is the word) that I have built up here over the last twenty years." This was not a gratuitous excuse. Canadian intellectuals were possessed throughout the early 70s with a ferocious fear of cultural and economic absorption by the American behemoth. Oddly enough, Frye then revealed to Bate that he wanted to use his accumulated authority not to be guru of the resurgent national culture but to be an avenging angel of English Canada in the face of troublesome Quebec separatism which, ironically enough, was fuelled by its own cultural nationalism.

The most important reason—his age—he said was more crucial. He reminded Bate that at 61, he had only a few years of active teaching left and was eager to "gather all my powers together for some complete and interconnected statement." He mentioned the Bible book and his study of structures of fiction which he would use for the Norton lectures. If he lived "long enough," there was also a more mysterious third work on conceptual myth. He eluded casually to his need of routine. "I am an introverted person heavily dependent on habitual routines and they have been set up in this environment."

Considering Harvard's rejection of Frye over 20 years before, he was surprisingly cordial. He only confessed privately his genuine dismay that Harvard was not looking for a younger man. The irrepressible Dean Rosovsky, however, followed up with his own offer. Harvard had been endowed with a fund for a William Lyon Mackenzie King Chair to be filled by a major Canadian scholar interested in Canadian subjects. This presumably would soften Frye's nationalist sensibilities by allowing him to be conscientiously Canadian outside Canada. Frye begged off because he said he didn't want to concentrate his efforts on Canadian subjects at the expense of everything else.

**NORTON PROFESSOR**

All the concentrated wooing was of course just a modest diversion
from the unnerving prospect of finding time for his heavy writing
commitments which was, he said, "rapidly reducing me to schizoid
fragments." He decided again to exploit his Oxford fellowship as
a retreat and arranged to go to Merton for much of June and July
to work on his Norton lectures. He even managed to avoid the
kind of distracting appearances which normally corroded his
energy. One major exception was the CRTC hearings on the CBC
in Ottawa in February, which elicited considerable newspaper
coverage, a *Time* (Canada) cover story, "What Ails the CBC?" and
a festering problem over the mandate of the CBC, which would
bedevil him three years later.

While his summer retreat at Oxford was productive, he continued to be preoccupied by the broader scope of the Norton lectures
which he sometimes tied to the theme of the Bible book and
sometimes to the more elusive book on Romanticism. At the end
of the summer, he pronounced the Bible book stalled, admitting
"an emotional crisis trying to blast some self-defensive carapace
off myself in order to tackle it again." After patiently waiting three
years beyond the contract delivery date, Paul Corbett naturally
wanted a progress report. In one of the most laconic exchanges in
publishing history, Corbett simply asked, "How *about* the book?"
Revealing little detail, Frye meekly replied that it was "a longer
process than I thought at first." A few days later, he and Helen
were on the plane to Boston for an intensive eight months during
which the Bible book would all but be forgotten.

The Fryes settled into the eleventh-floor penthouse of the F
Tower of Levrett House overlooking the Charles River. As assistant
dean of Levrett House, David Staines took the Fryes in hand and
helped with social ties including a dinner with Elizabeth Bishop
who swapped tales of her Nova Scotia upbringing with those of
Frye's in New Brunswick. Except for Jerome and Elizabeth Buckley, Frye tended to avoid socializing with the Harvard staff. Right
from the start he seemed most eager to give his attention to the
undergraduates. Somewhat to his surprise, he was an instant hit.

His first class on the Principles of Literary Criticism was so mobbed that it had to be moved immediately from the Science Center to the 955-seat Lowell Lecture Hall.

His reputation as systematizer had so preceded him that someone advertised in the student paper that Frye would draw large circles on the blackboard in his first class. When he did draw the circles, students applauded with the sense they were receiving the authentic man. Since the activism of 1968-70 was still fresh in his mind, Frye of course was surprised by students who enjoyed "much more of a sense of the genuineness of history and tradition." There were major hazards in this. Frye found himself keeping up an impossible schedule of house teas and being pressed for ideas. Although a veteran of decades of such gatherings at Vic, he was beginning to feel "MURDERED" by the social schedule by November. "Students of this generation are pets, really, full of good will and friendliness, but they *do* so want to know all the answers, and, what's worse, assume that I have them." This of course was the complaint of a happy man.

The resurgent student conservativism reinforced Frye's own fundamental recognition of what was wrong with contemporary society: its failure to recognize the strength of its own intellectual and religious past. Frye presented a rare ethnocentric image to a former student and Presbyterian minister, William Glenesk. "Students are not fools. They're asking what have *we* Christians got, instead of going all out for some damn guru." He admitted he saw himself as a kind of religious plainclothesman who might sneak students safely past the dragon of established religion.

Oddly enough, Frye didn't have to be a plainclothesman. When Rev. Peter Gomes asked him to preach a sermon just before Advent at Memorial Church right in the heart of godless Harvard, he readily agreed. Gomes was amazed to see his church fill with undergraduates who brought along notepads to scribble down Frye's ideas as if at a lecture. Taking Hebrews 11:1 for his text ("Now faith is the substance of things hoped for, the evidence of things not seen"), he flogged his favourite religious bogey, faith as mere acceptance of literal fact, rather than as an aspect of constructive human hope. On the one side he remembered the clergyman who resolutely insisted that "if the Bible had said that Jonah had swallowed the whale he would still believe it." Not mincing words, Frye identified this sort of faith as more "mental disease" than virtue. For his own part, there had to be reidentification of key religious terminology. "The wrath of God is the revelation, to man, of the kind of hell that man has made, and still·can make, of his own life in this world." At a luncheon put on in Lowell House, students then "crowded into the small dining room to catch his every word."

Frye clearly saw the danger of his own celebrity. He was becoming so involved that the Norton lectures themselves were in danger. Although he was "ploughing" through them in mid-November, he decided to leave Helen to entertain friends in Cambridge while he retreated to the isolation of Toronto through all of December. With the lectures approaching, he had to blitz them to finish on time. He only allowed three days to sneak away to a recording studio for some more work on the CBC documentary. By mid-January he sensed that haste would impair the subtlety of the lectures. Playing on an image of Geoffrey Hartman that an encounter with Frye's thought was like being in a planetarium, he confessed that his Norton lectures would be more like a wind tunnel.

Frye came out of his isolation in grandiose fashion. For the undergraduate Bible course Frye once more attracted a mob. The English 135 course, compulsory for English majors, normally drew from 50 to 75. Now there were 420 students turning up at the uncivilized hour of 9:00 am. There was actually a run on Bibles. Frye privately relished a student press description of his course as the first oversubscribed Bible course since the 7th century. The enthusiasm was evidently more than Frye-mania. For Christian students the courses offered an opportunity for learning about a key religious text without anxieties. Jewish students were more leery but still interested. Perhaps because of his own desire to be religiously neutral, Frye was delicate and careful in his lecturing. He early read out one of the Bible's "great epiphanies," Isaiah 6:1-4, describing the God-adoring seraphim. When Frye read verse four about the posts of the door moving "at the voice of him that cried," the class seemed to wait in expectant silence for the posts of the door to move. But Frye was not going to exploit the tension and the class was a bit deflated, deprived of a crying voice.

If Frye weren't busy enough, he undertook talks at Hollins College in Virginia and Boston College as well as the Witterbrynner Lecture on "The Ear and the Eye in William Blake." At Northeastern University he gave a talk, "Charms and Riddles," expanding on three pages of the *Anatomy* written two decades before. Although he delivered it off the cuff, the editor of his new essay anthology at the University of Indiana Press suggested he expand it to a whole book. In the midst of all this activity, Frye confessed by April that he was, to the contrary, "frantically anxious to get at" his Bible book. He feared a number of sleeping dogs, however, including the MLA presidency and the preparation of his Norton lectures, which he suspected were about to wake up and bite him in the rear.

For Frye, then, the Norton Lectures were curiously incidental. He would be simply relieved when they were over. He delivered them in grand fashion in the huge Lowell Lecture Hall. As often with prepared lectures, he ran through his text too fast for easy absorption. But, as usual, he didn't lose his audience over the course of the six lectures. An English PhD student, Tom Mallon, listening in the balcony with other graduate students, confessed bewilderment at the intimidating range of allusion in an area, prose romances, which he guessed only 1% of the audience, not including himself, knew.

When Frye faced the problem of what to do with his Norton lectures, he decided "simply to publish them as they were without worrying about the larger structure that they fitted into ..." As David Staines was making a round trip by car, he carried the Fryes' excess baggage back to Toronto including a bunch of eucalyptus leaves of Helen's, then returned in a fragrant car with the manuscript to Cambridge.

Frye then settled into some disconcerting paperwork. He had to face a heavy logjam of PhD theses. He wrote out "Charms and Riddles," then defended his own critical principles in answer to a critique of his ideas "Northrop Frye: The Critical Passion" by Angus Fletcher. While Fletcher's essay was casual and rambling, he managed to land some hard blows. Fletcher quoted and purred over a recent criticism in *A Map of Misreading* of another erstwhile Frye lieutenant, Harold Bloom, who accused Frye of being a latter-day Proclus or Iamblichus, two woolly gnostics who emphasized the power of magic. While explicitly denying the "gnostic mytho-poeia" Wimsatt argument of ten years before, Fletcher himself expressed dismay that Frye "assumes we can 'read' the mystery at the heart of light. If we cannot, then all is lost." Fletcher threw salt on the wound by denying the commonly held belief that Frye was *his* precursor. In other words, Fletcher managed in just a page and a half of a long essay to indicate that two of the brightest younger scholars he had deeply influenced in the early-60s were now drifting from the cause.

In a somewhat sloppy but passionate response, "Expanding Eyes," Frye showed a rare edge of pained anger and defensiveness. He restated his dislike of disciples, and now openly indicated his antipathy to revising the *Anatomy*. Revision, after all, would not "stop the flow of abusive nonsense which has also been directed at me, because most of that comes from people who know quite well what nonsense it is, but have their minds on higher things." Because it struck at his fundamental enthusiasm for liberating criticism from its mystery religion status, he was particularly stung by Bloom's putting him beside Proclus and Iamblichus, "both of them pagans, iniates of mystery-cults, and very cloudy writers ...." If Bloom displayed a very clear Oedipal complex about Frye, Frye wrote an uncharacteristically catty note in the back of *Secular Scripture:* "Except for the first clause in the next sentence, this passage was written before the appearance of Harold Bloom, *A Map of Misreading.*"

Because he was back fighting "old and tired problems," there was a tone of weary bitterness as he insistently restated and reaffirmed the basic tenets of his own theory. On the question of the verbal universe, for example, he sounded almost petulant. "The order of words is there, and it is no good trying to write it off as a hallucination of my own. The fact that literature is based on unifying principles as schematic as those of music is concealed by many things, most of them psychological blocks, but the unity

exists, and can be shown and taught to others, including children."
The whole point, however, was the possession of verbal power.

Never before was Frye so intellectually isolated. The predominant theoretical schools seemed hopelessly mired in impotence. If
Frye sinned by suggesting that everything could be decoded, now
the paragons of post-structuralism were suggesting that everything
was open to misinterpretation in a labyrinth of subtexts. The growth
of the new schools of criticism once more indicated a drift away
from a structure of literary theory to supposedly firmer outlying
areas. Frye quipped that there seemed to be "some Herculean
force in modern thought that would not be content to remain
spinning for a poetic Omphale." He didn't analyse them, but
suddenly they were all reappearing: the Marxist approach of
younger British scholars like Terry Eagleton, the psychoanalytic
borrowings of Bloom and Lacan, the pop anthropology of French
and Italian semiologists like Barthès and Eco. In all cases, literature
was a convenient, if secondary, entity to prove other non-literary
points about the world.

Frye wasn't done with enemies. His anger at Bloom and Fletcher
in fact spilled over in a Canadian direction in his new "Conclusion
to *Literary History of Canada.*" For a quarter-century, he'd seen
nonsense written about his influence on creative writing in Canada.
There was supposed to be a mob of Fryeish cookie-cutter poets
who wrote according to the formulas of the master. "There is no
Frye school of mythopoeic poetry; criticism and poetry cannot
possibly be related in that way; the myth of a poem is the structural
principle of that poem ..."

With so much irritating focus on old questions, it was logical
that Frye would show some zest in returning to the task of his
Bible book. While he did manage to work up a paper "History and
Myth in the Bible" for the English Institute at the end of the
summer, it was a somewhat colorless essay which barely hinted at
the grand proportions of what he was attempting. Compared with
his 1972 "Pistis and Mythos" essay, the paper made it into continuous prose, but revealed no great progress of thought. There was a
curious caution in picking up then dropping themes like iconoclasm, eye and ear opposition, repetition and re-creation.

Frye flushed out the *bête noir* of historicism, the inability of scholars to take seriously the "mythical and metaphorical aspect." The Bible was not fundamentally factual. Historical accuracy was not wanted and was purely coincidental. It accepted or twisted facts according to the internal needs of a myth. "We soon realize," said Frye, "that we are being told the same story over and over again, and that this story is U-shaped ..." This was the story of Adam "who loses the tree and water of life on the first page of Genesis and gets them back on the last page of Revelation." As the Bible used the primarily literary tool of mythical and metaphorical language, it shared the mythopoeic possibilities of all literature: " ... as the mythic and metaphorical language spoken by literature is primary language, and the only means of reaching any spiritual reality beyond language, then, if such reality exists, works of literature themselves represent a practically untapped source of self-transforming power."

Frye's tragedy at this point was that he was burdened with too many ideas. He had accumulated such a mass of notes that he started to bring them into his office for Jane to type up. With single-space typing, she appended new material as it came in and eventually produced a tome of over 250 pages. Richard Kostelanetz who interviewed Frye for a *New York Times Magazine* profile noted it on his desk when he visited and garnered Frye's prediction that it "would take several more years to complete." Not surprisingly, he confessed, "Most of my writings consist of an attempt to translate aphorisms into continuous prose." When he advanced further with his manuscript, he started trying to create form by arranging chapters by the names of the seven early planets including the sun.

## MLA PRESIDENT

At the year's end Frye found himself crowned as MLA president, the nominal head of literary studies in North America. As a Canadian who would serve through the American Bicentennial, his appointment represented an interesting irony. He joked, however, that in bringing the job home, he felt like Samson carrying the gates of Gaza. If this also suggested the phrase "eyeless in Gaza," he coincidentally recommended Blake's *Expanding Eyes* for a new book of essays, which was actually published as *Spiritus Mundi*.

*Spiritus Mundi* was a strong collection of writings that showed that all through the time that Frye was fretting over his Bible book, he could turn out quite stunning work like "Agon and Logos" on Milton's *Samson Agonistes* or "Blake's Reading of the Book of Job." In his introduction too, he at last publicly revealed the notion of the regenerative central purpose for his Bible work. Underlying all his earlier work, he said, was an assumption that literature was written within a mythological universe. The decidedly tautological reason was that like an atomic breeder reactor, "literature continues the mythological habit of mind." It was a basic function of the brain which could not be ignored in modernity.

But there was the eyeless aspect too. Frye started the year refusing appearances because he had to finish his "very large and complex book." At the end of June, though, he was again doubting the progress he could make. With the term approaching in late August, he admitted he was "struggling" with the project. Joking at first that it was sprouting "seven new heads whenever I cut one off," he considered even that analogy inadequate. It was now "so big" that it made the many-headed Hydra "look like a garter snake." He was a little more positive to Roy Daniells in announcing, quite inaccurately, that the summer's struggle, which involved distributing material, had led to a sense that he knew at least "what is to go where."

A serious complication was that on July 12, Frye was just one year from official retirement. This possessed a profound implication for the many graduate students and undergraduates who wanted a taste of Frye's teaching before he retreated to the Elysium of pensioned obscurity. Despite the enormity of the problem, the university administration ducked the question by telling him at the end of August that as his birthday was so close to the July 1 start of the university year, he could continue to the end of the term in 1978. As the years passed, though, this became a festering problem for Frye. His whole attitude was that of his grandfather Howard, that he wouldn't retire until he dropped. Because he was an internationally recognized name to the university and still attracted huge classes, there was no reason whatever for him to be put out to pasture. The university, however, continued to fret about pension rules. When his former student, Alvin Lee, who became Academic Vice-President of McMaster University in 1974, heard about the malingering, he received permission from his own President to raid Frye if Toronto ever faltered.

Despite his demoralization and increasing worry over the health of Helen, who was suffering bouts of insomnia and dizziness, he had the benefit of two restorative bursts. His Harvard lectures, *The Secular Scripture*, hit Toronto bookstores in February 1976 and was an instant sellout. In a replay of *The Modern Century* publication, Harvard had to go back for a fast reprint and was able to correct a mistake only on the third printing. Even then, the book was slow to get back into the stores, creating great headaches for academic bookstore managers like Bob Miller in Toronto. Although not extravagantly widely reviewed, it captured crucial full-scale reviews in the *Times Literary Supplement* by David Daiches and in *The New York Times Book Review* by Harold Bloom. While Daiches was neutral and accommodating, Bloom was ambivalent, praising "the Frye who matters most, the visionary of romance" while condemning him as potentially "the great homogenizer of literature." For Frye, Bloom said, "any story or poem is essentially a renewable archetype in a verbal universe, and so he is at a loss to account for just what makes it new in any particular story or poem." Bloom also threw the new "language centred" criticism at Frye, saying that he was "not much interested in the parallel vicissitudes of meaning within or between texts, the ways in which meaning changes when rival works collide."

Through the broadcast of *Journey Without Arrival* in early April, Frye also became an unlikely national TV star. *Journey Without Arrival* received enormous attention in the Toronto media, including publication of half of his script on the important op-ed page of *The Globe and Mail*. Intellectually it was about as good as television could get. Addressed to the Canadian identity obsession, the question of "where is here," it did not provide solutions so much as crucial reasons why the identity was hard to find.

While Americans created America and consulted their beginning "the way fundamentalists consult the Book of Genesis," Canada's "unwritten epic" was the ill-fated expedition of veteran Arctic navigator, John Franklin in 1845, who was "swallowed up, like another Jonah." Compared to such a miserably authentic Canadian destiny, the 17th century Europeans who plundered Canada were different. The world was confidently understood, by mathematics, through astrolabes and flat projection maps, and by the corollary assumption that "you could catch and control a universe in a net of abstractions and predictabilities." It was important "to keep in mind that the imaginative home was still somewhere beyond the shores of Canada itself." Since this kind of orientation was inauthentic, it put Canadians in the unusual position of having to find ground zero, identify it, acknowledge it, and build on it symbolically, mythically. It was also a warning that came out of Frye's work generally: when dealing with something so unreliable as reality, the logical approach was a dead end.

All this was a set-up for the voice crying in the wilderness, the poetic Baptist, E.J. Pratt. One of the great strengths of the show was the way the producer Vincent Tovell made Frye visually spontaneous and vibrant. In sitting over an old tape recorder and pushing the play button to produce Pratt's reading from "Newfoundland," Frye looked positively like Little Jack Horner ready for a plum. Pratt understood the bleakness of nature, the garrison mentality, but also "expressed the central comic theme of the Canadian imagination ... the successful accomplishing of a human act," which happened to be the less than romantic accomplishment of the National Dream, the transcontinental railroad. "For Pratt the real hero is not an individual but the group, the collective will to finish the job."

The success of the show seemed to give impetus to a vague TVOntario idea of doing a Frye series on literature. These were the days of extravagantly funded educational TV idea series hosted by such luminaries as Kenneth Clark, Jacob Bronowski, John Kenneth Galbraith and Malcolm Muggeridge. Frye had had a bit of trial run as commentator for part of a series on modern fiction for an American-based ETV producer in 1971, *Literature: Man's Search for Self.* Frye had to admit to "a powerful temptation to do a series like Malcolm Muggeridge's, given time, energy and unlimited financial support ... I can do that sort of thing all right, if I don't go pop first." By June 1976, TVOntario was emboldened enough to announce "a major new series, tracing the development of the entire body of western literature back to the Bible" to be based on Frye's Bible book "expected to be published at the end of the year." Because TVOntario considered it so important, the general manager, Jim Hanley, was resigning "to spend six months moulding the concept into a TV form." In his late thirties, Hanley was still basking in the glory of a popular and very polemical, nationalistic 1973 series *True North.* He was the subject of fawning Toronto magazine and newspaper profiles. He was the rising star who would energize frumpy ETV. Certainly for the increasingly nationalistic local media, there was a positive lust for any made-in-Canada product which might smell of international success. All the elements seemed to be there, Frye, Hanley, and a substantial ETV production unit.

But major problems cropped up from the start. The producers became leery about the religious dimensions of the series. This fear was not helped by premonitions of a violently controversial series under production at TVOntario, *The Jesus Trial.* Broadcast in 1978, it centred on the irreducibly controversial question of who actually killed Christ, the Jews or the Romans. Mixed in with garrulous and pretentious Toronto theologians, Frye made an explosive cameo appearance in which he simply said that in his reading of the Gospels, he thought that we all killed Christ. Because he was so preoccupied with other work Frye wanted someone he knew and trusted involved in the series. He chose Bob Sandler who wrote a master's thesis for Frye on Shakespeare and had recently worked as a TV comedy writer. Sandler and Hanley, however, developed such an antipathy for each other, they almost came to physical blows in one conference in Frye's office. Sandler felt that Hanley wasn't being faithful to Frye's ideas. He saw

Hanley forever trying to inject a pop culture element, including references to TV series like *Charlie's Angels*. Frye responded diplomatically that he wanted to see them take a popular not common approach.

Certainly Frye's central enthusiasm for a Bible and literature theme was steadily being eroded. By the summer of 1977 the series was no longer focussed on his Bible book but on *The Secular Scripture* with the theme of *de te fabula*, "the story is about you." This hearkened back to an earlier series Frye did for Hanley on the modern novel in 1971. In a little one-page sketch, Frye had laid down his own central theme: "Anything that's worth reading is about ourselves." Under this transmutation, and without so much as a minute of film in the can, the series still grabbed media attention. "Coming soon," trumpeted *Toronto Life* in September 1977, "*The Hero and the Quest*, the working title for the most ambitious educational television series yet." There was no mention that little had happened in a year. Nevertheless, the media still sucked stories out of its certain preeminence. A half year later, *Maclean's* news magazine gave lead attention to it in a profile on Frye.

Although Frye worked hard on the Bible book all through the summer, he made no direct mention of it in his correspondence. In December, he gave a major speech to the gathered luminaries at the MLA convention and seemed to prepare everyone for the possible failure. To those who didn't know, he offered the intelligence that he'd been "interested in the relation of the Bible to European literature." But he went on to confess that it was "the sort of topic that, whenever one gets at all close to it, sends one back again with a sense of total irrelevance of everything one knows, or thinks one knows. Yet the suggestion in it of infinite mysteries connected with *logos*, or articulate speech is as fascinating to the literary critic in me as a flame to a moth, even if in the end it proves equally destructive."

After years of struggle, he admitted he was "nowhere near really understanding" those great themes which had haunted him all his life, wisdom and prophecy. He'd in fact done a complete turnaround from 1961 when he arrogantly suggested in a National

Film Board clip that "the words wisdom and sin are completely meaningless to people who are operating, as I say, on 8-10% total capacity." The Newtonian image of the child on the edge of the sea now had a certain poignancy. He still had to confess that a central animating interest was the "discontinuous kind of wisdom, an insight for which all knowledge is only a symbol and literature only a means." He even injected an overtly mystical suggestion that "a drive toward some kind of 'zero degree of writing,' as it has been called, where the literary and all its conventions disappear and only the pure prophetic vision is left."

## JAPAN

Frye, as most English Canadians, was thoroughly shaken by the victory on Nov. 15, 1976, of the separatist Parti Québécois, in the Quebec provincial elections. The implications were enormous. The country could simply disintegrate through cultural factionalism. As a strong federalist who was also a native Quebecker, Frye was suddenly out of the MLA mystical clouds, preoccupied for nearly the whole next year with denouncing and working against the separatist movement. In a political motherhood speech in Washington in February, he threw in some bad press about it, calling it "a retrograde and counter-historical movement, both in its neo-colonial attitude to France and in its arrogant attitude to French Canadians outside Quebec."

The alarm about the Parti Québécois inevitably precipitated a great blow-up in Ottawa over alleged separatist bias in the French CBC. Prime Minister Pierre Trudeau sent a letter to CRTC Commissioner Harry Boyle requesting an inquiry into whether the English and French CBC networks were adequately "fulfilling the mandate of the Corporation" particularly in the news and public affairs programs. He also wanted advice on establishing a Royal Commission "to consider broader questions relating to the public broadcasting service in general." Although it was commonly perceived as a request for an anti-separatist witch hunt, the terms of the committee were glaringly wide. Trudeau in fact didn't even mention separatism. This hangar-size loophole permitted the CRTC to wriggle out of becoming an Uncanadian Activities Committee.

The problem for Frye was that Harry Boyle wanted him on the committee of inquiry. A wrenching irony lay in his business diary where Jane noted and heavily underlined "term ends as CRTC Commissioner" on April 3, just two weeks after the committee itself was established. For Frye there were obvious competing motivations to be involved. Although he was definitely on the side of excoriating separatism, he was also an ideological liberal who repudiated McCartheyite witchhunts. Critic Morris Wolfe saw Frye's involvement as some sort of gold-plated guarantee of integrity. The immediate headache was the time element. Writing on March 4, Trudeau wanted the report by July 1. Boyle considered this a "heavy burden" but promised to go ahead. Although the Committee of Inquiry consisted of Boyle, Frye, Alan Golden, Jacques Hébert, Gertrude Laing and Louise Martin-Côté, the report was really a concoction of Boyle's ideas, Frye's writing and whatever research CRTC could quickly dig out of the CBC and letters of comment solicited from the public.

Although Frye went to the Committee of Inquiry meeting on April 5 in Montreal, he soon departed on a long-planned trip to Japan. On the basis of translations of *The Educated Imagination*, *The Modern Century* and *The Critical Path*, he had a small but growing reputation there, which suddenly exploded with the translation of half of his works, including the *Anatomy*, in the 80s. There was of course something splendidly magnificent in penetrating a major non-western culture with his own ideas. Simply, the Japanese were finding that his analysis of English literature told them lots about their own, thereby proving there really *was* a universally comprehensible symbolism.

For his trip, Frye was under no compulsion to do anything but soak himself in Japanese culture; all expenses were nicely taken in hand by the Japan Foundation. Frye being Frye, however, he did give a few talks on Shakespearean comedy and romance at the universities of Tokyo and Doshisha and elsewhere but basically drained Japan for its essential cultural forms. Frye did some research among friends who knew Japanese culture and established certain basic "musts": the theatre of Noh and traditional Kabuki, the Katsura and Shugakuin Detached Villas in Kyoto, and the tea ceremony at Urasenke.

While Frye was no Alan Watts, donning kimono and experiencing satori over green tea, he was extravagantly receptive to the theatre forms, Kabuki, Noh and Bunraku, which reinforced his notions of a basic human symbolism. In Osaka's puppet theatre, the Asahiza, he saw a Bunraku *Romeo and Juliet*. Two lovers from feuding houses, facing an impossible love, commit suicide. With Japanese neatness, the remains of the lovers were sliced up, packaged and sent floating against the current across the river. Everything was done with elaborately costumed life-like puppets manipulated by black-dressed puppeteers. Sitting mesmerized for four or five hours in the hot theatre, Frye suffered an agreeable hallucination: " ... something suddenly occurred to me ... these puppets were quite certain that they themselves were producing all the movements and noises that the audience was hearing ... the great romances of Shakespeare's period ... seem to me to have been deliberately scaled down to puppet size ..." He was not so lucky with Noh. The particular play he saw had a *Tempest* feel about it, the *bardo* experience of figures recounting their lives between life and death. Although he was utterly enthralled by it, the Japanese insistently believe that westerners are immutably bored with Noh, and he was hauled out of the theatre by his guide. But the Fryes were so interested in the Kyoto-Osaka-Nara triangle, they decided to stay in Kyoto for two extra weeks until mid-May.

The return to Canada was not, of course, enticing. As soon as he was back he was deep into the CRTC report which he worked on until its publication in late July. Although Boyle and Frye acknowledged the separatist question right in their second sentence, they did little more than explore four of nine "typical" complaints from a total of 104 letters directed to the committee. In picking up unfinished business from the major CBC hearings from three years before, the harshest focus was on the weaknesses of both the English and French CBC networks. What came out of course was Frye's personal vision of a Canada in which both English and French elements of the country took note of each other. As Frye knew from his Governor General Award days, the failure of the "two solitudes" to communicate was a grave national deficiency. There was a related conception that only central Canada was worthy of news. "These assumptions," said the report, "are intolerable. They are also extremely stupid."

The report really came up with nothing new which had not already been said years before. It merely stirred up old fundamental questions about the CBC mandate. In the short term, though, it did serve to bury both the potential for a witchhunt and the suggestion of a politically-motivated Royal Commission. The press generally loathed it. Gordon Donaldson of *TV Guide* in particular heaped scorn on its "screaming sensationalism." Years later, political analyst Richard Gwynn considered it a flawed report "which predictably got nowhere."

Frye nevertheless kept up the polemics which showed him in a rather contradictory position of supporting cultural but not political regionalism. In a conference with an improbably bureaucratic name, Options Canada, Frye claimed to see "unreal abstractions" constantly blocking and thwarting "immense energies trying to find their proper regional outlets." "Painters and writers," he added, "are not acts of God: they come out of specific communities, and are the individual points where those communities have become articulate."

Through it all, however, Frye had to face up to the struggle with the Bible book. For the first time, he was no longer making brave attempts at joking it off and was now baldly calling it "this infernal book." When his old Harcourt editor, Bill Goodman, now at Harvard University Press, visited in early June, he understood from Frye that the Bible book would take three more years and then he would get back to the "balance" of his Norton subject, narrative structure, or telling in "mythos."

By the year's end, however, he had to admit to his old friend and MLA presidency successor, Walter Ong, that the Bible book, "goes very slowly: it seems to take its own time." Frye was clearly twisting uncomfortably in his attempt to make a dent in contemporary theory: "I have been soaking myself in Hegel's *Phenomenology* to try to figure out some kind of modern statement of the four levels of meaning. Then there is the whole Logos business and its relation to all the socio-linguistic people, so many of whom ... seem bent on avoiding it." Frye seemed to have little faith that his own symbolic analysis of the Bible, which he had taught for nearly forty years, would have sufficient authority and weight to impress younger scholars influenced by the French post-structuralists. Frye was not so much a martyr to the progressive notions of his own thinking as eager to make something new out of his old ideas.

## QUIET YEAR

At Christmas, he could once more avoid the headaches by packing for a trip to Guyana, one of the most bizarre of his trips as intellectual evangelist. Frye had met Wilson Harris in Toronto. Harris's Bible-permeated novels of the Guyana coast interested him enough to sniff out the ambience. But the Fryes were hardly jungle veterans. They had never been to a depressed "socialist" Third World country. Guyana was just eleven months from suffering the depradations of Rev. Jim Jones who poisoned nearly 900 members of his People's Temple cult in the bleak promised land of Jonestown.

The opening chapter of the nightmare, the attempt of an American couple to retrieve their child from Jonestown, was taking place in Georgetown precisely when the Fryes were there. There was certainly an unsettled atmosphere to the place, exacerbated in part by a festering racial split between East Indian and black political factions, both nominally Marxist and both manifestly incompetent in handling affairs of state. Frye was stunned that a country so wealthy in resources couldn't feed its people. In a land of sugar plantations, there were even shortages of sugar. Hardly exemplars of democracy, the government under Forbes Burnham coincidentally marked Frye's visit with a ban on imported books. Even innocuous university texts had to be read and approved by the authorities. There were already severe restrictions on newsprint and printing presses which effectively banned opposition papers.

The Fryes settled into the only real modern accommodation in Georgetown: the Pegasus Hotel which looked down on grey mud-roiled breakers, very unlike the tourist cliché of green crystalline Caribbean water. He had two obligations, a public lecture in Georgetown and a "seminar" on "Literature and the Educated Imagination" which drew 400 undergraduates at the University of Guyana. Seated before a full, short-sleeved, audience in the Town Hall, he wore tie and jacket, as he talked on the politically defensive topic of "Why Study Literature—A Rationale for the University Department of English." He parried anticipated Marxist questions such as "What is the university doing to involve the masses in the class struggle?" What he managed to focus on, however, was his old theme of new literature feeding on old literature. Nothing is new because the emotions which drove the Elizabethan greats were the same as those affecting writers today. Everything existed already: "Nowadays," he was quoted, "Shakespeare appeals to us because we have inside us everything he talks about." What was essential was an integration of writer and place to bring it all out. Stripped of a colonial mind-set, Canada was producing vibrant literature.

When he got back he was faced with yet another trial run of his Bible ideas, the Mathers Lectures at Queen's University in Kingston in mid-February. In three succeeding days, he delivered "The Language of Belief", "Diachronic and Synchronic Myths" and "Revolutionary Monotheism." Just from the titles, it's obvious that Frye was still grappling with the dimensions of the language of belief and power. *The Queen's Journal* quoted him as saying "the real history of the Bible begins when God spoke to Moses from the burning bush." As always this revolution is internal: "what is contained in the Bible has to be fought out on a battlefield, and that battlefield is the mind of the reader." Frye came out of this little series so exhausted, that he joked to an old friend, "They worked me so hard I came down with flu."

Soon after this, a profile on Frye in *Maclean's* magazine confidentally predicted that Frye's new TVOntario series was moving along so forcefully, the first episode would be filmed by the year's end. TVO was "quietly confident" that either the CBC or National Film Board would pick up part of the tab for the remaining programs. Even Frye seemed to be balancing excitement with apprehension. Despite the publicity, it was hard to know what progress the producer, Jim Hanley, was making. His conception of the series—now renamed "The Story About Us"—was still obdurately lowbrow. In a promotion portfolio of program outlines, he put together a medieval woodcut of the Holy Family with a bursting image of Superman, Blake's engraving of Christ's resurrection with a clip of John Travolta dancing in *Saturday Night Fever*. The outline of the concluding program tried to make the point that, as Hercules had his labors, The Beatles "have a string of gold records" and that, irrespective of million-dollar contracts, Reggie Jackson had to cop a World Series to prove himself a hero. Not surprisingly the potential series customer was hit with an ominous warning "the verbal universe is not easy to understand." Although this proved to be the last gasp of the project, TVOntario continued to woo Frye, hoping that he would continue to append his name to a self-destructing series. By November he diplomatically disassociated himself from the project by having a colleague write a very unfriendly letter about it.

TVOntario did soldier on to produce a pilot: *The Last Illusion*. Hanley took too seriously the theme—"The Story About Us." It mixed incongruous dramatizations of *Great Expectations* with confessions of various people, prostitute, dancer, war hero and preppy high school student about their life stories to link "real" life with Dickensian "fiction." The subjects often reflected lives of egoism, emotion, sense of alienation and defeat but unfortunately there was very little literary contact. As if to cover this, the narrator, ironically enough a Briton, who was mysteriously ensconced in a pretentious library of leather-bound books, passed out nostrums about the value of literature. There was throughout a disastrous and most unFryeish solicitude about the audience. The base audience appeared to be that of a sullen high school class who don't wanna read and might better relate to a whore's life story. The presumption seemed to be that literature *by itself* had little authority to say anything directly related to human concerns.

At the end of the school year, Frye again had to express quiet dismay about his progress. "I am still struggling with the book, which has been expanding and complicating itself in various directions, and I cannot say just now when it is likely to see light." His reason intimated a languishing sense of his own public idolatry: "My other long and complicated books were written at a time when I was less of a public figure and had fewer claims made on me." He confessed both to "alternating hope and despair" and even to "stage fright" created by a large public demand for a masterpiece which might be an anticlimatic disappointment. Despite this, none of his letters reflected the much greater anxiety of the year before.

The summer of 1978 was almost indulgently filled out with a lecture tour of New Zealand universities, preceded by a hugely un-Fryeish week-long stay at the Tahiti Beachcomber in Polynesia. Only five years after abjuring a beach holiday, here he was, heading for the South Pacific for two whole months with little chance of making important contacts or presenting new lines of thought. With Helen's Alzheimer's condition slowly worsening, he was determined to be more indulgent and easy with their lives.

Although an old Toronto friend, Jack Garrett, had been behind the trip, and his close Oxford friend, Mike Joseph, was at the University of Auckland, there was no great audience for Frye in New Zealand. There were even all the old hostile barriers he'd faced a decade before in North America. Faculty and students at Massey and Otago in particular were unhappy with his obdurate systemization, which made him seem like a "clever boy with his Meccano set." He waited until the latter part of the tour on the South Island to try out some Bible ideas at the universities of Canterbury and Otago. At Canterbury, Jack Garrett reported a good reception for his Bible lecture but complained that his central ideas seemed undemonstrable. At Otago in the southernmost city of Dunedin, where he lectured on the four levels, Frye seemed preoccupied with trying to catch glimpses of the "exotic South Pacific." Indeed, the Fryes broke the business part of their trip with a tour of the famous Mount Cook region.

Obviously eager to stay on vacation, the couple came back from New Zealand via Fiji and San Francisco. Not surprisingly he was mellowed by his experiences, noting that New Zealand was a "very relaxed country, as it has only three million human beings as against sixty million sheep, and the contemplation of all those sheep induces very pastoral thoughts." Pastoral thoughts were so little conducive to Biblical thoughts it seemed, he didn't mention his Bible book in his letters for the next three months.

Back home, there was a spectacular bit of pleasantness just after the start of the term: Frye's acceptance of a top cultural award in Canada, the Royal Bank Award. While the award garnered a cheque for $50,000 and a gold medal, the real joy was to be able to invite three hundred of his closest friends and students like Margaret Atwood as well as associates and even political celebrities to a formal banquet at the Royal York Hotel. This was an unimaginable luxury. Frye dressed up in requisite tuxedo with silk lapels and bow tie, and gave a speech so popular that photocopies had to be hurriedly made up and sent out.

Soon after, the man who had once so mercilessly ribbed Victoria College brass hats, particularly E.W. Wallace, stepped into Wallace's shoes as the Chancellor of Victoria. Although he clearly recognized the largely ceremonial nature of the job, he hoped that he could use some of his authority in the outside world to protect the identity and integrity of Victoria College within the university itself. Despite the shimmering full-length robe put on his shoulders during the Convocation Hall ceremony, which *The Varsity* coyly called a "gold lamé number," the photos taken at the ceremony hardly show an emperor. A *Varsity* photo shows him smiling with conspiratorial sheepishness.

Frye milked the incongruity himself. Nearly a half-century after writing the Bob Review, he was proud that the full authority of his office finally allowed a few bottles of ordinary Canadian ale to be placed in the refrigerator of the hallowed Methodist Burwash Hall so that staff members could indulge at noon. His chancellorship corresponded with a relaxing of his own shyness and formality. At High Table after he'd downed a Molson's ale himself, he was freer with junior staff members. He became the resident folklorist who dredged up anecdotes about Senior Common Room codgers of the 30s. He vividly remembered de Beaumont, who used to take out his frustrations with the SCR's stiff ecclesiastical furniture by cursing the chairs and roughly kicking and manhandling one or other of them across the room.

Exactly a week after his investiture, he gave a lecture on Castiglione, "Courtiers in a World without Courts: Castiglione and Twentieth Century Education," at Vic. He was asked by a flamboyant Vicenza native, Francesca Valente, a co-translator of the Italian *Fearful Symmetry*, who was then based at the nearby Italian Cultural Institute to come to Italy to lecture in the major universities. While the idea was not new to Frye—who had suspected Amleto Lorenzini of concocting a similar scheme before—he surprised Valente by agreeing immediately.

Unlike North America, where university-based literary intellectuals are still isolated and regarded with suspicion, those of France and Italy, like Roland Barthès and Umberto Eco, are celebrities, living in a world of popular intellectualism. To Italian intellectuals, Frye was simply another major contemporary literary thinker. While his ideas were not universally acclaimed, over a third of his books had been translated into Italian. What this meant, of course, was that Italy, unlike Japan and New Zealand, would be a merciless round of meetings, interviews and lectures. Fortunately Frye's speeches, an elaboration of his ideas on *The Tempest* and Castiglione's *The Courtier* would involve no great effort. A third theme, Literature and Myth, was of course instantly deliverable. Contentedly, Frye hoped to revisit his favorite cities of Pisa and Siena, which he and Helen hadn't seen since 1939.

Unfortunately, like a ghost he thought he had exorcised, the Bible book emerged once more, and genuinely spooked Frye for the next year and a half. At first he made a point of sounding philosophical about it and amiably groused that it "was taking all my time and energy" and that he really didn't know when it would be finished because he had to wait, not always patiently, for it to take its own shape. This was more brave than accurate. His hatred for the book was now palpable. In visiting his Oxford friend, Tom Allen, for lunch in Peterborough after an important appearance at

Trent University in January, he downed a double scotch and gloomily cursed it.

He now realized he had to break the manuscript up. Before
departing for Italy in May, he had his contract formally rewritten
to include two volumes: "Work #1: The Bible and Literature" and
"Work #2: Untitled Collateral Study." Months before he had
predicted he might be able to finish the first volume so quickly, it
could come out within the year.

## FRYE THE CONQUEROR

Frye was now very close to the formulations which would fill up
the first chapters of *The Great Code*. In his speech in January 1979
at Trent University, he outlined three stages of language: the
metaphorical, the abstract and the passive descriptive. He was
particularly eager to stress "the fact that society is best off when
all three phases of language are being used." He repeated his ideas
in mid-March at Emory and Henry College, Virginia, where he
admitted this Viconian scheme of hieroglyphic, hieratic and
demotic language was dubious as an historical model but handy
for looking at the way language fundamentally works. He was most
interested, of course, in the metaphorical level of language. He
mentioned its inherent alliance with magic where "a word is a
word of power." The importance of the Bible was that it was
centred in the first phase: "Most of the prose of the Bible is
oratorical prose, and oratory is the aspect of prose that is closest
to the metaphorical, magical approach to words, because the intention in oratory is to act on an audience and affect them by the
power of words." The primary function of literature, after all, was
"to recreate the original, primary, magical, and metaphorical use
of language." Never really buoyant at Emory and Henry, Frye
came back exhausted. As he now often did after trips he felt drained
and fluish. He nevertheless put himself back on the circuit again
refining his ideas in colleges in Fayetteville, Arkansas and Cedar

Rapids, Iowa. His theoretical ideas were now very close to the first chapter of *The Great Code*.

Unfortunately, the Italian trip now loomed, and he once more had to lay down his work. Despite initial hostility, his Italian tour was starting to generate genuine excitement in academic circles. Jane, who was desperate to get Frye back in one piece to work for three solid months on the Bible book, tried vainly to control the damage. She had insisted that the Fryes have three days to rest after arriving, only to find that the sponsors had set up a panel discussion the very first full day he was to be in Milan and had even sent out invitations. She was confident she could get it cancelled but Frye as usual went ahead with it. One of her few successes was to cut out one city, Bologna, which ironically enough, was the centre of Canadian Studies in Italy.

The cause for the simmering excitement in Frye's visit was not wholly mysterious. Official cultural ties between Italy and Canada were a natural by-product of the immigration to Ontario and Quebec in the 50s of several hundreds of thousands of Italians, some of whom kept a foot in both countries. A program in Canadian studies at the University of Bologna helped feed a voracious graduate student interest in original thesis topics. As for the specific interest in Frye, he seemed to fit very neatly into the predominating interest in structuralism and semiology in university circles. By the time Frye arrived in Italy, seven of his books, including the *Anatomy* and the only foreign edition of *Fearful Symmetry* had already been translated into Italian.

In Milan, in fact, Frye was taken out to dinner by an admiring Bologna-based semiologist by the name of Umberto Eco representing the journal *alfabeta*. While Eco had consulted with his fellow editors about appropriate questions, the "interview" itself was an impromptu performance. Far from thrusting a microphone in his face, Eco took Frye out to dinner and scribbled out questions on a napkin for Frye to answer later based on the recently translated *The Secular Scripture*. Eco himself was just a half-year away from finishing the phenomenally successful *The Name of the Rose*, and his non-fictional *Postscript* showed some interesting echoes from Frye's book.

After Milan, Frye gave three basic speeches, "Myth and Litera-ture" in Florence and Padua, "The Tempest" in Vicenza and "Cas-tiglione's Courtier" in Venice and Urbino. His audiences were wildly variable, from a high school audience at the Accademia Olimpico in Vicenza to the ominously named Circolo Filologico Patavino of the Instituto de Filologia Neo-Latina in Padua. He was so entranced with the knowledge and enthusiasm of the students at the former, that he had a rare sense of a true symposium unfolding. In Urbino, Frye was "in something of a dream state." While he didn't *quite* lecture on Castiglione in the Ducal palace itself, he did lecture in the Aula Magna of the Palazzo Bonaventura.

Besides a folder full of admiring newspaper profiles in many of the major national papers, he garnered the ultimate publicity: a TV show, produced in Florence by the national broadcasting net-work RAI, as one of the most influential personalities of the century. Immensely ironic after the TVOntario debacle, it showed him strolling down the medieval streets. The trip took its toll. After Vicenza, Francesca drove the Fryes in her family car from city to city through a hot Italian landscape which seemed to know no true *primavera*. Valente was almost too good, too efficient in setting up interviews, and by Rome Frye was exhausted and a little perturbed that there was no free time to see his beloved Pisa and Siena. Nevertheless, the Canadian cultural attaché, David Anido, who noted Frye's failing energy, suspected that few Italians would have particularly noted his exhaustion.

In Rome, Frye did not appear to have much to do except give one lecture in a small out-of-the-way theatre. There was nothing more than the odd banquet and resting. Settling into the Albergo Raphael on a little piazza off the Piazza Navona, he was, however, swept up by the Canadian community. Photographer Roloff Beny showed off the "Mussolini Mod" decor of his three-tiered "Tiber Terrace" on the Lungotevere Ripa overlooking the Forum on one side and St. Peter's on the other. He tried two shots of Frye. One had Frye standing in profile like a Caesar with arts bureaucrat Sergio Romano imperially towering over him against a red drape. Although Beny fussed and claimed he couldn't take a photo outside of someone with such strong features, he also took a stern solo shot of Frye sitting alone at a table outside on the terrace, holding a copy of *Fearful Symmetry*.

Frye also spent a fair bit of time with the director of the Canadian Cultural Institute, one-time English lecturer Gilbert Reid, whose home on Via Panico overlooked Hadrian's Tomb. Over dinner on a warm evening, Frye surprised Reid by his knowledge of Bachelard and his contention that he himself was "better known in Italy than perhaps anywhere else." By coincidence the Institute of Scientific Information in Philadelphia was at that very moment preparing a study, "Most-Cited Authors in the Arts and Humanities 1977-8" which discovered that in 150,000 items containing 900,000 citations, Frye stood eighth behind Marx, Aristotle, Shakespeare, Lenin, Plato, Freud and Roland Barthès. Furthermore, among the most cited works of authors born in the 20th century, the *Anatomy* stood first. Frye, of course, didn't know about this, but his obdurate sense of isolation in North America was clearly fed by the lack of *personal* warmth for himself as thinker which the Italians freely offered.

As Reid was also eager for good copy for a new magazine, *Canada Contemporaneo*, he fortuitously landed an interview with Frye. It was obvious that the Bible book dominated Frye's thought and he revealed yet more of its potentially evangelical scope. "I was brought up in a philistine tradition in which literature was considered a luxury, something you could do without ... I have decided to study the original function of literature and see what literature can still do for us ... Literature can in my opinion help us to discover, behind the various facades, the real origin and structure of imagination and as consequently also commitment and faith." Repeating his idea that language and consequently the Bible sprang from a metaphorical stage, he suggested its unceasing power: "Literature re-creates the metaphorical function of language continuously."

As at Harvard in 1975, the exhilaration of the trip was followed by a hangover. Because a DC-10 Jumbo jet fell out of the sky over Chicago on May 25, the Fryes' return was complicated by the grounding of DC-10 jets everywhere. This added to the accumulated exhaustion of the Italian tour. Faced too with pressure from

Harcourt to finish his manuscript by the end of the summer, Frye
decided to hide in his attic and have Jane refuse all requests for
appearances and interviews. Through an earlier commitment to
William French of *The Globe and Mail*, he went through a lunch
interview which resulted in the only Canadian article about his
trip, "Frye the conquerer wows them in Italy." He let slip a
suggestion of bitterness in his realization that the Italians seemed
"to treat me as a writer ... not as a scholar or critic." Ironically this
article generated a great deal of interest in the Canadian media
which had been caught napping on the Frye trip. When the CBC
called, Jane said that Frye was out of the country and had no idea
when he'd be back. When the CBC man thought the French
column suggested the opposite, Jane shot back, "Well, he was back
but now he's gone again."

Three weeks later, however, both the Fryes were still groggy
from the trip. Frye managed only 20 new pages and confessed to
"stage fright" over the book fearing it would be an anticlimax after
all the fuss over it. By the end of July he was more confident about
finishing much of the first volume. He felt it was best to ignore his
notes and get writing. With the school year upon him, he once
again realized that it would be impossible to finish it.

Frye even started competing against himself in another medium.
Bob Sandler, who'd been disturbed by the failure of the TVO
project, was now videotaping Frye's Bible course as potential base
stock for a Frye Bible TV series. Frye agreed to do it only if it
would not interrupt the class. In room 39 in Old Vic, where he
taught the course in the late 40s, there was now a Hitachi SK-80A
color video recorder aimed at him from mid-class. He was wired
up with a microphone, and, while the cord was long, he seemed
to feel reined-in. At the end of the first class, he murderously
fumbled with it, and asked a technician how "the f ... king thing"
came off. Despite a large class and the need to perform, he didn't.
Compared to his undergraduate Shakespeare course, his delivery
through much of the year was flat and wary. His head was cocked
back and immobile, a sea of green blackboard behind. Everything
indicated a tired man weary of untamed material. Because Sandler
was around at mid-day, he also decided to audiotape Frye's Shake-

speare course with the intention of preparing a general-audience book. This was the first time Frye had ever worked this way, but as long as Sandler was willing to do it, he saw it as a relatively painless way of producing his first popular book on Shakespeare which appeared in 1986 as *Northrop Frye on Shakespeare*.

Despite the interruptions of the term which invariably stopped work on any of his books, Jane expected that she would be busy handling new and revised manuscript all fall. Paul Corbett passed the news of the extra delay on to Julian Muller in New York with a protective rider that "this is not dalliance; he is labouring mightily." This time buying, however, did not soothe Frye himself and he was soon exhibiting real alarm when asked about its completion. Although he was travelling less, he was adamant about refusing all invitations for nearly a year. Since no one had looked at his manuscript or followed the vast expansion of his ideas over the 70s, no one understood his problems. How after all could Northrop Frye be going down to defeat on a subject so close to him for forty years?

In the next half year, there was little to allay suspicions that Frye wasn't battling panic. On a grey blustery day at the end of October, he delivered the inaugural Leland B. Jacobs Lecture at Columbia University on children's literature sponsored in part by Glenna Davis Sloan. In a dingy auditorium with seats spilling their stuffing, Frye spoke like a guru in a mad rush of ideas which no one followed. His speech was so disjointed that when he saw the verbatim transcription, he agreed to rewrite it completely. The central concern now fuelling the Bible was clear. The function of literature was "to recreate the primitive conception of the word of power, the metaphor that unites the subject and the object."

Frye was rattled by his speech. At the reception, with requisite sugared peanuts and white wine in plastic cups, he was unsettled. The press of the crowd managed to sweep him from the middle of the room into the safety of a space by the wall between the arm of a chair and a sofa table. Still, he received people, often like a cardinal giving a blessing. When he settled for dinner into a sofa in the Riverside Dr. co-op apartment of one of the organizers, he asked with jocular insistence for "Scotch and more Scotch." Frye later settled down beside Ron Campbell for a very earnest tête-à-tête about the problems of *The Great Code* manuscript. Like most people who believed it should have been an effortless operation, Campbell had been baffled by Frye's inability to finish his book. A week later, Frye wrote Paul Corbett reporting that his biggest problem was marking the line between the first and second volumes of the book. Because of his uncommon mix of theological interest and editing skill, Campbell seemed ideal as a consulting editor, which he considered he needed "badly." If it were to be an official Harcourt arrangement, Corbett was against the idea and Frye understood that Campbell would be in a conflict of interest.

## THE GREAT CODE

The sense of anxiety about Frye's progress was deepened when he started his Larkin-Stuart lectures, "Creation and Recreation" in January 1980. He delivered them to a packed audience in a grungy auditorium at the College of Education on Bloor St. and the free entry tickets went as fast as those for a hot musical. Despite the anticipation, Frye was oddly defensive right from start, declaring unnecessarily he was "not offering a rehash of lecture notes." Reading quickly from a typed copy of his speech, Frye had no real sense of the confusion of the audience who sat throughout for the most part shell-shocked by the quickly changing currents of the lectures.

As a bricolage of ideas and attitudes, the three speeches failed to develop a strong theme. Despite the fact that Jane coined them his "Bible lectures," they intimated little about his forthcoming book until the third lecture, in which Frye emphasized the importance of archaic language, which connoted process, over the rationalistic separation of subject and object. Borrowing from Buckminster Fuller, Frye suggested that perhaps God was a verb, "not simply a verb of asserted existence but a verb expressing a process fulfilling itself." The point was that while a mysterious unknowable God created nature, man reverses or neutralizes the sense of *the* creation through "decreation." Because it is mimetic, artistic realism cannot be of much help since bald reality has never offered much to man. Naturally, Frye recalled Oscar Wilde's excoriation of Zola.

This first step of decreation is followed by an analogous re-creation. Although the title promised an elucidation of Frye's obsession with the regenerated image, the remaking of old litera-ture, Frye at first walked around the possibly unanswerable on the softest of slippers. He touched on typology, the extension of *figura* through time, new events and people repeating, but also amplifying or giving meaning, to the past. This was not a mechanical process because of the "faith, hope, and vision" which promised to over-come calamity through a symbolic channelling and re-enactment of desirable ends. Baptism for example reflected but mitigated the Flood.

With the tiniest mention of typology in science fiction, he retreated to Milton, wondering why "so very great a poet" went in "the direction of retelling the story of creation." Frye put it in terms of possession: " ... the story of creation functions as a type or model of that inner state of mind in which Adam, at the end of the poem, begins the long climb up towards his original home again. Eden as an external environment disappears, to reappear as the 'paradise within thee, happier far' ..." The ideal reader of *Paradise Lost* is "the reader of the Bible, the person who under-stands it and possesses what Milton called the word of God in the heart." This obviously involved something which was already there, the implanted word of the Epistle of James 1:21. While this was a good, if tautological, answer, it begged the question of how far it went for all literature beyond Milton or Blake.

If anything came out of these raw but interesting lectures, it was that it most fully revealed the Frye that Bloom thought counted, the Romantic. Oscar Wilde suddenly becomes "one of our few genuinely prophetic writers." He saw the image of Noah's Ark all through the 19th century "bearing the whole surviving life of a world struggling to keep afloat in a universal storm." Although Frye didn't note if Noah was still in the ark, the book showed him struggling to raise typological issues with a contemporary audience which little understood the need for a Noah.

While Frye did not expect that the lectures would be published, Ian Montagnes of the University of Toronto Press phoned and suggested the possibility. Frye demurred then accepted, hoping that publication might serve as a prod for the big work. The University of Toronto Press moved so fast on them, that the editors barely seemed to look at them. They appeared in paperback form in August to no great attention, public or critical.

At the start of 1980 in fact it did look like Frye needed a boost. He admitted such slow progress on the Bible book generally, he even darkly joked that it had become "a consuming neurosis, rather like the building of the Canadian Pacific Railway at an earlier stage in Canadian culture." But once he cleared away the Larkin-Stuart lectures, he finally did get down to sock out a full manuscript of the first volume of *The Great Code*. Jane, who had learned word processing, sat in a glass-surrounded office off the stairwell of the New Academic Building and entered the manuscript into a University of Toronto mainframe computer. By early September she was able to produce a print-out of a manuscript which was substantially the final version. By early December, he was able to send the manuscript off to Harcourt, over eight years past deadline.

Frye loaded the early part of the book with all his theoretical obsession over the power of poetic language and its importance in balancing rational thought. Harcourt editors were concerned by Frye's heavily theoretical treatment, thinking correctly that it might lose all but the most determined readers right away. Frye felt that this might be to the good and wanted the book left as it was, with the exception of a few changes.

One of the great ironies was that after ten years of struggling with wider implications, Frye still believed that "the crux of the book" lay in chapters Six and Seven, which consisted of the material he had taught in his undergrad Bible lectures. For his former students, this was the most recognizable part of the book and seemed to say everything essential. As usual there was a simple direct image. Revelation is the "epitome" of the Bible's imagery as the Book of Job was the epitome of its narrative. Like the Bible itself, the story of Job is a comedy, which takes in all phases of the Bible, through creation and fall, wisdom and prophecy which brings us "to the final vision of presence and the knowledge that in the midst of death we are in life."

When the last of the manuscript went to Harcourt in New York, Frye then started preparing for The Tamblyn Lectures at the University of Western Ontario in March. In the lectures Frye found himself back in Shakespearean comedy, where he again pointed out the improbability of the comic plot, making marriages through bed tricks and other felicitous nonsense, amplified by great long recognition scenes which *only* happen in plays. Taking three "problem" comedies, *Measure for Measure*, *All's Well that Ends Well* and *Troilus and Cressida*, Frye suggested a bridge from the earlier comedies to the later romances through the recognition scenes, which lead to a final climax of "a vision of deliverance or expanded energy and freedom." Because of its message, it's a *socially* redemptive process: "... Eros triumphs over Nomos or law, by evading what is frustrating or absurd in law and fulfilling what is essential for social survival." By deliberately choosing "problem" comedies, Frye seemed eager to test the validity of his notions on the complicated borderlands where comedy joined irony and tragedy.

Although he had to do a bit of cut and splice, noting for example how *Measure for Measure* has an unmitigated ironic first half followed by a comedic second half, he was faced with a *real* problem comedy in *Troilus and Cressida* which seemed to combine a muddy concatenation of history, comedy, romance and tragedy. He evaded the question by detouring through the *Aeneid* and *Orlando Furioso* and finally solved the problem in a couple of paragraphs. As comedy promulgated a myth of deliverance, the crucial first step towards deliverance was the disillusionment with the way things are. *Troilus and Cressida* offers an illusory reality which the playwright attempts to reverse: " ... this play is about us, if not the aspect of us that we want to put on exhibition."

The final point is possession, "the last recognition, the incorporating of the play into our own creative lives and traditions."

Seizing on a couple of lines invariably excised in theatre productions of *The Tempest*, Frye had us take Prospero's island home with us as an apple and plant the seeds in our own lives and those of our children. As a result, "Prospero the dramatist practises a more credible and more useful art, the art of waking up of what is dead or sleeping within us, like Hermione stirring with Julio Romano's statue and responding to Paulina's challenge of 'Be stone no more.'"

For the summer, the Fryes had hoped to return to Japan for an extended vacation but the editing, then the horrendous production problems of *The Great Code* intervened. Everything that could possibly could go wrong did go wrong. The initial theory was extravagantly promising. The golden words of Frye would go straight onto computer tape and be directly typeset by the University of Toronto Press. Everything would be handed over from Toronto to New York in camera-ready pages for printing. At the end of May, Frye received his copy-edited manuscript back from New York. Harcourt editors hadn't understood that Northrop Frye was the only one to decide what is right for his style. Frye restored some 300 stylistic changes. In early July, Jane produced a new version of the manuscript and, during a Canadian postal strike, sent it back by a large but unreliable courier service which promptly lost it for ten days *en route* in Buffalo. Jane had to make furious phone calls to get the courier to track it down. Instead of sending correctable galleys, the University of Toronto Press sent Harcourt repros, the final version of set copy. Exasperated, Harcourt produced its own version patching material together according to need, hiring a freelance layout artist for three weeks to work up a paste-up. Still chasing its own dream, the UTP got set to run off a new version on a machine which promptly broke down. Finally, Harcourt finished its own version which simply vanished on its way to the printing plant in Binghampton in upper-state New York. A disbelieving Harcourt manager reported, "This was extraordinary. It hasn't happened twice in a quarter century!" The whole book then had to be reset the conventional way. As a result new mistakes were made in the reference section, which infuriated Frye who did not see the final proof.

The rumors about screw-ups, mostly inaccurate, were invariably more interesting than the facts. Jane's loss of a chapter on her master tape (easily recovered on a copy) became transformed into the loss of a whole tape which was supposed to have tumbled unseen behind her filing cabinet. The fact that the University of Toronto Press was having serious technical problems got translated into a demonological theory that the press was sabotaging it because it didn't get either to publish or print the book. The seed of this rumor may have been the University of Toronto Press which attempted to act as agent for the book in Canada, a request which baffled Frye and everyone at Harcourt. And, in the area of complete fantasy, wasn't it logical that the Prince of Darkness himself wanted to stop a book which laid open the heart of the Bible? The problems turned Jane from private secretary into virtual managing editor mediating difficulties between uncommunicative and sometimes bitterly hostile supervisors in Toronto and New York. The affair got so messy, it even hit the Toronto papers in mid-November. The media of course was enlivened by a situation in which a book called *The Great Code* was apparently trashing complicated computer hardware like an extremely nasty "trojan horse" program.

Although Jane prided herself on keeping Frye isolated from the fray, Frye knew exactly what was going on but was naturally mystified as to how he could help sort out the mess. Generally he kept the lowest possible profile all year. He spoke on bland topics, like "Criticism and Environment," which seemed unrelated to *The Great Code*. He made little obvious progress on the second volume. He even seemed unexcited by its impending publication. Just as he had for *Fearful Symmetry*, he was rather unimpressed with its complexity, calling it "relatively elementary and introductory." In a newspaper profile, he even appeared to be preparing readers for the possibility of eccentricity and failure. *The Great Code*, he said, was "unscholarly." "People will have to make out of it what they can."

There was a certain weariness about the whole subject which permeated the filming of Frye's Bible series which was now produced as a huge package of thirty programs with teacher guides.

Bob Sandler and the U of T Media Centre had refilmed Frye's Bible lectures once more on a new tape format. In the late summer, Sandler directed Frye through the introductions and seminar discussions for each theme. As a result, every so often that summer, the upper library of Massey was filled with klieg lights and an earnest production crew of technicians and the requisite bored script assistant. With a headphone-microphone headset, Sandler nervously tried to generate an emotional spark into the discussions. While invariably from the University of Toronto community the "students" were not always bona fide graduate students. They were well-scrubbed and mesmerized by the Occasion and the Man. Frye often gave his glum I'd-rather-be-home-writing look and seemed unable to fill Sandler's gentle demands for an emotionally more vibrant retake.

Normally in Canada, authors' personalities are mercilessly flogged in the service of their new books. They are forced into planes and taken across the country through a wearying round of radio and TV interviews and book-signings in major centres to boost sales. Frye, however, was not even interested in signing copies in local bookstores and his publisher's publicist, a former student, never pressed him. Because the book hit the market at a time everyone was eager to acquire a Frye ikon, it did not need the personal touch. Frye was nearly a household word. His name was even mentioned in a roll-call of famous Canadians on the lowbrow Wayne and Schuster comedy hour on national TV. There was also a pent-up demand among Canadian intellectuals who had heard of *The Great Code* for nearly a decade. This was combined with the demand of thousands of Victoria College graduates who had audited or enrolled in Frye's courses over four decades.

All of this was in turn fuelled by a cover story on Frye in May 1982 in the national newsmagazine *Maclean's* which enjoys a 600,000 circulation. The profile was even condensed and reprinted for the lowbrow Canadian *Reader's Digest*. The *Maclean's* cover photo showed Frye with stereotyped pill-box hat and ceremonial red hood draping his shoulders. There is a squint, almost glower on his face, occasioned not so much by deep thought as by caution over the photographer's moving in too close for the shot. Inside, the lead editorial by Peter Newman, the feature profile by Mark Czarnecki and the book review, were paeans by former Victoria College students, a benevolent conspiracy perhaps. The photos inside were revelatory of both Frye's past and present. One page featured a shot of the old college building rising above grimy snowy banks. Facing this was a photo of Frye in plain winter coat, cradling a copy of his new book. His tie was askew and his hair, now a mixture of brown and grey, was as long as it was when he was an undergrad. Frye looked like a veteran frontier preacher poised like Peter Cartwright to bring the Word to the masses.

Certainly in terms of sales, there was an immensely eager audience. When it finally appeared, a decade late, in the first week of April, the two academic bookstores near the University of Toronto, the SCM Bookstore and the Bob Miller Bookroom couldn't keep the book in stock. Bob Miller reported selling a hundred copies in the first week alone. By the third week in April, *The Great Code* jumped in a single leap to fifth place on the non-fiction list of the nationally surveyed "Maclean's Bestseller List." The first printing of 3,500, backed by an advance sale of 1,600, sold out quickly and Academic Press went back to press with three consecutive printings, each time pleasantly confusing Paul Corbett who didn't know where it might end. Through most of May and early June it was in fourth place and moved up quickly to second place in late June and stayed there until August, failing to dislodge its curious rival, *Jane Fonda's Workout Book*. It dropped a place until November 1, and then with the pressure of new Christmas season books, it quickly slipped off the list after eight months, going into healthy paperback sales. By the end of the year, Academic Press Canada reported sales in the first months of 8,769 with nearly 6,000 to year's end for a total of nearly 15,000 in the small Canadian market. There was something special about this particular book: the Great Code video series bombed and Frye's new collection of essays in July, *Divisions on a Ground*, slipped by without much notice.

After the years of struggle, Frye once more saw himself acting as simply as a puppy who'd broken some crockery and was scurrying away. He was more scatalogical later when he confessed that half of the first volume "had been on my mind so long that it was obsessive; just really to be excreted, to be dumped. The other half were things that were really coming in, and were new in my mind." Not only was he delivered of a ten years' struggle, he had at last produced another major book for critics to worry about. Despite his description of Frye's speculative linguisitic theories as "moonshine," Charles Wheeler allowed that Frye was still the northern giant, the Polaris of criticism. His amiable adversary Frank Kermode, went further by admitting the "return of the sensations I experienced when reviewing *Anatomy* twenty-five years ago." Hardly a fawning admirer, Kermode put Frye in the class of a "founder of a religion, a Swedenborg or a Marx," admitting that "the driving force of this amazing book is more mystical than skeptical. It is Frye's own antitype of the Bible; it ignores the improvisations of centurios of faith and doubt, and sets up its mirror before the Bible itself, as it really is or seems to be."

Like the sales, the critical reaction was immediate and extravagantly varied and widespread. Over 150 reviews, notices and review articles appeared, all the way from the *New York Times Book Review* on the book's publication date, April 12, to the back pages of obscure theological journals. In terms of widest attention it was probably Hugh Kenner's *Times* review which was decisive, but like the *Maclean's* pieces, it was amiable and rambling and not too critical. Kenner expressed relief that the book was not so structured as earlier tomes. He accepted Frye's basic thesis that the Bible is "our paradigm of all linguistic working, all interpretive challenge." But the impact was engaging and personal: the book had held his attention for two hours in the decrepit Newark train station.

At the other pole, there was the savage, uncomfortably close, reaction of Vic philosophy professor Francis Sparshott who, picking up on Frye's own previous self-criticism, called it "appallingly bad" for an academic tome. Brutally accusing Frye of writing "an old man's book," Sparshott then picked at the nerve by refusing to decide what kind of an old man's book it was, a sad memorial to an old reputation or an outline of an author's new world which was so private, many would decline to enter. Sparshott failed to find much of anything of note and particularly abused the book's central pretension "that reading the Bible is important, let alone essential, to the understanding of literature."

Although none were so brutal as this, there was a pervasive grouchiness among critics including even longtime admirers like Eli Mandel. Mandel's review, "Tautology as Truth and Vision," made a major point simply in the title. The tautological aspect was certainly evident in the expressed "double mirror" form of the book. Frye meant the two testaments reflected each other but there is the obvious implication of a sealed world of image which didn't see the world. The suspicion of such sterility compounded with the criticism of Charles Wheeler in *The South Atlantic Review* that "with the method of the kaleidoscope" the book was ultimately "tiresomely exhibitionistic": "Each shake of the machine produces a new symmetry ... there is always room for one more shake."

There was also a suspicion of a hidden agenda, "a powerful aura of something covert and withheld" which Louis Dudek and many others sensed. For some, it was the lurking bogey of religion. Dudek congratulated himself that he'd sniffed out Frye's "veiled Christianity" before. Frye was rather baffled by this conspiratorial theory. In an interview he said, "I wasn't out with a butterfly net to catch people's souls." Because of the "inexhaustible interest from a purely secular point of view," Frye said he "wanted to make it something that any cultivated person would normally take an interest in." For others the feeling was more generally applied. Mandel complained of "a curious sense of restraint that leaves the reader with the feeling that the final revelation has been deliberately withheld." Because it exerted an enormous demand for apocalyptic fireworks in the promised volume two, this was in some ways the most difficult of criticisms for Frye. The man apparently had no right to rest.

At the year's end, *The Great Code* was inevitably gathered up as a top candidate for the non-fiction category of the Governor General's Award. Since Frye had never won the award, he was a sentimental favorite and easily made the published short list the following May. Once again, however, kippers had the day, and Christopher Moore's *Louisbourg Portraits* won. Facing the inevitable outrage, the awards chairman, historian J.L. Granatstein, was defensive but unrepentant. While acknowledging the book was a "seminal" work by a "luminary of Canadian scholarship," Granatstein simply pointed out that it was no contest. His jury was unanimous for Moore. It was a bruisingly ironic reversal of Frye's own jury pressure-tactics to force a win for McLuhan's *Gutenburg Galaxy* twenty years before.

## WORDS WITH POWER

Despite the great popular success and an almost feverish amount of attention (135 reviews by the end of 1984) for the first volume of *The Great Code*, Frye started an early introduction to Volume Two with almost squeamish apologies. He considered his first volume "a kind of incubus to be got rid of ... a very vulnerable book." Assuming it was an almost obsessional, idiosyncratic book, he expressed relief that he was not more thoroughly drubbed by hostile critics. Nevertheless, he ostensibly started writing the second volume, as promised, on "the way in which the narrative and images of the Bible have infiltrated, so to speak, the later literary tradition ..." The original intent of the project, the promulgation of the power of metaphorical thinking, was also apparently intact.

At the same time, he was more cautious in pulling away from the magical-metaphorical assumptions that had put him too far out on the limb of necromancy. After a quarter century of using them, Frye finally admitted to the "pitfalls in the magical use of words:" "[the arts] do not work by magic, and are not mind-altering drugs: they cannot make people 'better' unless there is already a reasoning will to be made better." In naming his new manuscript he acknowledged this by making a small but crucial change of preposition. His key *Great Code* phrase "words of power" became "words with power" from the King James rendering of Luke 4:32.

On the face of it, Frye was nicely pressing ahead, addressing the critical demand that he show how the total form and imagery of the Bible lay behind the full extent of western literature. But he had a different idea of managing this than anyone could have imagined. Instead of surveying the apocalyptic array of "concrete" symbols redolent of everyday life, the images of city, mountain, river, garden, tree, oil, and so on, he more radically focussed on another complex of symbols, the artificial "verticals of Adam," the tower, ladder, winding staircase which symbolize man's efforts in both poetry and religion to work up and down the cosmology which lies behind and shapes all his thought patterns. In three essays between Oct. 1983 and June 1985, Frye indefatigably listed the staircases and spiral towers which ran through Egyptian and Persian myth to the Bible, thence to Dante, Milton, Eliot, Yeats, Pound and Joyce. This was an anthropology of symbolism which emphasized iconographic literature which possessed a lot of convenient stairways and towers. Their significance, however, was manifestly important: " ... the interest of modern poets in ladders and spirals is not nostalgia for outmoded images of creation, but a realization that such images stand for intensifying of consciousness through words, and so represent the concern of concerns, so to speak, the consciousness of consciousness."

Pared down, these images revealed the *axis mundi*, the pole which connected the levels of man's traditional cosmology, his underworld, his everyday reality, his ideal world and heaven. Simply, it was the vertical line in the quartered circle of the wheel. Frye was delighted to announce its usefulness simply because it *was* purely artificial. Outside the imagination, there'd never been an *axis mundi*. Repudiating Wallace Stevens's hope for "the great poem of earth" to counterbalance those of heaven and hell, Frye added, "It is not likely to be, as it seems entirely impossible to write a great poem of earth without reference to ascending and descending movements to what have to be metaphorically different worlds."

In his 1983 and 1984 addresses, "Romance as the Survival of Eros," "Repetitions of Jacob's Dream" and "The Koine of Myth: Myth as a Universally Intelligible Language," there was every indication that Frye was simply returning to the approach of the major essays on Milton and Yeats he published in *The Stubborn*

*Structure* in the late 60s. At that time he claimed that the essays were the basis of a new book on symbol clusters but since 1969, this project appeared only faintly in *The Secular Scripture* in the rather constricted area of Victorian sentimental romance. Now, clearly, he was dusting off the total conception without much regard to the preponderant weight of *The Great Code* themes. Ironically, the unrelenting critic of the counterculture recalled "the hopes and dreams" of precisely a period which at least, he now wistfully conceded, made the metaphorical process more acceptable.

With Jane ready to go, newly trained on the Unix computer system, Frye seemed to make good progress in the summer of 1983, eventually producing some 76 pages with an introductory Chapter One, a Chapter Two called "The Cosmos of Authority" and a ten-page start to a Chapter Three called "The Great Good Place." But he stalled. He was now feeling the pressures of competing with himself. The first volume was sufficiently weighty, he felt he had to produce a hefty sequel. He also confessed to the basic affliction of old age. There was no lack of ideas, only the necessary feverish ambition to sit down and make sense of a new panorama of ideas. He had started to suffer arthritis in his fingers which made hand-writing painful. He'd always composed his first drafts by hand, then typed cleaner copies later but now he had to experiment with composing on the typewriter.

Although it didn't affect his work particularly, Frye was discomfited by the creeping tendency at Vic to monumentalize him. It had started in the early 70s when a king-size portrait of him by Douglas Martin was raised high on the reading room wall of the Pratt Library, showing him sitting in the sky over a canyon. He looked like a bourgeois Jupiter sitting throneless with droopy socks. His pinched smirk was an unintentional reflection of his own self-consciousness. He relished someone's joke that the portrait showed Frye without visible means of support. His image loomed not only over innocent twenty-year-old students sweating over texts but even his own furtive self as he checked through cards in the adjoining card catalogue. As he admitted to a journalist, "One doesn't like to be turned into an ikon before one is dead."

Yet on June 3, 1983, the blandly named New Academic Building, where he spent much of his time working in his small third-floor corner office, was also renamed Northrop Frye Hall. At a ceremony attended by his own Class of '33, Frye and his classmate Laure Rièse cut the ribbon. A spot was cleared in the lobby for a new brass bust by Hanna Boos which was then unveiled in another ceremony in 1986. As this transpired, the University of Toronto was easing him out, requiring him to teach one less course a year until he would have none by the fall of 1987, then dithering as usual, authorizing him to continue his still popular Bible course. Jane, who daily had to contend with a pile of mail from abroad which was showing no signs of slowing, worried about how to stop the world once Frye was finally escorted into retirement. The world in fact blissfully ignored the possibility of his retiring. The Japanese in particular were developing such a strong interest in Frye, nearly half of his books was either translated or in the process of translation. The Italians were eager to have him back for a major conference.

Keeping an uncharacteristically clear appointments calendar all through the summer of 1984, Frye continued to work hard. As he headed into the school year, he expressed the hope of working out what was clear in his mind for Volume Two through the autumn and spring terms, then finishing up the following summer. Whatever work he managed, he had nothing to show to Jane for computer entry and she was starting to worry that a grant for computer time would run out. In the meantime, Bob Sandler's edited version of Frye's Shakespeare lectures had run into trouble at the University of Toronto Press which had sat on it for some time. Another firm, Fitzhenry and Whiteside, was interested in it but only if Frye reworked the fairly raw manuscript. The irony of course was that the book, which was to be effortless, managed to take up much of Frye's time and energies through the latter part of the summer of 1985.

As with *The Great Code*, Frye cloistered himself in his attic workroom and worked furiously on the manuscript. Beyond this stage there was no input from Sandler. Frye's insistence on the book's being "edited by Robert Sandler" was really a designation of thanks to Sandler for bringing the project that far along. The result was something which Frye had never before achieved, a genuine record of Frye the classroom lecturer. Here was a scholar who thought out loud, fleshing out complicated ideas with the kinds of direct examples often missing in his essays, even his formal lectures. In a sense it was Frye's first genuinely "practical" book aimed at his pristine *Anatomy* audience of intelligent 19-year-old undergraduates. It also faithfully followed Frye's irritating penchant for excluding index and notes.

Although critics strained to see either a pattern or abject lack of it in the choice of plays, the book in fact just followed Frye's share of the university's rather arbitrary syllabus which, for example, included *King Lear* and *Hamlet* but not *Macbeth*. Without drawing intimidating attention to them, Frye managed to slip in most of his career-long themes: informing antiquarian cosmology, the same old story, levels of nature, meaning, action and symbolism, levels of characterization, the cycle of seasons, colored time, historical degeneracy, the quest cycle and the wheel of fortune.

Frye thought the book unimportant, but he considered it at least a fair success in its genre. Most critics agreed. In an almost exact replay of *The Great Code*, however, criticism, which appeared in October 1986, ranged from adulatory to malicious. His perennial shadow, Robert Martin Adams, published an almost hysterical review in the *New York Review of Books*. Contrasting it unfavourably with Bradley's famous Shakespeare lecture book, Adams felt "not only regretful but embarrassed to report that the author of *Anatomy of Criticism* is hardly anywhere present in the new book." In the interjection of clear *Anatomy* themes, though, the *Anatomy* *was* everywhere. The book in fact recalled Frye's idea of a practical volume to back up the *Anatomy*.

More typical, fortunately, was the full-page spread of S. Schoenbaum in the *New York Times Book Review* who saw virtues precisely where Adams ground his teeth. While Adams savaged Frye's chatty style, for example, Schoenbaum welcomed it. While Adams thought it too directed to a simple audience of unwashed undergrads, Schoenbaum went so far as to suggest that "the sensibility and wisdom informing the book make it a delight for the expert too."

Although Frye did begin a new introduction to his Volume Two in the spring of 1986, he really didn't get very far with his writing. Again, with near indulgence, he planned to fill up much of the summer with a tour to Australian universities. The Fryes of course hoped to repeat the success of the earlier Pacific trip which had given them so much pleasure and relief from the pressures of both the Bible book and Helen's deteriorating health. Combining business with a vacation of their own, Jane and her husband Deryck planned to accompany them for much of the trip. Travelling via Vancouver and Honolulu, the Fryes flew on to Sydney for nearly a month of lectures and colloquia including a three-day "Northrop Frye Seminar" at the Australian National University at the end of June where Frye extemporaneously delivered a paper, "Myth: Metaphor and Reality," which was similar to his 1983 papers.

Once the work was over, the Fryes flew up to Cairns in Queensland to tour the popular Great Barrier Reef area. When Helen came off the five-hour flight from Sydney, however, she collapsed and had to be rushed to the hospital. She'd earlier noticed shortness of breath and her collapse proved to be the result of an embolism in the lungs. It appears that when older passengers, particularly overweight smokers, are unable to move around and get the circulatory system moving on long transoceanic flights, blood clots in the legs can break away and get trapped in the lungs where they can kill.

Deeply worried, Frye kept vigil at Helen's bedside through much of the daytime. When he realized that his open concern might be creating extra anxiety for Helen, he took an hour-and-half seaplane tour over the reefs at Jane's urging. Although semiconscious much of the time and unaware of where she was, Helen did try to alleviate the anguish. When her IV made an odd chirping sound when it ran out of fluid, she quipped, "Is that your pet cricket?" It was a small but crucial sign to her husband that in her last words to him, Helen's wit, and personality, remained intact.

Helen deteriorated the next morning, but the doctors assured Frye she would be stable enough for him to go out on a bus tour without worry. Frye went on the tour but suddenly at 3:10 pm felt an anguishing sense that her life had slipped away. When they returned to the hotel around 5:00 pm, he received the terrible news that she had died.

Extremely distraught, Frye sequestered himself in his hotel room. When Jane opened his curtains once to the brilliant sea and palms outside, he said she should close them again. Nature, he said, could never care about such a personal loss. With Jane, he flew home on one horrendously long 27-hour flight from Cairns through Honolulu and Los Angeles and stayed the weekend north of Toronto at the home of Jane and Deryck. For many months, Frye continued to fight depression. Jane became indispensible in setting up a part-time housekeeper and seeing that Frye settled into a new routine. A neighbour helped with a cold plate twice a week. He received a flood of condolence letters and felt it important to answer each one personally. He was able to come into work for a couple of hours to tend to correspondence, but was too distracted to make any progress on Volume Two. The college rallied with a memorial service in the Vic College chapel at the start of the school year. In the kind of socially adhesive ritual he often identified, Frye was surrounded by the community he now so personally needed, his Victoria College colleagues and old undergraduate friends. King Joblin read Frye's own memorial sketch of Helen and Art Moore delivered the sermon.

Just as he was recovering from the worst of his depression, Frye was again visited by major international attention. A once cancelled colloquium on his thought at Rome University went ahead at the end of May 1987 at the Villa Mirafiori in Via Carlo Fea. Twenty-six international scholars from Italy, Canada, Britain, and Denmark read papers at the end of the three-day symposium, called *Ritratto di Northrop Frye*. At the end, the gathered scholars stood up for an ovation to Frye. The Canadian media, which was caught napping on his 1979 visit, once more ignored a major Frye event. The Canadian Embassy, however, which had sponsored the conference, facilitated communications in the other direction, with early news that the Governor General's Award committee had finally seen fit to give Frye the non-fiction award for his 21st book, *Northrop Frye on Shakespeare*. Like a Hollywood actor clutching his first Oscar late in life, Frye wondered, of all his books, why *this* one.

Frye's only active contribution to the Rome conference was a speech, "Maps and Territories" which lamely hinted at the purpose but not the content of the now delayed Volume Two: "I ... still have hopes that I may be among those who will be studying over the next few years the inter-relations of education in words. Out of this study, I hope, would come something of a consensus on the social function and responsibilities of both poets and literary critics." There was a certain meekness here. A decade of the prevailing school of criticism, deconstructionism, had thoroughly unscrambled and demoralized the high purpose he'd confidently set for criticism forty years before. Naturally as much as he'd done as far back as 1933, Frye gave his perennial warning about distracting elements in criticism: "The real literal meaning of any verbal structure is to be sought in its own context, not in its relation to something outside it ... The false literal I identified with Paul's 'letter that kills', an infinity of signposts ..." His interest in the *axis mundi* now took on an especial significance. The *axis mundi* was uncompromisingly centripetal. It was a stark conductor of literary and philosophical energies, pulling a reader's mind through a layered cosmos of images.

Not long after Rome, Frye enjoyed perhaps the most delicious irony of his life, an honorary doctorate from Oxford, a month before his 75th birthday. It was his 35th honorary degree on a rather weighty list which now included Princeton, Chicago, Harvard, Columbia and Toronto. The unhappy Oxford inmate of the late 30s now saw himself given Oxford benediction. It was at Oxford too that he found his ideas starting to become less blocked by the trauma of Helen's death.

While Frye made a point of fighting reclusiveness, however, his climb from depression had still been difficult. For over a year, he had not worked well and his media interviews were bland, unoriginal, even listless. Conscious of his shaky morale, his close friends had made a point of keeping him socially active. For his

1987 Christmas present, Charles Heller, husband of his editor at Fitzhenry and Whiteside, Helen Heller, organized a concert in his honor at their home. A ten-singer chamber group, jokingly dubbed The Ad Hoc Singers, performed choral music, including the doctoral composition of his mentor, George Ross, "The Voice of the Wind," before Frye and a small group of friends.

It was his infallible ties with his graduating class of 1933, though, which set him firmly back on his feet. In the early 70s the Fryes started taking summer auto excursions to small Ontario resort and theatre towns like Blyth and Port Dover with former classmates. One of the key members of this group was Elizabeth Eedy Brown who'd first met Frye on registration day in 1929 when she was all of 16 and he two months over 17. Elizabeth, who later worked briefly in the 30s with Helen at the Toronto Art Gallery, had married James Brown and raised three children including writer Jamie Brown. Upbeat and forthright, she'd served as de facto home office secretary for her husband who was Member of Parliament for the Brantford riding for 15 years. Her husband had died in 1974 just after they retired.

In the spring of 1987, Elizabeth and Frye took a trip up into the Guelph, Elora and Elmira area. Possibly eager to forestall any rumors of romance or marriage, they acted like nothing more than a couple of old friends out for a little country excursion. They seemed carefully undemonstrative with each other. Even Elizabeth later admitted that while the thought was there, they themselves tended to skirt any direct question of marriage. In midsummer, though, they decided quite suddenly to throw caution aside. With just five days between decision and ceremony, it was the nearest thing to an elopement. They caught nearly everyone off guard. Jane and Deryck and many of their own friends and relatives, including two of Elizabeth's children, were away. They called one of their classmates Bob Bates down from his Muskoka cottage to officiate. In his living room, a few feet from his grand piano, Frye married again after 50 years, without music, fanfare or celebrity reception.

Frye's mood very much improved. Interviewed at Massey College in August by Bill Moyers of American Public Affairs Television, he appeared again in best form. Imperial in immaculately coiffed silver hair, he reminded Americans that there was, after all, a Canadian side to the border. Mildly but firmly he explained *why* the British had burned down the White House in the War of 1812. Moyers was excited and nervous throughout the interview and eagerly suggested doing a series with Frye analogous to his very successful series on myth with Joseph Campbell, "The Power of Myth," which had spawned a year-long bestselling book of the same name. The child of fundamentalism himself, Moyers was fascinated by the positive debt that people like himself and Frye owed to religion and wanted to explore this dimension.

There was a distinct turnaround in his work as well. In private Frye had talked uncertainly about Volume Two, now called *Words with Power*. He feared he might have to publish just a truncated first half. In late 1988, though, he plowed ahead and finished off a full eight chapters.

Throughout his career, he'd always recognized that he was the luckiest of men. He had almost always stepped through uncertainties and unhappiness to fulfil the work he had outlined with almost naive certainty decades before. Now it was perfectly clear how infallible was his fortune. Not only was he finishing off another major manuscript at age 76, he could confidentally say that in a world of radically changing literary criticism, he did not feel "wholly a member of an aging chorus either."

What he was offering, of course, was not the methodology of the 30s but a way into ever-present, ever continuing vision which survive the abrasions of time and scabrous ideology. As Frye reminds us in *The Tempest*, while the island may disappear, "when the magician leaves," the thought seeds can go back into the sea and "bring forth again the island that the world has been searching for since the dawn of history, the island that is both nature and human society restored to their original form, where there is no sovereignty and yet where all of us are kings."

## ACKNOWLEDGEMENTS

I would particularly like to thank Northrop Frye himself for having the courage and fortitude to put up with my seemingly interminable questions about every aspect of his life. Thanks of the highest order also go to his cousin Donald Howard for faithfully preserving letters from his Howard aunts, particularly Catharine Howard Frye, throughout his many moves among New England congregations in the 1930s. This material, now in the Victoria University Library, provides invaluable documentation about the Frye family in the 1929-1940 period. Another essential block of correspondence written by Frye himself in the 30s was graciously lent to me by the late Helen Kemp Frye. I later was able to use an important block of correspondence Mrs. Frye had sent her parents covering the 1947-1954 period. Charles Bell provided photocopies of relevant sections of his Oxford diaries, a copy of the only known photo of Frye in Oxford, as well as correspondence. Letters from Frye to George Johnston, in the Public Archives of Canada in Ottawa, were valuable for the period of the 1950s. David V. Erdman kindly sent me copies of correspondence concerning Frye's Blake-related activities and English Institute and MLA involvements in the 1950s and 1960s. James Nohrnberg also sent me material on Frye's advice and help in his own developing career in the late 1960s and 1970s. Two of Frye's publishers, Princeton University Press and

*The Hudson Review*, generously expended much effort in uncovering Frye-related correspondence.

Documentation for the 1960 to 1986 period is largely derived from Frye's office correspondence which emanated from his office at Massey College. Throughout the project, Frye's personal secretary since 1968, Jane Welch Widdicombe, cheerfully provided much assistance with office correspondence, unpublished manuscripts and other material. Letters from the 1960s to 1980s have now been transferred to the Victoria University library and been reorganized for research purposes. From his mountain home in southwestern Virginia, Frye's bibliographer, Robert Denham, was an unfailing source of difficult-to-obtain material about Frye's work. Denham's massively detailed *Northrop Frye: An Annotated Bibliography of Primary and Secondary Sources* was published in 1988 by the University of Toronto Press.

For their assistance with information and archival material, I would like to thank the following organizations:

Acadia University; Albert College; Archives Nationales du Québec, Sherbrooke; Art Gallery of Ontario; Bishop's University; Brandeis University; Brown University; Canada Council; Canadian Broadcasting Corporation; Carleton University; Western Reserve University; Claremont Colleges; Clarke, Irwin and Company; Columbia University; Concordia University; Cornell University; The Department of External Affairs, Ottawa; The Department of Consumer and Corporate Affairs, Ottawa; Emmanuel College, Victoria University; The English Institute; Georgetown University; Guelph Public Library; Harvard University; Haverford College; Indiana University; Institute for Scientific Information; John Simon Guggenheim Memorial Foundation; Kenyon College; Mary Washington College; McGill University; McMaster University; Michigan State University; Moncton Museum; Mount Allison University; National Council of Teachers of English; National Film Board of Canada; National Library of Scotland; New Brunswick Free Public Library, N.J.; New York Public Library; Ontario Archives; Osborne Collection of Early Children's Books, Toronto; Ottawa University; Princeton University; Provincial Archives of Alberta; Provincial Archives of New Brunswick; Public Archives

Canada, Ottawa; Queen's University; Royal Military College; Royal Ontario Museum; St. John's College, Annapolis; Saskatchewan Archives Board; Seminaire de Sherbrooke; Simon Fraser University; Smith College; La Societé d'histoire des Cantons de l'Est, Sherbrooke; Stanstead College; Skidmore College; Trent University; United Church of Canada Archives; United Empire Loyalists' Association of Canada, Toronto and the Sir John Johnson Centennial Branch, Stanbridge East; Union Theological Seminary, Richmond, Va.; University of Arkansas; University of British Columbia; University of California at Berkeley; University of California at Riverside; University of Chicago; University of Cincinnati; University of Guelph; University of Iowa; University of Kansas; University of Manitoba; University of Minnesota; University of Nebraska-Lincoln; University of North Carolina; University of Oregon; University of Tennessee; University of Texas (Humanities Research Center); University of Toronto; University of Utah; University of Virginia; University of Washington; University of Western Ontario; Vassar College; Victoria College; Wayne State University; Wellesley College; Yale University.

The following people provided useful material in interviews—either by phone or in person—often in conjunction with correspondence:
M.H. Abrams, Tom Allen, Don Amos, Margaret Atwood, Rodney Baine, John Bates, Munro Beattie, Charles Bell, John Bemrose, Earle Birney, George Birtch, Harry Boyle, William Blissett, John Branscombe, Jerome Buckley, Douglas Bush, Ron Campbell, Chau Wah-ching, Rod Chiasson, Carol Hickman Clark, Kathleen Coburn, Eleanor Cook, Paul Corbett, Kenneth Cousland, Dorothy Covert, Art Cragg, Florence Clare Cragg, Tom Daly, Kathy Daniel, Laurenda Daniells, Jim Davison, Michael Dolzani, David Dushkin, Robert Emerson, Wilma Howard Emory, David V. Erdman, Roy Faibish, Barker Fairley, Douglas Fisher, Angus Fletcher, Elizabeth Eedy Frye, Helen Kemp Frye, Roland Mushat Frye, Catherine Gillespie, Ray Godfrey, William B. Goodman, Jack Grainger, Margaret Graves, Don Harron, Eric Havelock, Helen Heller, Thomas Hernacki, Benjamin Houston, Donald Howard,

Kingsley Joblin, S.F. Johnson, Alexandra Johnston, George Johnston, Charlie Jolliffe, William Jovanovich, Pierre Juneau, Hugh Kenner, Fred Kirby, Margaret Newton Kirkpatrick, David Knight, M.L. Knight, Norman C. Knight, Roman Kroitor, Blair Laing, Norman Langford, Marshall Laverty, Lew Layhew, Alvin A. Lee, Hope Arnott Lee, Allan Logan, Evelyn Rogers Love, Thomas Mallon, Del Martin, Fredelle Bruser Maynard, Willard McCarty, Norah McCullough, Donald McGibbon, Pauline McGibbon, Hugh Maclean, Kenneth MacLean, Bill McMaster, Bernice McNaughton, Mrs. Walter Meyers, Lillian Noyce Miller, Barbara Moon, A.B.B. Moore, Margaret Moore, Hugh Moorhouse, James Nohrnberg, Robert O'Clair, Robert Patchell, Laure Rièse, Claire Rosenfield, Robert Sandler, Roy Sharp, Ernest Sirluck, Jon Slan, Glenna Davis Sloan, William Solomon, Datus C. Smith, John Speers, David Staines, Prudence Steiner, Margaret Stobie, Phyllis MacKenzie Thompson, Vincent Tovell, Neil Tracy, Memye Curtis Tucker, Francesca Valente, Harold Vaughan, Helen Vendler, Robert Weaver, Jane Welch Widdicombe, Drenka Willen, Mary Winspear, Rosemarie Schawlow Wolfe, Gordon Wood.

The following provided helpful information through correspondence:
Hazard Adams, David Anido, Carlos Baker, Sheridan Baker, J.E. Belliveau, Deanne Bogdan, Mary Elizabeth Bostetter, Alan Brown, Garth K. Calkin, Frank Carner, Edmund Carpenter, John Robert Colombo, Edward T. Cone, David Daiches, Margaret Dalziel, Dan Davin, Robertson Davies, Marion Davis, P.W. Day, Sylvia Johnstone Easton, Alma Howard Ebert, Umberto Eco, Richard Ellmann, W.R. Elton, Paul Engle, D'Iberville Fortier, Everett C. Frost, Edna Fulford, Robert Fulford, Paul Fussell, John Garrett, Mildred Shanas Gutkin, Andrew Hebb, Robert B. Heilman, Karl B. Hill, Gwenna Howard, C. Douglas Jay, E.D.H. Johnson, Rev. George Johnston, D.G. Jones, Michael K. Joseph, J.R.K. Kantor, Justin Kaplan, W.J. Keith, G. Wilson Knight, Richard Kostelanetz, Steven Langdon, Harold S. Lindenberger, Douglas Lockhead, Robin Lorimer, Alfred MacAdam, Mildred Winfree MacKenzie, Murdo MacKinnon, Jay Macpherson, J.C. McLelland, Joan

McNutt, Anne McWhirr, Dorothy Davison Maddison, Philip Marchand, Hazel Merrett, Robert Neale, Martin K. Nurmi, Sean O'Faolain, S. McKenzie Paige, Lou Palmer, Bob Rae, Helen Randall, James Reaney, Gilbert Reid, Jean Remple, David Robertson, Gordon Roper, Malcolm Ross, Robert Scholes, Francis Sparshott, George Winchester Stone, Jr., Earl Steeves, Carolyn Tate, Ruth M. Thompson, Diana Trilling, C.V. Wedgwood, Andrew Wernick.

I'm personally grateful to friends and relatives who provided especial encouragement and assistance during a seemingly endless project: Michael and Regina Ayre, Valerie Haig-Brown, Mary Jolliffe, Carmela Patrias and Fred, Ron, Harry and Jean Weihs. My cousin Ernest Watson, formerly of Shaunavon, toured me in grand style in air-conditioned van in 1980 and 1982 through The Bench of southwest Saskatchewan.

Grants from the Canada Council (Explorations) and the Ontario Arts Council (Writers Reserve) helped to defray the heavy research costs of this biography.

# NOTES

| | |
|---|---|
| MC | The Modern Century, *Northrop Frye* |
| MD | The Myth of Deliverance, *Northrop Frye* |
| NFCL | Northrop Frye on Culture and Literature, *Northrop Frye* |
| NFS | Northrop Frye on Shakespeare, *Northrop Frye* |
| NP | A Natural Perspective, *Northrop Frye* |
| OE | On Education, *Northrop Frye* |
| PL | Paradise Lost, *Northrop Frye, ed.* |
| RE | The Return of Eden, *Northrop Frye* |
| RR | Romanticism Reconsidered, *Northrop Frye, ed.* |
| SER | A Study of English Romanticism, *Northrop Frye* |
| SeS | The Secular Scripture, *Northrop Frye* |
| SM | Spiritus Mundi, *Northrop Frye* |
| SP | Sound and Poetry, *Northrop Frye, ed.* |
| StS | The Stubborn Structure, *Northrop Frye* |
| TSE | T.S. Eliot, *Northrop Frye* |
| WP | Words with Power, *Northrop Frye* |
| WTC | The Well-Tempered Critic, *Northrop Frye* |

## PEOPLE

| | |
|---|---|
| JA | John Ayre |
| NF | Northrop Frye |
| CF | Catharine Howard Frye |
| HK | Helen Kemp Frye |
| DH | Donald Howard |

## PERIODICALS

| | |
|---|---|
| AV | *Acta Victoriana* |
| CF | *Canadian Forum* |
| CL | *Canadian Literature* |
| HR | *Hudson Review* |
| KR | *Kenyon Review* |
| SN | *Saturday Night* |
| UTQ | *University of Toronto Quarterly* |

**PREFACE**

**p. 2:** uneventful life: SM 16
**p. 3:** academics ignorant of issues: an exception is Geoffrey Hartman in "Structuralism: the Anglo-American adventure," in Jacques
Ehrmann, ed.
**p. 4:** NF's doubts about biographical method: eg. FS 325-7
—— influence of Blake or evangelical Methodism: NF to William
Park, Dec. 3, 1976
—— "eternal newness of the same": CP 30
—— NF's criticism as autobiography: NF int. with Justin Kaplan,
OE 211; SM 104


## PART ONE

**NEW JERUSALEM**

**p. 9:** comedic and romantic tendencies: NP 1-2
**p. 10:** regeneration and sanctification: Simpson 24
—— city upon a hill: Miller 199
—— Zion appearing in Britain: Simpson 71; Barker 194-5, 381
—— Milton's vision of kingdom: Barker 196
—— Blake's "Jerusalem": *Milton* K481
—— "to anchor apocalyptic vision": FI 145
**p. 11:** "Jerusalem" hymn after Labour win: FI 140.
—— reenactment of mythology among Puritans: Tannenbaum 94;
Bercovitch 69-71. Both the Old (Ezek. 36:26) and New (James 1:
21-2) Testaments regard the believer as a vessel of the spirit or
word who then *acts* because of godly possession or (literal) inspiration. Bunyan was obsessed with both divine and demonic
possession. Bunyan, sections 101 and 174. NF suggests "self-resur-
rection" through recreation. AC 345-6
—— ffrie: The archaic ff form was the same as F. ffrie became Frie
in the second generation and Frye in the third.
**p. 12:** William Pierce Frye as jingoist: Senator Frye was a major
agitator for the annexation of Hawaii and the Philippines and
American influence in the Caribbean, including Cuba and Panama.
*Dictionary of American Biography*, Volume IV, 51-2.

—— Timothy Frye as Minuteman: Frye Barker 60

—— southern Britain: ffrie listed himself as native of Basing, probably Basingstoke, in Hampshire, a hotbed of peasant puritanism. Bridenbaugh 307

—— building a New England and New Jerusalem: See Bercovitch, Chapters 4 and 5

—— works of John Preston: will of John ffrie, Dec. 5, 1693

—— witch trials in Andover: Frye Barker 47; Thomas Brattle in Burr, ed. 180-1

—— Col. Joseph Frye escape: Fuess 135

—— Peter Frye the Loyalist: Frye Barker 57

**p. 13:** Peter Frye north of Sherbrooke: Day 434

—— ancestor Joseph Northrup: Northrop 147

—— Sarah Ann Northrop in Lowell factory: As a result of this, NF had particular interest in Melville's story, "The Tartarus of Maids".

**THE HOWARDS**

**p. 15:** item in Wellington, Ont. paper: McGill archives microfilm, undated clipping

—— NF's conjecture about Catholic Howards: SN, Oct. 1981, 21

—— Upper Canada: renamed Ontario in 1867

**p. 16:** Alma Howard's DNA research: Alma Howard Ebert to JA, June 11, 1980

—— CF's happiness at Stanstead: CF to DH, March 28, 1935

**p. 17:** walking circuit: Cf. Wesley 5

**p. 18:** Howard crisis at Nepean: CF to DH, Dec. 30, 1939

—— Rev. Howard's Bible readings: NF doesn't remember this.

**p. 19:** description of Harriet Howard: Lew Layhew int. with JA, Sept. 17, 1980

**A NINETEENTH-CENTURY HOME**

—— CF on her wedding: Howard Round Robin, Autumn 1913

**p. 20:** CF's depression in Lowell: CF to DH, Jan. 30, 1929

**p. 21:** Wolfe St. flat: *Sherbrooke City Directory for 1904-5*, 105

**p. 22:** Methodist Church: now razed

p. 23: Vera Frye to Danville cousin: CF to DH, Sept. 3, 1931

## NORTHROP

p. 23: NF's difficult birth: CF admitted this to NF many years later.

p. 24: NF's crying as infant: Howard Round Robin Autumn 1913, 9. There may be some relation between severe allergies and "colic." NF would later suffer from serious bouts of asthma and, like his father, hay fever.

p. 25: NF's performance of "The Acorn": Toronto *Telegram*, March 25, 1950

—— children's Christmas party at Methodist Church: Sherbrooke *Record*, Dec. 30, 1917

—— urban cast: Francis Sparshott has noted that despite the theoretical importance of the cycle of nature for NF, he is un-Canadian in exhibiting "no sense of *land*." This results in a curious "deadness" in his writing. CL, Winter 1979, 147

p. 26: NF's imagining heaven on other side of river: *Quest*, Sept. 1978

—— H.E. Frye hardware ad: *Sherbrooke City Directory for 1917-18*, 209

—— June 4, 1915 troop ceremony: *Men of Today in the Eastern Townships*, 52

—— Lt. LaBreque ad: *Record*, Mar. 30, 1917

p. 27: Howard Frye's letter: *Record*, May 7, 1917

—— Howard Frye to 14th Battalion: *Record*, Aug. 9, 1918

p. 28: RATS! RATS! ad: *Record*, Apr. 20, 1917

—— adjutant report, Aug. 18, 1918: War Diary, 14th Canadian Battalion, Royal Montreal Regiment

p. 29: CF's loneliness after losing Howard: CF to DH, Jan. 15, 1939

p. 30: bankruptcy: There is no registration of bankruptcy listed with the courts.

## MONCTON EXILE

**p. 33:** CF's enthusiasm for Bible as poetry: CF to DH, Apr. 26, 1939

**p. 34:** "penal servitude": SN May 1973, 20

—— "sentence lengthened": DG 139-40

**p. 37:** NF's athletic clumsiness: Dorothy Davison Maddison to JA, Jan. 25, 1980

—— NF in cold tub: NF to HK, June 14, 1932; cf. Victorian schoolboy practice of "cold dips at dawn": Girouard 170

—— sequence of novels: undated autobiographical sketch

**p. 38:** music composer ambition: ibid.

**p. 40:** entertainment badge test: Jim Davison to JA, Apr. 15, 1979

**p. 41:** Howard Frye's wanderlust: Howard Round Robin, Autumn 1913

## ABERDEEN HIGH

**p. 43:** Egyptian sorceress: Dorothy Davison Maddison to JA, Oct. 7, 1979

—— Catholic boy: In Canada, Catholics and Protestants rarely go to the same schools.

—— Ned Belliveau on NF: *Atlantic Advocate*, Oct. 1978

**p. 44:** NF's loss of fundamentalism: NF int. with Bob Sandler, Sept. 20, 1979, ms. 5

**p. 45:** NF's religious attitudes: NF to Roy Daniells, Apr. 1, 1975

—— CF's latent religious doubts: NF int. with Bob Sandler, ibid. ms. 5; also NF int. with Deanne Bogdan, *Studies in Canadian Literature*, Fall 1986, 255

**p. 47:** NF's dislike for piano practice: ibid. 257

—— "puerile attitude": Dorothy Davison Maddison to JA, ibid.

**p. 50:** NF as Devotional President: Wesley Memorial Church calendar, Jan. 20, 1929

**CHAMPION TYPIST**

**p. 52:** pianist earnings of $5.00: CF to DH, Jan. 30, 1929
—— relief over no recording: NF int. with Ian Alexander, Feb. 1, 1985, Denham transcription 3
—— Underwood contest: Toronto *Telegram*, Apr. 8, 1929

**VICTORIA COLLEGE**

**p. 54:** "panic of time": CR 19
—— Buttercup: There's also a Buttercup in the operetta *H.M.S. Pinafore*.
**p. 57:** CF on NF's missionary zeal: CF to DH, Mar. 12, 1930
—— Underwood contest: Toronto *Telegram*, Sept. 30, 1929
**p. 59:** Kathleen Coburn's Coleridge work: Coburn, Chpt. 1
**p. 60:** unemployment in Amherst: Robert Emerson int. with JA, June 12, 1980
**p. 61:** role of Moore: Pakington, in John Hampden, ed. 50

**SCHERZANDO**

**p. 61:** chop-suey menus: SN, May 1973, 21
**p. 62:** NF's reading Saurat: NF to Pelham Edgar, Aug. 9, 1948; Edgar 85
—— Blake's coherency: Saurat 191
**p. 63:** Edgar's car accident: This was a favorite Douglas Bush anecdote. Edgar's unfortunate passenger was the Marquis of Dufferin.
—— Edgar's study of Henry James: *Henry James, Man and Author*. Toronto 1927
—— Edgar's literary taste: Edgar's taste was not infallible. He promoted John Masefield and groused about the later Yeats.
**p. 64:** *The Tempest* and Sixth Aeneid as comparable accounts of the Eleusinian mysteries: Irrespective of this speculation, NF thought there was a connection between the two works simply because Shakespeare kept reminding everyone of Virgil. Because T.S. Eliot mentions it in his preface to Wilson Knight's *Wheel of*

*Fire*, NF thought he saw the influence of Still's book in *The Waste Land*. TSE 68

**p. 65:** Hamlet as successor to Norse mythological figures: Hudson xi

—— "almost perfect essay in ... Comparative Religion": Still 205

—— impact on NF of Spengler: SM 193-4

**p. 66:** "pure forms which underlie": Spengler 104

—— "same characters repeated again and again": K567

—— "repeating themselves true to type": Spengler 4

**p. 67:** photo of Stanley Kemp in Mellen 19

—— not "love at first sight": *Today*, June 3, 1981

—— NF's cancelling summer mission: CF to DH, June 26, 1931

**p. 68:** failure to publish "Eccentricity": CF to DH, Mar. 28, 1932

**p. 69:** CF's copy of "Eccentricity" schema: CF to DH, ibid.

—— "encyclopedic ranges of association": FS 193

—— trunks from Alberta: CF to DH, June 26, 1931

**p. 70:** scholarships: CF to DH, Sept. 3, 1931


**OWL AND BIRD OF PARADISE**

**p. 70:** Herb Norman: Despite the similarity of character, wraith-like appearance and formidable intellectual appetites, NF and Norman were never close.

—— "if the professors wanted to pluck him": CF to DH, Jan. 9, 1932

—— NF's exploration of Blake prophecies: Edgar 85

**p. 71:** "Something moves, anyhow": StS 162

—— Ken Johnstone: Johnstone, who worked as a clerk for a meat packer, nursed an ambition to become a writer and eventually became a journalist in Montreal.

—— NF's talk on Greek tragedy: a result perhaps of his interest then in Nietzsche's *Birth of Tragedy*

—— Maurice Spector as founder of Can. Communist Party: Buck 97

—— Spector's starting Trotskyite cell: ibid. 131

**p. 72:** NF's dismay over Knight's politics: NF to HK, Aug. 25, 1932

—— Earle Birney: Birney wrote the novel *Down the Long Table* about the group.

—— Egon Friedell's survey: *A Cultural History of the Modern Age*; Birney 27

**p. 73:** Norman Knight on NF's debating: AV, April 1933, 36-7

—— night trek along Bloor St.: Apparently there was a fad among some students for these treks, which also included Toronto's north-south axis, Yonge St.

**p. 74:** NF on spring exams: AV, April 1932

**p. 75:** "too strong a sense of humor": NF to HK, June 1, 1932

**p. 76:** "bigger fools in the world": NF to HK, June 14, 1932

—— NF's failing Religious Knowledge: The University of Toronto had a requirement for a one-hour-a-week course in either religious knowledge or other subject remote from a student's area of concentration. The exams and essays were often easy but if neglected, could result in technical failure.

—— "determining factors" of exam writing: NF to HK, July 6, 1932

—— "very clogged thoughts": NF to HK, July 15, 1932

—— "the natives stare at me": NF to HK, Aug. 1, 1932

—— Sinclair Lewis's style: NF to HK, June 23, 1932

—— *Elmer Gantry*: NF to HK, Aug. 25, 1932

**p. 77:** United Church as epitome of Canadianism: NF to HK, Aug. 25, 1932

—— "life of a misanthropic clam": NF to HK, Aug. 1, 1932

—— "going to be professor": NF to HK, July 15, 1932

**p. 78:** "great tradition to sustain": NF to HK, Sept. 2, 1932

—— "thick skin": NF to HK, Aug. 25, 1932

—— "very definite heroisms": NF to HK, Sept. 12, 1932

—— origin of dog collar: NF to HK, Aug. 25, 1932

**GOLD MEDALIST**

**p. 79:** United Church cradle of Can. philosophy: AV, Nov. 1932, 18

—— satirizing leading figures: Professors often turned up at performances and took the ribbing with good humor.

—— outline of NF's Bob Revue: "The Way of All 'Fresh' " program, Oct. 14, 1932. The script itself doesn't seem to have survived.

**p. 80:** "Question of Maturity": AV Dec. 1932, 24-6

**p. 81:** telling poets how to write: AV, Feb. 1933, 7

—— "horizon defined by myths": Nietzsche 135 (Section 23)

—— Edgar's sorting out NF's writing: *Graduate*, Spring 1961, 32

**p. 82:** CF's description of poor business: CF to DH, May 11, 1933

—— antidote to depression gloom: Cf. MC 48 for a darker view of depression anxieties

—— description of pavilions: *Popular Mechanics*, May 1933

—— fair gardens: NF to HK, June 20, 1933

—— "unsavoury-looking kitchens": NF to HK, June 20, 1933

**p. 83:** NF's move to boarding house: NF to HK, July 14, 1933

**p. 84:** "sponger and parasite": NF to HK, July 26, 1933

—— typing all day, reading detective fiction: NF to HK, ibid.

—— NF between Liberal and CCF: NF to HK, Sept. 4, 1933

—— "established cooperative church": NF to HK, ibid.

**p. 85:** no Spengler "east of the Don": NF to HK, Sept. 22, 1933

—— "Parable of the Brown Agate": NF to HK, Sept. 12, 1933

## PART TWO

### EMMANUEL COLLEGE

**p. 90:** Jim Lawson's Group of Seven collection: Laing 24

**p. 91:** NF's Edgar review: AV, Christmas 1933, 17-20

**p. 92:** "alphabet for the symbolic figures": NF to HK, Dec. 28, 1933

—— meaning in a cluster of symbols: Yates 1983, 25

—— cabalistic arrangements: see Rembrandt's etching in Jung 1968, 116; astrological: Boehme's quadernal zodiac in Jung 1968, 356; philosophical: John Dee used a skimpy zodiacal arrangement to represent the essential elements of philosophy, Yates 1983, plate 10; biblical: Friedrich Heer notes an arrangement at Schongrabern, Austria, of magic symbols and shapes which outline the history of mankind from the Creation to the apocalypse, Heer 364

—— "alphabet of forms": FS 417

—— "committed to a book on Blake": NF to Pelham Edgar, Aug. 9, 1948; Edgar 85-6

**p. 93:** Blake's borrowing from the Bible: StS 170

—— "hymn to the eternal newness": CP 30

—— NF's thinking about academic career: NF to HK, Apr. 17, 1934

**p. 94:** NF's idea of Brown's theology bias: CF to DH, March 29, 1934

—— no competition for Travelling Scholarship: NF to HK, Apr. 17, 1934

—— Bachelor of Divinity thesis topic: NF to HK, Apr. 17, 1934

**p. 95:** "why Bach is greater": NF to HK, Apr. 24, 1934

### STONE PILE, GARDEN HEAD

**p. 95:** United Church's lack of interest in ordaining scholars: Even Emmanuel College was staffed largely by foreign scholars.

**p. 96:** NF to HK's critical promise: NF to HK, Apr. 24, 1934

—— Currelly's bitterness: Currelly 14-28

—— arcades of geometry: Stegner 19. Stegner grew up just to the west of NF's mission field.

**p. 97:** "fitful tossing country": NF to HK, May 10, 1934

—— "all you can see is your own farm": NF to HK, ibid.

**p. 99:** grasshopper plague: NF to HK, June 19, 1934

—— suicide: NF to HK, May 19, 1934

**p. 100:** "collect my remains": NF to HK, July 9, 1934

—— "Bible is magnificent": NF to HK, May 19, 1934

—— NF on idolatry and tyranny: NF to HK, May 10, 1934

**p. 101:** "absurd scale of values": NF to HK, May 19, 1934

—— "cultural deadness": NF to DH, June 1, 1934

—— local tales and popular music: Cf. Stegner 26 and Currelly 20. Currelly specifically mentions stories about early settlement years, singing at well-attended church gatherings, clog dancing.

—— tunes "so light and lilting": NF to HK, May 19, 1934

**p. 102:** no second summer: NF to HK, May 19, 1934

—— insects "driving me nuts": NF to HK, July 23, 1934

**p. 103:** "eternity" since talking to someone like John Bates: NF to HK. Aug. 17, 1934
—— "marriage with the right woman": NF to HK, May 19, 1934
—— HK to explore "the art side": NF to HK, ibid.
—— "only devouring enthusiasm": NF to HK, May 19, 1934
—— book to buy engagement ring: NF to HK, July 23, 1934
—— "I don't give a damn": NF to HK, Aug. 17, 1934
**p. 104:** "final and culminating effort": NF to DH, June 1, 1934


**BLAKE, BLAKE, BLAKE**

**p. 104:** "I have got to smash them": NF to HK, Oct. 19, 1934
—— "getting good instruction across": NF to HK, ibid.
**p. 105:** Brown's superstitions: ibid.
—— Pratt's doubts about NF's teachings: Significantly, Pratt had the reputation of being an undynamic teacher who preferred pass course students to those in honors.
—— "rasped nerves, bad dreams": NF to HK, Nov. 9, 1934
—— dubbed Bucket of Blood: by John Creighton
—— "excessively morbid: NF to HK, Dec. 4, 1934
—— Frazer's *Golden Bough*: NF to HK, Oct. 19, 1934
**p. 106:** insights into Blake: StS 189-190; Walt Disney: CF, Apr. 1938, 453
—— Gilbert Murray's Hamlet paper: "Hamlet and Orestes" in Murray 180-210
—— significant details repeated: Murray 208
—— "originality": ibid. 24
**p. 107:** agon: AC 187; alazon: 172-5, AC 226-8
—— komos: Cornford 4-5; "release and *renouveau*": ibid. 9
—— anatomies common: Burton xi
—— adhering qualities of Eliot's poetry: TSE 28
—— "literature of Europe from Homer": Eliot 1964, 49; AC 18
—— idolization of Eliot's poetry: e.g. Delmore Schwartz, Atlas 154
—— stunned and sickened: SM 14
—— "free-thinking Jews undesirable": Eliot 1934, 20
—— "anyone who wasn't completely anti-fascist": NF int. with JA., Dec. 1, 1976

**p. 108:** "why there has to be critics": ibid.

—— PhD thesis: NF to HK, Dec. 4, 1934

—— hanging on with "luck, gall, overwork": NF to HK, Dec. 12, 1934

—— "I slept and slept": NF to HK, Jan. 1, 1935

**p. 109:** "straw thrashing" lower criticism: GC xvii

—— Hugh of St. Victor: David Staines overemphasized the Victorine influence on NF in his essay "The Holistic Vision of Hugh of Saint Victor" in CL

—— Christ as second Adam: Mâle 186; TSE 69

—— "historical, allegorical, tropological and anagogical": Mâle 184-85

—— four levels of meaning: Douglas Bush noted levels of meaning in his 1932 book on Elizabethan mythographers. By conveying Erasmus's sarcasm, Bush was hardly fostering a revival. Bush 69; Erasmus 91-2

**p. 110:** Blake the greatest: NF to HK, Jan. 25, 1935

—— "mysterious super-chemical way": NF to HK, Apr. 23, 1935

**p. 111:** "masterpiece": NF to HK, Mar. 11, 1935

—— doubts about Massey money: NF to HK, Mar. 11, 1935

—— NF's fear of being outflanked: NF to HK, undated letter, c. June 1935

—— Wilson Knight's understanding NF's ideas: NF to HK, May 3, 1935

**p. 112:** 'The Flood in Genesis": Knight 1934, 198

—— works of intellectual history: One of Woodhouse's graduate students remembers that he was uncomfortable with Milton's poetry, much preferring the safer ground of Milton's polemics and thought.

—— "weird bird": Mary Winspear int. with JA, Sept. 20, 1980

—— Wilson Knight's admiration for NF's Blake knowledge: Wilson Knight to Edmund Blunden, July 14, 1936

**p. 113:** Knight's apparent confusion over folio and quarto: SM 12-3

—— "mass of pencilled annotations": ibid.

—— Knight's urging NF to write book on comedy: Knight was no stranger to the comedies and noted in "Jesus and Shakespeare" written at the time he saw NF: "... in his final plays Shakespeare creates a series of love-parables whose plots of loss in tempest and reunion to music correspond ... from *Pericles* to *The Tempest* the interest is almost entirely concentrated on personal love, loss and reunion." This pattern is similar to NF's basic concept of initial disruption followed by social harmony.

—— impact of Knight's work on NF: SM 13

**p. 114:** "Read Blake or go to hell": NF to HK, Apr. 23, 1935

—— failed to obtain money: NF to HK, ibid.

—— "every problem of the universe": NF to HK, Apr. 23, 1935

—— exceptional letter: NF to HK, May 3, 1935

**p. 116:** NF's defence of religion: NF to HK, July 24, 1935

—— interest in Rabelais, idea for novel: NF to HK, May 22, 1935

**p. 117:** "profound ignorance": NF to HK, June 28, 1935

—— antipathy to Victoria mentors: NF to HK, June 28, 1935

—— trip to Kemp cottage: NF to HK, June 28, 1935

### LAST YEAR

**p. 118:** Arthur Lismer: Although Lismer was one of the Group of Seven, his heavy canvases never achieved the commercial or critical success of many of the others. He had a genius, however, for enlivening gallery tours with lectures which helped break down deficiencies in the artistic taste and knowledge of Toronto's stodgy middle class. He ran a celebrated Saturday morning art class for as many as 700 Toronto-area children who were nominated for ability in art.

**p. 119:** spheres of heavens: PL 546

—— NF's fellowship on Blake: *Royal Society Proceedings for 1936*, xxiv; general meeting, May 20, 1936

—— NF's review *Madame Butterfly*: AV, Oct. 1935, 12-14

**p. 120:** "Ballet Russe": AV, Dec. 1935, 4-6

—— Jooss performance: CF, Apr. 1936, 18-19

**p. 122:** "golden rain": WTC 133. The image is overtly sexual in the Ovidian version of the Perseus myth, quite common in Rennaisance art, in which Zeus's golden rain or light falls on Perseus's half-naked mother, Danae.

**p. 123:** conversion experiences: *The Toronto Star*, June 13, 1936.

In resigning from the Methodist ministry in 1907, the prominent Christian Socialist, J.S. Woodsworth, confronted this ticklish Methodist problem by admitting he had never had a conversion experience. Woodsworth 7

—— names of Tiriel: FS 242-3

**p. 124:** "after-image of Howard": NF to HK, Aug. 14, 1936

—— CF's dreams like *Pilgrim's Progress*: NF to HK, Aug. 13, 1936

—— backwoods Methodism: NF to HK, Aug. 17, 1936

—— *The Winter's Tale* and fertility festivals: Cf. FI 108

**p. 125:** "mountain must be lonely": NF to HK, Aug. 20, 1936


**MERTON COLLEGE**

**p. 125:** "supreme gift": NF to HK, Sept. 12, 1936

—— description of passengers: ibid.

**p. 126:** NF's reaction to countryside: NF to HK, Sept. 15, 1936

—— "I belonged to London": NF to HK, Oct. 1, 1936

—— "grey horror of this dying world": NF to HK, Sept. 21, 1936

**p. 127:** "one Constable after another": NF to HK, Oct. 5, 1936

—— "two most important classes of myth": Jackson Knight 144. There's an echo of this in NF's notion of *The Tempest* as submarine version of Virgil's underground *Sixth Aeneid*. TSE 68-9, 71; MD 89

—— swastikas as labyrinths: Hooke 1935, 10, figures 11 and 12; Bayley 81-2; cf. "hooked cross" FS 212. Although Knight was conservative, NF had no sense of his being a crypto-fascist.

—— "the Knights ... speak my language": NF to HK, ibid.

—— NF's analysis of fascism: NF to HK, ibid.

**p. 128:** NF on his Merton room: NF to HK, Oct. 11, 1936

—— CF's approval of NF's living style: CF to DH, Jan. 2, 1937

—— hazing of newcomers: NF's classmate, Howard K. Smith, gives an account of this in Smith 31-4.

—— NF's dislike of moral snobbery: NF to HK, Oct. 27, 1936

—— NF's depression, love of cities: NF to HK, Oct. 11, 1936

**p. 129:** fascists at Oxford: The Mosleyite fascists had an office in Oxford but enjoyed little support. They suffered a humiliating defeat at a May 1936 rally in the Carfax Assembly Rooms when the blackshirts were so badly beaten, four ended up in hospital. Benwick 209-11

—— cricket: While not interested in cricket or rowing, NF considered learning badminton.

—— Paul Engle's poem: from "Edmund Blunden on his Sixty-Fifth Birthday," Engle 27

p. 130: NF on first tutorial: NF to HK, Oct 10, 1936

—— second tutorial: NF to HK, Oct. 27, 1936

p. 131: NF's murderous mood: NF to HK, Nov. 30, 1936

—— Michael Joseph on NF as critical thinker: Michael Joseph to JA, June 22, 1979. NF stole this back for NFS 16.

—— "endless niggling": NF to HK, Oct. 27, 1936

p. 132: imaginative possibilities of patterns: Lewis 1967, 202-3

—— cosmological approach inherently non-evaluative: In the 1954 introduction to *English Literature in the Sixteenth Century* Lewis reaffirms, "Bad books may be of importance ... and if they are passed over too briefly, the student's picture of the period may be distorted." In *The Discarded Image*, Lewis like NF at the time seriously entertained the notion that scholarship may "achieve the steady progress of the sciences." Lewis 1967, 15

—— Lewis's mistrust of historicism: ibid. vii

—— Beckett-like statement: NF to HK, Nov. 10, 1936

p. 133: bleakness, discomforts: NF to HK, Dec. 11, 1936; Nov. 3, 1936

—— NF's anger over *New Yorker* delivery: NF to HK, Nov. 3, 1936

—— "most of the beer in Oxford": NF to HK, Dec. 11, 1936

p. 134: "glorious Mantegna": NF to HK, Dec. 30, 1936

—— NF at *Murder in the Cathedral* : NF to HK, ibid.


**BIONDINO INGLESE**

—— Fulke Greville in "neat little sack": NF to HK, Feb. 3, 1937

—— "very saleable pages": NF to HK, Feb. 9, 1937

p. 135: NF's proposed Europe trip with HK: NF to HK, Mar. 9, 1937

—— work on Blake in Rome: CF to DH, Apr. 1, 1937

—— "biondino inglese": NF to HK, Mar. 24, 1937

—— haste to get to Rome: Michael Joseph remembered that with reduced train fare, they were possibly trying to reach a philatelist conference, thus keeping up an appearance of sponsored travellers. Michael Joseph to JA, Mar. 17, 1980

**p. 136:** Mussolini as "Protector of Islam": *The Toronto Star*, Mar. 23, 1937

—— NF's disgust with Roman art: NF to HK, Mar. 24, 1937

**p. 137:** Cimabue greatest artist: NF to HK, Apr. 5, 1937; FS 89

—— half hour "for the great ones": Charles Bell diary, Apr. 2, 1937

—— Bell and NF both wrong: Lou Palmer to JA, Nov. 14, 1985

—— "that hideous church": Santa Maria del Carmine

**p. 138:** impact of Lowlands art in Uffizi: NF to HK, Apr. 28, 1937

—— NF on raping a Baroque angel: Charles Bell diary, Apr. 12, 1937. In *The Half Gods*, Bell changed NF's line to "When Ah git deah, Ah hope ole Peter let me bugger a baroque angel." Bell 102

**p. 139:** finding lost manuscript: NF to HK, ibid.

—— NF's impressions of Venice: NF to HK, ibid.

**p. 140:** MUST COME HOME: NF cable to HK, May 1, 1937

—— Brown promised $600: NF to HK, May 18, 1937

—— deeper in debt: NF to HK, May 21, 1937

—— NF's sending first chapter: NF to Pelham Edgar, June 10, 1937

**p. 141:** NF's dreams of recognition with book: NF to HK, June 8 and 9, 1937

—— "heartily sick of Oxford": NF to HK, May 28, 1937

—— B.M.: British Museum

—— freezing my feet: NF to HK, May 21, 1937

—— NF's not "getting enough out of Oxford": NF to HK, May 18, 1937

**p. 142:** Last Judgment theme: Although Blake was perhaps the last major artist to work the theme, Romantic painter John Martin produced a huge canvas of the Last Judgment as late as 1852. In Chapter VII of *Under the Volcano*, Malcolm Lowry describes a contemporary version, which encapsulates the whole novel.

## TORONTO ILLUSION

**p. 143:** return on Empress of Australia: on June 20

—— terms of Travelling Scholarship: Board of Regents minutes, June 24, 1931

—— terms of NF's position: Board of Regents minutes, Nov. 15, 1937

**p. 144:** CF's complaint about wedding announcement: She may have meant a formal, engraved card.

—— NF's working on honeymoon, rejection slips: Edgar 86

—— "a lot of growing": ibid

—— "What was everything else about?": *Today*, June 3, 1981

**p. 145:** Hollywood's "two authentic geniuses": CF, Apr. 1938, 453

—— "complete turnout": *Varsity*, Feb. 10, 1938

—— "If you ain't got that swing": *Varsity*, Feb. 11, 1938

**p. 146:** Mexican mural painting: This was the great era of the left-wing muralists, Rivera, Orozco and Siqueiros who realized Blake's dream of public art.

—— "Face to Face" story: AV, Mar. 1938

**p. 147:** "all night it rained": cf. fertilizing rains AC 153

—— NF as exam supervisor: CF to DH, June 1, 1938

—— "building of a new world": Breton 216; cf. the New Apocalypse group in Britain in Ray 290-2; cf. Hesse's fictional League and apocalyptic counterparts which hoped "for the Dawn of a Third Empire" after WW1 in Hesse 1972, 39; the demonic version, of course, was the New Order of the Nazis which fed on the German spiritual need for redemption through a Messiah: Pauwels and Bergier 171

—— "how far the surrealists can go": cf. FS 406. Although the European surrealist dream may have been a romantic fantasy crushed more by self-indulgence than fascism, the 1949 surrealist manifesto *Refus Global* of Quebec artist Paul-Émile Borduas seems to have precipitated the not-so "Quiet Revolution" which over-hauled conservative Quebec society. Fetherling, ed. 112-27. Fundamental to this was "the power of speech," an insistent NF theme. Bourassa 265

## OXFORD

**p. 149:** NF on voyage and London: NF to HK, Sept. 29 and 30, 1938

**p. 150:** NF and Baine's intercepting Bell: Charles Bell diary, Oct. 18, 1938

**p. 151:** year "to have its difficulties": NF to HK, Oct. 7, 1938

—— NF's review of Canadian show: CF. Jan. 1939, 304-5

—— NF's reaction to Nazi art: NF to HK, Oct. 21, 1938

—— "however bad Naziism may be": CF, ibid.

**p. 152:** NF's reaction to Oxford lecturing: NF to HK, Oct. 21, 1938

—— Jewish refugee stories: NF to HK, Dec. 6, 1938

**p. 153:** Paris "incredibly cheap": NF to Chancellor Wallace, Jan. 13, 1939

—— "real or artificial": Michael Joseph to JA, Nov. 20, 1979

**p. 154:** Versailles: NF to HK, Dec. 22, 1938

—— "I shall become a sot": NF to HK, Apr. 4, 1939

—— Amien's "messianic, prophetic cathedral": Mâle 390

**p. 155:** Notre Dame de Mantes rose window: Cowen 105

—— "completeness ... of the medieval achievement": NF to Chancellor Wallace, Jan. 13, 1939. NF had earlier mentioned to Helen a growing fascination for the Dark Ages which he viewed as culturally inspired.

## OXFORD AND ITALY, 1939

**p. 155:** NF's return to London: NF to HK, Jan. 12, 1939

**p. 156:** bursar's delaying payments: NF to HK, Feb. 2, 1939

—— "fairly good teacher": NF to Chancellor Wallace, Jan. 13, 1939

—— "scholarship in a university such as ours": Chancellor Wallace to NF, Jan. 31, 1939

—— NF as HK's housekeeper: NF to HK, Feb. 24, 1939

**p. 157:** NF's lectures "twenty-five times as good": NF to HK, Mar. 14, 1939

—— "stuff of an unusually good writer": NF to HK, May 15, 1939

—— no "danger of war": NF to HK, Apr. 17, 1939

**p. 159:** "would rather work there": NF to Chancellor Wallace, July 22, 1939

—— Mussolini homilies: "Two Italian Sketches: 1939," AV, Oct. 1942

**p. 160:** reporter's prediction of war: Michael Joseph to JA, Nov. 20, 1979


## WAR GOVERNED THE NATIONS

**p. 160:** Casa Loma towers: StS 57

**p. 161:** "books I should be reading": CF to DH, Dec. 30, 1939

—— CONTINUE YOUR STUDIES: *Varsity*, Sept. 28, 1939

—— no "man left on this bloody continent": Jack Mason to NF, Sept. 13, 1939

—— Michael Joseph's wartime activities: int. with M.K. Joseph, *Islands*, Nov. 1979 and novels *I'll Soldier No More* and *A Soldier's Tale*

**p. 162:** CF's reaction to war: CF to DH, June 18, 1940

—— two choices for an epic: This probably reflects his ideas from Milton. FS 313

**p. 163:** Margaret Atwood's fascination: *The CEA Critic*, Nov. 1979, 21

—— serpentine swiggle: GC 171

**p. 164:** Christina McCall on NF's teaching: *Maclean's*, Jan. 1972, 56

**p. 165:** Dante's influence: Although NF never wrote an essay directly on Dante's work or his influence, his AC is full of observations about Dante's cosmology and these virtually take over an essay on Yeats, "The Top of the Tower." StS 257-77

**p. 169:** Borge's story: in Frye, Baker and Perkins, eds. 1980

—— "War on the Cultural Front": CF, Aug. 1940

**p. 171:** NF's worry about father: NF to HK, undated

## HUNTING THE FINAL SYNTHESIS

**p. 171:** R.H. Charles's commentary: *A Critical and Exegetical Commentary on the Revelation of St. John.* Edinburgh 1920

**p. 172:** "jeweller's paradise": Lawrence 122

**p. 173:** titles of NF Bible course: Listed each fall in the *Varsity* notice column. While NF's typological approach may have been unusual, Bible courses for English students existed in such universities as Harvard as far back as the late nineteenth century.

—— NF's on CF's funeral: NF to HK, Nov. 27, 1940

**p. 175:** roses on chamber pots: StS 56

**p. 176:** "final synthesis": "The Anatomy in Prose Fiction," *Manitoba Arts Review*, Spring 1942, 43

**p. 177:** unity that can be felt: SM 111

**p. 178:** *The Four Zoas* as code book: FS 314-5

—— Los "genius of civilized life": FS 332

—— attraction of Nazi myth: NF int. with Imre Salusinszky, Salusinszky 41; note 66, FS 449

## SATIRE BEGINS AGAIN

**p. 178:** "Satire begins again": AC 239

—— fiction as term for all prose: *Manitoba Arts Review*, Spring 1942, 35

**p. 179:** "old Ptolemaic view": ibid. 36

—— Bunyan's only important contributor to novel: ibid. 46

—— "observer of men thinking": ibid. 38

—— Menippean satire as literary guardian: ibid. 43

—— "dust blown out of a library": ibid. 43

**p. 180:** "dealing with an unmusical poet": UTQ, Vol. 11, 168

—— "mobilizing Canadian artists": War Policy Statement, Federation of Canadian Artists, 1942. Queen's University Archives.

**p. 181:** NF on Alan Creighton's poetry: NF to A.J.M. Smith, undated, c. late 1942

**p. 182:** "The Truant" as "greatest poem": BG 173

—— "voice of humanity": CL, Summer 1964, 9

—— "The Truant ... foreshadows the poetry of the future": BG 250

—— "The Truant" as "important influence": NF to J.R. Struthers, May 30, 1977

—— satire's breaking up stereotypes: UTQ, Vol. 14, 79

p. 183:  Dante's image of devil's behind: AC 239, SM 71

—— irony a corrosive acid: ibid. 82

p. 184:  irony and tragedy melding: ibid. 85

—— CF reviews: Apr. and June 1943

p. 185:  Mildred Shanas on seminar: Mildred Shanas Gutkin to JA, July 26, 1984

p. 186:  NF's new baby: ibid.

—— ersatz beauty contest: Varsity, Dec. 8, 1942

—— NF on art exhibit: Varsity, Feb. 12, 1943


# PART THREE

**VE 1945**

p. 191:  "complete and systematic interpretation": NF to Princeton University Press, March 8, 1945

—— "ready to print": NF to Datus C. Smith, Mar. 17, 1945

p. 192:  MacLachlan report: Mar. 28, 1945

—— FS ms. no longer exists: For much of his writing career, NF was insensitive to the archival value of different drafts of his work and consistently threw material out. HK scolded NF about this and the FS ms. fragment in the Victoria College Archives is said to have been retrieved out of the garbage can by HK.

—— Carlos Baker's PUP report: dated Apr. 24, 1945

p. 193:  Smith's not bluffing: Datus C. Smith int. with JA, May 27, 1983

—— NF's request for advice: NF to Datus C. Smith, Apr. 28, 1945

—— Baker's plan: Baker memo, undated

p. 194:  Smith still interested: Datus C. Smith to NF, May 19, 1945

—— NF on another rewrite: NF always claimed he rewrote the book five times.

—— "so personal a book": NF to Datus C. Smith, May 28, 1945

p. 195:  cathode-anode theory: FS 386

**p. 196:** "good old 'general reader' ": MacLachlan report, Sept. 28, 1945

—— plumber's rates: HK to parents, July 16, 1952

**p. 197:** spell on "household matters": NF to George Johnston, Nov. 30, 1953

—— Cardinal Newman's notion of gentleman: Cf. StS 11; NF shared the Victorian period's neo-chivalric interest in the gentleman. Girouard, Chapter 17

**GREAT TEACHER**

**p. 199:** oriental references: e.g. FS 431

—— "nearly walked out again": Fisher, Editor's Preface

**p. 200:** "Yeats and the Language of Symbolism": FI 218-37. The paper was delivered at Cornell University, May 2, 1947.

—— Douglas Fisher's battlefield anecdote: Douglas Fisher to JA, Feb. 25, 1985

—— Gurka anecdote: HK to parents, July 16, 1947

**p. 201:** Blake course with Joyce: The course was the basis of "Quest and Cycle in *Finnegans Wake*." FI 256-64

—— Hugh Kenner on NF's thinking: Hugh Kenner int. with JA, July 5, 1979. A decade later NF suggested "it is possible a new construct will be found and a new table of metaphors organize the imagery of our poets." FI 66

—— "If Joyce or Yeats had read it": Hugh Kenner to Irving Layton, Sept. 23, 1955, in Cameron 243

—— "clear and complete solution": Information for Sales Promotion, PUP, *Fearful Symmetry*, undated

**p. 202:** "value to practicing artist": application to John Simon Guggenheim Memorial Foundation, Oct. 31, 1949

—— "coherent tradition of criticism": FI 220

**GOD**

—— NF's delight over FS design: NF to Datus C. Smith, Apr. 8, 1947. The book won a design award.

—— NF's hope for Edmund Wilson review: NF to Jean MacLachlan, Jan. 25, 1947

—— Wilson's favourable review: *The New Yorker*. Aug. 5, 1944

**p. 204:** FS between popular and academic: NF to Earle Birney, Aug. 15, 1947

—— FS 1962: "Preface to the Beacon Press Edition"

—— reading FS overnight: *Alphabet*, No. 1, 3; cf. FS 7

—— "what did God say today?": Linguist Edward Sapir was also once dubbed "God" by students. Howard 51

**p. 205:** FS as sleeper: NF to Datus C. Smith, Oct. 15, 1947

—— problems of British edition: Datus C. Smith to NF, Feb. 18, 1948

—— Edith Sitwell's review: *The Spectator*, Oct. 10, 1947, 466

**p. 206:** NF to Edith Sitwell: Apr. 12, 1948

—— Edith Sitwell to NF: Apr. 29, 1948

**p. 207:** FS as father-swallowing: 1949 diary, Feb. 1, 1949

—— Edmund Blunden to NF: Nov. 6, 1947

—— Pelham Edgar to NF: Aug. 2, 1947; NF's reply, Edgar 85-7

—— Geoffrey Keynes's response: *Time and Tide*, Dec. 27, 1947

**THE ARGUMENT OF COMEDY**

**p. 209:** reflecting idea in FS: FS 304-5

—— "fairies, dreams": Downer, ed. 1949, 72; cf. C.S. Lewis's 1956 essay, "Sometimes Fairy Stories May Say Best What's to be Said," in Lewis 1984

—— "follies of the 'normal' world": ibid. 72

—— "just completed" article: NF to Frederick Morgan, Oct. 12, 1948

**p. 210:** fifth "quintessential" prose form: HR, vol. 2, 595

—— romances not bad novels: ibid. 585

—— fictional forms in Jungian terms: Cf. mandala in Jung 1968, 107

—— "six possible combinations": ibid. 593

—— *Moby Dick* as romance-anatomy: ibid. 593

—— separate anatomy category: Cuddon 40-1; also Frye, Baker and Perkins, eds. 1985, 32

p. 211: "start slugging again": CF, Dec. 1946, 195
—— "invisible communion of the Christmas feast": CF, Dec. 1947, 195
—— "kingdom of heaven is within": CF, Dec. 1948, 194

## ACTIVE AND SELF-COORDINATING

p. 213: idea of a Pentateuch: undated autobiographical sketch
p. 214: Peter Grant's "Concrete Conception": see Douglas Fisher's column, *The Toronto Sun*, Jan. 1, 1981
—— thrown penniless: Tenure was still imperfectly established.
—— opinion piece on censorship: "Dr. Kinsey and the Dream Censor". CF, July 1948, 85-6
p. 215: Christian Socialist dogma: CF, Dec. 1948, 194
p. 216: NF's denying strong Jungian influence: SM 117. In the 1941-2 period, NF was intrigued with the extensive footnotes on mythology of the 1916 Hinkle translation of *The Psychology of the Unconscious* but abandoned it, fearing that FS could be overwhelmed by Jungian thought. He seriously returned to Jung in the 1947-8 period. NF int. with JA, March 3, 1980; NFCL 122
p. 217: no publicity or coverage: There was a comment about the published essay in SN, Dec. 13, 1949.
p. 218: "bald chronicle of name and dates": UTQ, Vol. 19, 10
—— "whole tradition of Western poetry": ibid. 16
—— "different levels of meaning": ibid. 12
—— "literature exists in a verbal universe": ibid. 13-4
—— "ocean of super-verbal significance": ibid. 15
p. 219: "miscellaneous pile": ibid. 15
—— Herbert Davis's pressure: HK to parents, Aug. 4, 1949
—— Havelock's nomination for NF: Although professors were directly affiliated with General Education, they were appointed through the mainstream departments. The appointments committee was expected to rubber-stamp names provided by the departments. There had been a tiff in an earlier committee which rejected a name and when Havelock suggested NF over another person, he was admonished for creating the same problem. Eric Havelock to JA, Mar. 10, 1982

—— barroom anecdote: HK to parents, Sept. 18, 1949

## SCHOLARLY PROSPECTUS

**p. 220:** ten or 15 years: Toronto *Telegram*, Mar. 25, 1950
**p. 221:** two-page defence: NF to Henry Moe, Feb. 16, 1950
**p. 222:** John Danby on four levels: Danby 122-3
**p. 223:** "place to start looking for a theory": KR, Spring 1950, 246
—— "powers of words": ibid. 259
—— "surrounding fields": ibid. 262
—— "Adam and Samson our own story": PL xxx; also "the story is about you": SeS 186; "this play is about us": MD 85
—— "important series": *CBC Times*, June 18-24, 1950

## ON THE EDGE OF HARVARD

**p. 225:** "cards close to his chest": Eric Havelock phone int. with JA, June 6, 1982
—— "calculus for all their criticism": Downer, ed. 1951, 194; cf. "keys to poetic thought" StS 178
—— four moods or state: ibid. 178
—— "true hero": ibid. 186
—— "theories ... belong to criticism": ibid. 192
**p. 226:** "work of Los": ibid. 185; cf. NFCL 106: "purifying the imaginative dialect of the tribe"
—— code of modern art: ibid. 192
**p. 227:** "what the great religious are talking about": NFCL 212
—— NF's review of *Boswell's London Journal*: NFCL 165-9
**p. 228:** "imaginary stock exchange": FI 8. NF's anti-evaluative stance was probably his most controversial position. It was an attempt to remove irrelevant personal biases in studying literature in the same way anthropologists purged ethnocentrism and personal feeling in their formal, presumably scientific, studies of primitive cultures. NF is a brilliant evaluative critic when privately judging other writer's manuscripts.
—— "converging patterns of significance": FI 13

—— Farrer's diamond-shaped schema: Farrer, chart following 348; cf. Blake's fourfold diagram, K523

—— drama, lyric, epic: FI 17

**p. 229:** "Shakespeare's Comedy of Humors": Through at least one permutation, it appeared three years later as "Characterization in Shakespearian Comedy," *Shakespeare Quarterly*, vol. 4, 271-77

—— "Aristotle": ibid. 272

—— conflict over hiring NF: W.J. Bate to JA, March 15, 1983

**p. 230:** "not a banner year": BG 3

**p. 231:** "grass like Persian carpet": HK to parents, June 21, 1951

—— "scribbling notes furtively": NF to Charles Bell, Feb. 8, 1952

**p. 232:** description of class: Herbert Lindenberger to JA, Oct. 29, 1982

—— pigeon-holing procedure: FI 19-20; see also FT 16 and FS 277-8. NF also associated the Books of David and Solomon with the "stages" of Luvah (eternal name of Generation) and Urizen (Eden) in FS. 370. NF resented the pigeon-holing metaphor and later suggested that of a map: "A map is not the territory being explored but is normally the best guide to it, and maps improve in refinement and accuracy ...." "Maps and Territories" ms. 2; cf. negative map analogy in Wimsatt 20

## PERMANENT AFFECTIONS

**p. 233:** whole shelf of books: *Varsity*, Feb. 21, 1952

**p. 234:** "how deeply intertwined": NF to Robert Heilman, Nov. 12, 1951

**p. 235:** "every god-damned jingle": NF to Frederick Morgan, Jan. 2, 1952

—— buttocks and buttercups: BG 8

—— "Mr. Butchevo Phrye": Layton 1952, 55

—— NF's ambivalence about CanLit: articulated most fully in "Conclusion to a *Literary History of Canada*," BG 213-5

—— "Preface to an Uncollected Anthology": BG 163-79

**p. 236:** rumor of new book: Datus C. Smith to NF, June 22, 1951

—— "unorganized jig-saw puzzle": NF to Datus C. Smith, Sept. 30, 1951

—— "Towards a Theory of Cultural History": UTQ, vol. 22, 325-41

p. 237: outline in Raglan: Raglan 180-1


CHAIRMAN (1952-1953)

p. 238: deprived of "faculty of reading": NF to Frederick Morgan, July 28, 1952

—— "article you like of levels of meaning": NF to Benjamin Houston, Nov. 12, 1952. This paragraph was copied into Houston's notes from a missing original.

—— NF "terribly happy": HK to parents, c. early July 1952

p. 239: "getting papers written": NF to George Johnston, Dec. 8, 1952

—— "hell of a year": NF to George Johnston, Feb. 20, 1953

—— "logrolling": NF to Lisa Dyer, Apr. 8, 1952

—— NF's review of Inquiring Spirit: NFCL 170-77

—— critical self-consciousness of 1950s: Cf. Howe 172-3. Wayne Booth bitterly complained of this in College English, Oct. 1965, 1-13.

p. 240: "Great Western Butterslide": NFCL 132

—— as with Austin Farrer: Farrer 14, 17

p. 241: "Mr. Tate's angels": NFCL 135

—— "until the pilgrim reaches": NFCL 138

—— symbolism of red dress and white parasol: AC 101

—— pairing city of destruction and Acrasia garden: Cf. AC 150

p. 242: outline for a book on the Bible: not entered into diary

—— unexpected letter from Princeton: E.D.H. Johnson to NF, Mar. 18, 1953

—— no place for Jay Macpherson: NF to George Johnston, undated note


PRINCETON

p. 243: "pages of the manuscript accumulated": E.D.H. Johnson to JA, Aug. 31, 1983

—— NF on house: NF to Gordon Wood, Mar. 12, 1954

**p. 244:** Robert Martin Adams's disbelief: "Dreadful Symmetry," HR, vol. 10, 618
—— "fell into bed": NF to Gordon Wood, Mar. 12, 1954
**p. 245:** "saucer of milk": NF to Gordon Wood, ibid.
—— NF on America: NF to George Johnston, June 18, 1954
—— "nothing but timetables": NF to George Johnston, ibid.
—— "cool, comfortable": NF to George Johnston, ibid.

## PART FOUR

### STRUCTURAL POETICS

**p. 249:** "scrofula of footnote numbers": NF to Benjamin Houston, June 22, 1955
**p. 250:** Douglas Bush's cut-up: *Sewanee Review*, vol. 64, 591-6
**p. 251:** classicism to romanticism: Cf. FS 175-6
—— "do not care about terminology": FI 130
—— "oracular and half ecstatic process": FI 137
—— important discussion of metaphor: AC 122-5
—— lion-man discussion: NF earlier discussed in FS 116-7
—— importance of rational thought: Jung 1965, 34 OE 146
**p. 252:** 25 Clementi sonatas: NF int. with Deanne Bogdan, *Studies in Canadian Literature*, Fall 1986, 259
—— CBC radio talk on Spengler: CBC Nov. 23, 1955
—— NF's writing David Erdman about AC: NF to David Erdman, Oct. 8, 1955
—— "essay" implying "disjointedness": Benjamin Houston to NF, Oct. 14, 1955
**p. 253:** list of titles: Benjamin Houston to NF, Oct. 3, 1956
—— "Criticism of Structure": NF to Benjamin Houston, Oct. 7, 1956
**p. 254:** "anatomized cadaver": FS 350; Wimsatt 19: NF "stands before us in the shining white garments, the rubber gloves, of the anatomist—the passionately neutral dissector."
—— NF's offer to review Robert Graves: NF to Frederick Morgan, Nov. 8, 1955
—— "where we invent our own myths": NFCL 234

—— dream in *Horses of Instruction*: Adams 6

—— NF's production line: NF to John Crowe Ransom, Jan. 21, 1956

**p. 255:** "meteorologically close to the mouth of hell": NF to David Erdman, Apr. 21, 1956

—— no "systematic work on Stevens" until AC in proof: NF to James Thorpe, May 27, 1966; AC proofs were first available on Oct. 18, a month after NF submitted his essay to HR

—— "sense of a world disintegrating": FI 245

—— "auroras of a vanished heroism": FI 244

—— theory and practice of poetry "inseparable": FI 238

—— Stevens "centrally in the Romantic tradition": FI 240

—— "surrender to heaven": FI 245

—— "neo-paganism": FI 245

—— motive for metaphor: FI 248; also EI 11

**p. 256:** "world of total metaphor": FI 249

—— "separation between subject and object": FI 251

—— "reservoirs yet untapped": *The Daily Student,* July 6, 1956

—— "principle of the Bloody Mary": NFCL 239

—— "aphorisms to be recreated": NFCL 140

—— "primitive gift of charm": SP xxvii

—— "involuntary physical response": AC 278


## ANATOMY OF CRITICISM

—— "work of genius": NF to Benjamin Houston, undated postcard, c. late Jan. 1957

**p. 258:** "smiling public man": NF to George Johnston, Nov. 15, 1957

—— photo of NF at Blake exhibit: *The Saratogian,* Nov. 15, 1957

—— NF's breakdown of Blake's *Milton*: "Notes for a Commentary on *Milton*." This was generally applied in AC 158-60

—— Blake's lack of sentimentality of irony: FI 139. The real attraction to Blake for most university students was closer to that of Allen Ginsberg who had a transforming mystical experience reading "Ah, Sunflower," "The Sick Rose" and "The Little Girl Lost." His search for a New Jerusalem was of a radically different sort. *Paris Review* 299-309

**p. 259:** "immediate form of imaginative experience": "Blake after 200 Years," Wellesley College, Mass., Apr. 17, 1957; reported in *Wellesley College News*, Apr. 25, 1957

—— "pure critical theory": AC vii

—— AC as ironic: GC II ms. 8; cf. "detached vision" AC 348; cf. NFCL 106: "effort ... to turn away from crisis and commitment"

—— "this is the engine room": *Culture and the National Will*

**p. 260:** "central part of this training": DG 122; cf Blake, K604

—— "keys to the whole imagination": DG 123

—— OLD SCHOLARS ON WAY OUT: Canadian Press release, June 17, 1957

—— "relation of symbolism and imagery to faith and conduct": "The Study of English in Canada," *Dalhousie Review*, Spring 1958, 2; also OE 23

—— "The Anagogic Man": Macpherson 56. The poem was prompted by seeing NF in the morning hurrying along Charles St. towards his office in the Birge-Carnegie library. Although it started as light verse, with "Norrie" instead of "Noah," it developed a deeper tone, influenced by Douglas LePan's "Images of Silenus." Jay Macpherson to JA, July 30, 1987

**p. 261:** essays basis of practical volume: Benjamin Houston to NF, Sept. 18, 1957

—— FS to go out of print: Benjamin Houston to NF, Sept. 18, 1957

**p. 262:** "great to-do about the theory of criticism": NF int. with Andrew Kaufman, *the newspaper*, Oct. 27, 1982

—— "best book I'd ever read": Harold Bloom int. with Imre Salusinszky, Salusinszky 62

—— "very great book": Harold Bloom, *Yale Review*, Sept. 1957, 133

—— "seminal for the next decade": Frederick McDowell, *Western Review* 22, 309

—— one of most quoted books: *Current Contents, Aug. 6, 1979*

—— "strangest and most interesting literary minds": Robert Martin Adams, HR, vol. 10, 616

**p. 263:** "so much of it is perverse": George Whalley, *Tamarack Review*, Summer 1958, 101

—— Eli Mandel's awe: CF, Sept. 1958, 129

—— "mind is not freed, but trapped": Winnipeg *Free Press*, July 26, 1958

—— Abrams's complaint about "Fearful Symmetry": Robert Scholes to JA, Apr. 12, 1984; Scholes 118

—— "square yard of tabular diagram": UTQ, vol. 28, 191

**p. 264:** "artefacts of the conceptual scheme": ibid. 192

—— resemble almost any archetypal shape: ibid. 194-5

—— "medieval encyclopedic tables": ibid. 191

—— circle of fifths section: AC 177

**p. 265:** "lens of field glasses": *The CEA Critic*, Jan. 1980, 34

—— "fairy tales in the low mimetic displacement": StS 218

—— Frank Kermode's complaint: Kermode 72

—— "five most respectful readers": *College English*, Oct. 1965, 6

**p. 266:** Robert Denham's charts and mandalas: in Denham

—— "model only": SM 118-9; cf. "a mere dictionary or grammar of symbols": CP 103

—— critics like William Wimsatt: Kreiger 102

—— "easier to work with": NF to Earle Labor, May 20, 1975

**p. 267:** "Byron type": FI 188-9


PRINCIPAL

—— NF's excitement over Pratt's new poems: NF to John Gray, Mar. 7, 1958

**p. 268:** "Ford Salesman's Handbook": NF to John Gray, Feb. 9, 1958

—— NF to the Learneds: NF to David Erdman, June 20, 1958

**p. 269:** Milton's interest in elegies: FI 125

—— "The starry floor": B, dedication page

—— "work which had engaged so much of his attention": Board of Regents Minutes, Jan. 15, 1959

—— "grit and oyster theory": SN, Apr. 1973, 20

**p. 270:** "by-products of the Spenser": NF to Benjamin Houston, Oct. 28, 1958

—— book on "continuous prose forms": Benjamin Houston to NF, Mar. 10, 1959. This was a response to NF letter of Mar. 6, which seems to have been misplaced.

—— "distinguished" Canadians: *Hansard*, July 9, 1959, 5731

—— "combat Soviet ideological warfare": *Hansard*, ibid. 5733

**p. 271:** "very deeply honored": NF to Richard H. Henneman, July 5, 1959

—— "The Truth Shall Make you Frye": undated mimeographed copy of *The Strand*

—— "communion of wisdom": BLT 9

—— "current of mental energy": BLT 18-9; cf. "university is the powerhouse" DG 104

**p. 272:** "sources of creative power": BLT 22

—— maladjusted Davids: BLT 16

—— "root of all the nonsense": BLT 17

—— Bible book "a bit vague": NF to R.W.W. Robertson, Dec. 23, 1959

—— "One banks one's fires": NF to George Johnston, Nov. 18, 1959

**p. 273:** "nightmare of irrelevant ritual": NF to Charles Bell, June 16, 1960

—— listing college toilets: Robert B. Heilman to JA, April 26, 1982

—— "solve *ambulando*": NF to George Johnston, Nov. 18, 1959

**p. 274:** "focus of articulateness": ibid.

—— "would have died a happy man": *The Globe and Mail*, Oct. 3, 1981


**EXECUTIVE RHYTHM**

**p. 274:** "executive rhythm": NF to Esther and Earle Birney, Nov. 23, 1960

—— "pseudo-theses": BLT 16

—— "all commentary on Joyce, Eliot and Yeats": NF to Hazard Adams, Feb. 11, 1960

—— "exciting" assignment: NF to Frederick Morgan, Feb. 15, 1960

**p. 275:** front page headline: *Varsity*, Feb. 27, 1959; cf. DG 55 for a later view

—— "no ghosts or cycles": ibid.; the idea was developed in NF's 1975 essay "Haunted by Lack of Ghosts," Staines ed., 22-45

—— "hundreds of designs for poems": *Poetry*, June 1959, 188

**p. 276:** James Reaney's experimentation: James Reaney to JA, July 21, 1987

—— build a New Jerusalem through art: Woodman 24-5

—— "nimbus of eminence": *The CEA Critic, Nov. 1979, 20*

—— NF's equivalence of critical and creative: "Academy Without Walls," *Canadian Art*, Sept-Oct. 1961, 297; also OE 42

**p. 277:** "celebration not cerebration": CF, Apr. 1962, 16

—— "sterile ideologue": Layton 1972, 172

—— "young, impressionable writers": ibid. 174

—— "never worried much": NF to Irving Layton, Feb. 8, 1965

**p. 278:** "models in the head": Bruner 184

—— Bruner's "most controversial statement": ibid. 185

—— "study of myths and folk tales": Stanley and Sylvestre 25

**p. 279:** "further voyages": ibid.; also NFE 31

—— 19-year-old: AC 14

—— formation of Joint University-Board Committee: DL 4; also OE 46

—— Liberal Party suspicions: *The Globe and Mail*, Sept. 17, 1962

—— "avuncular avalanche": *Interchange, Vol. 7. No. 4, 1976-7*

—— two friendly critics: William Blissett, UTQ, vol. 33, 408; George P. Elliott, HR, vol. 16, 467

**p. 280:** poetry "central powerhouse": WTC 26

—— "holy of holies": *The CEA Critic*, Jan. 1980, 37

—— "rhythm and leisure slowly soaking into the body": WTC 26; cf. Plato 90

—— "Good writing must be based on good speech": WTC 34

—— expurgation of stock response: WTC 145

**p. 281:** "annihilate what is legal and historical": FS 346

—— Jesus for Moses, Blake for Milton: FS, ibid.

—— poet as "lost leader": TSE 24

—— "bob sled" theory: TSE 7

—— Civil War had not ended: TSE 20

—— "permanent achievement": TSE 6

**p. 282:** draw a cross, then a circle: TSE 77

—— "innocence and experience": TSE 77

—— not quite the Last Judgment: TSE 77

—— "archetype of this cycle is the Bible": TSE 79

—— idea for expanding TSE: Robin Lorimer to A.N. Jeffares, Nov. 20, 1961

—— TSE "a bust": NF to Anne Bolgan, Jan. 9, 1962

—— NF's brazen prediction: NF to Robin Strachan, Sept. 19, 1962

—— Julian Muller rejects WTC: Julian Muller to NF, Nov. 29, 1961

**p. 283:** William Jovanovich offers advance: NF to Arthur Stocker, Dec. 6, 1961

—— "horizontal in a darkened room": NF to J.W.E. Newberry, Jan. 26, 1962

—— "unending series": NF to George Johnston, Mar. 26, 1962

—— commitment of articles and books: NF to Frederick Morgan, June 26, 1962

—— expand TSE with bibliography: Robin Lorimer to NF, May 28, 1962

**p. 284:** typology of Bible idea: NF to Grayson Kirk, May 25, 1962

—— AC sequel: NF to Robert Johnston, Mar. 9, 1962

—— AC successor: NF to Gordon Ray, Dec. 14, 1962

—— contradiction of spring-romance, summer-comedy: FI 16 vs. AC 163, 186

**p. 285:** anti-Romantic attitudes of Hulme *et al*: RR v

—— Garden of Adonis: RR 16

—— "looking in the wrong direction": RR 17

—— Massey Lectures contract: Robert McCormack to NF, May 25, 1962

**p. 286:** "carefully edited by me": NF to J.A. Gonsalves, Oct. 20, 1962

**p. 287:** Mentor Books: NF to Harriet Anderson, Apr. 23, 1963

—— Cinderella or Bluebeard: EI 15

—— literature literature-like: EI 37

—— "ideals and great visions": EI 32

—— wish dream and anxiety dream: EI 43

—— to return with vision: EI 68; cf. Erasmus 22.
—— emotion was dangerous: EI 59
**p. 288:** "full of the energy of repudiation": EI 41
—— "unthinking pleasure": EI 42
—— "constructive power of the mind": EI 50

## MILTON, ELIOT, SHAKESPEARE

**p. 288:** "black pall of commitments": NF to Frederick Morgan, Feb. 6, 1963
—— "very browned off" with TSE: NF to Anne Bolgan, May 3, 1963
—— "state of Blake scholarship": NF to David Erdman, June 10, 1963
**p. 289:** "brows never seemed to unknit": *Gazette*, Mar. 8, 1963
—— "more important to study the world than change it": RE 58
—— "the Word ... that releases the power": RE 59
—— Divine power releases energy "by creating form": RE 50
—— Protestant emphasis on recreation of the Word: RE 95
—— "verbal liberty": RE 95
**p. 290:** Eliot's fascist sympathies: Evident as early as 1923. Ackroyd 143
**p. 291:** "elementary handbook": TSE 5
—— TSE not "a simplified exposition": CL, Winter 1964, 51-2
—— TSE a "potboiler": CL, Winter 1979, 152
—— NF's sharp instruments: UTQ, vol. 33, 404
**p. 292:** typology and its influence: NF to Grayson Kirk, May 25, 1962. There's a trace of this in NP 148-9.
—— idea of romanticism: NF to Henry van Dusen, Feb. 13, 1963
—— "direction of the four Romances": NF to Edward McMenamin, June 18, 1963
—— through tragedy and irony to comic restoration: Cf. NP 107: " ... the imagery of the final recognition scene [of A *Comedy of Errors*] suggests a passing through death into a new world."
**p. 293:** "most heroic effort of criticism": FS 405
—— eve of Shakespeare's 400th anniversary: NP vii
—— "comic framework": NP 133

—— "logical evolution toward romance": NP 7

**p. 294:** "Odyssean critic": NP 2

—— "plays like *Pericles*: NP 59

—— "drama is born in the renunciation of magic": NP 59

—— "Magic attempts to repeat": NP 59-60

**p. 295:** world "not real enough": *The Educational Courier,* Jan. 1964, 23

—— "world of the tiger": MC 121

—— "this neo-fascist age": DG 154


## SABBATICAL

**p. 295:** "trying to spin a web": NF to Lewis Leary, Dec. 24, 1963

—— "large idea" for third book: NF to Cudworth Flint, Mar. 2, 1964

**p. 296:** NF "ghostly colossus": F.W. Watt, CL, Winter 1964, 51

—— NF "most powerful critical force": R.W.B. Lewis to NF, Nov. 9, 1964

—— "absolute hold": Kreiger 1

**p. 297:** "Burnt Norton": Paul Fussell to JA, May 31, 1985

—— Wizard of the North: Angus Fletcher to NF, Mar. 23, 1967

—— HBJ project sputters out: The last letter was Feb. 7, 1975

**p. 298:** "the blitz": NF to William Jovanovich, Mar. 10, 1965

**p. 299:** NF didn't believe theories until implemented: *The CEA Critic,* Jan. 1980, 33

—— "absence of a coherent teaching programme": StS 91

**p. 300:** legend of NF as NFB guru: See James Reaney in *The CEA Critic,* Jan. 1980, 30

**p. 301:** Exodus cycle in AC: AC 191

—— "We're in the desert": Daly notes 7

—— "attack the monster": ibid. 20

—— "the story of your life": ibid. 51, SeS 186

**p. 302:** *In the Labyrinth:* NFB film 106C 0179 133

—— *The Bottomless Dream:* NP 108; NF stole this back for the fourth chapter of SeS; *Offered Fallacy:* from A *Comedy of Errors,* Act 2, Sc. 2

**p. 303:** terms of New York University offer: William Buckler to NF, Jan. 18, 1965

—— Bissell promise to match NYU offer: Claude Bissell to NF, Feb. 10, 1965

—— sabbaticals and illness: NF to William Buckler, Mar. 3, 1965

—— "difficulties are with leaving here": NF to George Winchester Stone, Mar. 16, 1965

—— read without guilt: NF to Bunny Mellor, May 5, 1965

—— behind in work: NF to John Fisher, Sept. 24, 1965

**p. 304:** NF's depression over Richard Blackmur's death: NF to E.B.O. Borgerhoff, Apr. 27, 1965

—— suggestion for nursing care: John A. McRae to NF, Oct. 22, 1965

—— "no writer who is not completely paranoid": Kreiger 27

—— Hartman's nervousness about system: ibid. 131; history-scrubbed myth: ibid. 126-7

—— NF as Haussmann: ibid. 31-2

—— "virile man standing in the sun": ibid. 109; Marshall McLuhan, who was hostile to NF's thinking, later admitted, "Norrie is not struggling for his place in the sun. He is the sun." Quoted in Richard Kostelanetz, *Michigan Quarterly Review*, Fall 1978, 441

**p. 305:** Hartman's denial of NF as occultist: ibid. 117

—— "optimistic Magi of the north": Ehrmann, ed. 148

—— AC "virtually contraband": *Sewanee Review*, Fall 1984, 623

—— fourth-of-July pinwheels: Kreiger 103

—— spring-summer, comedy-romance inconsistency: ibid. 102

—— "primitive response": from NP 64

—— "gnostic mythopoeia": For a conservative Catholic like Wimsatt, an association with gnosticism would be poisonous. The term implied secret knowledge, excessive absorption in form and repudiation of earthbound reality. NF however always insisted on critical openness and a necessary return from vision to use vision. Another conservative Catholic, Marshall McLuhan, went so far as to see Frye's ideas as part of an evil Masonic or Rosicrucian conspiracy. Marchand 103-5

—— "New Critics, grovelling": Kreiger 101

**p. 306:** "Frye is a neo-Ricardian": Memye Curtis Tucker notes

—— literature "there to serve mankind": Kreiger 145; AC 354
—— "society's anxious response to mythopoeia": ibid. 146; cf.
Lewis 1984, 132


## MYTH OF CONCERN

**p. 307:** apocalyptic circle: AC 141
—— "life is better than death": NF to Betty Cole, Apr. 17, 1974
—— "All genuine art ...": OE 44
—— "state of perfection": Carpenter 1978, 151; also Carpenter
1979, 42-4; also Green and Hooper 116
—— "dialectical separation": StS 86
**p. 308:** "detachment from detachment": StS 34-5
—— "taking charge of his own world": StS 52
—— "identifying ourselves": StS 35
—— "cult of objectivity": StS 25
—— "prestige of subject-object relationship": StS 49
—— "demythologizing" religion: StS 23
—— word "God": StS 24
—— "fully conscious vision": EI 43
—— "leisure class remote": FT 8
**p. 309:** "reducing our wants": FT 6
—— "expressions of despair": FT 101
—— "end of a tragedy": FT 120
—— "fantastically difficult genre": FT Preface
—— "three-fold structure": FT 95-6
—— "not pigeon-holes": FT 16
—— "three-fold pattern of characterization": FT 17
—— wheel of fortune: Marion B. Smith, UTQ, vol. 37, 401. Actually
the wheel did appear in Renaissance iconography: e.g. Yates 1986,
plate 14a. The wheel was a favorite NF motif applied to Shakespearean histories in NP 120 and later throughout NFS. Although
analogous to the Last Judgment, it is an historical, not apocalyptic,
model.
—— "three concentric tragic spheres": FT 38
**p. 310:** Tantalus and Sisyphus: FT 66
—— Prince Henry as "emerging sun king": FT 68

—— Cleopatra: FT 71-2

—— "78 small drawers": Christopher Ricks, "Dead for a Docket," *The Listener,* May 9, 1969

—— Vera Frye memorial: Porter Orr to NF, July 21, 1966

—— "first phase in an imaginative revolution": SER 15

—— evolutionary pattern in his lectures: SER 48-9

**p. 311:** "Poetry speaks ... language of concern": SER 88

—— reviving counter movement: SER 116; cf. NF's "Comment to Peter Hughes's Essay." *Yale Italian Studies,* Winter 1977: When "mythical and heroic language are recovered within a total demotic context," art also can mediate historical cycle by moderating decline by "spiral expansion."

—— "parade of stubborn facts": SER 121

—— abstraction "experience without fresh thought": SER 122

—— "any God who can die": SER 90. At almost the same time, Thomas Merton similarly addressed the God is dead problem as an exhaustion of symbols not of deity. Merton quoted in Campbell 265

—— "paralyzing world of dream": SER 131

—— necessity of Endymion's quest: SER 135

—— Endymion must descend: SER 138

—— "he awakens the dream into his world": SER 143

**p. 312:** second printing: NF to Martha Springer, Oct. 10, 1968

## THE MODERN CENTURY

**p. 313:** "this nightmare": NF to James Nohrnberg, Apr. 14, 1967

—— "no-woman" much more useful: NF int. with Robert Sandler, Sept. 20, 1979

—— "lunatic and suicidal": *The Globe and Mail,* Jan. 26, 1967

**p. 314:** "ants in the body of a dying dragon": MC 37

—— "genuine human destiny": MC 48-9

—— "immersion in the international style": MC 57

—— question of the accuser: MC 74

**p. 315:** "whole structure of society": MC 86

—— "test of one's inner resources": MC 89

—— "long and tired tradition": MC 95

—— Narcissus reflection: MC 49; StS 68
—— more articulate than usual: NF to Ivor Owen, Aug. 28, 1967
—— "world of the tiger": MC 121
p. 316: "irresistible power of renewing life": StS 239
—— "black can never ultimately win": ibid.
—— "colonial means to be mature": MC 15
—— MC "antidote" to McLuhanism: *American Scholar,* Summer 1968, 522


# PART FIVE

## LATE SIXTIES

p. 319: "unify the subject of mythology": NF to Stephen Graubard, Feb. 19, 1968
—— "mythological subjects": SM 44; also SER 5
—— "very barren scenery": NF to Ivor Owen, May 13, 1968
p. 320: "book on patterns of imagery": StS x
—— "mythical habit of mind": Cf. "once again a great mythopoeic age" FS 423
—— "mythical confronts the logical": "Mythos and Logos" 36; also CP 96
p. 321: "shallow roots": *The Toronto Star,* Sept. 19, 1968; also OE 77
—— "moral superiority" of social withdrawal: DG 161
—— "Society does not hate them enough": DG 166
p. 322: "aggregate of individual bewilderments": SM 47
—— "university *qua* university": SM 47
—— "Little Bourgeois Cultural Revolution": Kampf and Lauter, eds. "Introduction"
p. 323: "robots or bug-eyed monsters": CP 146
—— "ice death": Convocation Address, York University, May 5, 1969, 5
—— Mircea Eliade: Eliade 114-5; Alan Watts: Watts 359-61; cf. ambivalence of another myth scholar, Joseph Campbell. Campbell 215
—— "Narcissus mirror": StS 68

—— Emily Dickinson's literary universe: NF int. with Deborah Shackleton, *Descant,* vol. 12, nos. 32-3, 225

—— spiritual experiment of Eliade: Eliade 40-6

—— Jung in robe and skull cap: Brome 13 *et passim*

**p. 324:** "poetry which is not primitive": "Mythos and Logos," 36

—— myth orientation in audiences: CP 143; in cinema: CP 145

—— Land of Cockaigne: NF quote in *Time,* July 7, 1967

—— "poetry of impersonal nexus": CL, Spring 1968, 45

—— "gigantic Methodist movement": NF int. with JA, AV, Jan. 1970

—— patina of guru: One Indian student actually wrote NF to request that he become his guru. NF politely declined. M.L. Sharma to NF, Sept. 9, 1977

**p. 325:** quasi-official acceptance: Fekete 114, 247

—— "growing pressure from within": NF to Warren Anderson, Jan. 15, 1969

**p. 326:** myth of concern "central part": NF to Harold Bloom, Feb. 19, 1969

—— criticism and comparative religion: NF to Bernard Perry, Jan. 2, 1969

—— "study of very wide range": NF to William B. Goodman, Aug. 7. 1969

—— remythologizing Bible: "Literature and Society" speech ms. 14; GC 30

—— "language of symbols ... of love": AV, Nov. 1968, 33-4

—— "The Critical Path" essay: *Daedalus,* Spring 1970, 268-342

**p. 327:** sprawling list of themes: Vico's three stages of language CPe 276-8, CP 38, GC 5; the Deuteronomic reform CPe 279, CP 46, GC 201; pericopes CPe 306, CP 41, 113, GC 215-6; I John Epistle: doctrine of Trinity later insertion CPe 279, CP 47, GC 163; Israel as defeated and subjected nation CPe 279, CP 47, GC 83, 89; "God" CPe 305, CP 111, GC 16-7; believing in the Bible, Jonah and the whale CPe 305, CP 111, GC 45; no evidence in NT about Jesus which would interest a biographer CPe 307, CP 114, GC 41; Bible as comic romance CPe 322, CP 124, GC 169; Bible as the Great Code of art CPe 323, CP 128, GC xvi

—— book on typology: NF to Daniel C. Noel, Dec. 16, 1969

—— request for McGill lectures: Eric Jay to NF, Dec. 16, 1969

—— Rev. George Johnston's tip-off: although Jay and Johnston remember the details only vaguely, Johnston thought that a NF book on the Bible seemed imminent at the time of lectures. Rev. George Johnston to JA, Sept. 13, 1983; Eric Jay to JA, Mar. 8, 1985

—— NF's condition for McGill Bible lectures: NF to Eric Jay, Dec. 23, 1969

—— "concerned prose": Cf. CP 110-6

—— *Laocoön*-like list of ideas: When shown this list in Nov. 1986, NF didn't understand all the items.

**p. 328:** NF about Bultmann: NF to John Dancey, Jan. 14, 1970

**p. 330:** "all you got was two amoebas": *Time Canada,* Mar. 4, 1974

—— "Tell me what to do": CRTC int. transcript, 15

**p. 331:** "decline in the sense of festivity": *The Listener,* July 9, 1970, 34

—— sketch on iconography: NF to Rod Chiasson, Jan. 11, 1971

—— "The Word not only causes": SM 212

## THE CRITICAL PATH

—— dissatisfied with CP: NF to Bernard Perry, Feb. 23, 1970

**p. 332:** no "material changes": NF to Bernard Perry, Apr. 29, 1970

—— CP "transitional book": NF to Edward Jayne, Oct. 18, 1973

—— CP "farce": CP 7

—— "vulnerable on all fronts": NF to Harry Levin, Mar. 3, 1972

**p. 333:** "major work of criticism": NF to E.E. Temple, Oct. 5, 1970

—— trip to London and Ankara: NF to M.S. Gaull, Sept. 16, 1970

—— "starting point": NF to Ralph Cohen, Nov. 16, 1970

**p. 334:** "no book by me on the Bible": NF to Paul Corbett, May 3, 1971

—— "length of the book": Paul Corbett to NF, May 10, 1971

—— "form of a handbook": NF to Martin Kessler, July 6, 1971

—— "stupidity of biblical scholars as literary critics": NF to Roland Frye, July 19, 1971

—— "stuck like the Ancient Mariner": NF to Martin Kessler, Sept. 27, 1972

—— "big book": NF to Lenore Horowitz, Aug. 5, 1971

—— Wallace Stevens paper: SM 275-94

**p. 335:** Robert Fulford's ignorance of CP publication: His review finally appeared in *The Toronto Star*, Dec. 24, 1971. Fulford's exasperation: Midway Column, *Canadian Reader*, Vol. 20, no. 3

—— *Time* (Canada) review: Apr. 26, 1971

—— what CanLit specialist could surpass BG: UTQ, vol. 41, 170-3

—— NF on utility of BG: NF to Ramsay Cook, Mar. 25, 1971

—— "mass of rubble": NF to Dennis Lee, Oct. 6, 1971

**p. 336:** Dennis Lee's title ideas: Dennis Lee to NF, Dec. 22, 1970

—— NF's title choice: NF to Dennis Lee, Dec. 22, 1970

—— "trying to get out of the bush": NF to James Purdy, July 7, 1971

## FACES OF THE BIBLE

**p. 337:** Old Testament as folk epic: *Athenaeum,*Feb. 17, 1972

**p. 338:** "The Gospels were myths": "Pistis and Mythos," paragraph 13. Myth-oriented Bible scholars had suggested this but not quite as forcefully (e.g. Hooke 1963, 166). Prevailing thought still insisted on hard historical fact beneath the narratives of, for example, Exodus. Albright 249-257, GC 39-40. Revisionist Syro-Palestinian archeology of the mid-1980s abandoned this thesis, thus validating NF's opposition to demythologizing the Bible. GC 30

—— "releasing power by creating form": RE 50

—— "the command, the starting point": CRTC review, "Reflections on Nov. 5" [1971]

—— chant of Trobriand magician: Malinowski, Chapter IV

—— astronauts reading creation hymn: "Leap in the Dark" sermon, Dec. 12, 1971

**p. 339:** *Enuma Elish,* "magical energy": GC 6

—— NF's ignorance of Hebrew and Greek: NF to Richard Macksey, June 9, 1972

—— "gigantic book": NF to Stephen Graubard, Aug. 14, 1972

—— "barking up a tree": NF to Leeds Barroll, Aug. 14, 1972

—— NF can't do fiction theory paper: NF to Harry Levin, Aug. 15 1972

**p. 340:** "enormous honour": NF to Harry Levin, Aug. 30, 1972

—— "John Wesley blood in me": NF to Harry Levin, Oct. 12, 1972
—— "Search for Acceptable Words": SM 3-26
—— "no biographer": SM 16
—— NF's nervous mention of Bible project: NF to James Nohrn-berg, Oct. 13, 1972
**p. 341:** "imaginative world": OE 116
—— preserve metaphorical processes: OE 115
**p. 343:** "heavy and unportable typewriter": NF to Sandra Black, Jan. 16, 1973
—— "Four Last Things": NF to Carl Woodring, June 12, 1973
—— "beach on Antigua": NF int. with JA, Mar. 5, 1973
—— "academic bad debts": NF to Lenore Horowitz, Jan. 18, 1973
—— "return to Romanticism": NF to Martha England, Feb. 5, 1973
—— "dithery and demoralized": NF to Carol Orr, Apr. 16, 1973
—— revision of AC: Sydney Feshbach to NF, Mar. 15, 1973
—— "man who wrote it is dead": NF to Sydney Feshbach, Sept. 13, 1974
—— NF in panic: NF to Sydney Feshbach, Feb. 27, 1976
**p. 345:** "bankruptcy of knowledge": "Wisdom and Knowledge" sermon, Newman Chapel, Sept. 27, 1973
—— Bible book "getting so big": NF to Alan Heimert, Nov. 20, 1973
**p. 346:** "greatest honour": NF to W.J. Bate, Oct. 18, 1973
—— NF's rejection of Mackenzie King Chair: NF to Henry Rosov-sky, Dec. 4, 1973

**NORTON PROFESSOR**

**p. 347:** "schizoid fragments": NF to Angus Fletcher, Jan. 25, 1974
—— *Time Canada* CBC cover story: Mar. 4, 1974
—— Norton lectures tied to Bible book: SeS vii
—— book on Romanticism: NF to Martha England, Feb. 5, 1973
—— "self-defensive carapace": NF to Hazard Adams, Aug. 16, 1974
—— "How *about* the book?" Paul Corbett to NF, Sept. 3, 1974
—— "longer process": NF to Paul Corbett, Sept. 6, 1974

p. 348: "genuineness of history": NF int. with Justin Kaplan, OE 208

—— students "pets": NF to James Nohrnberg, Nov. 16, 1974

—— "what have *we* Christians got": Glenesk's article was commissioned for the *United Church Observer* but not published.

—— "religious plainsclothesman": NF used the same phrase in the *United Church Observer,* Jan. 1984, 40

p. 349: "mental disease": cf. GC 45

—— "The wrath of God": Dec. 12, 1971 sermon

—— "catch his every word": Peter Gomes to JA, Aug. 2, 1983

—— "wind tunnel": NF to Lenore Horowitz, Jan. 16, 1975

—— Bible course oversubscribed: NF to Kathleen Coburn, Jan. 20, 1974

—— "great epiphanies": GC 116

p. 350: "Charms and Riddles": AC 278-80

—— "frantically anxious": NF to Goldwin French, Apr. 1, 1975

—— graduate student bewilderment: Tom Mallon phone int. with JA, Feb. 21 1980

—— "simply to publish them": NF to Fred Sternfeld, Feb. 26, 1976

p. 351: "mystery at the heart of light": *Critical Inquiry,* June 1975, 755

—— "Expanding Eyes" essay: SM 99-122

—— "flow of abusive nonsense": SM 100

—— "both of them pagans": SM 117

—— "Except for the first clause": SeS 193

—— "old and tired problems": SM 107

—— "order of words is there": SM 118

p. 352: possession of verbal power: SM 119

—— "some Herculean force": SM 106

—— "no Frye school": DG 72

p. 353: "mythical and metaphorical aspect": Fletcher 12

—— "same story over and over": ibid. 7

—— "untapped source": ibid. 19

—— Richard Kostelanetz's profile: Commissioned and accepted but not published, it appeared in *Michigan Quarterly Review,* Autumn 1978

—— "several more years": *Michigan Quarterly Review,* ibid., 437
—— "attempt to translate aphorisms": ibid. 436

## MLA PRESIDENT

**p. 354:** Samson carrying the gates: NF to Rodney Baine, Jan. 7, 1976
—— "literature continues the mythological habit": SM ix; see GC 23
—— "large and complex book": Hamilton Southam, Jan. 5 1976
—— doubting progress: NF to Stephen Graubard, June 24, 1976
—— "struggling": NF to Goldwin French, Aug. 30, 1976
—— sprouting "seven new heads": NF to Paul Fleck, Aug. 13, 1976
—— "garter snake": NF to Elizabeth von Klemperer, Aug. 18, 1976
—— "what is to go where": NF to Roy Daniells, Oct. 1, 1976
**p. 355:** NF wouldn't retire: *Regina Leader-Post,* March 6, 1982
—— HK's insomnia and dizziness: NF to Roy Kemp, Apr. 5, 1976
—— David Daiches review: *Times Literary Supplement,* Nov. 5, 1976
—— Harold Bloom's review: *New York Times Book Review,* Apr. 18, 1976
**p. 356:** "Book of Genesis": *Journey Without Arrival* script 18
—— "like another Jonah": ibid. 24
—— "net of abstractions": ibid. 14
—— "imaginative home": ibid. 20
—— poetic voice in wilderness: NF to Robertson Davies, Apr. 21, 1976
—— "central comic theme": ibid. 32; from BG 169
—— "real hero": ibid. 32
**p. 357:** "powerful temptation": NF to Gordon McLennan, Apr. 20, 1976
—— "Jim Hanley to develop NF series": Jack Miller column, *The Toronto Star,* June 26, 1976
**p. 358:** *de te fabula:* SeS 186; MD 85
—— *Maclean's* profile: March 6, 1978, 36b
—— "infinite mysteries connected with logos": DG 100

**p. 359:** "wisdom and sin": National Film Board *University* script 12

—— "discontinuous kind of wisdom": DG 101

—— "pure prophetic vision": DG ibid.


## JAPAN

**p. 359:** "counter-historical movement": DG 64

—— Royal Commission idea: CRTC v

—— anti-separatist witch hunt: eg. Gordon Donaldson, *TV Guide*, Aug. 6, 1977

—— guarantee of integrity: SN, June 1977, 56

**p. 361:** "puppets were quite certain": DG 133-4

**p. 362:** "These assumptions are intolerable": CRTC 30

—— Gordon Donaldson's scorn: *TV Guide* ibid.

—— flawed report: Gwynn 318

—— "unreal abstractions": *The Globe and Mail*, Oct. 18, 1977

—— "writers are not acts of God": The *Globe and Mail*, Oct. 18, 1977

—— "this infernal book": NF to R. van Fossen, May 25, 1977

—— balance of Norton subject: William B. Goodman to NF, June 22, 1977

—— Bible book "goes very slowly": NF to Walter Ong, Dec. 22, 1977


## QUIET YEAR

**p. 363:** Wilson Harris's novels: DG 31

—— shortages of sugar: Naipaul 7 and 27

**p. 364:** restrictions on newsprint: Naipaul 78

—— just from titles: There was no official audiotape made.

—— "the real history of the Bible": *The Queen's Journal*, Mar. 2, 1978

—— "came down with flu": NF to Pauline McGibbon, March 9, 1978

**p. 365:** "quietly confident": *Maclean's*, March 6,1978

—— excitement with apprehension: NF to John Fraser, Apr. 7, 1978

**p. 366:** "other long and complicated books": NF to Martin Kessler, Apr. 19, 1978

—— "alternating hope and despair": NF to Gabriella, Apr. 18, 1978

—— "stage fright": NF to Dorothy Swartz, June 7, 1978

—— "quiet year": NF to Gabriella, ibid.

—— "Meccano set": Robert Neale to JA, Sept. 2, 1985

**p. 367:** "very pastoral thoughts": NF to Marnie Edison, Aug. 24, 1978

—— Royal Bank Award speech: reprinted as "The Rear-View Mirror," DG 181-90

—— *Varsity* photo: "Frye joins the best-dressed list at Victoria," Oct. 13, 1978

—— Molson's Ale. Alex Pugsley, "Northrop Frye a real Canadian," *the newspaper*, Jan. 19, 1983

**p. 368:** "taking all my time": NF to Laure Riese, Dec. 11, 1978

## FRYE THE CONQUEROR

**p. 369:** "society is best off": *Arthur*, Jan. 23, 1979

—— "word of power": "Reconsidering Levels of Meaning" ms. 4

—— "oratorical prose": ibid. 9

—— primary function of literature: ibid. 12, cf. GC 23

**p. 370:** Can. Studies at Bologna: see *The Globe and Mail*, Aug. 22, 1978; SN, Nov. 1979, 65-8

—— *The Name of the Rose*: started in March 1978, introduction dated Jan. 5, 1980

—— Fryeish interest: Eco 73-5

**p. 371:** "dream state" in Urbino: OE 140

**p. 372:** "better known in Italy": Gilbert Reid to JA, Mar. 23, 1985

—— "Most Cited Authors": *Current Contents*, Aug. 6, 1979

—— NF int. with Gilbert Reid: *Canada Contemporaneo*, Feb. 1980, 8-9 and 11

**p. 373:** "Frye the conqueror": *The Globe and Mail*, June 14, 1979

—— "stage fright": NF to Dorothy Swartz, June 26, 1979

—— ignore notes and get writing: NF int. with JA, July 27, 1979

**p. 374:** "not dalliance": Paul Corbett to Julian Muller, Sept. 13, 1979

—— "metaphor that unites": OE 146; cf. GC 23

**p. 375:** line between first and second volumes: NF to Paul Corbett, Nov. 7, 1979


**THE GREAT CODE**

**p. 375:** God was a verb: CR 70

**p. 376:** "decreation": CR 11; analogous re-creation: PL xviii

—— "faith, hope, and vision": CR 60

—— Milton's retelling story of creation: CR 62-63

—— "inner state of mind": CR 63

—— Oscar Wilde "genuinely prophetic": CR 5

—— Noah's Ark image: CR 53

**p. 377:** "consuming neurosis": NF to James Nohrnberg, Jan. 21, 1980

—— "crux of the book": NF int. with Andrew Kaufman, *the newspaper*, Oct. 27, 1982

—— Revelations and Job as "epitome": GC 193

**p. 378:** "the final vision of presence": GC 197

—— "vision of deliverance": MD 14

—— "Eros triumphs": MD 61

—— *Troilus and Cressida* as muddy concatention: MD 62; cf. "pure irony" NP 119

—— "this play is about us": MD 85

—— "the last recognition": MD 89

**p. 379:** take Prospero's island home: MD 89; NFS 186

—— Paulina's challenge: MD 90

—— 300 stylistic changes: *Maclean's*, Apr. 5, 1982

—— "extraordinary": anonymous Harcourt memo

**p. 380:** GC "relatively elementary": NF to James Nohrnberg, Apr. 28, 1981

—— "unscholarly": *The Globe and Mail*, Oct. 3, 1981

—— Things: William French column, *The Globe and Mail*, Apr. 7, 1973

**p. 382:** skirring away: NF int. with Andrew Kaufman, *the newspaper*, Oct. 27, 1982

—— "on my mind so long": NF int. with Imre Salusinszky, Salusinszky 42

**p. 383:** "moonshine," Polaris of criticism: Charles Wheeler, *South Atlantic Quarterly*, Spring 1983, 154-5

—— "return of the sensations": *The New Republic*, June 9, 1982

—— "driving force of this amazing book": ibid.

**p. 384:** central pretension: *Philosophy and Literature*, vol. 6. 189

—— "double mirror"; GC xxii

—— "method of the kaleidoscope": Wheeler, ibid. 159

—— NF's "veiled Christianity": UTQ, vol. 52,.

—— "catch people's souls": *United Church Observer*, Jan. 1984, 39

—— "curious sense of restraint": CF, Sept. 1982, 30

**p. 385:** jury unanimous: *Quill and Quire*, May 1984

**WORDS WITH POWER**

—— "kind of incubus": GC II ms., chpt. one, 1

—— "images of the Bible have infiltrated": ibid., 1

—— "pitfalls": NF int. with Stan Correy, Australian Radio, Sept. 20, 1982

—— arts "do not work by magic": Wiegand Lecture, Sept. 29, 1982, *Descant*, Spring 1983, 20

—— "words of power": GC 6, 7, 17

**p. 386:** "concrete" symbols: GC xiii

—— "interest of modern poets in ladders": WP ms., chpt. 5

—— "impossible to write a great poem of earth": WP ms., chpt. 8

**p. 387:** "hopes and dreams": GC II ms., chpt. 1, 19

—— "ikon before one is dead": SN, Oct. 1981, 24

**p. 389:** pristine *Anatomy* audience: AC 14

—— career-long themes: antiquarian cosmology: NFS 8-9; same old story: NFS 29-30; levels of nature, meaning: NFS 105-7; levels of characterization: NFS 45, 132-3; cycle of seasons: NFS 41-2; generically coloured time: NFS 77, 178-9; historical degeneracy: NFS 122; the quest cycle: NFS 176-8; the wheel of fortune: NFS 62, 76, 111, 120, 158

—— Robert Martin Adams review: *New York Review of Books*, Nov. 6, 1986

—— S. Schoenbaum review: *New York Times Book Review*, Nov. 30, 1986

**p. 390:** "Myth: Metaphor and Reality" similar: see Imre Salusinszky, "Frye in Canberra," AUMLA, No. 66, Nov. 1986

—— "pet cricket": NF memoir of HK, Victoria College Chapel, Sept. 9, 1986, ms. 4

**p. 391:** nature could never care: NF int. with Deanne Bogdan, *Studies in Canadian Literature*, Fall 1986, 269

**p. 392:** "Maps and Territories": ms. 8

—— "infinity of signposts": GC II ms., chpt. 1, 2

**p. 394:** "member of an aging chorus": WP ms., Preface

—— "when the magician leaves": NFS 186

## BIBLIOGRAPHY

Peter Ackroyd. *T.S. Eliot*. London 1985
Hazard Adams. *Horses of Instruction*. New York 1968
William Foxwell Albright. *From the Stone Age to Christianity*.
    Garden City, NY 1957
James Atlas. *Delmore Schwartz*. New York 1978
Arthur E. Barker. *Milton and the Puritan Dilemma 1641-1660*.
    Toronto 1942
Ellen Frye Barker. *Frye Genealogy*. New York 1920
Harold Bayley. *The Lost Language of Symbolism*. Secaucus, N.J.
    1988
Charles Bell. *The Half Gods*. Boston 1968
Robert Benwick. *The Fascist Movement in Britain*. London 1972
Sacvan Bercovitch. *The Puritan Origins of the American Self*. New
    Haven 1975
Earle Birney. *Spreading Time*. Montreal 1980
André G. Bourassa. *Surrealism and Quebec Literature*. Toronto
    1984
André Breton. *Manifestoes of Surrealism*. Ann Arbor 1969
Carl Bridenbaugh. *Vexed and Troubled Englishmen 1590-1642*.
    New York 1968
Vincent Brome. *Jung: Man and Myth*. London 1978
Jerome Bruner. *In Search of Mind*. New York 1984

Tim Buck. *Reminiscences of Tim Buck*. Toronto 1977

John Bunyan. (Roger Sharrock, ed.) *Grace Abounding to the Chief of Sinners*. Oxford 1962

George Lincoln Burr. *Narratives of the Witchcraft Cases 1648-1706*. New York 1963

Robert Burton. (Holbrook Jackson, ed.) *The Anatomy of Melancholy*. New York 1977

Douglas Bush. *Mythology and the Renaissance Tradition in English Poetry*. Minneapolis 1932

Morley Callaghan. *A Fine and Private Place*. Toronto 1975

Elspeth Cameron. *Irving Layton: A Portrait*. Toronto 1985

Joseph Campbell. *Myths to Live By*. New York 1973

Canadian Radio-Television and Telecommunications Commission. *Committee of Inquiry into the National Broadcasting Service*. Ottawa 1977

Humphrey Carpenter. *J.R.R. Tolkien: A Biography*. London 1978
— *The Inklings*. Boston 1979

Kathleen Coburn. *In Pursuit of Coleridge*. Toronto 1977

Eleanor Cook *et al*, eds. *Centre and Labyrinth*. Toronto 1983

Kenneth H. Cousland. *The Founding of Emmanuel College*. Toronto 1978

Painton Cowen. *Rose Windows*. London 1979

J.A. Cuddon. *A Dictionary of Literary Terms*. Garden City, NY 1977

C.T. Currelly. (Northrop Frye, ed.) *I Brought the Ages Home*. Toronto 1967

Foster Damon. *Blake's Job*. Providence, Rhode Island 1966

John Danby. *Shakespeare's Doctrine of Nature*. London 1949

Mrs. C.M. Day. *History of the Eastern Townships*. Montreal 1869

Robert D. Denham. *Northrop Frye and Critical Method*. University Park, Penn. 1978

Alan Downer, ed. *English Institute Essays, 1948*. New York 1949
—, ed. *English Institute Essays, 1950*. New York 1951

Stan Dragland, ed. *Approaches to the Work of James Reaney*. Toronto 1983

Umberto Eco. *Postscript to the Name of the Rose*. New York 1984

Pelham Edgar. (Northrop Frye, ed.) *Across My Path*. Toronto 1952

Mircea Eliade. *Ordeal by Labyrinth*. Chicago 1984
T.S. Eliot. *After Strange Gods*. New York 1934
— *The Sacred Wood*. London 1964
Richard Ellmann. *Yeats: The Man and the Masks*. New York 1978
Paul Engle. *A Woman Unashamed*. New York 1965
Desiderius Erasmus. *The Praise of Folly*. New York 1941
Austin Farrer. *A Rebirth of Images*. Philadelphia 1949
John Fekete. *The Critical Twilight*. London 1977
Douglas Fetherling, ed. *Documents in Canadian Art*. Toronto 1987
Peter Fisher. (Northrop Frye, ed.) *The Valley of Vision*. Toronto 1961
Angus Fletcher, ed. *The Literature of Fact*. New York 1976
Claude M. Fuess. *Andover: Symbol of New England*. Andover, Massachusetts 1959
Northrop Frye. *Anatomy of Criticism*. Princeton 1957
—. *The Bush Garden*. Toronto 1971
—. *Creation and Recreation*. Toronto 1980
—. "The Critical Path." *Daedalus*, Spring 1970
—. *The Critical Path*. Bloomington 1971
—. *Divisions on a Ground*. Toronto 1982
—. *The Educated Imagination*. Toronto 1963
—. *Fables of Identity*. New York 1963
—. *Fearful Symmetry*. Princeton 1947
—. *Fools of Time*. Toronto 1967
—. *The Great Code*. New York 1982
—. *The Myth of Deliverance*. Toronto 1983
—. "Mythos and Logos." *The School of Letters, Indiana University: Twentieth Anniversary, 1968*. Bloomington 1968
—. *A Natural Perspective*. New York 1965
—. (Robert Denham, ed.) *Northrop Frye on Culture and Literature*. Chicago 1978
—. *Northrop Frye on Shakespeare*. Toronto 1986
— *On Education*. Toronto 1988
—. *The Return of Eden*. Toronto 1965
—. *The Secular Scripture*. Cambridge, Mass. 1976
—. *A Study of English Romanticism*. New York 1968
—. *The Stubborn Structure*. London 1970

—. *Spiritus Mundi*. Bloomington 1976

—. *T.S. Eliot*. New York. 1972

—. *The Well-Tempered Critic*. Bloomington 1963

Northrop Frye, ed. *Blake: A Collection of Critical Essays*. Englewood Cliffs, New Jersey 1966

—, ed. *Paradise Lost*. New York 1951

—, ed. *Romanticism Reconsidered*. New York 1963

—, ed. *Sound and Poetry*. New York 1957

Northrop Frye, Sheridan Baker, George Perkins, eds. *The Practical Imagination*. New York 1980

—. *The Harper Handbook to Literature*. New York 1985

Mark Girouard. *The Return to Camelot: Chivalry and the English Gentleman*. New Haven 1981

Roger Lancelyn Green and Walter Hooper. *C.S. Lewis: A Biography*. New York 1976

Richard Gwynn. *Northern Magus*. Toronto 1980

John Hampden, ed. *Ten Modern Plays*. London 1926

Friedrich Heer. (Janet Sondheimer, tr.) *The Medieval World*. New York 1962

Hermann Hesse. *The Journey to the East*. London 1972

S.H. Hooke, ed. *The Labyrinth*. London 1935

—. *Middle Eastern Mythology*. London 1963

Jane Howard. *Margaret Mead: A Life*. New York 1985

Irving Howe. *A Margin of Hope*. New York 1982

Henry Norman Hudson, ed. *The Tragedy of Hamlet*. Boston 1909

C.G. Jung. (Aniela Jaffe, ed.) *Memories, Dreams, Reflections*. New York 1965

C.G. Jung. *Psychology and Alchemy*. Princeton 1980

Louis Kampf and Paul Lauter, eds. *The Politics of Literature*. New York 1972

Frank Kermode. *Puzzles and Epiphanies*. London 1962

Geoffrey Keynes, ed. *Blake: Complete Writings*. London 1966

G. Wilson Knight. *Atlantic Crossing*. London 1936

W.F. Jackson Knight. *Cumaean Gates: A Reference of the Sixth Aeneid to the Initiation Pattern* in *Virgil: Epic and Anthropology*. New York 1967

Murray Kreiger, ed. *Northrop Frye in Modern Criticism*. New York 1966

G. Blair Laing. *Memoirs of an Art Dealer*. Toronto 1979

D.H. Lawrence. *Apocalypse*. Cambridge 1980

Irving Layton. Louis Dudek and Raymond Souster. *Cerberus*. Toronto 1952

Irving Layton. (Seymour Mayne, ed.) *Engagements: The Prose of Irving Layton*. Toronto 1972

Hope Arnott Lee and Alvin A. Lee, eds. *Wish and Nightmare*. New York 1972

C.S. Lewis. *The Discarded Image*. Cambridge 1967

—. (Walter Hooper, ed.) *Of This and Other Worlds*. London 1984

Jay Macpherson. *The Boatman*. Toronto 1957

Emile Mâle. *The Gothic Image: Religious Art in France of the Thirteenth Century*. New York 1972

Branislaw Malinowski. *Coral Gardens and their Magic, Volume 1*. Bloomington 1965

Philip Marchand. *Marshall McLuhan: The Medium and the Messenger*. Toronto 1989

Peter Mellen. *The Group of Seven*. Toronto 1970

Perry Miller and Thomas H. Johnson, eds. *The American Puritans: Their Poetry and Prose*. New York 1963

Gilbert Murray. *The Classical Tradition in Poetry*. New York 1957

Shiva Naipaul. *Black and White*. London 1981

Friedrich Nietzsche. (Walter Kaufmann, tr.) *The Birth of Tragedy*. New York 1967

A. Judd Northrop. *The Northrup-Northrop Genealogy*. New York 1908

Paris Review. *Writers at Work: Third Series*. New York 1967

Plato. (Francis MacDonald Cornford, tr.) *The Republic of Plato*. New York 1945

Lord Raglan. *The Hero*. London 1949

Paul C. Ray. *The Surrealist Movement in England*. Ithaca, New York 1971

Imre Salusinszky. *Criticism in Society*. New York 1987

J.E. Sanderson. *The First Century of Methodism in Canada*. Toronto 1908

Denis Saurat. *Blake and Modern Thought*. New York 1964

Robert Scholes. *Structuralism in Literature*. New Haven 1974

Alan Simpson. *Puritanism in Old and New England*. Chicago 1961

Howard K. Smith. *Last Train from Berlin*. New York 1942

Oswald Spengler. *The Decline of the West*. New York 1932

David Staines, ed. *The Canadian Imagination*. Cambridge, Massa-
chussets 1977

Wallace Stegner. *Wolf Willow*. Toronto 1966

George Stanley and Guy Sylvestre, eds. *Canadian Universities
Today*. Toronto 1961

Colin Still. *Shakespeare's Mystery Play: A Study of "The Tempest."*
London 1921

Leslie Tannenbaum. *Biblical Tradition in Blake's Early Prophecies*.
Ithaca, NY 1982

Alan Watts. *In My Own Way*. New York 1973

John Wesley. *The Journal of the Rev. John Wesley, Vol. 2*. London
1907

W.K. Wimsatt. *Hateful Contraries*. 1965

Ross Woodman. *James Reaney*. Toronto 1971

J.S. Woodsworth. *Following the Gleam*. Ottawa 1926

Frances A. Yates. *The Art of Memory*. Chicago 1966

— *The Occult Philosophy in the Elizabethan Age*. London 1983

W.B. Yeats. *A Vision*. New York 1966

# INDEX